THE
BUSINESS OF INDEPENDENT
COMIC BOOK PUBLISHING

BY GAMAL HENNESSY

DISCLAIMERS

THE
BUSINESS OF INDEPENDENT
COMIC BOOK PUBLISHING

The Business of Independent Comic Book Publishing
ISBN: 978-0-578-72892-6
First Edition: October 2020
Published by Nightlife Publishing, LLC. Copyright © 2020
Text Copyright © 2020 Gamal Hennessy
Covers Design © 2020 Nicola Black Design, LLC

Printed in United States

Contents

DEDICATION

To Gina, for giving me the support and the
space I needed to write this, and to all the
creators who have welcomed me into the
comic book community, even though
I never created a comic of my own.

FOREWORD

In 1988, during my first year as a student at New York City's School of Visual Arts, a classmate of mine lost the rights to his original artwork to a magazine.

He was one of the most talented artists I had ever met during those formative years, and every time I saw him, whether it was in class or outside one of the college buildings, I noticed his demeanor, his body language, his manner of communicating with me and others, and it was always pleasant. The kind of pleasant that comes from knowing your worth, and the innate confidence that you have a place in the world.

The day he stood up in front of the class and told the story about losing the rights to his precious art because he did not thoroughly read the contract before signing it, I saw another side of my classmate and friend. He was embarrassed, deflated, and defeated. That was my first understanding of the need for the artist to wear the hat of the businessperson.

Five years later, I began my career in the comic book industry, and started to earn a living founded in dreams.

Dreams made manifest in the form of characters and stories centered around hero fiction. Writers and artists from various walks of life and personal struggles, overcoming the seemingly insurmountable odds of becoming published creators by some of the most influential comic book publishers of the twentieth century.

In my dealings with those creators and friends, whether in the office or after work for drinks and dinner, conversations would revolve around personal hopes, inspirations for story ideas, legendary illustrators who influenced childhoods and careers, and the emotional value of our dreams.

What we never discussed in those early idealistic days, to my memory, was the business of comics. Discussion of such things would serve to be a killjoy, an unwanted commercial interruption, and a blight on the evening's overall tone of victory, accomplishment, and happiness. We lived in the realm of imagination, plot devices, and the structure of myths, while pushing aside the truth of the contract as the underpinning of creative business.

The filmmaker Alfred Hitchcock once said "…drama is life with the dull bits cut out.", and while he was speaking about the craft of cinema, his words have a profundity regarding a career in comics. Ignoring the dull bits of business and legal issues will inevitably lead to a life of drama. How, then, do we leverage the comic book industry to our advantage?

The answer lies in embracing information.

Just as creators are emotionally inspired and enriched by narratives based on the written word, beautiful illustrations, music, cinema, or another form of art, the artists of the future can train themselves to be intellectually stimulated by the business of their art so they can learn how to protect their rights and their future.

The need for a book that recognizes the needs of the artist, and explores the power of business models to secure the long-term viability of a creative career is where The Business of Independent Comic Book Publishing comes into play, and the intentions of its author.

Gamal Hennessy has a wide and varied career spanning the most popular forms of media and creative business, and his knowledge is thoroughly and patiently displayed in this book, but what makes this educational narrative unique is the author's understanding of his purpose as a servant to the community of independent comic book creators and publishers.

We are living in the time of a global paradigm shift, from a business culture that wanted to marginalize, trivialize, and ignore the stories and lives of people from diverse communities, lifestyles, life conditions, and gender identifications, to a global corporate complex that invites new stories, diverse narratives, and creators of different cultures.

The business relationships of the future will be determined by an understanding of mutual value between the creator and the publisher, making it more important than ever that both sides are armed with the knowledge to protect their intellectual properties.

The Business of Independent Comic Book Publishing is the roadmap to a secure creative future, a journey that begins with personal and tough questions. Questions requiring the aspiring entrepreneur to be self-aware and honest.

Most people have ideas, but only a percentage of them have the drive to turn those ideas into a real product, and only a small percentage of those people have the specific vision of utilizing their ideas to create a business with growth trajectory and a feasible chance of financial prosperity.

The comic book industry, and business of intellectual properties based on characters and worlds, can be both exciting and perilous. A journey of great importance and substantial reward is best undertaken with the aid of a guide, and the dawning clarity of a clear path.

You have found your guide, and the means through which to illuminate your path.

Build something with a strong foundation, and a spire that can touch the clouds.

Joseph Illidge
July 2020

Introduction

Do you want to publish comics?

If you read and enjoy comics, then the answer is probably "yes". Most of the creators I know read comics as fans before they got into the business of comics as professionals.

Do you want a chance to create and own the next generation of iconic characters?

I'm willing to bet your answer to this question is also "yes". Over the past eighty years, comic books have produced characters and ideas that can compete with musicians and organized religion in terms of popularity and cultural impact. Who wouldn't want to create the next *Superman?*

Do you understand the comic book industry well enough to create the foundation for a lifelong career?

If you do, this book might be entertaining. If you don't, this book is *essential*.

The business of comics is chaotic, complex, and on a certain level, crazy. Few other industries transform fantasies and nightmares into profitable products. But having a career in comics isn't like becoming a doctor or a lawyer. There is no license you can obtain or a standard path for you to take to superstardom. Everyone who works in comics has a unique story on how they rose to their position. Everyone in the industry used some combination of talent, perseverance, connections, and luck in order to succeed.

Some people find their way into comics through other forms of professional illustration or visual art. Some began their careers in theater. Some have been found through art portfolio reviews at conventions or through a formal story submission process. There have been people who learned their craft in staff jobs at established publishers and some who broke into the business working at retail stores. There is no *one door* that you can open to get into comics. Everyone has to find their own key.

If there is one common thread I've heard from successful creators, established publishers, and industry watchers, it can be summed up in the following statement:

"You need to self-publish and get work out into the public. Many good creators never get anywhere. You have to be good, but you also have to be persistent and lucky[1]"

The Business of Independent Comic Book Publishing (or ICP for short), is designed to help you understand both the comic book publishing industry in general and the needs of your comic book in particular. While ICP can't guarantee your story will be good, it can facilitate your persistence and help you capitalize on your luck. It can't teach you how to create comics, but it can teach you how to become an independent comic book publisher.

What Is Independent Comic Book Publishing?

A **business model** is a company's plan for making a profit[2]. There are hundreds of specific business models in comics, but they all fall into three basic types.

I define **independent comic book publishing** as the development, production, and commercial distribution of narrative sequential art without the support or assistance from any larger corporate owner or third party publisher. The independent is responsible for all aspects of production and retains ownership and control of the entire book. Under this definition, companies like Aftershock or Mad Cave Studios and webcomics creators are independent publishers. DC, Marvel, and Valiant are not independent because they are owned by larger corporations.

By contrast, **creator-driven comic book publishing** is the development, production, and commercial distribution of narrative sequential art with the support or assistance of a third party publisher[3]. In most cases, the creator is responsible for making and promoting the book, and the publisher is responsible for distribution, advertising, sales, and other business functions. This business model could be structured like an Image or Source Point Press deal, or it could be closer to the traditional publishing arrangements of companies like Random House or Simon & Schuster.

Finally, **freelance comic book publishing** is the development, production and commercial distribution of narrative sequential art on behalf of a third-party publisher. Here, the creator is brought in to develop certain aspects of the story in exchange for payment. The publisher is

---

[1] Johnston, R. (2017, August 30). The Reality of Trying to Break into Comics, By Top Cow's Matt Hawkins. Retrieved May 14, 2020, from https://www.bleedingcool.com/2017/08/29/reality-trying-break-into-comics-top-cow-matt-hawkins/

[2] Kopp, C. (2020, April 24). Understanding Business Models. Retrieved May 14, 2020, from https://www.investopedia.com/terms/b/businessmodel.asp

[3] Crowell, T. A. (2015). *The pocket lawyer for comic books: A legal toolkit for indie comic book artists and writers.* Burlington, MA: Focal Press. P. 76

responsible for all aspects of publishing and retains ownership and control of the book. Most major and minor publishers utilize freelance talent in modern mainstream publishing.

This book isn't a book about the complex roles of freelance comic creators, or creator-driven artists. All facets of comics are interrelated, and all of them can build their foundations on independent comic publishing, so we'll touch on those roles at various points of the book, but to paraphrase an old Conan movie. "*Those are stories for another time*".

How Am I Qualified to Write a Book About Publishing Independent Comics?

When someone says they're writing a book on a certain topic, the first thing I want to know is what makes them qualified to write the book in the first place. Do they have the credentials to be an expert? Have they done their homework? Where is their information coming from? Here's some background about me and where I got my information.

The Author
I've been working in and around the comics industry since 1999. I started as the general counsel for an anime and manga company called Central Park Media. Following that, I became the International Publishing Manager at Marvel Comics to help them break into the Japanese comics market. In 2004, I opened a boutique law firm called Creative Contract Consulting and started working with freelance creators, independent publishers, and large companies like Amazon. Finally, I wrote six espionage novels between 2013 and 2018 in a connected universe of my own. While this didn't make me famous or get me a movie deal, the experience gave me first-hand insight into the independent publishing process. **I'm hoping that being in the business for almost twenty years gives me the perspective to understand what this kind of book needs**.

The Editor
Although I've been in the business for a long time, I've never actually made a comic. I have no byline and no credits to my name. Before I started writing, **I asked my good friend and longtime client Mike Marts to join ICP as the editor because he's been on the front line of comics for decades**. For years, he was the lead editor for the *Batman* line of books for DC Comics and the *X-Men* line of comics for Marvel. These days he runs AfterShock Comics, where he finds critical and commercial success in an extremely tight market. If anyone knows what it takes to get comics out the door Mike does, so he can provide a reality check to my theory and ideas.

The Research
A lot of information about the business of comics has been written over the past thirty years. In addition, there are dozens of books and hundreds of articles about the publishing industry in

particular (and business in general) that can be applied to independent comic book publishing. **I've written some of these articles and spent the past five years researching other sources. I've shared many of them online and in my Professional Comics Creator Newsletter[4]**. Combining the published knowledge of the industry will serve to reinforce the professional experience Mike and I bring to the book.

The Interviews

As an entertainment attorney, I've had a lot of creator clients and I've listened to a lot of people at various levels of the industry about their experience in making comics. **ICP contains information I've collected from several dozen of my interviews as well as podcasts, published interviews, and convention panels I've sought out on this subject.** By pulling all these viewpoints and knowledge together, I want to create a comprehensive picture of the industry.

What Information is Covered in This Book?

We're going to cover elevator pitches later, but I understand why you might hesitate to buy this book. Comic creators don't often have a lot of extra money floating around, so you want to know what you're getting before you part with your hard-earned money. Without giving away the whole plot in the trailer, **ICP is broken down into three main parts, which I've illustrated with the following three circles.**

- **Pre-Production**: putting all the elements together to make your book
- **Production**: making your comic
- **Post-Production**: getting your book out into the market in exchange for revenue

Each major stage has several moving parts within it, and some of those parts start moving while the prior steps are still in motion, but we've laid the process out in a way that will make sense once you understand the broader framework.

---

[4] You can sign up to the newsletter at http://www.creativecontractconsulting.com/professionalcomicscreator/

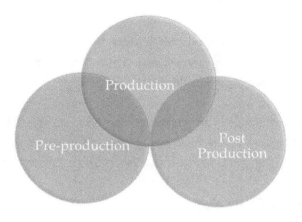

How is the Book Structured?

A big part of being a lawyer is asking and answering questions, so I'm going to stick with what I know in this book. **In each chapter, I'll pose basic and important questions about various aspects of comic book publishing**. Then, I'll attempt to provide information and ideas you can use to create your specific publishing program to help you get books out the door.

Having said that, ICP is not all questions and answers. Publishing comics is not a one size fits all process, so I try to explain the different options you have at each stage of your book's development, as well as the positive and negative aspects of each choice. Using this method, you can decide what is best for your unique situation.

The book also includes ideas, theories, aspirations, and possible outcomes in a multiverse of futures for you and the industry. Use this book not just as a guide to what is, but also what might be possible. After all, comics are about exploring your imagination.

How Should I Read This Book?

ICP is one-part instruction manual, one-part reference guide, and one-part inspirational program. I've combined practice and theory to create something you can use from the moment you decide to publish comics to the point your business is running like a well-oiled machine. Because of the range of topics it covers, this is a book that needs to be read, consulted, and questioned.

The first time you read this book, I suggest just trying to understand the general framework of independent comic book publishing and how the different options might relate to your project. Once you've completed the book, you can go back and review the various forms I provide to build a specific plan that works for you. While you are in the process of publishing your book, you can refer back to this text and the references I provide whenever you get stuck or need to go deeper into a specific idea.

I wrote this book under the presumption that the reader has no business or legal background, so if you're an MBA or a hedge fund investor reading this to understand the comic book industry, please forgive the time I take explaining the fundamentals.

You might not agree with the ideas and concepts in this book. I'm not trying to claim any authority as the single source of truth when it comes to publishing independent comics. As long as you understand the options I offer and why you might reject them for your projects, ICP can still be helpful to you.

What Can This Book Do for Me?

A book on independent comic publishing isn't necessarily a book you're going to read for fun (although I hope you'll at least find it interesting). Any decision you make for your book, including reading ICP, needs to give you a good return on your investment (ROI)[5]. If you read this book and follow its process to a reasonable degree, here's what you'll get for your purchase price and time spent reading:

- Intellectual property (in terms of characters and stories) that you own
- A business plan for publishing comics
- Experience in the comics publishing industry
- Contacts within the industry[6]
- A market for your ideas
- A process you can replicate with other books
- A finished product
- A little cash left over...maybe

What *Can't* This Book Do for Me?

This book is not the Infinity Gauntlet. It can't do everything for your independent comic. As a general concept, this book does not guarantee:

- That your book will be profitable
- That your book will be popular
- That your book will be successful (depending on your definition of success)
- That the things you read in this book will be applicable outside the United States.

---

[5] We'll cover ROI in more detail in Chapter 60

[6] This only works as long as you don't alienate everyone while making your book.

Specifically, while I cover a lot of legal concepts in this book, this isn't legal advice. If you have particular questions about your situation or a project you're working on, you need to contact a legal professional.

Finally, this book shouldn't stifle your creativity. There is no contradiction between being creative and understanding the business of creativity[7]. Some comic creators feel that they need to avoid business and legal issues to focus on their art. Others feel that treating comics as a business will suck the fun out of the medium. The creators who have the opportunity to turn their publishing into a viable full-time business can have just as much fun as the part-time publisher. In fact, gaining a grasp of the business of publishing comics can remove doubt and frustration from the process and make the experience of comics more enjoyable in the long run. If you want to publish comics and possibly create the next generation of modern mythology, you need to learn the business as well as the art.

---

[7] MacKee, R. (2010). *Story: Substance, structure, style, and the principles of screenwriting.* New York, NY: ItBooks.

STAGE 1: PRE-PRODUCTION

PART 1: THE FOUNDATION

Or "Why Are You Publishing Comics?"

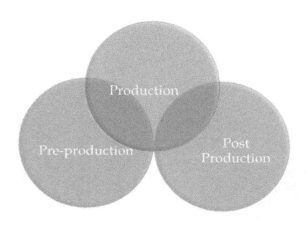

This question might seem ridiculous.

If you want to publish comics, then you already know what a comic is. If you didn't, then why would you decide to get involved in this business?

Well, an exploration of basic principles helps to create the foundation for any major endeavor. It doesn't make sense to spend time, money, and effort on something you don't understand. So it makes sense to start at the beginning.

In his groundbreaking book *Understanding Comics*, Scott McCloud defined the medium of comics as *"juxtaposed pictorial and other images, in a deliberate sequence, intended to convey information and/or to produce an aesthetic response in the viewer."*[8]

Later, author and comics editor Andy Schmidt expanded on this broad concept in *The Insider's Guide to Creating Comics* when he asserted that the goal of comics is to *"communicate a story in an entertaining way."*[9]

The ideas of both gentlemen can be distilled into the thought that **comics are narrative sequential images and text**. We'll get into the specific comic formats in Chapter 50, but as a general narrative art form, comics share qualities with other types of storytelling[10]. It is the unique nature of comics that create opportunities and challenges for you in both a business and legal sense.

Are Comics the Best Form of Storytelling for You?

Communications theorist Marshall McLuhan once said, *"The medium is the message."*[11] This is especially true in storytelling, since the medium that a storyteller uses influences the way the story is told. In his seminal book *Story*[12], Robert McKee broke down these narrative constraints in terms of internal, interpersonal, and extra-personal conflict.

---

[8] McCloud, S., & Martin, M. (2018). *Understanding comics: The invisible art*. New York, NY: William Morrow, HarperCollins.

[9] Schmidt, A. (2009). *The insider's guide to creating comics and graphic novels*. Cincinnati, OH: Impact.

[10] Tate. (n.d.). Narrative – Art Term. Retrieved May 14, 2020, from https://www.tate.org.uk/art/art-terms/n/narrative

[11] McLuhan, M., Agel, J., & Fiore, Q. (2005). *The medium is the massage: An inventory of effects*. Corte Madera, CA: Gingko Press.

[12] MacKee, R. (2010). *Story: Substance, structure, style, and the principles of screenwriting*. New York, NY: ItBooks.

- Prose: Novel, novellas, and short stories are best at showing the <u>inner life</u> and struggles of the characters. The novelist can take the reader inside the mind and thought process of anyone in the story, whether it's the inner dialogue of Albert Camus or the stream of consciousness monologues of Anais Nin.

- Theater: Plays and musicals are the perfect stage (pun intended) to display <u>interpersonal conflict</u>. Because all of the action and reaction is played out in dialogue (or song), the playwright and the actors can focus on elevating language to its highest expressive form, whether you're talking about *Waiting for Godot*, *Rent,* or *Hamilton*.

- Video: TV, film, and video games can create <u>extra personal conflict</u> that might be too cumbersome to describe in words or too impractical to put on stage. One only needs to look as far as the opening scene in *Saving Private Ryan*, the expansiveness of *Grand Theft Auto 5,* or the inventiveness of *Horizon Zero Dawn* to see the power and potential of the medium.

I'm not trying to suggest that inner life can't be captured on film or that grand spectacle can't be described in prose. **Every narrative medium can explore all three types of conflict at a high level.** What I am suggesting is that each medium has its inherent strengths and weaknesses. I'm also suggesting that comics can take advantage of the strengths of all other narrative media at the same time and produce an impact greater than the sum of its parts.

- <u>Inner Life</u>: Through thought bubbles and caption boxes, we can be privy to the inner lives of all the characters on the page.

- <u>Interpersonal Conflict</u>: With facial expressions and word balloons, dialogue can be subtle, ironic, efficient, and powerful all at once.

- <u>Extra personal Spectacle</u>: The art on the page can go anywhere and show anything, from the microverse to the multiverse to a quiet kitchen table, all in the blink of an eye.

There is also the unique balance of activity in the comics compared to other media. When I refer to activity, I'm talking about how active or passive the audience is when experiencing a particular story.

In prose, the audience is most active, because they are translating the author's words into sensory sensations, perspectives, and events based on their personal histories. One hundred people can hear a story from the Bible and each one will come away with a different interpretation of those words. Video is the most passive, because the sights and sounds are curated by the director to create a specific story. Every camera angle, every prop, every facial expression is seen by every member of the audience the same way. Video games exist on the active side of the spectrum, because depending on the game, your successful participation in the story is required to get to the end. Plays tend to be more passive because like a film, what the audience sees and hears is dictated by the director.

Comics provide a unique level of activity for the reader based on the line between panels. According to McCloud[13], the words and images inside the panel give the creators a chance to tell the story. They choose the camera angles, establish the settings, design, and position the characters, and choose the dialogue and text. The line between the panels gives the readers a chance to imagine aspects of the story for themselves. The line represents a passage of time that might be a millisecond or an eternity. Within the confines of the two panels it separates, anything and everything could happen in the mind's eye of the reader. When the reader's eye moves to the next panel, control of the story goes back to the creator. The dance between artists and the audience creates a unique type of participation that is hard to replicate in other media.

But this same dance between reader and creator has also tended to limit the audience of comics after World War II. Some have referred to this as a lack of **comic book literacy**[14]. Independent comic editor Steve Colle explained it to me this way:

"Different forms of narrative are processed in different ways by the audience that can limit the appeal of comics. For example, prose fans often have difficulty with the introduction of graphics to assist in telling the story because they are accustomed to the exclusive use of words creating the images in their heads. Likewise, those who like the fluidity of film and television often have difficulty adapting to the static medium of comics because there is not only the introduction of reading, but also a need to fill in the blanks between panels with their imaginations. In both cases, there is also the pace and time commitment that disinterests those audiences from outside of comics, as graphic narration is typically a very quick read relative to the price."

But despite the potential behavioral limitations created by modern comics, the nature of the medium creates two powerful benefits. First, there are no barriers or constraints on the type of story you want to tell. Independent comics are not bound by corporate or creative barriers. They are not limited to a single genre or paradigm. **The storyteller who uses comics as their media of choice can create any story and every story in ways that other media can't for financial or practical reasons.**

Second, **your story has the potential to connect with an audience, spread like a virus, and find expression in all media** when it starts in comics. The characters, stories, and ideas created in comics have found their way into books, Broadway shows, television, movies, video games, toys, merchandise, and the popular consciousness. There are very few novels, TV shows, or movies that can reinvent

---

13 McCloud, S., & Martin, M. (2018). *Understanding comics: The invisible art.* New York, NY: William Morrow, HarperCollins.

14 Lopes, P. D. (2009). *Demanding Respect.* Temple University Press.

themselves and expand their fan base over multiple generations. That potential for popularity can translate into millions of dollars in revenue and could become the basis for a dominant global business, if you take the right steps in the beginning and maintain that focus throughout the life of your book.

Obviously, the vast majority of comics do not find multimedia success and there is no formula or technique to determine which book will catch fire or when it might happen. **From a business and legal standpoint, any comic you invest time, energy, and resources into should be treated as The Next Big Thing**. You never know when your entertaining narrative of sequential images could turn into something more.

Comics may not be the best media for telling a story, but it has the most freedom of expression and the most potential to expand beyond the medium and into the public consciousness.

Comics might be an amazing vehicle for telling a story, but is it the right medium for you? Before you start thinking about characters, sales, or social media, it is important to figure out exactly what you're trying to accomplish and why. Making comics, like any artistic or business endeavor, involves substantial effort and investment. If you're going to make comics a part of your life beyond the Wednesday ritual of picking up your pull box, it makes sense to take a step back and look at the big picture.

To answer this broad personal question, I suggest you take yourself out for a cup of coffee or a cocktail (if you're old enough, of course) and figure out the answers to the following smaller questions. Keep in mind that the answers can and will change over time, so don't be afraid to revisit these questions as your circumstances or the industry changes.

Goals (or *What Do You Want to Do in Comics?*): "I want to make comics" is a start, but there are different aspects to the industry, and figuring out where you want to be will help you make decisions on which opportunities to pursue and which ones to avoid. Maybe you want to make your own books and sell them at cons. Maybe you want to work for the Big Two[15]. Maybe you want to be the next Stan Lee or Todd McFarlane. Maybe you want it all. You can have any goals you want. The purpose of goals isn't to limit you. They just guide you on your path.

Reasons (or *Why Do You Want a Career in Comics?*): It's one thing to know what you want to do. Knowing *why* is a different type of insight. Are you doing this because you have a story to tell, because you want to be a part of the comics community, or because you want more money than Tony Stark?

Like your goals, your reasons are personal. They don't have to define you, but keeping them in mind can motivate you to overcome the inevitable setbacks and pitfalls of publishing comics. You can have any reason or motivation you want for getting into comics. **There are opportunities for artistry, creativity, and profit at almost every level of the industry, but at the end of the day, a love of the art form will keep you going.**

Plan (or *How Are You Going to Get into Comics?*) After you understand your goals and your reasons for wanting those goals, you need to develop a plan to help you get from where you

---

[15] In comics, any mention of "The Big Two" is a reference to DC Comics and Marvel Comics which account for the majority of sales and revenue in comics publishing, as well as owning some of the most popular characters in popular culture. Albert, A. (2018, June 26). Here is a List of the Top Comic Book Publishers and Companies. Retrieved May 14, 2020, from https://www.thoughtco.com/top-comic-book-publishers-and-companies-804427

are to where you want to go. As you read this book, you can begin to figure out which path you want to adopt for your purposes and take the appropriate steps.

Of course, no plan survives contact with reality. The industry is in a state of constant flux. The impact of changing trends will often be outside of your control. You're going to need to modify your plan to adapt to new conditions, so the plan you make might not be the path you ultimately take. But you have to start somewhere and making your comic is a good place to begin, no matter where you ultimately want to go.

Resources (or *What Do You Have to Offer the Industry?*) The secret to success in the comics business involves making consistent ritual sacrifices on the altar of the industry. What you get from comics is based in large part on what you put in. Your offering might be a creative vision, artistic skill, a network of eager professionals, or an investment of time and finances. In many cases, the creators who came before you had to offer all these things and more. Now is the time to figure out what you bring to the table and what you need to find in the community to make your goals real.

Milestones (or *How Will You Track the Progress of Your Plan?*) No one goes to sleep wanting a career in comics and wakes up where they want to be. Your development as a creator will grow in stages. You get to determine what those stages are and, to a large extent, in what order you want them to happen. You can start with putting your first team together, getting your first issue online, or any other basis that's right for you. You can decide whether your goals are books created, copies sold, or views on your website. Milestones give your goals a concrete structure you can use to measure your efforts.

Motivation (or *What Gets You Started and Keeps You Going?*) Despite the view from the outside, the business of comics is not easy. It can be a long road from your initial inspiration to holding your book in your hands and the road is seldom a straight line. There will be obstacles and pressures to stop. This isn't just true in comics. It's true in life.

Even if you get your vision into the world, success (whatever your definition of it is) may not come quickly. It is not hyperbole to say some creators did not live long enough to see their stories become a fixture in mainstream culture[16].

What is it about your comic that's going to bring you back to the project month after month and year after year? What is going to pick you up when life knocks you down? What drives you might be very personal or it could be the universal desire for fame and fortune.

---

[16] Jonathan Larson. (n.d.). Retrieved May 14, 2020, from https://www.pbs.org/wnet/broadway/stars/jonathan-larson/

Yes, there are movies, merchandise, and money to be made. Yes, comics are one of the driving forces in 21st Century pop culture. But the comics business is not a get-rich-quick industry. For every *Walking Dead*, there are thousands of other titles that lose money or never get off the ground. **If you don't love comics, it might not make sense to spend the time and effort of getting into the business**.

Do You Love Publishing Comics?

As I write this book, comic book related entertainment has dominated pop culture for more than ten years. Characters, stories, ideas, and even methods of consuming entertainment have emerged from the pods of comic shops to infect the whole world like *Venom*. It is only natural that creators from other media start looking at comics as a place to make a name for themselves before they move on to "the big time". If this applies to you, don't worry. There's nothing wrong with jumping on the comics bandwagon, as long as you do it out of love—and not *lust*—for comics.

What is the difference between love and lust in publishing independent comics? It's similar to the difference between feeling love and lust for another person.

When a person falls in love, they offer their time, energy, and creativity to the loved one with enthusiasm. They bring the best aspects of themselves to the experience. They make an effort to keep the relationship going because they want it to last as long as possible. They are always looking for new ways to express their love. They are proud to display that affection in public. Part of what defines the lover is the person they are in love with.

A person in lust wants to get something from the object of their desire as quickly as possible. They are often single-minded and ruthless in their pursuits. They jump from target to target, never taking the time to establish a bond or relationship with anyone. They often repeat a scripted pattern of behavior with each new target. They often act in secret or with a certain amount of shame. They are more defined by their hunger than their connections to others.

All this might seem very abstract, but the concept of love vs. lust has concrete applications for an independent comic book publisher:

- A creator in love with comics wants to publish as many books as they can in their lifetime. A creator in lust with comics wants that one book that will give them money, recognition, sex, or whatever it is they are after.

- A creator in love with comics creates books about things that they are passionate about. A creator in lust with comics creates stories that they think are "hot" or take advantage of a pop culture trend.

- A creator in love with comics takes time to learn their craft and find their voice. A creator in lust doesn't want to invest time and effort because they think publishing comics is fundamentally easy.

- A creator in love with comics uses social media to make connections with readers and other creators. A creator in lust with comics uses every social media post to scream "Buy my book!"

- A creator in love with comics reads a lot of comics. A creator in lust is only interested in other creators when he's trying to sell them his book.

- A creator in love with comics will start on a new project soon after the current one is done. A creator in lust checks the sales figures on their book every thirty minutes instead of making comics, hoping they'll see a magical flood of revenue.

- A creator in love with comics will experiment and try new things to improve both their artistic craft and their publishing business. A creator in lust is looking for that one gimmick or magic bullet that will make their book sell.

- A creator in love with comics takes pride in their catalog and tries to expose it to as many people as possible in as many ways as they can. A creator in lust will reject independent comics as dead after the first book fails because their book isn't a bestseller.

Moments of lust are inevitable in the creative process, but it is an emotion that is hard to sustain over a long period because publishing comics is not all drawing, drinking, and attending movie premieres. "*You will have setbacks. You will get rejected. This will happen more than a little bit. But you can't let that stop you from making comics if that's what you love to do.*"[17]

If you get into comics based on a love of the medium, it will be easier to maintain the persistence that can lead to success.

What Are Your Chances of Success?

Comics are similar to other forms of narrative art when it comes to competition. It wouldn't be an exaggeration to say that every person who has ever read comics is a potential comic creator in an age where technology allows the production, marketing, and distribution of content by anyone and everyone.

---

[17] Manning, D., Lederman, L., & Reddington, J. (2012). *Write or wrong: A writer's guide to creating comics*. San Bernardino, CA: Transfuzion Publishing. p. 210

But no matter what your definition of success might be, keep in mind that your competition might not be as overwhelming as you might think. Screenwriter Corey Mandell once addressed this issue in *Script* magazine.[18] I'm borrowing his logic and substituting comic creators for screenwriters:

- Competitors who start production: If there are a million potential independent comics creators in the world every year, only twenty percent of them will sit down and try to create a comic.

- Competitors who finish production: Out of those two hundred thousand potential competitors, only a fraction of them will finish their books because they'll burn out, or life gets in the way, or whatever. That fraction might only be ten percent.

- Competitors who publish: Just because a book is created and thrown out into the world doesn't mean it's published in an optimal manner. The number of books out of that remaining twenty thousand that are published with any thoughtful consideration to marketing, printing, distribution, advertising, and sales are going to be very low even if you take into account webcomics and titles available in a combination of print and online. Even if we assume a generous twenty percent of potential titles fall into this category, the number isn't very big.

- Competitors in your niche: The number of competitors gets even smaller when you consider that your comic isn't really competing with every other comic in the market. We'll talk more about genre and target market in Chapter 28, but when you focus on the particular niche your story falls into, the number of fish in your pond shrinks to a manageable level.

- Competitors who last: You can't have a successful life as a comic publisher with one great book in the same way you can't have a successful sports career with one great game. Persistence in comics means publishing book after book, year after year. Some creators can crank out a book. They might even catch lightning in a bottle, but not many of them can keep doing the work after the first book. The ones that do will be successful.

I have a friend named Paul Azaceta. I met him at Central Park Media and we both found a way into Marvel at different points in our careers. He went on to publish *Graveyard of Empires* at Image and do

---

[18] Mandell, C. (2017, July 05). What Are Your Real Chances of Screenwriting Success? Retrieved May 14, 2020, from http://www.scriptmag.com/features/career-features/what-are-your-real-chances-of-success

work for both of the Big Two. I met him for drinks while he was working on *Outcast* with Robert Kirkman and during the conversation, he summed up everything I've tried to say here in one thought:

"*A lot of people love comics. Some of them talk about making comics. A handful might start making comics, but only a few of them will actually ever make a comic and almost none of them keep making comics.*"

If you get into publishing independent comics with an eye to sustaining your effort, your chances of success expand over time.

In addition to looking at the potential for success in relation to your comic book publishing competition, you also need to consider the potential for success or failure in a wider business context. According to the Bureau of Labor Statistics, 20% of small businesses fail in their first year, 30% fail in their second year, 50% fail after five years in business and 70% of small business owners fail in their 10th year regardless of what industry they are in[19]. This business failure could come from negative cash flow, poor business models, too much competition or not having the right team to run the business. These statistics aren't meant to discourage you from publishing comics. I'm only trying to place the importance of the business concepts contained in this book in context with your potential success.

---

[19] McIntyre, G. (n.d.). What Percentage of Small Businesses Fail? Retrieved May 14, 2020, from https://www.fundera.com/blog/what-percentage-of-small-businesses-fail

There's a lot more to the comics business than writing and drawing. The different tasks involved in pre-production, production, and post-production all take time. Weeks, months, and years can easily be consumed by your book. At the same time, most of us can't pause our lives to publish comics. Making sure everything gets done requires planning and forethought, but luckily the way to fit comic publishing into your life can be found in the pages of classic superhero stories.

What Is Your Secret Identity?

Anyone who has read comics from the Big Two is familiar with the trope of the secret identity. The hero or villain exists with two personas. One is the powerful masked combatant. The other is the unassuming civilian. Each one has its uses, but the secret identity is kept hidden to protect the character's loved ones and their status in the community.

Comic publishers can live this reality as well as write about it. **If your identity as a comic book professional is like your superhero persona, then your secret identity includes all aspects of your life outside of comics.** This is your day job, your family and friends, your entertainment, and your overall health. You need both aspects of your life to publish comics, and in a perfect world, one side doesn't overwhelm the other.

But we don't live in a perfect world. Balance takes effort.

How Do You Maintain Your Double Life?

You only have so many hours in a day to get things done. You only have a finite amount of energy to devote to any task. The key is getting the most done to complete your book in the most efficient way. **Time management** is defined as the organizing and planning of how to divide your available time[20]. Like the crime-fighter who practices law during the day and patrols the streets of Hell's Kitchen at night, you're going to need a plan if you want to get both jobs done.

Business journalist Mario Peshev created a useful framework in an article for *Entrepreneur Magazine*[21]. I'm going to paraphrase it here and then point out how this book will help you develop the tools for independent publishing time management.

---

[20] Bill T, Chrystal, & Mind Tools Content Team. (n.d.). What Is Time Management?: Working Smarter to Enhance Productivity. Retrieved May 14, 2020, from https://www.mindtools.com/pages/article/newHTE_00.htm

[21] Peshev, M. (2017, March 29). 7 Time Management Strategies for Busy Entrepreneurs. Retrieved May 14, 2020, from https://www.entrepreneur.com/article/292112

- *Create a long-term roadmap*: Start with where you are, figure out where you want to be (Goals), and then determine your path (Plan). This book provides a linear framework to guide your project from start to finish to the beginning of the next book.

- *Manage Priorities*: Accept the reality that you can't do it all. Your secret identity is going to have to sacrifice something if you want to publish comics. Storenvy CEO Jon Crawford put it succinctly: "*Work, sleep, family, fitness, or friends—pick three. It's true. In order to kick ass and do big things, I think you have to be imbalanced.*[22]"

- *Break down the project into simple problems*: Instead of trying to handle all aspects of publishing your book at once, figure out what needs to be done in what order to make sure you're not wasting time. My method breaks publishing down into digestible tasks which will get you from idea to published comic.

- *Start with a simple task:* It's easy to get overwhelmed with all the different aspects of publishing. Start your roadmap with a manageable first step and you won't sabotage yourself before beginning. This book starts with the basic assignment of managing your ideas to give you a foundation for action.

- *Adapt to Changing Circumstances:* As we said, no plan survives contact with reality[23]. Things will change in the industry and your life during the development of your book. Adjust your time management as you move through the process and take advantage of your small size relative to the established publishers and adjust your plans quickly.

What If You Realize You Don't Have Time to Make Comics?

Time management is a powerful tool, but it can't create, pause, or rewind time. If you make an honest assessment of your schedule and you don't see a reasonable amount of time left over for publishing even after you've given up the gym, TV, video games, and your relatives, then it doesn't make sense to pile more on to your plate.

---

[22] Stillman, J. (2016, February 03). Work, Sleep, Family, Fitness, or Friends: Pick 3. Retrieved May 14, 2020, from https://www.inc.com/jessica-stillman/work-sleep-family-fitness-or-friends-pick-3.html

[23] Projects, C. (2019, October 03). German Field Marshal. Retrieved May 14, 2020, from https://en.wikiquote.org/wiki/Helmuth_von_Moltke_the_Elder

This doesn't mean you need to give up on comics forever. Continue to collect your ideas and give your plans a chance to incubate until you can devote the proper time to your efforts. Just don't confuse patience with procrastination.

How Many Independent Comic Creators Have a Secret Identity?

If I knew how many comic creators and publishers had secret identities, then it wouldn't be a secret, but it's safe to say that you are not alone in your double life. Based on my anecdotal experience, the vast majority of comic creators who are not working in the offices of a major publisher as a day job, or have exclusive contracts with major corporations, or are full-time freelance artists probably have a secret identity. Jim Zub may have said it best: *"I've been writing Avengers for years and I still haven't quit my day job."*[24]

How Long Do You Have to Maintain Your Secret Identity?

While living a double life can add layers of complexity and stress, shedding your secret identity isn't a realistic goal for most independent publishers, and in some cases, it shouldn't be. Even if you had the financial success to quit your day job and publish comics full time, there would still be personal, social, and other outside obligations to deal with. But those aspects of your life help you maintain balance. It's always a good idea to have some portion of your life outside of comics, both for your sanity and because creative people need outside experience to fuel their ideas.

This leads us to a discussion about the creative ideas for your comic.

---

[24] Zub. J (n.d.). Retrieved May 14, 2020, from http://www.jimzub.com/cliff-diving/

STAGE 1: PRE-PRODUCTION

PART 2: INTELLECTUAL PROPERTY MANAGEMENT

Or What Is Your Comic About?

What is an Idea?

Comics at their heart are based on ideas. Since we're starting from the beginning, it makes sense to establish what I mean by an idea, because from a legal standpoint, ideas have a specific status in terms of how they are protected and how they can be used. While there are over a half a dozen definitions of an idea in the dictionary[25], for our purposes, **an idea is any single thought that inspires the creation of a comic story**.

Where Do Ideas Come From?

A metaphysical discussion on the source of ideas is too abstract for this book, but in my experience as an author, **ideas come from the organic interaction between the different stimulus you are exposed to and your imagination and perspective at the time you encounter the stimulus.**

Using myself as an example, my novels were inspired by an idea cobbled together like Frankenstein's monster. I took a concept that I thought was missing from the spy genre, focused on an actual practice from real-world spying, based my antagonist from horrible men in the news, copied the writing styles of four great but widely divergent authors, created characters based on prominent actors and musicians and I published six novels in five years.

Your comic idea might develop from a similar process, but the results will always be different. If you and ten other comic creators could be exposed to the same stimulus (everything from media, everyday conversations, the events of your day, and so on), you would arguably still generate at least ten different ideas for comics. Similarly, the ideas you create today will be different from the idea you come up with tomorrow, because you are not the same person you were yesterday. As the Greek philosopher Heraclitus allegedly said *"No one can step in the same river twice, for it is not the same river and they are not the same person.*[26]*"* It might be a little theoretical, but if ideas are a river, you'll never have exactly the same idea more than once.

This means as a creator you need to expose yourself to as many different ideas from as many different sources as possible. You may be focused on a particular type of story in a specific genre, but your ideas and ultimately your project will benefit from diversity. You might love comics, but the ideas for your comic needs exposure to books, television, plays, film, video games, relationships, travel, architecture, and art.

---

[25] Idea. (n.d.). Retrieved May 14, 2020, from https://www.dictionary.com/browse/idea

[26] Heraclitus, Haxton, B., & Hillman, J. (2003). *Fragments*. New York: Penguin Books.

This also means that **recording your ideas as they come is essential**. We've all heard it before, especially if you're a writer. You're supposed to carry something around with you all the time to record your ideas. This cliché advice is based on bad news and good news. The bad news is that you will not remember the brilliant idea you had during your commute, or over a dinner conversation, or drifting off to sleep. Some versions of it might come back to you later, but it will be at a different point in the river of ideas. The good news is that you can record your thoughts on your phone with text, voice, or even video. Just try not to do it over dinner if you're with family or friends. If you do record all the comic ideas you have, it won't be long before you have so many ideas you might have a hard time deciding which one to pursue.

How Do You Decide Which Ideas to Pursue?

You have an unlimited imagination for potential comics. You have a limited amount of resources to publish your comics. You need to curate your ideas and move forward with one book, at least in the beginning. As Stan Lee once said "To have an idea is the easiest thing in the world. Everybody has ideas. But you have to take that idea and make it into something people will respond to – that's hard.[27]"

Fortunately, choosing the right book is easy. All you have to do is **run with the idea that you love and obsess over more than all the others**.

Whatever book you make, there's a good chance you will spend more time with this idea than you do with your family, your friends, your partner, and your day job. You are going to sacrifice time, money, brain cells, emotions, and risk physical injury to turn this idea into a published comic. You are going to have to fight for this idea from an intellectual, social, political, and financial standpoint, not just with other people, but with yourself. If everything works out in the best possible way, this idea could be what you are known for in the industry forever. This idea could impact your career like *Batman* did to Bob Kane or *Usagi Yojimbo* for Stan Sakai.

There is no reason to put in all that energy for just any random idea. Let your imagination run wild, but only invest in the idea that you love. And don't let anyone take your idea away from you, unless they give you what that idea is worth. No matter what your goal as an independent publisher, your product needs to be closer to art rather than content.

What is Art?

When we talk about "Art" here, we're not talking about the images that make up your comic. Instead, we're discussing the aspirational and idealized concepts of human expression. **Art** is defined as the

---

[27] Stan Lee's 16 Quotes to Inspire Success in Your Life and Business. (2019, September 29). Retrieved May 14, 2020, from https://thinkmarketingmagazine.com/stan-lee-quotes-on-life-and-success/

conscious use of skill and creative imagination, especially in the production of aesthetic objects.[28]"
While this broad definition can be applied to any comic book, in theory, there are elements of quality, craftsmanship, and outside critique that elevate a particular comic to the level of art[29]. There is an ongoing and often malicious debate about who is qualified to critique comics and what they can say, but we'll explore that issue more when we talk about social media[30].

What Is the Difference Between Comic Art and Comic Content?

Established publishers have the luxury (or the burden, depending on your perspective) of being in a business that revolves around producing content on a consistent basis. They have to keep their titles in circulation. They need to provide products to retailers. They need to give their readers something to consume. They all want to deliver quality content, but publishers aren't necessarily shooting for an Eisner award with every issue of every comic.

But those publishers aren't in the same position as you. To one extent or another, they have established books, talent, and retail accounts. Some of them have been consistently publishing content for years. Some of them have created art. The best of them have done both. If you have limited resources and limited experience as an independent comic publisher, then you want your ideas to translate into art. **Any story can serve as content, but only some books rise to the level of art.**

Like all determinations of art, the elements that constitute comic art are subjective. Some stories have defined or redefined the media in the modern era. *Contract with God, Devil by the Deed, Watchmen, Dark Knight Returns, Superman: Red Son, The Phoenix Saga*, *The Elektra Saga, Monstress,* and *Lone Wolf and Cub* are the kind of books I think of when I think of milestones in comic book art, but I'm sure you have your list of books that stand apart from the weekly releases[31].

When thinking about the differences between content and art for your book, look at content as forgettable stories, with a limited shelf life, and limited relevance to a fan of the book. Art, on the other hand, is classic. It's something that will be in high demand years after its release and be seen as the seminal work to understand both the characters in the story and the creative team that brought it to life. As a practical consequence, content is usually cheaper and faster to produce. Art takes time and often isn't cheap, especially to the creators with limited resources.

---

[28] Art. (n.d.). Retrieved May 14, 2020, from https://www.merriam-webster.com/dictionary/art

[29] Id.

[30] Plummer, J. (2019, March 14). Comics Twitter Perfectly Illustrates What's Wrong with Comics. Again. Retrieved May 14, 2020, from https://bookriot.com/2019/03/13/whats-wrong-with-comics/

[31] The comics I reference in lists like this aren't meant to be absolute or definitive. There are several shelves of graphic novels on the shelf where I write. When I need an example of any type of comic, I just look around and pick a good one.

Focus on the ideas you love and use them to create the best book you can. Strive to cultivate ideas that lead to books better than your favorite comic[32], but don't chase perfection. No book is perfect. "Perfection is the enemy of done"[33]. As we will see in Chapter 53, missed deadlines can kill even the best book.

Does Your Idea Have to Be New?

If you try to make a comic based on a new theme, you will probably never make a comic. Since Homer dropped *The Iliad* in 850 B.C., we've had almost three thousand years of narrative art in the Western World. Storytelling traditions probably go back farther in Asian and African cultures, and Neanderthal cave paintings are the original narrative sequential art[34]. Depending on who you believe and how you count them, in the history of narrative art, humanity has only come up with seven basic plots.[35]

Even if you ignore all of the literature and focus just on comics, you'll find novelty isn't a required element of the ideas. *Superman* and *Batman* were the original comic book superheroes but they didn't spring up from nowhere. They both borrowed concepts from pulp heroes like *Doc Savage* and *The Shadow*, and those titles borrowed ideas from even older literature[36]. The modern comic itself isn't original as a narrative medium, since it's a hybrid media combining newspaper comic strip funnies of the early 20th century with pulp mystery and science fiction[37].

Your idea needs to be unique and original, not new. You have to tap into your perspective and create something only you can create with elements that set it apart from similar work. You have to create something that isn't a copy of someone else's work. The *Walking Dead* wasn't the first zombie comic, but it might be the most successful one. *Deadpool* wasn't the first character to break the 4th wall, but he might be the most well-known. According to the comic creators at Make Stuff Studios, the key is to strike a balance between building on established ideas and inventing a unique experience[38].

---

[32] Manning p. 202

[33] Patel, D. (2017, June 16). Why Perfection Is The Enemy Of Done. Retrieved May 14, 2020, from https://www.forbes.com/sites/deeppatel/2017/06/16/why-perfection-is-the-enemy-of-done/

[34] McCloud, Understanding Comics

[35] Booker, C. (2016). *The seven basic plots why we tell stories*. London: Bloomsbury.

[36] Lopes, P. D. (2009). *Demanding Respect*. Temple University Press.

[37] Id.

[38] Oscar, J. (Director). (2019, October 6). *Building Vs. Inventing: The Problem With Studios* [Video file]. Retrieved May 14, 2020, from https://www.youtube.com/watch?v=eE5vngd0eNk&t=74s

When Should You Stick with an Idea and When Should You Give Up on It?

Part of the process in choosing a comic idea to publish is deciding what not to publish. Even after you settle on a specific idea and start to run with it, some ideas may not reach their full potential as published comics. Your job as an independent publisher is to choose which ideas to stick with over time and which ones to drop to conserve resources.

Don't give up on an idea because you get negative feedback about it, or because your marketing isn't an instant hit, or based on any rejection you might receive[39]. *Star Wars*, *Back to the Future*, and *ET* were all famously rejected when they were first pitched to studios[40], but the writers and creators stuck with their vision and created enduring stories. As we'll see in Chapter 27, a large part of the success of a story lies in connecting it to its proper target market. Of course, there are many examples of ideas that never got off the ground despite the dedication of their creators, but that doesn't justify abandoning your idea. *"Strive to publish the comic that you believe in, even if the readers, editors, your family, or friends don't believe in it."*[41]

Give up on an idea when you are no longer in love with it. As we discussed earlier in this chapter, larger publishers don't have to be in love with every book they release. Independent publishers who have to do (and often pay for) everything themselves need something beyond money to justify their efforts because making money is not a guarantee. Gravitate towards the ideas you obsess over, not the temporary flashes of inspiration.

But while you can't publish every idea you have, it is important to **never throw an idea away**. Artists and creators from different media stress the concept of revisiting, reworking, or improving ideas over time[42]. My experience as an author is a perfect example. Between the ages of twenty and thirty, I spent ten years writing the worst science fiction novel ever committed to paper. I see that work as a horrible failure of creativity, but the characters and concepts from that disaster became the basis for novels I'm very proud of today. Creators often need to work through the bad ideas to get to the good ones, so record every idea, whether you love it or not.

---

[39] Ng, M. (Adapter). (2019, May 6). *Stan Lee Keynote at the 2017 Graduation Ceremony* [Video file]. Retrieved May 14, 2020, from https://www.youtube.com/watch?v=c_SXIUTwfvo

[40] 8 Hit Movies That Were Originally Rejected by Studios. (2016, April 30). Retrieved May 14, 2020, from http://mentalfloss.com/article/79197/8-hit-movies-were-originally-rejected-studios

[41] Manning 202

[42] Questlove, & Greenman, B. (2018). *Creative quest.* New York, NY: Ecco, an imprint of HarperCollins.

Why Can't Anyone Legally Protect an Idea?

It is inevitable in your career as a creator for you to say something along the lines of "They stole my idea!"

You'll come across something, a book, movie, or TV show that reminds you of an idea tucked away in your notepad or on your phone. You may have never shared your idea with anyone, but somehow the world got access to your thoughts and rushed them to market before you could capitalize on them. You might wallow in anger and regret. You tell your friends how you thought up the idea for that hit show years ago. You might even contemplate a lawsuit to get paid for what you see as your rightful property. While artists of all types are at risk of having their work stolen, you might be wasting valuable time you could be using to publish comics.

Consider this example: Imagine I told you I just read a comic about a rich man who suffered a life-changing criminal tragedy and then used his wealth to acquire the skills and technology to become a vigilante fighting outside the law. What comic did I read? Was it *Batman*, *Moon Knight*, *Green Arrow*, *Iron Man*, *Knight Hawk*, *The Shadow,* or a dozen other books? Remember, a comic doesn't need to have an original idea. It just needs to have a unique expression of that idea.

Your ideas might come to you as dreams, nightmares, or flashes of brilliance. When you first get them, you might write them down on napkins, the notepad of your phone, or in insane little scratches on your bedroom wall. Your method of capturing your ideas can be as unique as the idea itself, but at some point, you're going to have to articulate your idea to other people if you want to publish comics. A nightmare scrawled on a wall probably isn't the best long-term strategy, especially if you're renting that apartment.

There is a uniform structure you can use to express your ideas after the initial inspiration. This structure is something you can use with every idea you have. Over time, you can build a library of ideas that can be easier to combine and manipulate as you build the one idea for your comic art. The structure borrows conventions from both novel and film, but they can be used to develop any type of narrative art.

The structure consists of a synopsis, a pitch, a tagline, and a query letter.

What is a Synopsis?

A synopsis is a summary of the entire story. It lays out all the major plot points of the narrative (premise, inciting incident, progressing complications, climax, and resolution[43]). A comic synopsis also needs to have descriptions for all the major and supporting characters, a description of the setting, and any unique features of the world where the story takes place. The setting and unique features can be baked into the narrative, but the characters should be given additional focus as part of the overall synopsis.

The synopsis is the basis for your entire idea structure. You reduce the synopsis to its fundamental elements to create the pitch and the tagline. You expand the synopsis to its full strength in the script and finished pages. You cut and repurpose elements of the synopsis for your marketing, advertising, and sales. The synopsis is the heart of your idea. If you have an idea that you can't express as a synopsis, there is a good chance it won't work as a comic.

While a synopsis usually tells a linear story, it doesn't have to be created in a linear form. Maybe your first inspiration is a character. Maybe the ending of your story comes to you before any other element. Maybe it's a setting. You can start from anywhere and build the synopsis in any direction. The synopsis doesn't have to lay out every story beat and every panel at this stage. You just need to define the answers to the core questions.

---

[43] McKee, Story

What are the Core Questions?

Sometimes referred to as the Five W's and How[44], these are the core questions the synopsis has to answer:

1. Who is the story about (who are the characters)?
2. What happens in the story (what is the plot)?
3. Where does the story take place (what is the setting)?
4. When does the story happen (what is the time period)?
5. Why did the characters do what they did (what is their motivation)?
6. How did the characters do what they did (what is their rationale)?

The synopsis is the heart of your idea. Make sure you love it before you try to turn it into a comic.

What is an Example of a Synopsis?

In 2014, I published a book called *A Taste of Honey*[45]. This is a modified version of the synopsis I used. I'm not using this because it's the greatest synopsis ever written. I'm using it because I control the rights to the book and everything associated with it, so I know I can use it without legal repercussions.

A Taste of Honey

Nikki Siriene is a spy who uses her beauty to steal secrets for her lover Chris. She travels to Argentina for him to seduce the leader of an arms smuggling ring named Manuel Cruz. Her mission is to get close enough to the womanizing shipping magnate to steal the secrets of his crimes without being caught.

Nikki attracts the attention of Manuel, but she also catches the eye of his mysterious wife Dominique. Nikki tries to focus on the mission, but she tumbles into a love triangle with the married couple. The two women eventually fall in love, and Nikki keeps up the pretense of spying on Manuel just to stay close to her new lover.

After months of simmering jealousy, Chris explodes. He forces Nikki to make a choice. She has to finish her mission or watch both her lovers die.

---

[44] Hart, G. (2002). The five w's of online help systems. Retrieved May 14, 2020, from http://www.geoff-hart.com/articles/2002/fivew.htm

[45] Hennessy, G. (2014). *A Taste of Honey*. Jackson Heights, New York: Nightlife Publishing LLC.

Nikki complies, stealing the files that prove Manuel's guilt. But before she can escape, Dominique exposes her own identity as a secret agent and her mission to spy on Manuel. The lovers agree to shut down Manuel's operation and find a way to stay together.

But Chris won't accept Nikki's plan. He tries to end the operation and send Nikki back to America, but she threatens to blackmail him if he doesn't comply with her wishes. Chris pretends to agree, but when he meets Dominique alone, Chris has her tortured and records video of the sexual violence.

Nikki is forced to deliver the data in exchange for Dominique's life. In the end, she is able to escape from her brutal lover's trap, but Manuel and Dominique die and Nikki is forced into a life of hiding from the man who taught her everything she knows.

These six paragraphs summarize the major plot points in the story. The first paragraph defines the premise. The second adds the inciting incident. The third fourth and fifth paragraphs build progressing complications. The final paragraph provides both the climax and the resolution. At the same time, my synopsis answers the core questions in a way that ties the narrative together.

What is a Pitch?

A pitch is a full sentence that can explain your entire story. Like the synopsis, it shows the unique nature of your story and the stakes involved. Unlike the synopsis, it is shorter, normally doesn't use the names of the characters, and doesn't give away the end of the story.

The pitch is a quick snapshot of your story. It's what you use when you only have a short period of time to get someone's attention. Because of its rapid nature and lack of spoilers, it has multiple uses in the development of your book. At different points, you'll use the different versions of the pitch (or a modified version of it) to:

- Recruit creators
- Build your website
- Talk to retailers
- Talk to the press
- Talk to fans

In general, there are two types of narrative pitches; *the convention pitch* and *the high concept pitch*. Both of them are similar, they just use different language to get their point across.

The **convention pitch** is supposed to convey the essence of your book between fifteen seconds and one minute, or the time you might have to talk to someone when they walk up to your booth at a comic convention. In other industries, it's known as the elevator pitch, but the central idea remains the same.

When crafting a convention pitch, boil down the essence of your synopsis. It needs to highlight the genre, the protagonist (and perhaps antagonist), the setting, and the stakes. Think about the blurbs Netflix uses with each one of its films and TV shows and you'll get a decent idea about the convention pitch. For example, "A group of diverse superheroes band together to stop an insane alien from destroying half the universe" works pretty well as a convention pitch.

By contrast, a high concept pitch combines well known pre-existing ideas to describe a new idea in an effective manner[46]. It relies on both the popularity of the existing idea and the potential novelty of joining different elements together. High concept pitches are usually in the form of "It's X meets Y" or "It's what you get if X and Y had a baby."

Depending on your personality and the nature of your story, it might make sense to use your synopsis to create both types of pitches. This will give you more options to convey your story idea before they have a book in their hands.

A pitch is the face of your idea. It is the first thing (and maybe the only thing) people will hear about your book before they decide to invest in it.

What Are Some Examples of Pitches?

I wrote two pitches for *A Taste of Honey*. I'm sure the pitch for your comic will be better.

- Convention Pitch: *A Taste of Honey* is a spy thriller about one woman's descent into the worlds of gun running, human trafficking, and sexual obsession.

- High Concept Pitch: *A Taste of Honey* combines the dangerous sensuality of *Basic Instinct* with the international espionage of *Casino Royale*.

What is a Tagline?

A tagline is a short, memorable phrase that becomes identified with a story or product. It conveys the essence of the story without giving away any details about character, setting, or plot. It is designed to pique interest, convey a mood, or capture the theme of your story. It is a teaser that sums up the whole idea in a few words.

---

[46] Schmidt, A. (2020). Why "X meets Y" loglines are usually ineffective. Retrieved May 14, 2020, from https://www.facebook.com/100001633638895/posts/2760957897301971

Your tagline will be key to advertising and marketing your book. If it's not done well, a tagline is extraneous and forgettable. If done well, it can come to define your idea. Consider these classics and then the one I developed for *A Taste of Honey*:

- "In space, no one can hear you scream"[47]
- "A long time ago, in a galaxy far, far away..."[48]
- "With great power comes great responsibility."[49]
- "In the wrong hands, seduction is a deadly weapon"

Writing a tagline is both an art and a science, but the most important aspect is becoming so intimate with your story that you can describe the central idea in a few words. The best approach might be to play with several examples as you write and edit your synopsis and choose the option that packs the most power in the fewest words. If you're like me, the tagline will probably come to you as you imagine watching the trailer of the movie based on your book.

What is a Query Letter?

In literary circles, an author uses a **query letter** to convince an agent or an editor to read their unsolicited manuscript[50]. As an independent comic publisher, your query letter will be used for three main purposes:

- To determine if you love your idea enough to turn it into a comic
- To determine how difficult it will be to secure the intellectual property rights to your idea
- To convince potential members of your team to join you in making this comic

The query letter is comprised of your tagline, your pitch, your synopsis, and a short introduction of you and what you're trying to accomplish. You will probably have to tailor the introduction depending on who you send the package to, but the core of the query letter is the same.

The first purpose of your query letter will be achieved when you sit down with yourself and look at the idea in a concrete form. How do you feel about it? Is it love or lust? Are you willing to invest years of your life in it? Can you imagine your comic book career being defined by this one book? If so, then keep going.

---

[47] Aliens, Twentieth Century Fox (1986)

[48] Star Wars, Twentieth Century Fox (1977)

[49] Spider-Man (all of it)

[50] Brown, J. (2018, January 05). What Is a Query Letter - How to Write an Agent Query for Literary Agents. Retrieved May 14, 2020, from https://query-letter.com/how-to-write-a-query-letter/what-is-a-query-letter/

The second purpose will be served after you find a competent attorney and retain them to help protect your book. The query letter will have the information they need to help you get started, so you can send them that as soon as the attorney-client relationship is established[51].

The third purpose will be served when you're ready to go out into the world and find the people to make your comic. Armed with a tight query letter, you'll probably have a lot more success than trying to explain your idea to other creators using the weird scratches on your wall.

You might worry about having your idea stolen before your comic gets started, so pay attention to the timing and the relationships involved.

- The person helping you secure the IP rights to your idea will be your attorney and they probably won't be in a legal or ethical position to run off with your idea.

- You won't send the query letter to potential members of the team before you submit the IP applications and registrations, so your idea should be legally protected from other creators.

As a guide to developing a query letter, I've attached a template on the next page to get you started. Feel free to modify it for your own purposes, and don't be afraid to let your idea change and grow over time. This structure is designed to help you wrap your head around your idea. It's not the final expression of your intellectual property.

The template also focuses on written expressions of ideas because most of my independent comic publishing clients tend to be writers—but there is no reason artists, illustrators, and other visual artists can't develop comic ideas. As long as you can summarize the story, answer the key questions, and express your vision to the people who need to understand it, words don't have to get in your way.

---

[51] In most cases, an attorney-client relationship is established when a person seeks and receives legal advice from an attorney. This relationship often involves a retainer and a fee. A Practical Guide to the Attorney-Client Privilege. (n.d.). Retrieved May 14, 2020, from https://www.smu.edu/ola/BriefingPapers/AttyClientPrivilege2

Independent Comic Book Publishing
Form 1: Idea Structure

1. **Creation Date** (*The date you record the idea*):

2. **Creator(s)** (*The people involved in creating the idea*):

3. **Working Title**:

4. **Tagline**: (*a short, memorable phrase that becomes identified with the story*):

5. **Pitches** (*a full sentence that can explain your entire story*):
    a. Convention Pitch (*convey the essence of your book in fifteen seconds*):
    b. Elevator Pitch ("It's X meets Y"):

6. **Synopsis** (*a short summary of the entire story that answers the core questions*):
    a. Who is the story about (who are the characters)?
    b. What happens in the story (what is the plot)?
    c. Where does the story take place (what is the setting)?
    d. When does the story happen (what is the time period)?
    e. Why did the characters do what they did (what is their motivation)?
    f. How did the characters do what they did (what is their rationale)?

7. **Character Details**:
    a. Protagonist(s):
    b. Antagonist(s):
    c. Supporting characters (if any):

8. **Random notes, information, and art**:

Ideas are infinite, but they can't be legally protected until and unless they meet some minimum requirements. Ideas gain the legal status of intellectual property at the point when you meet those conditions.

Experts define **intellectual property** (or IP as it is often referred to) as "intangible creations of the human intellect"[52]. Unlike real property (real estate that doesn't move) and personal property (the material goods that you can move), intellectual property focuses on the ability to own, control, and profit from ideas. Patents, trade secrets, and trade dress are types of intellectual property, but they aren't usually relevant to comics. As a publisher, **your main concerns are copyright and trademark**.

What is the Difference Between a Copyright and a Trademark?

Copyright (normally represented in the US with the symbol ©) is the intellectual property right protected by federal law for original works of authorship in any tangible medium of expression[53]. In its most basic form, a copyright gives the owner the right to make a copy (hence the name), but it also governs who can use or exploit the work for any type of gain.

By contrast, a **trademark** (normally represented in the US with the symbols ™ or ®) is a word, phrase, symbol or design that identifies the source of the goods of one party from those of others.[54]

Over the years, I've found the easiest example I can give a comic book reader to help them understand the difference between copyright and trademark goes something like this:

Let's say someone (we'll call him Bob) creates a story about a rich boy whose parents are killed right in front of him after a night at the theater. After that tragic night, the boy grows up obsessed with fighting crime and making criminals feel the same fear he felt in that alley. He trains for decades and takes on a persona modeled after an animal associated with the fear and the night (for the sake of this example, let's say this guy decides to use a bat). He goes on to create a series of tools based on his symbolic totem. While many people in the city see this mysterious man as a vigilante and a criminal, he becomes the one thing that keeps the city from descending into chaos.

---

[52] Understanding Industrial Property. (2016). Retrieved May 14, 2020, from
https://www.wipo.int/publications/en/details.jsp?id=4080

[53] 17 U.S.C. Section 102(a)

[54] Trademark, Patent, or Copyright? (2019, October 15). Retrieved May 14, 2020, from
https://www.uspto.gov/trademarks-getting-started/trademark-basics/trademark-patent-or-copyright

Maybe you've seen or read a story like this in comics, TV, film, and video games dozens of times over the past eighty years, but as an example, it still works very well. **There is a copyright created for every story of the masked crime fighter. The images associated with him and his story become trademarks and those symbols can be put on anything and everything to help sell stuff.**

Why Is Controlling IP important to Comic Creators?

Whoever controls the copyrights and trademarks to a particular piece of IP decides how that IP is used and who gets paid for it. Keep in mind I didn't say whoever creates a particular piece of IP. **In many cases, the creator is not the ultimate owner, and it is very easy for a creator to give away control over the IP they create if they don't understand their legal and business relationships concerning their creations.** If you remember nothing else from this chapter, remember this:

You can only sell what you own, and you cannot sell what you do not own.

The Big Two have built a multi-billion-dollar business on IP that they own but didn't necessarily create. In 1938, Jerry Siegel and Joe Shuster sold the rights to *Superman* to DC Comics for one hundred and thirty dollars.[55] As of 2016, the licensing rights to *Superman* (not counting the comic book sales) are worth $277,000,000.[56] At the same time, Marvel defines itself as a "character-based entertainment company"[57], whose entire value is based on characters created by hundreds of in-house and/or freelance talent[58]. These comic powerhouses dominate the market because of what they own, not particularly because of what they made.

In Chapter 21, we're going to cover the difference between a collaboration agreement and a work-for-hire agreement, but all you need to be aware of right now is the fundamental difference between the two legal relationships. **In a collaborator deal, the creators share ownership of the IP. In a work-for-hire relationship, an owner hires a creator to create IP that the owner will own exclusively.** This idea might seem simple, but many of the major lawsuits in comics from *Walking Dead* to *Ghost Rider* to *Fantastic Four* came about because it wasn't clear who owned the characters and stories[59].

---

[55] Mcg, R. (1996, January 31). Jerry Siegel, Superman's Creator, Dies at 81. Retrieved May 14, 2020, from https://www.nytimes.com/1996/01/31/us/jerry-siegel-superman-s-creator-dies-at-81.html

[56] Sun, C. (2016, March 17). Batman vs. Superman: Who Makes More Money? Retrieved May 14, 2020, from https://www.entrepreneur.com/article/272554

[57] About Marvel. (n.d.). Retrieved May 14, 2020, from https://www.marvel.com/corporate/about/

[58] List of Marvel Comics superhero debuts. (2020, May 13). Retrieved May 14, 2020, from https://en.wikipedia.org/wiki/List_of_Marvel_Comics_superhero_debuts

[59] Rogers, V. (n.d.). 10 Major Creator Disputes Throughout Comic Book History. Retrieved May 14, 2020, from https://www.newsarama.com/15504-10-major-creator-disputes-throughout-comic-book-history.html

I'm not explaining all of this to discourage you from making comics, frighten you about the concept of IP, or suggest that you don't work with other creators to publish your book. I just want to highlight the importance of owning and controlling the IP of your independent comic and put you in the best position to profit from your creativity.

The first step in owning your IP is to make sure someone else doesn't already own it. One of the major violations of intellectual property law is called infringement. **Infringement occurs when "a work protected by IP laws is used, copied or otherwise exploited without having the proper permission from an entity who owns those rights."**[60]

For example, if you decided you were going to publish a space opera about a battle between a dictatorial empire and a group of rebels that revolved around several generations of a family called Skywalker and their relationship to a semi-mystical energy called "The Force", you would be infringing on the *Star Wars* IP. Things would not end well for you or your book.

If you want your comics to avoid infringement issues, you need to make sure someone else can't make a credible claim on your potential IP. You need to figure this out before you spend limited time, money, and energy on an idea that you don't own. The most efficient way to make this determination is to have your lawyer conduct an **IP review** for your idea.

What Elements of My Potential IP Needs Review?

As you develop the ideas for your comic, every element that could be an aspect of IP needs to be reviewed. That includes:

1. The title of your book
2. The characters in your book
3. The locations and settings
4. Any unique weapons or equipment
5. Logos or symbols

Remember, your story needs to be unique and original, not new. You can have a superhero that runs fast. Every superhero publisher has someone that can run fast. You can publish a fantasy story about an intrepid group of adventurers on a quest to vanquish an ancient evil, but you will run into trouble if you're trying to publish a story about a group of Hobbits trying to destroy the One Ring to Rule Them All.

---

[60] What is an IP infringement? (n.d.). Retrieved May 14, 2020, from http://www.iprhelpdesk.eu/node/3188

How Does a Lawyer Conduct an IP Review?

Different lawyers use different methods for their review. At the minimum, they will compare the elements of your IP to information in government IP databases, domain name registries, internet searching, social media searches, and online store searches. They will then let you know about any potentially conflicting IP they find so you can decide whether or not to move forward with your IP. Under most circumstances, your lawyer will not tell you if you are allowed to register your IP or not. **They will offer advice on the potential risks involved with the ideas you have, but it will be up to you to decide if you want to move forward.**

While your lawyer may conduct an in-depth review on your behalf, it may not capture every potential problem with your IP. As I am writing this book, Image is going through a trademark dispute for the title *Dead Rabbit*, because a bar in New York City published its menu as a comic and secured a trademark just before the Image book titled *Dead Rabbit* went to press. At this point, Image was forced to recall all the copies of *Dead Rabbit* #1.[61] An IP review is important, but it isn't a guarantee.

Does Your Idea Belong to Your Co-Creators, Employers, or Friends?

As you're trying to figure out if anyone in America already owns your potential IP, you also need to give special consideration to your creative and work relationships. Those potential claims of ownership will never show up in your attorney's IP review, but they can be even more damaging to the growth of your book.

Certain types of employment contracts contain language transferring the IP you create to your employer as a condition of your employment. The severity of these contracts varies, but some of them will strip away ownership of your IP even if you don't create it during working hours and even if it has nothing to do with your job[62]. This kind of IP transfer is most common in creative, entertainment, media, and technology jobs, but it makes sense to have your attorney review any employment contract you have to ensure you're not creating the next million-dollar property for your employer.

Creative people often congregate to talk shop, swap ideas, and bond over their art. They also brainstorm, workshop, and attempt to get projects off the ground together. Comics are no exception to this phenomenon. You might find an idea that you love in this free-flowing stew of creativity, but **before you go too far down the pre-production path, it pays to insulate yourself from a potential co-creator or friend trying to make an ownership claim on your IP when it gets off the ground.** Your

---

[61] Johnston, R. (2018, November 19). Image Comics Issues Mandatory Recall Of Dead Rabbit #1 and #2... Over Trademark? Retrieved May 14, 2020, from https://www.bleedingcool.com/2018/11/19/image-comics-mandatory-recall-dead-rabbit-1-2-trademark/

[62] Klein, D. (2020, March 18). Work-For-Hire Clauses and Agreements. Retrieved May 14, 2020, from http://www.kleinmoynihan.com/work-for-hire-clauses-and-agreements-one-key-to-intellectual-property-ownership/

best solution will be based on your situation, so discuss things with your attorney as part of the overall IP review.

Can You Use Celebrities or Famous Historical Figures in Your IP?

If your potential IP is about real people living or dead, then you need to add another layer to your analysis. Using real people in fictional work raises three different legal concepts:

1. **Defamation**[63] is a false statement of fact that exposes a person to hatred, ridicule, or contempt, causes them to be shunned, or injures them in their business or trade. Your main concern here is whether or not your story is based on facts, since prior case law has established that impossible flights of fancy are not considered defamatory[64].

2. **Invasion of Privacy**[65] is actually a set of legal concepts bundled together. The bundle includes the appropriation of name or likeness for commercial gain, intrusion, undue publicity, and false light. A person's right to the use of their name or likeness has been balanced by the First Amendment and the desire for public expression[66]. The cases are often decided on the way a name or image was used[67]. Basically, **if a celebrity's name is used just to sell goods, then it's not protected by the First Amendment**[68]. **If the celebrity's name is used in a way that promotes artistic expression or literary criticism, then it is protected**[69]. These principles apply whether the celebrity in question is alive or dead[70] and no matter what type of literary work created, so a comic book or graphic novel is a relevant art form.

3. **Trademark infringement**[71] occurs when a trademark is used on an unauthorized product in such a way that creates confusion in the minds of consumers. Many celebrities trademark their name and image. If you decide to use their name without their permission,

---

[63] Digital Media Law Project. (n.d.). Retrieved May 14, 2020, from http://www.dmlp.org/legal-guide/what-defamatory-statement

[64] Kimerli Jayne Pring, Plaintiff-appellee, v. Penthouse International, Ltd., a New York Corporation, Andphilip Cioffari, Defendants-appellants, 695 F.2d 438 (10th Cir. 1983)

[65] LII Staff. (2015, June 19). Publicity. Retrieved May 14, 2020, from https://www.law.cornell.edu/wex/Publicity

[66] Frosch v. Grosset & Dunlap, Inc., 75 A.D.2d 768, 427 N.Y.S.2d 828 (1st Dept. 1980)

[67] Zacchini v. Scripps-Howard Broadcasting Co. 433 U.S. 562 (1977)

[68] Estate of Elvis Presley v. Russen, 513 F.Supp. at 1358

[69] Frosch v. Grosset & Dunlap

[70] GROUCHO MARX PRODUCTIONS V DAY AND NIGHT CO. 523 F.SUPP. 485 (1981)

[71] Is It Trademark Infringement? (n.d.). Retrieved May 14, 2020, from http://www.nolo.com/legal-encyclopedia/is-it-trademark-infringement

they have a potential case against you.

There are several methods you can use to avoid claims like this if you want to use celebrities in your work including trademark searches, disclaimers, and licenses from the holders of the IP rights. Again, your best solution will be based on your situation, so discuss things with your attorney as part of the overall IP review.

The second step in owning your IP is securing registrations for your ideas with the proper government agencies. There is a different process for copyright and trademark applications, and different considerations you have to give each one in the development of your book.

Why Should You Register Your Copyright?

You only have a limited amount of time and money to spend on your book. Does it really make sense to go through the motions of paying money and filling out forms before the book is even created? The answer to that question depends on your goals and how much you value the benefits of copyright protection.

If you don't see your comic as a viable commercial concept or if you think it is viable, but for whatever reason, you are comfortable with the characters and story being used freely by anyone and everyone, then registration might not make sense for you. Legally, you are not required to register a copyright for your comic[72]. But if you plan to invest time, money, and energy into your idea and you want a better chance to benefit from your investment, the benefits of registration will be helpful to you.

The benefits of copyright registration include[73]:

- Before you can sue anyone for infringement, registration (or refusal) is necessary for works of U.S. origin.

- Registration establishes **prima facie**[74] evidence of the validity of the copyright and facts stated in the certificate when registration is made before or within five years of publication.

- When registration is made prior to infringement, a copyright owner is eligible for statutory damages, attorneys' fees, and costs[75].

---

[72] 17 U.S.C. Section 408(a)

[73] Copyright Basics. (2019). Retrieved May 14, 2020, from https://www.copyright.gov/circs/circ01.pdf

[74] Prima facie is Latin for "on its face". In legal terms it means that the information provided is sufficient to establish a fact.. Lawyers love to use Latin terms for some reason, probably because it makes us sound smarter. Prima Facie: Legal Dictionary - Law.com. (n.d.). Retrieved May 14, 2020, from https://dictionary.law.com/Default.aspx?selected=1598

[75] This means that if you sue someone for infringement and you win, the other side has to pay you for your attorney, your court costs and an additional penalty between $750 and $30,000 (17 U.S.C. Section 504)

Registration permits a copyright owner to establish a record with the U.S. Customs and Border Protection for protection against the importation of infringing copies from other countries.

Basically, registration gives you peace of mind when it comes time to share your ideas with other creators. When you know you can pursue someone for infringement and collect money from anyone who steals your IP, the © on your inquiry letter can be powerful.

Somewhere in the mists of time, a creative person decided to try and get the benefits of copyright registration without paying the costs for the registration. Under the concept of a "poor man's copyright", a person mails a potentially copyrighted work to themselves and uses the postmark to establish the latest date on which the work was created[76]. This is a waste of time. While there is no legal requirement to register a copyright, *"there is no provision in the copyright law regarding any such type of protection, and it is not a substitute for registration"*[77]. Besides, it doesn't cost much to file a copyright application, and the process to file an application for a narrative work is fairly straightforward.

When Should You Submit Your Copyright Application?

You can submit a copyright application at any time, but to get the full benefits listed above, you have to apply within three months of publication[78]. As an independent publisher who plans to share their ideas before publication, there are two other dates to consider.

First, you should only submit your application after your attorney has completed their IP review and you've decided to move forward with the idea. Second, you should submit your application before you begin looking for any outside investment in the book or reaching out to other creators to build a team to make the book. Keeping this timing in mind will protect you both from infringing on the rights of someone else and having someone infringe on your IP rights.

How Do You File a Copyright?

You need three basic elements to file a copyright application:

- A completed online copyright application[79]

---

[76] Goldman, E. (2016, October 26). How Will Courts Handle A "Poor Man's Copyright"? Retrieved May 14, 2020, from https://blog.ericgoldman.org/archives/2016/10/how-will-courts-handle-a-poor-mans-copyright.htm

[77] Copyright in General. (n.d.). Retrieved May 14, 2020, from https://www.copyright.gov/help/faq/faq-general.html

[78] Copyright Basics. (2019). Retrieved May 14, 2020, from https://www.copyright.gov/circs/circ01.pdf

[79] U.S. Copyright Registration Step One: Category. (n.d.). Retrieved July 05, 2020, from https://copyright-application-online.com/apply/

- An electronic or print version of the work you want to copyright
- Payment of the copyright application fee

The Application

The copyright office has posted a useful tutorial video to walk you through the process[80], and the online application has simple instructions for each piece of information required once you create an account[81].

The Fee

The fees for copyright applications in 2019 is $65 if you file online. Copyright registration fees are subject to change, so before you submit your application, check the fee page of the copyright office[82]. This fee will be in addition to any lawyer fees you decide to pay for copyright registration, but unlike trademarks, my clients normally handle copyright registration on their own.

The Deposit

Once your application is complete and your fees are paid, the copyright office will send you a confirmation email and a request for your deposit. The email will list all the different formats the copyright office will accept, including text and image file types. The regulations call for the best and most complete edition of the work[83]. While you're applying for a copyright to your comic, you'll be applying before the comic is complete, so the Idea Structure form and/or some version of the script should be the first deposit. Of course, the book itself will inevitably change as you develop the final product. The Copyright Office has supplemental forms you can use when you're ready to submit the finished work, or if the book changes completely, you can file a new form[84].

Why Should You Register Your Trademark?

Your goals for your book may go beyond the initial publication. You might see your book as the anchor to an ongoing line of comics. You might envision a wide variety of merchandise and licensed products based on the characters and stories you create. You might have plans for the logo of your company to

---

[80] The United States Copyright Office (Producer). (n.d.). *Copyright Registration Basis* [Video file]. Retrieved May 14, 2020, from https://www.copyright.gov/eco/standard.mp4

[81] U.S. Copyright Registration Step One: Category. (n.d.). Retrieved July 05, 2020, from https://eco.copyright.gov/eService_enu/start.swe?SWECmd=Start&SWEHo=eco.copyright.gov

[82] United States Copyright Fees. (n.d.). Retrieved May 14, 2020, from https://www.copyright.gov/about/fees.html

[83] Mandatory Deposit of Copies or Phonorecords. (2019). Retrieved May 14, 2020, from https://www.copyright.gov/circs/circ07d.pdf

[84] Copyright Form CA. (2019). Retrieved May 14, 2020 https://www.copyright.gov/forms/formcawi.pdf

be more recognizable in fifty years than the Big Two. If any of this fits your goals, then at some point you'll need a trademark.

Like copyrights, registered trademarks confer specific benefits for IP owners including:[85]

- Public evidence of ownership of the trademark.

- The ability to sue for trademark infringement in federal courts.

- Registration can be used as a basis for obtaining registration in foreign countries.

- Registration may be filed with U.S. Customs Service to prevent importation of infringing foreign goods.

When Should You Register Your Trademark?

The choice and timing of comic trademark registration is more complex than copyright registration. Even if your potential trademark doesn't infringe on someone else's IP, it might not be eligible for trademark protection. Once you review all the potential factors you might decide not to file for trademark registration until you are further along in the development of your book.

First, the title of a book can't be trademarked unless it is part of a series[86]. So if you have a single issue or a graphic novel you can't use that as the basis for a trademark. If you have an ongoing series, the name and the logo can get a potential trademark. The name and logo of your overall publishing company can also get a trademark, as can the logos for your characters.

Second, a trademark must be used in commerce at some point to be eligible for trademark registration[87]. This means that the mark has to be used on goods actually sold in the marketplace[88]. You can file what is referred to as an "intent to use"[89] application for a trademark to secure your potential trademark before the book comes out, but that application is only valid for a limited time. If you

---

[85] Trademark FAQs. (2020, February 19). Retrieved May 14, 2020, from https://www.uspto.gov/learning-and-resources/trademark-faqs

[86] Trademark Manual of Examining Procedure Section 1202.08

[87] 15 U.S.C. Section 1051

[88] Back to Basics: Trademark Use In Commerce. (2014). Retrieved May 14, 2020, from https://www.stites.com/resources/trademarkology/back-to-basics-trademark-use-in-commerce

[89] Trademark applications – intent-to-use (ITU) basis. (2018, August 27). Retrieved May 14, 2020, from https://www.uspto.gov/trademarks-application-process/filing-online/intent-use-itu-applications

don't start using the mark before the time limit on the intent to use application expires, then the mark is abandoned.

Finally, the trademark application process is longer and more expensive than the copyright process. In most cases, it makes sense to have a lawyer handle your trademark application because, in addition to conducting the IP review, they can manage the application process, any responses or negotiations with the examining attorney reviewing your application, any subsequent filings, the notice period where other potential trademark holders can contest your mark, and keep track of all the renewals and subsequent filings after you get your mark[90]. This process normally takes nine months to a year, and as we'll discuss later, some parts of independent publishing should be handled by professionals.

In general, you should consider filing a trademark when you have the book and the finances to make the process worthwhile. If and when you branch out into merchandise or any kind of licensing, a trademark application will be vital.

How Do You File a Trademark?

You need three basic elements for a trademark application:

- A completed application
- Proof of use in commerce (or an intent to use)
- Payment of the trademark application fee

Applications might also include images of your logo, but that is a discussion you should have with your attorney. They will also walk you through the overall application process, but I'll provide some information here that you can have ready when they ask for it.

The Application

Your attorney will need the following information to complete the initial trademark application:

- The exact spelling of the mark and any font, style, color, or image you plan to use for the mark.

- The owner of the mark, whether that is an individual or a company. If you are using a company, the state of incorporation is also required.

---

[90] Trademark process. (2020, February 15). Retrieved May 14, 2020, from https://www.uspto.gov/trademarks-getting-started/trademark-process

- The physical address, phone number, email address, and website of the trademark owner

- The specific type of goods you plan to associate with the mark. You might initially start with comics, or the mark can be for any category of merchandise.

Proof of Use

At some point (not necessarily when you first apply for the mark), you'll need to prove you're using it by submitting what is referred to as a specimen. Your attorney can guide you on what the best types of specimens are for your book, but some examples include:

- Actual copies of the comic
- Advertising for the comic
- Webpages selling the comic

The Fee

Depending on your application method the fees for trademark applications in 2019 range from $225 to $400. Application fees are subject to change, so before you submit your application, check the fee page of the trademark office[91]. Keep in mind, this fee will be in addition to any lawyer fees you decide to pay for the application.

Completing the copyright registration and the trademark applications are major steps in turning your ideas into intellectual property and assets for your independent publishing. Unless you plan to make comics based on someone else's ideas, legal ownership of your IP is essential to the process.

---

[91] Trademark fee information. (2020, February 15). Retrieved May 14, 2020, from https://www.uspto.gov/trademark/trademark-fee-information

If for whatever reason, you don't have a viable IP of your own, you can still publish comics without infringing on the IP rights of someone else. The key is to **either use a story that everyone owns (public domain works) or to get permission from the IP owner (licensing)**. Both types of IP have their own properties, so it makes sense to look at each one separately.

What Are Public Domain Works?

The IP protections granted by copyright law do not last forever. "Depending on when a work is registered copyright lasts for a number of years. The years that copyright lasts is called the copyright term [92]. When that term ends and can no longer be renewed, the work becomes part of **the "realm of materials that is unprotected by intellectual property rights and free for all to use and build upon."**[93] This realm is referred to as the **public domain.**

Why Do We Have Public Domain Works?

The stated purpose of the public domain is to stimulate creativity in the present by drawing inspiration from the works of the past[94]. As I mentioned in Chapter 3, ideas come from the organic interaction between the different stimulus you are exposed to and your imagination and perspective at the time you encounter the stimulus. **The public domain argument is if no one could build on the ideas of the past because they were always worried about infringement, progress would diminish because creators would have to continuously reinvent the wheel.** It is the doctrine of public domain that allows companies like Disney to create new works based on classic stories like *Snow White*, *The Little Mermaid*, *Beauty, and the Beast,* and many others. It is also cynically ironic that many claim that Disney manipulates the public domain system to protect its characters while at the same time using public works to improve its bottom line.

---

[92] The Copyright Society of the USA. (n.d.). Copyright Terms and Definitions. Retrieved May 14, 2020, from https://www.csusa.org/page/Definitions

[93] Public Domain Day - Frequently Asked Questions: Duke University School of Law. (2012). Retrieved May 14, 2020, from https://law.duke.edu/cspd/publicdomainday/2012/faqs/

[94] Why the Public Domain Matters: Duke University School of Law. (2012). Retrieved May 14, 2020, from https://law.duke.edu/cspd/publicdomainday/2012/why/

How Can You Tell If a Work Is in the Public Domain?

Because of persistent lobbying by Disney to retain the copyright to Steamboat Willy (the original Mickey Mouse story)[95], copyright term is somewhat of a moving target. If you come across a pre-existing story that inspires you to spend years publishing it as a comic, there is a four-step process you can take to make sure you're working with a public domain story.

- **Find the copyright notice** of the story. It will usually say something along the line of "© The year it was published and who published it.

Selected Copyright Terms in the United States

Date of Publication	Conditions	Copyright Term
Before 1924	None	None. In the public domain due to copyright expiration
1924-1977	Published without a copyright notice	None. In the public domain due to failure to comply with required formalities
1924-1963	Published with notice but copyright was not renewed	None. In the public domain due to copyright expiration
1924-1963	Published with notice and the copyright was renewed	95 years after publication date
1964-1977	Published with notice	95 years after publication date
1978-3/1/1989	Created after 1977 and published with notice	70 years after the death of the author. If a work of corporate authorship, 95 years from publication or 120 years from creation, whichever expires first
1978-3/1/1989	Created before 1978 and first published with notice in the specified period	The greater of the term specified in the previous entry or 31 December 2047
3/1/1989-2002	Created after 1977	70 years after the death of the author. If a work of corporate authorship, 95 years from publication or 120 years from creation, whichever expires first

---

[95] Schlackman, S. (2018, November 16). How Mickey Mouse Keeps Changing Copyright Law: Artrepreneur. Retrieved May 14, 2020, from https://alj.artrepreneur.com/mickey-mouse-keeps-changing-copyright-law/

3/1/1989-2002	Created before 1978 and first published in this period	The greater of the term specified in the previous entry or 31 December 2047
After 2002	None	70 years after the death of the author. If a work of corporate authorship, 95 years from publication or 120 years from creation, whichever expires first
Anytime	Works prepared by an officer or employee of the United States Government as part of that person's official duties.	None. In the public domain in the United States (17 U.S.C. § 105)

- Based on the copyright year, **determine which term length applies**. Cornell University posted a chart that was valid as of January 1st, 2019[96] that I've reprinted below, but depending on when you're reading this, Disney might have changed the law again.

- If the copyright year falls between 1924 and 1963 and you're unsure if proper notice was given or if the copyright was renewed, you can check databases like the one maintained by Stanford University[97] or New Media Rights[98] to check on the status of your particular work. You can also check the records of the copyright office for any work published after 1978[99].

- Once you have an idea of the status of your potential public domain work, **run it by your lawyer**, just to put a set of experienced eyes on your work.

How Do You Develop an Idea Based on a Public Domain Work?

Once you determine the book you want to use is in the public domain, the next step is to **decide how you're going to turn this book into a comic idea**. The Idea Structure form in Chapter 5 can help, but since this isn't an original idea, part of your decision will be deciding between creating a straight adaptation, where you tell the original story using comics as a medium, or if you reimagine the original story with new elements. Examples of adaptation include Espinoza's *Alice in Wonderland* or Hind's *Macbeth*. Examples of reimagining include all the variations of *Sherlock Holmes* published over the

[96] Hirtle, P. (2020). Copyright Term and the Public Domain in the United States. Retrieved May 14, 2020, from https://copyright.cornell.edu/publicdomain

[97] Copyright Renewals. (2020). Retrieved May 14, 2020, from https://exhibits.stanford.edu/copyrightrenewals?forward=home

[98] How do you find out if a book still has a valid copyright? (n.d.). Retrieved May 14, 2020, from https://www.newmediarights.org/book/how_do_you_find_out_if_book_still_has_valid_copyright

[99] United States Copyright Public Catalog. (2020). Retrieved May 14, 2020, from https://cocatalog.loc.gov/cgi-bin/Pwebrecon.cgi?DB=local

years[100]. Whichever direction you choose, your comic will be an original work under copyright law, so you should follow the same copyright registration process discussed in Chapter 8.

What Are Licensed Works?

Licensed works are comics based on IP owned by a specific person or company. They get their name from the license the publisher gets from the IP owner to make the book in exchange for a fee or a royalty[101]. **The license serves as permission from the IP owner that protects the publisher from an infringement claim.** Several major publishers, including BOOM Studios[102], Dark Horse [103], Dynamite[104], and IDW[105] publish licensed comics as part of their catalogs. Marvel also published licensed comics in the past, including *Transformers* and *G.I. Joe*[106].

Why Do We Have Licensed Works?

Licensed works are useful because, **if used properly, they can leverage the existing popularity of an established title to increase the potential success of the comic.** As we will see in Chapter 28, appealing to a specific set of potential readers can be the difference between success and failure for a comic. When you create a new IP, you have to build your market based on elements like demographics, genre, and psychographics. Creating the right narrative to appeal to the right group of people can be challenging, even for experienced creators. The theory behind a licensed work is that the market already exists. Licensed comics can be developed from books, film, games, or television, and depending on what IP you select and how you position the comic, the right license can tap into a group eager to read what you publish.

How Do You Acquire a License?

The key to getting a license to make a comic lies in making a deal with the IP owner that works for both of you. If you find a property you're willing to spend years publishing as a comic, there are four steps you need to take to secure the license.

---

[100] Sherlock Holmes Search - Comics by comiXology. (2020). Retrieved May 14, 2020, from https://www.comixology.com/search/items?search=Holmes

[101] Licensing of Intellectual Property Rights. (n.d.). Retrieved May 14, 2020, from https://www.wipo.int/sme/en/ip_business/licensing/licensing.htm

[102] Boom! Studio Online Catalog. Retrieved May 14, 2020, from http://www.boom-studios.com/SERIES/

[103] Dark Horse Comics Online Catalog. (n.d.). Retrieved May 14, 2020, from https://www.darkhorse.com/Comics/

[104] Dynamite Comics Online Catalog. Retrieved May 14, 2020, from https://www.dynamite.com/htmlfiles/titles.html

[105] IDW Publishing Online Catalog. Retrieved May 14, 2020 from https://www.idwpublishing.com/comic-series/

[106] Marvel's Licensed Titles. (n.d.). Retrieved May 14, 2020, from https://comicvine.gamespot.com/profile/rubicon/lists/marvels-licensed-titles/58780/

1. **Find the actual IP owner**: This could be an individual, a company, or an estate if the original owner is dead. This might take some research and due diligence, since IP rights can change hands over the life of the property. When in doubt, enlist your attorney to help you track down the current IP owner.

2. Contact the IP owner and **determine if the property is available**: The owner may have given the comic license to someone else, or they might not want anyone to make a comic based on their property. Either way, you can't buy the rights that aren't available for sale.

3. **Work out a deal memo** with the IP owner: A deal memo is a document that outlines the basic structure of the deal. While it is not a contract, it includes most of the business terms agreed to by you and the IP owner. It makes sense to hammer out these points before you get your lawyer involved, since lawyers charge by the hour and you don't want to pay them any more than you have to. The basic outline for a comic book deal memo includes the following specifics:

    a. Title: *What is the exact name of the IP you're licensing? Is it one story, one character in a story, or all the characters and stories the IP owner controls?*

    b. Rights Granted: *What rights are you being granted? Is it just digital publishing and print publishing, or does the deal include merchandise or other media rights?*

    c. Format: *What kind of comics can you make? Are you limited to single issues or graphic novels?*

    d. Number of Issues: *How many issues are you allowed to make?*

    e. Number of Pages per Issue: *How long can each comic be?*

    f. Term: *How long can you publish and distribute the comic?*

    g. Territory: *Where can you distribute the comic? Is it just in the United States, all over the world, or something in between?*

    h. Language: *What language does the text have to appear? Are you limited to English or can you translate the book into another language?*

    i. Advance: *How much (if anything) do you have to pay the IP owner upfront to acquire the rights?*

      j.   <u>Royalty Rate</u>: *How much (if anything) do you have to pay the IP owner for every copy of the book you sell?*

    4. **Bring the deal memo to your attorney** so they can draft and negotiate the final license agreement.

How Do You Develop an Idea Based on a License?

Once the contracts are signed and you've got your license, you'll need to develop your idea within the creative, financial, and production restrictions of the license. **Depending on the nature of the owner and the property, the IP owner might impose restrictions on what you can and can't do**.

    1. On the creative side, they might impose limits on what can or can't happen in the story. For instance, you might not be allowed to turn a G-rated kid's phone app into an NC-17 horror comic. Or you might not be allowed to reveal a potential spoiler in an ongoing series.

    2. On the financial side, the advance and/or the royalty rate might limit the amount of money you have to offer talent when it comes time to build your creative and business teams.

    3. On the production side, you might be required to release the book before or after a certain time frame (often referred to as a window), to either coincide or avoid conflict with, another license or use of the property. This will become an important factor when you start to develop your production, marketing, distribution, advertising, and sales schedules.

There is a distinct difference between developing your own or public domain IP and licensed IP. That difference is monetary. If and when you decide to make a book based on a licensed property, there is a very good chance you're going to have to come up with some money to pay for your comic. In most cases, you'll have to pay this money before the book is made and before you make any money from it. Where that money can come from and how you manage the use of your comic book production money is the subject of the next part of this book.

STAGE 1: PRE-PRODUCTION

PART 3: INVESTMENT

Or How Are You Going to Pay for Your Comic?

Any discussion about financing comic book publishing has to begin with a disclaimer:

What you are going to read in the next 4 chapters isn't financial advice and or legal advice. These are concepts you can consider when deciding if and how to fund your project, but before you do anything concerning money, consult your financial advisor. You should also speak to anyone in your life who might be relying on your finances.

What are the Three Economic Realities of Independent Comic Book Publishing?

Some creative projects don't get produced because the creators fail to acquire the funds to get the project off the ground. Other projects are produced, but at a cost that ruins the creator financially or forces them to lose the ownership of their creation. While managing the finances of your book might not be as exciting as seeing your vision come to life or as inspirational as seeing your book on the shelf of a comic shop, it is a critical aspect of independent publishing that revolves around three basic economic realities[107].

The first economic reality you have to come to terms with is that **before your IP can make money for you, you have to put money into your IP**. Who puts the money in, when the money is spent, how (or if) you pay it back are all factors you can influence, but it will be difficult to make comics without getting some startup money from somewhere.

I define this initial money as your **investment**. It includes all the cash and other financial assets spent to develop the IP. Investment is different from **revenue**, which is all the money generated by the actual IP at any stage. Basically, investment goes into the project and revenue comes out.

The second economic reality of comics is that **you have to be willing to lose your entire investment**. When you put money in the stock market, real estate, or gambling, you are making a bet. You're hoping to win back the money you put in and acquire additional money for your efforts. Some bets are more calculated than others, but all investments have some risk of loss.

Investment in your comic follows the same dynamic. You're betting you can get back the money you put in and acquire additional money for your creativity. But there are no financial guarantees in comics. **For your financial security and mental sanity, you should only invest funds that are not vital to your survival.**

---

[107] Mooney, R. (2019, August 24). The terrifying REAL cost of creating a comic issue. Retrieved May 16, 2020, from https://richardmooneyvi.wordpress.com/2019/08/24/the-terrifying-real-cost-of-creating-a-comic-issue/?

The amount you are willing to lose on any investment is referred to as your **risk tolerance**[108]. Determining your risk tolerance for independent publishing will be based on several factors, including:

1. Goals: If you plan to publish comics as an entry into a new career, you're going to have a higher risk tolerance than someone trying to publish comics as a way to pay off their current debts.

2. Timeline: If you plan to publish comics for the next four or five decades, you're going to have a higher risk tolerance than someone who needs their comic to make a profit in the first year of release.

3. Life stage: If you have little or no financial responsibilities, you're going to have a higher risk tolerance than someone who has a mortgage to pay, kids to support, or medical bills to cover.

4. Relationship to comics: If you love comics, you're going to have a higher risk tolerance than someone who lusts after comics.

5. Personal comfort level: If you have a personality that enjoys risk, you're going to have a higher risk tolerance than someone who likes to play it safe.

Everyone's risk tolerance in comics is unique. The goal of determining your risk tolerance is not to take on as much risk as possible. The goal is to find out how much you can invest in your IP without endangering other aspects of your life.

The third economic reality of comics is that **comics is a discretionary investment** for both you as the publisher and for your readers. You may have a burning passion to tell your story. Publishing comics might be your singular goal in life. You may be willing to risk everything for your comic. These are admirable traits that are valuable to independent publishing. But in most circumstances, your publishing of comics has to occur in the context of other aspects of your life.

If you consider comics in terms of Maslow's Hierarchy of Needs[109], you will find that you can only use comic publishing to address your growth needs of self-esteem, recognition, and creativity after you have

---

[108] Marquand, B. (2020, January 31). Risk Tolerance: What It Is and Why It's Important. Retrieved May 16, 2020, from https://www.nerdwallet.com/blog/investing/what-is-risk-tolerance-and-why-its-important/

[109] Burton, N. (2012, May 23). Our Hierarchy of Needs. Retrieved May 16, 2020, from https://www.psychologytoday.com/us/blog/hide-and-seek/201205/our-hierarchy-needs

satisfied your needs for food, shelter, and stability. You need to make sure you can continue to pay for a place to live, food to eat, and basic life necessities before you can invest in your comic. At the same time, your readers might want your comic, but it's not something they have to have. If they need to choose between buying gas for their car or buying your comic, your comic might not be purchased.

How Do the Economic Realities of Independent Publishing Determine the Investment?

The key to your investment is finding the funding mechanism that fits in with the rest of your life. First, you need to determine how much money you need to publish your comic. Then you need to understand the impact of your potential investment on your personal or family finances. After that, you can explore additional forms of investment from outside parties or the public. This analysis will lead you to a better understanding of how much cash you have to work with and shape your various budgets.

Understanding of the three realities shouldn't prevent you from independent publishing. They are designed to help you be more strategic about your financial investment.

Before you sell your house, beg your grandmother for money, or rob a bank to publish your book, it helps to know how much money you need in the first place. It doesn't make any sense to spend a lot of time stressing about cash when you don't have a clear idea of the costs you're trying to cover. Of course, **prices change and unexpected expenses are more common than you think[110], but if you have a basic idea of your costs, it will help you focus your revenue collection efforts**.

In general, **there are seven types of costs you need to consider when you decide to publish your first comic**:

1. *Initial Costs*: This is the money to get off the ground. It includes the costs to set up your publishing company[111], buy the URL for your website, draft the initial creative contracts, and conduct the initial IP review for your idea.

2. *Ongoing Operating Costs*: This is the annual cost to keep your publishing empire afloat. It will include the fees for your accountant, lawyer, website fees, and other recurring costs.

3. *Creative Costs*: This is the cost to pay your creative team to make the actual book, including your artist, colorist, editor, designer, etc.

4. *Marketing Costs*: This is the cost to pay for both your offline and online marketing, including your website development and maintenance, convention attendance, direct market, and book trade interactions.

5. *Printing Costs*: If you decide to distribute a print version of your book, this will be the cost to print physical copies.

6. *Distribution Costs*: This is the cost to get your book in the hands of readers. This will include storage and shipping costs of physical books and/or any download or bandwidth costs for digital distribution.

---

[110] Vincent, H. (2020, February 22). What does a comic cost? Part 1: Getting Started. Retrieved May 16, 2020, from https://www.andrastecomic.com/post/what-does-a-comic-cost-part-1-getting-started

[111] We'll look more at the benefits of forming a company in Chapter 16:

7. *Advertising Costs*: This is the cost to let your readers know that your book exists. This includes any paid online advertising, app advertising, ads in distributor catalogs like Diamond Previews, convention guides, etc.

These different types of costs represent an overall budget that will give you an idea of how much money it will cost to publish your book[112]. Again, the costs you wind up paying may be different than your initial budget, but this will give you a baseline of the funds you need to collect.

Before you start to worry about all the different types of costs on this list, keep in mind five factors:

1. Singular costs: The initial costs are one-time payments. If your goal is to publish comics over an extended period of time, this cost won't be a factor after the first book.

2. Avoidable costs: Depending on how you structure your publishing plans, certain costs, like printing, might not apply.

3. Managing costs: A resourceful independent publisher can keep costs low by utilizing various low cost or no-cost options for things like marketing and distribution.

4. Timing of costs: All these costs don't become payable as soon as you decide to publish a comic. Certain costs are triggered at different stages of the publishing process, which will give you more time in certain cases to secure the funds you need.

5. Deductible costs: If you decide to establish a company to manage your publishing efforts, many of the costs listed above are tax-deductible expenses that can alleviate the overall burden of the costs over time[113].

Every budget is going to be different depending on your goals, creative choices, marketing focus, distribution methods, and other factors, so I won't try to force you into a one-size-fits-all kind of budget here. One thing you do need to keep in mind when looking at these costs is that **each category will impact your book whether you decide to pay for them or not**. Some creators decide to skip everything but the creative costs in an attempt to save money. That tends to be short term thinking that can have detrimental effects on your book in the long run. We'll explore the impact of each type of cost throughout the rest of the book, but your book will require some level of investment if it's going to have a chance to achieve your definition of success.

---

[112] Kal. (1970, January 01). Comics Economics 101: Comic Book Budgets. Retrieved May 16, 2020, from https://enigmaresolve.blogspot.com/2017/08/comics-economics-101-comic-book-budgets.html

[113] We will cover business deductions in Chapter 16

If you need to put money into your comic before the idea can become a reality, the next logical question is "where will the money come from?"

In general, there are two sources of money: *your money* and *someone else's money*. Let's look at your potential as an investment source first, before we go reaching into someone else's pocket.

What Are the Advantages of Investing Your Money to Make a Comic?

It is not unusual for an independent publisher to dip into their own pockets to publish their comic. Even in cases where someone else contributes funds to the cause, your outside investors will be more at ease if you contribute money first. After all, if you're not willing to pay for your dream, why would anyone else?

Outside of the optics, there are several advantages to using your own money to publish your comic[114], including:

1. Certainty: You know exactly how much is available to spend.

2. Time: You won't spend time chasing money, so you'll have more time to focus on your comic.

3. Control: You can make the comic you want the way you want if no one else is holding the purse strings.

4. Independence: You don't need to pay back or rely on outside investors or lenders, who could decide to withdraw their support at any time.

5. Revenue Potential: You get to keep all the money your book might make.

6. Responsibility: You might be less inclined to engage in excessive spending if the money is coming out of your pocket

---

[114] Advantages and disadvantages of using your own money to start a business. (2019, August 16). Retrieved May 16, 2020, from https://www.nibusinessinfo.co.uk/content/advantages-and-disadvantages-using-your-own-money-start-business

What Are the Disadvantages of Investing Your Money to Make a Comic?

Of course, investing in something as risky as comics has downsides, but these can be relatively low in the long run.

1. Stress: As discussed before, there is a chance with any comic that it will never be completed, never get published, or sell zero copies once it gets published. If any of those things happen, all the money you sank into the project is gone[115]. While you can get more from publishing comics than just a return on your investment, the potential financial failure of the book creates a natural level of stress. However, **if you only used the money that didn't impact your day-to-day existence, the stress won't be as high**. It will certainly be lower than if your book failed AND you had to pay back a loan or other interest-bearing investment.

2. Time: Depending on how much cash you're sitting on before you get started, and how much disposable income you generate on a regular basis, it might take some time for you to save up enough to collect the funds for your comic. While no publisher wants to wait to see their comic book out in the world, **the various other aspects of publishing comics can take a considerable amount of time to develop**. If you're saving cash while working on other aspects of your book, then time can be an asset instead of a liability.

3. Limited funds: Your ability to save money for your comic may be limited based on your income and other life obligations. But you aren't limited to just using your own money. Your investment can be supplemented by other forms of money and revenue as the project begins to take shape. Once interested parties see you're willing to invest skin in the game, they will be more likely to join you[116].

What Factors Should You Consider When Investing Your Money in Your Comic?

Tony Stark money isn't the same as Peter Parker money. Different people have access to different levels and sources of personal finances. Each circumstance has unique advantages, disadvantages, and factors to think about in relation to your comic. Again, these are broad overviews of complex financial instruments and they shouldn't be used without understanding the risks and rewards.

---

[115] There are ways to reduce the pain of loss through the proper use of business deductions, but we'll deal with those in Chapter 16.

[116] Freeburn, C. (n.d.). How to Get Money to Start a Business – 8 Startup Financing Options. Retrieved May 16, 2020, from https://www.moneycrashers.com/money-start-small-business-financing-options/

1. **Savings**
   a. <u>Description</u>: This is the money you already have in the bank. It could come from money you save over time, tax refunds, or selling Vibranium on the black market.
      i. <u>Advantages</u>:
         1. It is the easiest source of personal investment to access.
         2. There is no direct financial penalty if you don't put the money back into your account.
      ii. <u>Disadvantage</u>: Money you take out of your savings account stops earning interest when you withdraw it[117], but at the time of the writing of this book, the loss of current levels of interest isn't a significant barrier for many publishers.
      iii. <u>Consideration</u>: While it might be tempting to invest your entire savings account into your book, it makes more sense to set aside a contingency fund to deal with unforeseen personal or business costs. This will help increase your risk tolerance for the money that you do invest. Depending on your circumstances, financial writers suggest setting aside $5,000 or 50% of your current savings[118].

2. **401K**
   a. <u>Description</u>: A **401(k)** is a savings plan that uses pre-tax money from an employer to contribute towards retirement[119]. Many 401(k) plans allow you to borrow against the plan before retirement and many people use it to fund personal businesses.
      i. <u>Advantage</u>: Many plans allow you to borrow up to 50% of your vested account balance up to a maximum of $50,000[120].
      ii. <u>Disadvantage</u>: If you lose your day job, you might have to pay back any money withdrawn from the 401(k) within 60 days of the job ending. Since paying back a loan at the same time you become unemployed is not an ideal situation, you should consider the security of your job before you tap into this source of money.
      iii. <u>Consideration</u>: Understand both the penalties and fees for withdrawal for your particular plan and discuss the potential implications with your financial advisor and/or significant other.

---

[117] Blackman, A. (2014, February 10). Funding a Business From Your Own Pocket. Retrieved May 16, 2020, from https://business.tutsplus.com/tutorials/funding-a-business-from-your-own-pocket--cms-19437

[118] Advani, A. (2006, June 05). Tapping Your Personal Savings to Fund Your Startup. Retrieved May 16, 2020, from https://www.entrepreneur.com/article/159522

[119] The Wall Street Journal. (n.d.). What Is a 401(k)? Retrieved May 16, 2020, from http://guides.wsj.com/personal-finance/retirement/what-is-a-401k/

[120] Staff, E. (2010, September 22). Self-Financing Your Startup. Retrieved May 16, 2020, from https://www.entrepreneur.com/article/217376

3. **IRA**
    a. <u>Description</u>: An **IRA** (either a traditional or a Roth IRA) are long term savings plans that allow you to purchase investments and offers significant tax breaks over the life of the account[121].
        i. <u>Advantage</u>: You can withdraw money from an IRA any time you want, as long as you replace it within 60 days. This is not a loan, so you don't pay interest[122].
        ii. <u>Disadvantage</u>: If you don't pay the money back, you can be hit with a substantial early withdrawal fee and taxes on the money you didn't put back into the account.
        iii. <u>Consideration</u>: This could be a good source of short-term cash, as long as you can avoid the penalties.

4. **Personal Property Sales**
    a. <u>Description</u>: Using online tools like eBay or offline methods like garage sales to trade in the things you own and no longer need for cash.
        i. <u>Advantages</u>:
            1. Selling your stuff gives you cash without tapping into your bank account
            2. It could be a way to remove clutter from your living space or garage
        ii. <u>Disadvantages</u>:
            1. The amount you make from selling your stuff isn't fixed and can fluctuate over time.
            2. You might have to invest a considerable amount of time selling that you could be using to make your comic.
        iii. <u>Consideration</u>: Be aware of the potential tax implications depending on what you sell and how you sell it[123]

5. **Second Job / Freelance Work**
    a. <u>Description</u>: Acquiring employment outside of your regular job to fund your comic.
        i. <u>Advantage</u>: Depending on what job you have, your side job could allow you to acquire skills that will be useful in publishing your comic
        ii. <u>Disadvantages</u>: Your time and energy are finite. The time and effort you take working for someone else is time that you can't spend on your book.

---

[121] Yochim, D. (2020, May 13). Individual Retirement Account (IRA): Definition & How to Start. Retrieved May 16, 2020, from https://www.nerdwallet.com/article/learn-about-ira-accounts

[122] Staff, E. (2010, September 22). Self-Financing Your Startup. Retrieved May 16, 2020, from https://www.entrepreneur.com/article/217376

[123] Freeburn, C. (n.d.). How to Get Money to Start a Business – 8 Startup Financing Options. Retrieved May 16, 2020, from https://www.moneycrashers.com/money-start-small-business-financing-options/

No matter what type of personal investment you use to publish your comic, try to leverage the relationship between time and money to your benefit. **You can publish very quickly if you are willing to drop more money into the project. You can publish the same book at a lower personal cost if you are willing to take your time**. You shouldn't wait forever to publish. We only have so much time to pursue our dreams. But finding a balance between time and money will help maximize your personal investment.

Of course, the other alternative is finding outside sources of funding...

After you figure out how much you can invest in your comic, you may find that you don't have enough to fully fund your publishing based on your initial budget. That's when it's time to go out into the world and find more money.

Before we go into details about getting investors and the different types of investment, we should understand that in many cases, **it is very difficult to convince anyone to invest money in an untested comic book idea**. The three economic realities of comic publishing we discussed earlier reduce the risk tolerance of most potential investors to the point where your offer isn't attractive to them. From their standpoint, your idea has no track record, all the money they put in could be completely lost, and you're making something that no one really needs.

In the instances where someone is willing to invest, they might want something from you that has less to do with your idea and more to do with some other personal or real property you own. Don't look at this resistance as a statement about the quality of your idea or your commitment to the project. It is simply an expression of economic prudence.

What Do You Need to Show Investors to Convince Them to Invest?

Every potential investor will have different requirements depending on the type of investment you're looking for. Some will want detailed information about your idea, so you'll need to be ready with the following documentation:

1. Your idea structure, including pitch, tagline, and synopsis

2. Your IP review to prove you own the idea

3. Your copyright registration, public domain analysis or license agreement

4. Your marketing data, planned distribution channels, and projected sales

Other investors are looking for specific financial information including:

1. Your financial contribution to the project

2. Your budget for the project

3. Your credit score

4. Your collateral

We'll go into details about credit scores and collateral in this chapter, but as a general rule, it makes sense to have both your creative and financial information ready for whatever type of investment might come along.

What Are the Different Types of Outside Investment?

Like personal investment, every type of outside investment has unique benefits and risks that you should take into account while you're trying to collect funds. These broad categories can give you an idea of the options that might be available, but you'll need to understand your risk tolerance for each one depending on your situation and discuss the options with your financial advisor and anyone impacted by your economic decisions.

1. **Credit Cards**
   a. Description: A **credit card** is an account that allows you to borrow money from a bank to make purchases on a short-term basis. If you pay back the money within a specified period (typically 30 days), you don't have to pay any additional funds. If you take longer than 30 days to pay, you'll have to pay interest (a percentage of the money you owe to the bank) on top of the money you borrowed[124].

   b. Advantages[125]:
      i. Credit cards are relatively easy to acquire, depending on your credit rating
      ii. The revolving credit of a card is more convenient than a bank loan
      iii. Credit cards don't require you to give up ownership of your book or your company
      iv. They don't require collateral
      v. They make it relatively easy to track costs

   c. Disadvantages[126]:
      i. Credit cards require a personal guarantee, which means if you don't pay off the credit card, the bank can attempt to recover the money from your real or personal property
      ii. Credit cards have generally low limits compared to loans
      iii. Credit card interest rates can start high and get higher over time
      iv. Failure to repay credit card debt will harm your credit rating.

   d. Considerations: Understand your credit rating and the impact that credit cards will have on your secret identity if you make or miss payments.

---

[124] NerdWallet. (2020, April 27). What Is a Credit Card? Retrieved May 16, 2020, from https://www.nerdwallet.com/blog/nerdscholar/credit-card/

[125] How to Fund a Business: 13 of the Best Ways to Fund Your Small Business. (n.d.). Retrieved May 16, 2020, from https://www.fundera.com/blog/using-credit-cards-to-fund-your-business

[126] Id.

e.   Your **credit rating** is a number that represents your ability to pay back a loan. It is based on your payment history, the amount you owe, the length of your credit history, and the types of credit you use[127]. You can currently determine what your credit rating is by using free services like Credit Karma[128] or similar sites.

2. **Gifts**

    a.   <u>Description</u>: A **gift** is defined as something given without expectation of anything in return[129]. This could be anything from a family member giving you money to support your comic to a creator offering a service to help get your book off the ground.

    b.   <u>Advantages</u>: True gifts are investments with no strings attached. You get money for your comic. The person who gives you the gift gets to see you fulfill your dreams.

    c.   <u>Disadvantages</u>:
        i.   Personal manipulation: Some gifts are given with an unspoken expectation of reciprocation in material or emotional terms[130]. In many cases, these social transactions aren't detrimental, but if you sense a gift is a form of negative manipulation, it might make sense to look for money elsewhere[131].
        ii. Gift Tax: Gifts over a certain amount are subject to a federal gift tax. As of 2018, any person who gives a gift over $15,000 is subject to a tax[132] of up to 40% and must be reported to the IRS[133]
        iii. Future expectation: If your book happens to become the next *Walking Dead*, your generous donor might expect to share in the success their money helped create.

---

[127] Papadimitriou, O. (2018, May 14). What Is a Credit Score? Credit Score Definition & More. Retrieved May 16, 2020, from https://wallethub.com/edu/what-is-a-credit-score/19569/

[128] Credit Karma. (n.d.). Retrieved May 16, 2020, from https://www.creditkarma.com/

[129] Gift. (n.d.). Retrieved May 16, 2020, from https://www.dictionary.com/browse/gift

[130] Spragins, E. (2003, December 07). When Parental Gifts Come With Strings Attached. Retrieved May 16, 2020, from https://www.nytimes.com/2003/12/07/business/love-money-when-parental-gifts-come-with-strings-attached.html

[131] Shortsleeve, C. (2018, October 16). How to Tell If Someone Is Manipulating You-And What to Do. Retrieved May 16, 2020, from http://time.com/5411624/how-to-tell-if-being-manipulated/

[132] United States Internal Revenue Service. (n.d.). Frequently Asked Questions on Gift Taxes. Retrieved May 16, 2020, from https://www.irs.gov/businesses/small-businesses-self-employed/frequently-asked-questions-on-gift-taxes

[133] Ebeling, A. (2018, June 06). IRS Announces 2018 Estate And Gift Tax Limits: $11.2 Million. Retrieved May 16, 2020, from https://www.forbes.com/sites/ashleaebeling/2017/10/19/irs-announces-2018-estate-and-gift-tax-limits-11-2-million-per-couple/

    d.   Consideration: While gifts on this level don't normally require formal contracts, it would help you and your donor if you both understood the tax implications and what could happen if the book blows up and becomes a huge hit. If they do want a piece of the pie, then it might make more sense to structure this money as a private investment instead of a gift.

3. Grants

    a.   Description: A **grant** is financial assistance given by a government, organization, or person for a specific purpose[134]. Unlike a loan or a line of credit, this money does not have to be paid back in a majority of cases.

    b.   Advantages[135]:
        i.   Grants have all the advantages of gifts with none of the potential disadvantages.
        ii.   Once you get a grant, you can likely get other grants because once you get the first one you will be seen as a more reliable candidate.

    c.   Disadvantages[136]:
        i.   The research and paperwork for grants can take up a lot of time that you could be using to make your comic,
        ii.   There is no guarantee that the time you spend will result in grant money.
        iii.   There is a lot of competition for grants of any type.
        iv.   There is a limited amount of grants specifically available for comic book publishing.
        v.   There are often restrictions on how grant money can be used.

    d.   Considerations:
        i.   Make sure you follow the exact instructions for any grant you apply for. Submissions with errors or completed incorrectly are often rejected regardless of the quality of your idea.

---

[134] Singer, M. (2020, May 02). What is a grant? Definition and meaning. Retrieved May 16, 2020, from https://marketbusinessnews.com/financial-glossary/grant-definition-meaning/

[135] 8 Advantages and Disadvantages of Business Grants. (n.d.). Retrieved May 16, 2020, from http://www.businessgrants.org/2018/12/8-advantages-and-disadvantages-of-business-grants.htm

[136] Ibid

        ii.   Start your search for a grant that will fit your publishing plans with the lists creators Melanie Gillman[137] or Stephanie Cooke put together in 2018[138].

4. HELOC

    a.   Description: Home Equity Line of Credit Loans (**HELOC**) is a loan that provides a line of credit using your home as collateral[139]. The amount of money available to you depends on the amount of equity you have in your home and your credit rating.

    b.   Advantages[140]:

        i.   HELOCs are similar to credit cards in that you only pay interest on the amount of the credit line that you use, not the entire amount of the credit line[141].

        ii.   The interest rates on HELOCs are typically lower than the interest rates on personal loans.

    c.   Disadvantages[142]

        i.   Failure to pay a HELOC loan will result in a negative impact on your credit rating and could force you to lose your home to foreclosure.

        ii.   Interest rates are variable, which means monthly payments can be unpredictable for both your secret identity and your publishing budget.

        iii. In the event the value of your home falls, your home could go underwater meaning that you could end up owing more money than your home is worth. This will make it harder for you to sell your home or refinance your mortgage in the future.

    d.   Considerations

        i.   Be sure that you read and understand the terms of any loan agreement you are considering. Consult your accountant and attorney whenever possible.

---

[137] Gillman, M. (2016, August 14). Grants, Fellowships, and Residencies for Cartoonists! Retrieved May 16, 2020, from http://pigeonbits.tumblr.com/post/148910645278/grants-fellowships-and-residencies-for

[138] Cooke, S. (2018, June 12). Grants, Fellowships, and Residencies. Retrieved May 16, 2020, from http://www.creatorresource.com/grants-fellowships-and-residencies/

[139] Home Equity Line of Credit (HELOC) Rates for May 2020. (n.d.). Retrieved May 16, 2020, from https://www.bankrate.com/finance/topic/heloc.aspx

[140] Johnson, H. (2020, April 21). Home Equity Lines Of Credit: Pros And Cons. Retrieved May 16, 2020, from https://www.bankrate.com/finance/home-equity/pros-cons-of-home-equity-lines.aspx

[141] Fay, M. (2020, April 21). Home Equity Line of Credit (HELOC) - Pros and Cons. Retrieved May 16, 2020, from https://www.debt.org/real-estate/mortgages/home-equity-line-of-credit/

[142] Johnson H. (2020, April 21). Home Equity Lines of Credit: Pros and Cons

ii.   Consider developing alternative methods for paying off any loan that are not tied to the financial success of the comic as a contingency position

iii.   Remember the economic realities of comics and only invest funds that are not vital to your survival.

5. **Personal Loans**

    a.   Description: A **loan** is money borrowed from a bank, credit union, or individual. Depending on the terms of the loan, you'll have to repay the money within a certain period of time with an additional amount of interest paid on top of the money you borrowed[143]. There are two major types of loans: secured or unsecured.

        i.   Secured Loans: You can get a secured loan if you have an acceptable form of real or personal property to serve as **collateral** for the loan[144]. If you repay the loan amount and interest, you get to keep the collateral. If you fail to repay the bank, they can take ownership of your collateral and sell it to recover the unpaid loan amount. If the sale of your collateral does not cover the full loan amount, you are still responsible for the unpaid balance[145].

            1.   Advantages:

                a.   A secured loan does not necessarily require a high credit score because the loan is backed more by your collateral than your promise to pay.

                b.   A secured loan amount is often higher than an unsecured loan amount depending on the value of the collateral

            2.   Disadvantages:

                a.   Failure to pay a secured loan could result in the loss of your collateral. Because publishing comics is an inherently risky investment, using a secured loan to fund a comic puts your collateral at substantial risk.

                b.   Failure to pay a secured loan will also result in a negative impact on your credit rating.

            3.   Considerations:

---

[143] NerdWallet. (2020, January 30). What Is a Personal Loan? Retrieved May 16, 2020, from https://www.nerdwallet.com/blog/loans/personal-loans-exactly-250-words/

[144] Irby, L. (2019, March 12). How Secured Loans Are Different From Unsecured Loans. Retrieved May 16, 2020, from https://www.thebalance.com/how-secured-loans-are-different-from-unsecured-loans-960032

[145] Ibid

a. While there is a loan market for intellectual property[146], **it is highly unlikely that any bank would accept your unproven comic book concept as adequate collateral for a secured loan.** Because there are no sales, there is no proven value in the property. While loans based on entertainment IP are common in Hollywood[147], you're probably going to need more than your pitch package to get a secured loan.

ii. <u>Unsecured Loans</u>: You can get an unsecured loan if you have a good credit rating. Even if your credit score is less than ideal, you can still get an unsecured loan with a co-signer[148]. If you repay the loan amount and interest, there is no penalty. If you fail to repay the bank, they will have to recover the unpaid money through collections, garnishment[149], or other means.

1. <u>Advantages</u>: Your loan is tied to your perceived ability to pay and not any specific collateral that you own.

2. <u>Disadvantages</u>:
   a. Loan amounts are generally lower because of the lack of collateral.
   b. Failure to pay an unsecured loan can lead to prolonged harassment from the banks, including litigation and possible bankruptcy.
   c. Failure to pay an unsecured loan will result in a negative impact on your credit rating.

3. <u>Considerations</u>:
   a. Be sure that you read and understand the terms of any loan agreement you are considering. Consult your accountant and attorney whenever possible.
   b. Whether you get a secured or unsecured loan, when constructing an overall budget, be sure to include repayment of the loan and interest as part of the financial calculations.

---

[146] Financing Alternatives for Companies: Using Intellectual Property as Collateral. (n.d.). Retrieved May 16, 2020, from https://www.stout.com/en/insights/article/financing-alternatives-companies-using-intellectual-property-collateral/

[147] Cpip. (2017, May 11). From Star Wars to La La Land: How Intellectual Property Fuels Films. Retrieved May 16, 2020, from https://cpip.gmu.edu/2017/05/11/from-star-wars-to-la-la-land-how-intellectual-property-fuels-films/

[148] NerdWallet. (2020, January 30). What Is a Personal Loan? Retrieved May 16, 2020, from https://www.nerdwallet.com/blog/loans/personal-loans-exactly-250-words/

[149] Pyles, S., NerdWallet, & New York Times. (2019, September 12). Wage Garnishment: How It Works and What You Can Do. Retrieved May 16, 2020, from https://www.nerdwallet.com/blog/finance/wage-garnishment/

         c. Consider developing alternative methods for paying off any loan that are not tied to the financial success of the comic as a contingency position. The personal investment concepts in the previous chapter might be useful here.

         d. Never take a loan, structured or unstructured, from anyone named Wilson Fisk.

6. Private Investment:

         a. <u>Description</u>: **Private investments** come from individuals or groups who provide money to help businesses get off the ground in exchange for ownership of part of the business[150]. Private investments are different from gifts because the money is provided in exchange for the potential in the IP. While independent comics are still a rare choice in the investment world, the continuing success of comics-related properties in film and television could inspire investors to try and get a piece of the next new cinematic universe[151].

         b. <u>Advantages</u>[152]:

            i. Money that comes from a private investment does not need to be paid back. If the business fails, the investor loses their money and can't go after any of your property.

            ii. The criteria private investors have for their business can be more flexible and open than other types of financing.

            iii. Investors familiar with business in general or comic book publishing in particular can offer expertise in addition to funding.

         c. <u>Disadvantages</u>[153]

            i. You have to give up a portion of ownership and control of your company to the investor. This could limit both the types of comics you create and your ability to enjoy the profits from the business if the book is successful.

            ii. Private investors often focus on being able to get their money back from their investment plus interest within a certain period of time. This can be a challenge in an industry where profits are not guaranteed.

---

[150] Ganti, A. (2020, March 05). Angel Investor. Retrieved May 16, 2020, from https://www.investopedia.com/terms/a/angelinvestor.asp

[151] Hennessy, G. (2018, December 10). Positioning Your Book for the Coming Content War. Retrieved May 16, 2020, from https://www.creativecontractconsulting.com/c3blog/2018/12/10/positioning-your-book-for-the-coming-content-war

[152] Shteyn, R. (2018, January 19). Weighing the Pros and Cons of Angel Investors. Retrieved May 16, 2020, from https://www.business.com/articles/pros-and-cons-of-angel-investors/

[153] Id.

      iii.   Finding and pitching your idea to potential investors could take up a lot of time that you could be using to create your book.

      iv.   The demeanor and personality of an affluent investor could create friction in a creative environment like comic book publishing.

   d. <u>Considerations</u>

      i.   Evaluate every potential investor from a personal interaction perspective as well as from a financial perspective.

      ii.   Every potential investor must sign some sort of investment agreement.

      iii.   Be sure that you read and understand the terms of any investment agreement you are considering. Consult your accountant and attorney whenever possible.

If you decide to get outside funding for your comic make sure you understand how much you are receiving, what you have to pay back, and what you are giving up. Avoid any deals based on vague or unclear terms and don't believe any promises of "free" or "easy" money. Comic book publishing is not an easy money business. Don't sacrifice your IP or your secret identity chasing a financial scam.

After all this talk about using your money and other people's money to fund your comic, I'm sure you're wondering why I haven't talked about one of the biggest sources of comic book funds in the last few years: **Kickstarter**. I didn't forget about it, but Kickstarter and other forms of crowdfunding are sources of revenue, not investment. Once you begin making your comic, you can use your IP to generate revenue through crowdfunding, donations like Patreon, subscriptions, advertising, merchandise, and of course, sales of your comic. But you have to put the investment into your business before you make any revenue.

STAGE 1: PRE-PRODUCTION

PART 4: BUSINESS MANAGEMENT

Or How Are You Going to Protect Your Idea and Your Investment?

Management is the organization and coordination of business activities to achieve defined objectives.[154] **As an independent publisher, this means using your resources in the pre-production, production, and post-production phases of your book to achieve the milestones and goals you defined in Chapter 2.**

As a creative individual, you might consider business management a subject to avoid. If your goal is to spend your time and energy making comics, then dealing with budgets, contracts, and schedules might be the last thing you want to do. But before you dive into making your comic, consider the possible negative outcomes of avoiding business management:

1. Vital aspects of your publishing process either won't be done properly, won't be done on time, or (worst of all) they won't be done at all.

2. Some or all of your investment could be wasted on issues and problems that could have been avoided.

3. The idea that you own and love will fail despite the quality of the idea or the creative work you invested into it.

4. You could lose control of your idea completely.

If you are a creative who doesn't feel they have the time or the headspace to handle the business side of publishing, you could bring in someone to handle those tasks. Either way, you'll still need a basic understanding of your business plan to achieve your goals.

What is a Business Plan?

A **business plan** outlines the strategies and tactics a business intends to utilize to achieve its specific goals.[155] As I mentioned earlier, business plans are often used to attract outside investment, since most experienced investors want to know how you plan to use their money. They can also serve as a valuable roadmap in the publishing process. Your actual publishing experience probably won't match the details of your plan, because reality has a habit of deviating from our intended schemes. But a flexible and thoughtful business plan, combined with your IP and your investment, can get you closer to your objectives.

---

[154] Management (n.d.). Retrieved May 16, 2020, from http://www.businessdictionary.com/definition/management.html

[155] Kenton, W. (2020, February 19). Business Plans: The Ins and Outs. Retrieved May 16, 2020, from https://www.investopedia.com/terms/b/business-plan.asp

How Do You Write a Business Plan?

To build a roadmap for publishing your book, you need to:

1. Understand your business environment.

2. Envision the process of publishing from acquiring the idea to collecting the revenue for the book.

3. Break down every step in the process and figure out how you're going to complete it, taking into account the realities of your business environment.

4. Summarize the assets you have to complete the process

5. Explain how the business makes money

6. Predict the possible outcomes of your business

Form 2 on the next page is a template you can use to get started. Some of the terms might not be familiar to you at this point, and you might not have answers to the questions I pose, but the later chapters of this book will give you the guidance you need. Feel free to modify this template for your own purposes. Like your idea structure, don't be afraid to let your business plan change and grow over time.

Independent Comic Book Publishing
Form 2: **Business Plan Template**

1. **Business Description** (*What kind of business is it?*):
    a. Intellectual Property: (*What is the idea?*)
    b. Goals (*What do you want to accomplish with this business?*):
    c. Ownership (*Who owns or controls the IP?*):

2. **Investment**: (Where will the initial funding come from?)

3. **Costs** (How much investment is required to make the Product?)

4. **Talent** (*Who is working for the business and what skills do they bring to the business?*)

5. **Market** (*Who is going to purchase the Products?*)
    a. Ideal Reader (*What are the demographics and psychographics of the Market?*)
    b. Competition (*Who is delivering similar products to the Market?*):
    c. Differentiation (*How will the Product stand out against the Competition?*):
    d. Size: (How many ideal readers are in the Market)
    e. Growth: (What are the opportunities to increase the size of the Market?)
    f. Interaction Methods: (*How will you connect and communicate with the Market?*):

6. **Distribution** (*How will you deliver the Products to the Market?*):

7. **Products** (*What goods or services does the business provide?*):

8. **Sales Strategy**: (*How will you sell the Product to the Market?*)

9. **Revenue**: (*How will the Product make money?*)

10. **Finances**: (*How will the Revenue be distributed?*)

11. **Next Steps**: (*How will the business react to the success or failure of the Product in the Market?*)

As an independent publisher, there are a lot of tasks you'll need to take care of on your own. But there are at least three situations where a do-it-yourself attitude will be detrimental to your book. After you develop your initial business plan, your next step in business management is bringing in professionals for your book. In this context, I'm defining professionals as accountants, attorneys, and editors.

Please note if you happen to be in one of these professions as part of your secret identity, then some aspects of this chapter might not apply to you. But to paraphrase Abraham Lincoln *"A person who represents themselves has a fool for a client",* so it might make sense to bring in a professional even if you share the same profession.

A cynical reader might see this chapter as a not so subtle advertisement for my services as a comic book attorney. That perspective might have some merit. I don't practice this type of law because I'm independently wealthy. More clients mean more money, and I do enjoy the money. But even if this is true, three other factors should convince you to hire professionals for your business.

- **You need to protect your investment**, especially if you're using someone else's money. Without professionals on your team, you could not only lose your investment, but you could also put yourself in a situation where you lose additional money on top of your investment.

- **You need to protect your IP**[156]. Without professionals on your team, you could spend years developing your book only to lose ownership of it.

- **You need to protect your reputation**. The book that you publish will not only be the public expression of your IP, it will also form the basis of your reputation in the industry. Without professionals on your team, your book has an increased risk of being over budget, or come across as substandard content instead of celebrated art.

This is not to say that the other business and creative people you hire to publish your book are any less important to the process or less professional than an accountant or an editor. I'm simply discussing these three professionals first because you need to have them in place before you bring in a colorist or a web designer. Besides, independent comic book creators often know what they need from a creative team. What they get from professionals isn't always as clear, so let's take a look at each one of them to understand their benefits and costs.

---

[156] Rogers, V. (n.d.). 10 Major Creator Disputes Throughout Comic Book History. Retrieved May 16, 2020, from http://www.newsarama.com/15504-10-major-creator-disputes-throughout-comic-book-history.html

Why Is an Accountant Important for Your Independent Publishing?

An **accountant** is a qualified person trained in bookkeeping, and the preparation, auditing, and analysis of accounts. Accountants prepare annual reports and financial statements for planning and decision making, and advise on tax laws and investment opportunities.[157] While anyone who performs these functions can claim the title of accountant, most accountants have a Bachelor's or Master's degree in accounting and the more advanced accountants have been licensed by their states as Certified Public Accountants[158]. An accountant can maximize and protect your investment and potential revenue in three important areas:

1. Analyzing your financial plans to ensure they match the realities of the market.

2. Developing your budgets to avoid both overspending and missing required payments.

3. Ensuring your business pays all the local, sales, state, and federal taxes that apply to your business, as well as taking advantage of all the available deductions.

Why Is an Attorney Important for Your Independent Publishing?

An **attorney** is an agent authorized to act in a legal capacity for a client[159]. Attorneys advise their clients on legal issues related to their business, analyze and draft documents related to the business, and represent their clients in legal matters[160]. While anyone who graduates from law school can be considered a lawyer, an attorney is someone who has graduated from law school and who has been licensed by the Bar in one or more states[161]. Lawyers are similar to doctors in that many tend to specialize in a specific area of expertise[162]. Comic book law, for example, is a focused form of publishing law that deals with broader aspects of entertainment law[163]. An attorney can protect your intellectual property and your overall business in three important ways:

---

[157] What is an accountant? (n.d.). Retrieved May 16, 2020, from http://www.businessdictionary.com/definition/accountant.html

[158] CPA vs. Accountant. (n.d.). Retrieved May 16, 2020, from https://www.accountingedu.org/cpa-vs-accountant.html

[159] What is attorney? (n.d.). Retrieved May 16, 2020, from http://www.businessdictionary.com/definition/attorney.html

[160] Rivera, J. (2018, July 04). What Is a Business Attorney? Retrieved May 16, 2020, from https://www.legalmatch.com/law-library/article/what-is-a-business-attorney.html

[161] Attorney vs. Lawyer Definition. (n.d.). Retrieved May 16, 2020, from https://www.lawyeredu.org/attorney-vs-lawyer.html

[162] Brown University: Fields of Law. (n.d.). Retrieved May 16, 2020, from https://www.brown.edu/academics/college/advising/law-school/fields-law/fields-law

[163] Hennessy, G. (2019, February 24). What is Comic Book Law? Retrieved May 16, 2020, from https://www.creativecontractconsulting.com/c3blog/2019/2/23/what-is-comic-book-law

1. Analyzing, drafting, and negotiating the various contracts associated with your book.

2. Researching, registering, and protecting the intellectual property connected to your book

3. Representing the business with other creative professionals, companies, and government organizations.

Why Is an Editor Important to Your Independent Publishing?

An **editor** is a person having managerial and sometimes policy-making responsibility related to writing, compilation, and revision of content for publishing[164]. Comic book editors handle structural, stylistic, and copy editing. They are also involved with proofreading, formatting, and overall project management[165]. While many editors have college degrees in fields such as English, journalism, or communications[166], the editorial industry does not have a state licensing system like accountants or attorneys. There are several aspects of comic book publishing where an experienced editor can enhance the quality of your book[167], including:

1. Project management: which covers everything from finding talent, developing a production schedule, and making sure the book is published on time and under budget[168].

2. Developmental editing: focuses on the overall structure of the story before it is written, from the basic structure of the narrative to the pacing of the story[169].

3. Substantive editing: focuses on the distinct elements that make up the story, including the target audience, underlying ideas, characters, and themes[170].

---

[164] Editor. (n.d.). Retrieved May 16, 2020, from https://www.dictionary.com/browse/editor

[165] Definitions of Editorial Skills. (n.d.). Retrieved May 16, 2020, from https://www.editors.ca/hire/definitions-editorial-skills

[166] Book Editor: Education Requirements and Career Information. (n.d.). Retrieved May 16, 2020, from https://study.com/articles/Book_Editor_Education_Requirements_and_Career_Information.html

[167] Cooke, S. (2020, January 02). What Is Comic Book Editing? Retrieved May 16, 2020, from http://www.creatorresource.com/what-is-comic-book-editing/?utm_source=dlvr.it

[168] Comic Book Project Management Tips. (n.d.). Retrieved May 16, 2020, from http://www.comixtribe.com/2011/04/25/comic-book-project-management-tips/

[169] Williams, E. (2017, November 21). Description of Developmental Editors. Retrieved May 16, 2020, from https://work.chron.com/description-developmental-editors-17300.html

[170] Comparison: Copyediting, Proofreading and Substantive Editing. (n.d.). Retrieved May 16, 2020, from https://www.editage.com/all-about-publication/english-editing/copy-editing-vs-proofreading-vs-substantive-editing.html

4. Copy editing: ensures that the final book is easy to follow and free from error, omission, inconsistency, and repetition[171].

How Should You Hire a Professional for Your Book?

Because having professionals on your team is vital to the success of your book, you need to put some time and thought into choosing the right people. Once you determine who you need and how much of your initial investment you can spend on professionals, it's time to research potential candidates.

Online research, social media searches, and personal referrals can all be sources of professional contacts, but it might make sense to research their experience and give preference to professionals who some background in comic book publishing. An attorney who specializes in medical malpractice or an editor who only works on academic textbooks might not be able to help you.

When you have your shortlist of candidates, reach out to each one and see if they're willing to give you a free consultation. Make appointments with the ones that do, and be prepared to explain your goals and ask how they can help your business. Try and talk to several professionals in each category to give yourself more opportunities to find the right person.

If they can help, the professional will offer their services. At that point, your choice will be based on whatever criteria is important to you (personality, price, reputation, etc.) Before working with any professional, keep three things in mind[172]:

1. Make sure there is a written contract between both parties and that you understand the terms of that contract.
2. Make sure you understand the nature of the relationship between you and the professional, including their scope of work, how they will bill you, and the length of time they will be working for you.
3. Start with a small project to determine if the relationship is mutually beneficial. This will give you a chance to confirm the quality of their services without risking too much of your investment.

Depending on your goals, the first small task for your professional team could be the creation of a company for your business. The next chapter will explain the benefits of creating a company and the different types of companies you can create to publish your comic.

---

[171] Max, T. (2020, January 14). Copyediting vs. Proofreading: What's the Difference? Retrieved May 16, 2020, from https://scribewriting.com/copyediting-vs-proofreading/

[172] Hennessy, G. (2017, June 29). A freelancer's guide to hiring a lawyer. Retrieved May 16, 2020, from https://blog.freelancersunion.org/2017/05/24/a-freelancers-guide-to-hiring-a-lawyer-2/

AfterShock, Archie, BOOM, Dark Horse, DC, Image, Marvel...these are some of the major players in the comic book industry. I did a broader survey of comic book companies in 2018 and found that there were over three hundred publishers in the United States and Canada. Some of these were individuals working with one book. Some of them had hundreds of employees, thousands of freelancers, and were themselves smaller branches of a vast multinational corporation. The one thing they all have in common is they aren't publishing their books in their own names. Every publisher made a conscious decision at some point to take advantage of the benefits of working as a formal company instead of as an individual.

What is a Company?

A **company** is an artificial person, established by the laws of a specific state or country, formed to operate a business enterprise[173]. A company does not require a building, an office, a logo, or any of the outward symbols of modern corporations. It does require compliance with the laws of the state where the company was formed in terms of its creation and its ongoing business. There are several different types of companies available in most states of America, and even if the corporate form that you are looking for isn't available in your state, in many instances, you can live and do business in one state and form your company in another state.

Why Should You Form A Company?

There are several legal and financial benefits of forming a company. The specific impact of each of these benefits will be based on the type of company you choose to form, but in general, companies have the following main advantages[174]:

Liability Protection: is designed to protect your personal assets if your business runs into debt. For example, if you order a large print run for your book and fail to pay the printer on time, the printer can sue to recover the unpaid fees. Depending on what kind of company you form and how closely you conformed to the rules of your state, the printer could only come after the assets owned by your business and not your bank account, car, or house.

Tax Advantages: Some types of companies can claim tax deductions for certain business expenses. A tax deduction reduces a person's taxable income, which can reduce the amount

---

[173] Kenton, W. (2020, April 07). Understanding Companies. Retrieved May 16, 2020, from https://www.investopedia.com/terms/c/company.asp

[174] BizFilings. (2020, May 14). The 7 Benefits of Forming a Corporation. Retrieved May 16, 2020, from https://startupnation.com/start-your-business/plan-your-business/benefits-of-forming-a-corporation/

of tax they have to pay[175]. For example, let's say you make $50,000 a year. You attend a convention and had to pay $2,000 for flights, hotel, meals, and other related costs. As an individual, you wouldn't get any benefit from spending that money beyond the pleasure of being at the con. Depending on the company you create, some or all of that $2,000 could be deducted from your income which could lead to more money coming your way at tax time.

What Are the Different Types of Companies?

The limited liability and tax advantages will vary based on the type of company you create. This short chapter can't capture all of the nuances and subtleties of US corporate forms, but in general, there are five main types of companies[176]:

1. A **sole proprietorship** is the most basic form of legal entity. If you do business of any type and don't form another type of business, you are considered a sole proprietor.

   a. *Liability protection*: None. Sole proprietors are personally liable for all debts of the business.
   b. *Tax advantages*: Income and losses from the business are taxed on the individual's tax return[177].

2. A **partnership** is where two or more people form a business together. In most states, there are two types of partnerships: general partnerships and limited liability partnerships[178]:

   a. *Liability protection*: In general partnerships, all the partners are equally liable for all the debts of the company. In a limited liability partnership, each partner is only liable for the actions they have taken.
   b. *Tax advantages*: Income and losses from the business are taxed on each partner's tax return based on their share of the partnership[179].

---

[175] Kagan, J. (2020, January 29). What Is a Tax Deduction? Retrieved May 16, 2020, from https://www.investopedia.com/terms/t/tax-deduction.asp

[176] Choose a business structure. (n.d.). Retrieved May 16, 2020, from https://www.sba.gov/business-guide/launch-your-business/choose-business-structure

[177] Sorensen, M., Kohler, M., & Herzog, K. (n.d.). Sole Proprietorship Definition - Entrepreneur Small Business Encyclopedia. Retrieved May 16, 2020, from https://www.entrepreneur.com/encyclopedia/sole-proprietorship

[178] Kopp, C. (2020, February 05). Partnerships: What You Should Know. Retrieved May 16, 2020, from https://www.investopedia.com/terms/p/partnership.asp

[179] How are Partnerships Taxed? (n.d.). Retrieved May 16, 2020, from https://obliviousinvestor.com/how-are-partnerships-taxed/

3. A **corporation** is a legal entity separate from its owners. Unlike sole proprietorships, partnerships, and LLCs, corporations can exist regardless of who owns shares in the company. Corporations are the easiest business entity to transfer, since the stock can be sold in various ways. Corporations have the highest cost to form and maintain because they require more formal operational and reporting protocols[180].

   a. *Liability protection*: Corporations have the highest level of liability protection for the owners of the company
   b. *Tax advantages*: There are three different types of corporations, (B, C, and S) each with slightly different tax advantages.
      i. B Corp (or benefit corporation) exists for both a public benefit and for-profit and is taxed the same as a C Corp.
      ii. C Corp is the most common form of corporation and is subject to a double tax. They are taxed first on their profits and again on the dividends paid to shareholders[181].
      iii. S Corp is a corporation which is subject to a single tax similar to a partnership. The price for enjoying this special tax rate includes special formation and limitations on the way the S corp can conduct business[182].

4. A **limited liability company** (LLC) combines the liability protections of a corporation with the tax advantages of a sole proprietorship[183]. Because of the flexible nature of the LLC structure and the less stringent formation and operating requirements, I advise my clients to form LLCs more than any other corporate form[184]. Check with your professionals to make sure your goals and circumstances fit this form before you make your choice.

   a. *Liability protection*: In general, members of an LLC are not personally liable for the actions or debts of the business.
   b. *Tax advantages*: Income and losses from the business are taxed on each member's tax return based on the operating agreement.

---

[180] Choose a business structure.

[181] Kagan, J. (2020, January 29). Double Taxation. Retrieved May 16, 2020, from https://www.investopedia.com/terms/d/double_taxation.asp

[182] *The S-Corporation Election; Advantages & Disadvantages* (Rep.). (2015). Retrieved https://www.irs.gov/pub/irs-utl/2015_NTF_Advantages_Disadvantages_S-Corp.pdf

[183] Kenton, W. (2020, April 30). The Truth About Limited Liability Companies. Retrieved May 16, 2020, from https://www.investopedia.com/terms/l/llc.asp

[184] Hennessy, G. (2017, January 31). The Benefits of Forming an LLC for Your Independent Comic. Retrieved May 16, 2020, from https://www.creativecontractconsulting.com/c3blog/2017/1/30/the-benefits-of-forming-an-llc-for-your-independent-comic

5. **Nonprofit corporations** (often referred to as a 501c3) are organized to do charity, educational, religious, literary, or scientific work[185]. Because the IRS sees this work as a public benefit, nonprofits do not have to pay state or income tax[186]. Depending on your goals and the nature of the books you plan to make, it is conceivable for your company to fall into the literary category. But keep in mind that in addition to forming a standard corporation, a non-profit has to secure tax exemption from the IRS and there are ongoing rules governing how the corporation can operate.

   a. *Liability protection*: In general, owners of a nonprofit are not personally liable for the actions or debts of the business.
   b. *Tax advantages*: If the business attains 501c3 status, then it is exempt from both state and federal taxes.

How Do You Choose Which State to Form Your Company?

Every state has different laws governing companies, so choosing where to form your company might be just as important as what type of company you decide to create. In general, there are five factors to consider when choosing a home state for your company[187]:

1. *Formation fees*: Each Secretary of State charges a fee to form a corporation, and there may be other fees required to satisfy all the legal requirements. For example, New York has a publication fee for LLCs that can run several hundred dollars[188].

2. *Annual fees*: Many states charge an additional amount to maintain the company. This can be a relatively small amount to several hundred dollars a year.

3. *Franchise tax*: In addition to the formation and annual fees, some states charge a fee for the privilege of doing business in the state. Several states have no franchise tax as a way to attract more business.

---

[185] Choose a business structure. (n.d.). Retrieved May 16, 2020, from https://www.sba.gov/business-guide/launch-your-business/choose-business-structure

[186] Kenton, W. (2020, April 29). Nonprofit Organization (NPO). Retrieved May 16, 2020, from https://www.investopedia.com/terms/n/non-profitorganization.asp

[187] Akalp, N. (2015, February 02). The Many Variables to Consider When Choosing In Which State to Incorporate. Retrieved May 16, 2020, from https://www.entrepreneur.com/article/241528

[188] Odegard, J. (2018, April 05). What's The Deal With New York's LLC Publication Requirement? Retrieved May 16, 2020, from https://www.forbes.com/sites/jennyodegard/2017/09/06/whats-the-deal-with-new-yorks-llc-publication-requirement/

4. *Legal system*: Many states attract companies (or certain types of companies) because the courts of that particular state specialize in certain types of business-related law. For example, sixty-four percent of the Fortune 500 are incorporated in Delaware because they specialize in business law[189]. In my experience, many entertainment and publishing companies are formed in New York or California because courts in those states have more experience with that type of business.

5. *Investment*: Experienced private investors have usually worked with Delaware, New York, or California law before for the reasons stated above, so if you plan to seek out this type of investment, you might be forced to incorporate in the state of their choosing.

6. *State corporate income tax*: Some states do not require companies to pay a corporate income tax, making them more attractive to business owners, but keep in mind you often can't take advantage of this tax benefit if the physical address of your business is located in another state.

How Do You Form a Company?

To take full advantage of a corporate form, and to avoid confusion in the process, it's best to get input and support from your professionals, especially your accountant and attorney. They can walk you through the process and help you make the best choices, but there is some information you'll have to give them before your company can be created. Form 3 on the next page is a template you can use to get started, although some professionals might ask for additional or different information.

Keep in mind that your professionals will be a valuable resource for your long-term business management and not just the formation of your company, since the financial and legal obligations of the business last as long as you continue publishing.

No matter what type of company you decide to create and no matter where your investment is coming from, **you need to establish a separate bank account for your company when it is created**. You can't take full advantage of the limited liability protection or tax advantages of forming a company if you co-mingle your personal funds with the funds of your company[190], even if you are the only person in your company. Separate bank accounts also make your accounting easier, proves your publishing isn't

---

[189] About the Delaware Division of Corporations. (n.d.). Retrieved May 16, 2020, from https://corp.delaware.gov/aboutagency/

[190] Commingling. (n.d.). Retrieved May 16, 2020, from https://legal-dictionary.thefreedictionary.com/Commingling

just a glorified hobby, and provides a clear audit trail in case your books need to be examined in the event of a dispute with the IRS or your talent[191].

[191] Carlson, R. (2020, January 11). 5 Reasons to Keep Personal and Business Finances Separate. Retrieved May 16, 2020, from https://www.thebalancesmb.com/reasons-to-open-a-business-bank-account-393378

Independent Comic Book Publishing

Form 3: Business Formation Template

1. What is the proposed name of your limited liability company?

2. What is the planned address of your company?

3. What is the contact information for the organizer of the company?
    a. Name:
    b. Mailing Address:
    c. Phone number:
    d. Email Address:

4. What type of company do you want to form?

5. What state do you want to form the company in?

6. What is the contact information for the owners of the company?

7. What is the fiscal year of the company[192]?

8. How long do you want to company to last?[193]

9. What is the purpose of the Company[194]?

10. Who is going to manage the company on a day to day basis?

11. Who will have the right to sign documents on behalf of the company?

12. Who will be the officers of the Company:
    a. President:
    b. Treasurer:
    c. Secretary:

---

[192] A fiscal year is a twelve-month period that a company uses for accounting purposes. Talk to your accountant to determine the best fiscal year for your company Tuovila, A. (2020, January 29). Fiscal Year (FY) Definition. Retrieved May 16, 2020, from https://www.investopedia.com/terms/f/fiscalyear.asp

[193] Many companies exist on a perpetual basis, but you should discuss this with your professionals

[194] In many cases this will be comic book publishing, but you can create a broader purpose if you want

13. What will each of the Owners contribute to the initial company? The contributions can be money, goods, services, scripts, or other valuable items agreed upon by all the owners.

14. How will profits and losses from the company be handled for tax purposes?

15. What salaries or other compensation will the owners and officers of the company receive?

16. What is the name and address of the registered agent who will receive official documents for the company?

STAGE 1: PRE-PRODUCTION

PART 5: TALENT MANAGEMENT

Or Who Is Going to Make Your Comic?

Before we take another step in the publishing process, let's take a breath and appreciate what we've accomplished so far. In the first four steps, you have:

- Determined your goals for making comics
- Found an idea that you love and own
- Conceived how to pay for the comic before it's created
- Formulated a plan to turn your idea into a comic
- Created a legal structure to protect both your idea and your investment.

With these building blocks in place, it's time to start thinking about the talent management of your comic book.

I define **talent management as the discovering, employing, organizing, and utilizing of individuals with specific skill sets to achieve your goals**. For independent publishers, this means building a team to make your book and get it into the hands of your readers.

The importance of talent management to the life of your book can't be overstated. Putting the right team together can turn your comic book into a long-term artistic and financial success far beyond your original goals. The wrong team can waste money, damage your reputation, and squander an idea you love.

Remember, while the next several chapters discuss different types of contracts and the language within those contracts, this is not a comprehensive education on contract law by any stretch of the imagination. My goal here is only to give you the knowledge and vocabulary you need to discuss contracts with your attorney and understand what they're talking about.

The next nine chapters will explore different aspects of the talent management process in-depth, but before we can talk about finding the right people, negotiating their contracts, and putting them in a position to publish art, we have to understand what roles go into independent comic book publishing.

What Roles Do You Need to Publish a Comic?

Critical acclaim for comics is similar to the accolades that movies or television shows receive. Actors, directors, and sometimes showrunners get the glory in film and TV. What little admiration exists in comics is often reserved for the publisher, artist, and writer. But like movies, publishing comics normally requires a variety of different skill sets and functions in an industrial production process[195]. And those skills go beyond the tasks seen as creative. The comic book industry is a business. **Successful independent publishing requires both business and creative roles**. Focusing on only one side limits the potential of the project.

The Creative Team

These are the roles that transform your idea into a finished comic book. Some roles can overlap, but **the common structure of a comic book creative team includes[196]**:

1. The **editor** who oversees the entire process to ensure that the best possible finished product is created on time and under budget as we discussed in Chapter 15.

2. The **writer** creates the overall plot of the book and the script.

3. The **artist** creates the images on each page. They may also create the basic character designs, settings, logos and the cover for the overall book

4. The **inker** enhances the images created by the artist, altering the tone and weight of the images by emphasizing some visual aspects over others.

5. The **letterer** inserts all the words in the book including dialogue, captions, and "sound effects" in a way that guides the reader's eye in a natural progression from one image to another.

6. The **flatter** prepares the inked images for the colorist to enhance the color rendering process.

7. The **colorist** adds moods, energy, and texture to the images to give them more impact to the eye

8. A **production designer** is responsible for the overall visual look of the project.

---

[195] Lopes, P. D. (2009). Chapter One. In *Demanding respect: The evolution of the American comic book*. Philadelphia: Temple University Press.

[196] This list was compiled from several sources, including Love, C., & Withers, A. (2015). *The complete guide to self-publishing comics: How to create and sell your comic books, manga, and webcomics*. Berkeley: Watson-Guptill, Blaylock, J. (2006). *How to self-publish comics not just create them*. Chicago: Devil's due. and Schmidt, A. (2009). *The insider's guide to creating comics and graphic novels*. Cincinnati, OH: Impact.

The Business Team

The creative side of comics is intense and time-consuming, but it is only part of the process. One of the goals of a professional comic creator is publishing books that generate a profit. **Without someone (and more often several people) running the business side of things, even the best comics will not make money**. The elements of the business team vary from book to book, but every book needs to fill these roles as part of the process:

1. **Accounting**: As discussed in Chapter 15, you need someone responsible for the financial health of the project.

2. **Advertising:** informs the public about the book, including offline and online ads, promotions, and sponsorships[197].

3. **Distribution**[198]: handles the relationships with Diamond, other distributors, and the direct market shops for the print book. They are also in charge of managing digital distribution, and other emerging distribution channels.

4. **Legal**: protects the intellectual property of the book, handles the internal and external contract negotiations, and the other tasks outlined in Chapter 15.

5. **Marketing**[199]: creates the website, maintains the social media presence, runs the crowdfunding campaign, and handles the interactions with the comic book press.

6. **Printing**[200]: manages the printing process (if the book is being distributed in a printed format).

7. **Publisher**: oversees the overall creative and financial success of the book from a management perspective.

8. **Sales**[201]: uses the intellectual property to generate money, either through direct sales of the book, advertising sales, merchandise sales, or other forms of monetization.

---

[197] Advertising will be discussed in Part 9

[198] Distribution will be discussed in Part 7

[199] Marketing will be discussed in Part 6

[200] Printing will be discussed in Part 7

[201] Sales will be discussed in Part 10

Finding, employing, organizing, and utilizing fifteen separate skill sets is not a simple or short-term endeavor. Talent management involves juggling time, money, personalities, and technology, all while living your secret identity. This is one of the many reasons I suggested you only pursue an idea that you love. Independent publishing often involves wearing several hats and performing different tasks at different stages of the development of your project. The next chapter will explore the division of labor in comics and how you can make the most of the resources at your disposal.

Independent comic book publishers often have limited resources compared to other publishers. Depending on the levels of investment and secret identities, many independent comics don't' have fifteen people working on them[202]. Creating independent comics is a startup experience. This means flexibility and ingenuity replace an abundance of resources in three main ways.

1. In the absence of a full staff, multiple publishing tasks can be distributed amongst certain members of your team.

2. Certain tasks can be outsourced to freelance professionals

3. You could attempt to perform all the roles yourself.

We'll explore each one of these options separately so you can decide which method works best for your book.

How Do You Assign Multiple Roles Among a Few Individuals?

There is a school of thought supporting small groups over larger ones to complete a project,[203] because each team member is more engaged and the group can move and react faster than a large organization. **If you select members of your creative team that can also provide business services, you can reduce the size of your team by more than half.** Just keep these things in mind before you ask people to start wearing different hats.

1. **More work often means more money.** If you give a person several roles, expect to give them increased or multiple forms of compensation. We'll talk about forms of compensation more in 24, but for now, just keep in mind that people who do work expect to be paid. People who do more work often expect to be paid more.

2. **Leverage secret identities and personalities.** Some comic book creators you meet might have skill sets in their day jobs that could be perfect for your business or creative needs. The scriptwriter who writes ad copy, the colorist who does web design, or the editor who has experience in the direct market can be secret weapons for your book. When you're out looking for talent, pay attention to the secret identities that can reduce

---

[202] If it's any consolation, some established publishing companies don't have fifteen people working on each individual book.

[203] Morgan, J. (2015, April 15). Why Smaller Teams Are Better Than Larger Ones. Retrieved May 16, 2020, from https://www.forbes.com/sites/jacobmorgan/2015/04/15/why-smaller-teams-are-better-than-larger-ones/

your overall team size. To the extent you understand your talent's personalities, factor them into the equation as well. Let the introvert handle the quiet jobs and leave the promotional and marketing work to the extroverted.

3. **Enthusiasm is not a replacement for skill.** This is the flip side of secret identity leverage. You might find people willing to help with your publishing, especially if you pay them. But each one of the roles is a distinct profession that people spend their entire careers trying to perfect. You might want (and need) some of your creatives to step into business roles, but they won't be able to replicate years of experience if it's not part of their secret identity.

4. **Use time to your advantage.** You have control over the marketing and production schedules, the release date, and some of the other timing issues for your book. Extend and manipulate these to maximize your limited resources. Build in time in your schedules for people to jump on a business role while they're waiting for their turn to contribute to the creative side. Don't pile on too many tasks onto one person (including yourself) with deadlines that don't conform to reality or the secret identities.

5. **Make it clear in the contract.** Every member of your team needs to sign a contract. If you want a member of your team to handle multiple roles and you're going to give them multiple forms of compensation for that work, then each one of those roles and forms of compensation needs to be spelled out in writing before the work starts. There will invariably be small unforeseen tasks that come up in a start-up business, but adding on surprise jobs in the middle of a project isn't helpful for either side.

6. **Create milestones for each role.** In the same way you establish creative milestones in the production of your comic[204], it helps to build similar milestones into the business roles you assign to members of your team. This will help everyone understand when each deliverable is due and help you stay on schedule.

7. **Things will not magically fall into place.** Any job that you don't assign to someone will not be done, or it won't be done well. It does you no good to spend two years making a book and then realize no one is prepared to sell it or collect the money.

---

[204] We'll explore more of that in Chapter 24.

8. **There are no guarantees in comic book publishing**. Your chances of success are greater if all jobs are assigned, everyone agrees on the terms, and the schedules for production, marketing, sales, and payment are established well before making the book. But **all this preparation does not guarantee a hit book**. The Big Two have dozens of people involved in each book and some of them still fail. As Jean-Luc Picard once said on *Star Trek*: "*It is possible to commit no mistakes and still lose. That is not weakness. That is life.*"[205]

Can You Do Everything Yourself?

There are several reasons why an independent creator might want to handle all of the publishing tasks on their own.

1. You might not want to burn through your investment paying other people.
2. You might want to keep control of the project for yourself.
3. You might not be a good manager of people.
4. You might want to retain as much of the potential revenue as possible.

While there are more than a dozen skills involved in publishing a comic book, solo operations are not unheard of. Many of the auteur and literary graphic novel creators insist on doing everything themselves to retain complete control over their creative vision[206]. Jason Brubaker, author of the *ReMIND* series, wrote about his experiences as a solo publisher in his book *Unnatural Talent*[207]. Some of the advice for small group publishing is even more important in a solo effort, but there are two other considerations Brubaker mentions when doing it alone.

1. **You have to learn what you don't know**. If you don't happen to know everything from advertising, to crowdfunding, to scriptwriting, to web design, you're going to have to learn it from someone or teach yourself. This means your book might take significantly more time to publish. It also means you'll have a wide range of skills when the project is complete.

2. **Solo doesn't mean you have to do everything**. There are publishing tasks that can be outsourced to freelance professionals on a short-term basis without making them a formal part of a team. For example, Brubaker brought in someone to handle his color flatting work and as we discussed in Chapter 15, professional work still needs to be handled by

---

[205] "Star Trek: The Next Generation" Peak Performance. (n.d.). Retrieved May 16, 2020, from https://www.imdb.com/title/tt0708753/characters/nm0001772

[206] Definitions for cartoonist. (n.d.). Retrieved May 16, 2020, from https://www.definitions.net/definition/cartoonist

[207] Brubaker, J. (2013). *Unnatural talent: Creating, printing and selling your comic in the digital age*. Place of publication not identified: Jason Brubaker.

professionals.

How Do You Outsource Tasks to Freelance Professionals?

Maybe the members of your creative team are not willing or able to take on business roles. Maybe you decide not to do everything yourself. Your third talent management option is outsourcing. **Outsourcing** is defined as hiring a party outside the company to perform services normally performed in-house[208]. From a technical standpoint, using work-for-hire creators[209] is similar to the outsourcing concept, but for our purposes, I'm using outsourcing for business roles and work-for-hire for creative roles.

In 2018, there are approximately fifty-seven million U.S. workers in what is referred to as the "gig economy.[210]" Freelance consultants can be found in every role an independent creator needs. Services like Fiverr, UpWork, and WeWork allow you to find talent and process payments. This pool of talent can fill crucial roles in your publishing, if you manage them correctly:

- Set aside some portion of your investment for outsourcing.
- Attempt to verify the quality of their work with references or online research
- Get some form of a contract signed[211].
- Set clear deliverables and delivery dates.
- Start with small projects to determine who to work with long term.

I've described three separate methods of dividing labor, but you may find the best solution for your publishing is a combination of all three methods in a configuration that is best suited to your resources. As long as you make the best use of the people you discover and add to your team, how you use them is up to you.

---

[208] Twin, A. (2020, April 07). Why Companies Use Outsourcing. Retrieved May 16, 2020, from https://www.investopedia.com/terms/o/outsourcing.asp

[209] Work-for-hire creators are discussed in Chapter 23.

[210] McCue, T. (2018, August 31). 57 Million U.S. Workers Are Part Of The Gig Economy. Retrieved May 16, 2020, from https://www.forbes.com/sites/tjmccue/2018/08/31/57-million-u-s-workers-are-part-of-the-gig-economy/

[211] Services like Fiverr have contractual terms in their terms of use that cover the provision of services, ownership of intellectual property and other legal issues, so be sure to look at them or have your attorney review them before you commit to a major outsourcing project. One Small Step. (n.d.). Retrieved May 16, 2020, from https://www.fiverr.com/terms_of_service?source=footer

What is the Most Important Aspect of Talent Management?

I imagine putting together the right team for your comic is like building a rock band or assembling the Avengers. You can find great people in strange places. You might share more than a few memorable experiences with them. But in the end, **the long-term relationships you build are often more important than whatever specific book you are trying to publish**.

Of course, your goal is to publish art, not to make friends. The ironic thing about comic books is that when you look at the celebrated creative teams like Claremont and Byrne, Loeb and Sale, Miller and Janson, Wolfman and Perez, Snyder and Capullo and all the others, you realize that they didn't just make one great book. They created dozens of books using a variety of characters for many years[212]. They may not have been the best of friends, but they did create good working relationships that translated into art.

As you build a team for your book, you need to build positive relationships at the same time. **The comic book industry is small**. Reputations, good and bad, travel quickly. Power and influence are relative. Positions shift all the time. Relationships last.

The enthusiastic fanboy I first met at a small anime company twenty years ago is now the editor-in-chief of Marvel. The confused sales assistant I met at the same place is now a manga executive at Random House. Assistants and interns at that same defunct company became successful artists and writers for DC, Image, and Marvel. Beyond my circle of friends, every comic book writer with a Netflix deal now was once rejected by dozens of publishers. Some of the top older names in the industry have faded into obscurity. So, don't abuse or neglect comic book professionals. **Be nice, even when you have to say no**.

The person who isn't right for this project might be perfect for the next one, or they might fit a need of another creator you meet. The person who wants you to hire them today might be in a position to hire you tomorrow. You don't have to be artificial in your interactions. You don't have to like everyone, even the people you work with. But for the sake of the idea you love, for your professional reputation and your career in comics[213], be nice, because relationships matter.

---

[212] Hennessy, G. (2017, May 02). Is the Golden Era of Comic Collaborations Over? Retrieved May 16, 2020, from https://www.creativecontractconsulting.com/c3blog/2017/5/2/is-the-golden-era-of-comic-collaborations-over

[213] Lesser, C. (2019, February 27). Artists Become Famous through Their Friends, Not the Originality of Their Work. Retrieved May 16, 2020, from https://www.artsy.net/article/artsy-editorial-artists-famous-friends-originality-work

What Type of People Are You Looking For?

In a perfect world, you could hire and pay the top talent in the industry to focus on one specific role for your book. If that isn't your situation, you're going to need to shift your focus to recruit people who match your resources.

- **Level of Experience**: If this is your first independent publishing project, and you have limited experience or reputation, it will be hard to recruit Eisner-award winning creatives or Fortune 500 business professionals to work on your book. You would be much better served at this stage by **building relationships with people at or below your level** because "you'll get more opportunities from your peers than you will with creators who are further along in their careers than you.[214]"

- **Multiple Skill Sets**: As we discussed in the last chapter, it makes sense to recruit people who have multiple skill sets. If each creative person you hire has one or more viable business skills as well, your search time can be faster and your team can be smaller.

- **Complimentary Goals**: You have a better chance of building a long-term relationship with your creative team if they are looking for the same things you are. If you're trying to build a long-term property and they are trying to get rich quick, the friction could damage the project and the relationship.

- **Complimentary Styles**: For both the business and creative team, bringing in people who have an approach that matches or complements yours is better for the overall team. You need artists who will enhance your idea. You need professionals who gel with the business plan.

- **Budgetary concerns**: You don't want to hire the professional who breaks your budget, no matter how great they might be.

- **Timeline**: If they can't meet the deadline, they aren't right for your team. Missed deadlines kill both comics and reputations in comics.

- **Temperament:** Some people get along from the moment they meet. Some people warm to each other over time. Some people just don't. Pay attention to personalities in your group, not just between you and each team member, but also among the team itself.

- **Reputation:** As we discussed, reputations carry weight in comics. Bringing in the right

---

[214] Greg Pak quote Ramon, G. (2019). *The Comics Career Manual.*

person can elevate your book before it hits the stands. The wrong person can taint an otherwise promising concept.

- **Communication:** The clear exchange of ideas is critical in collaborative art. It does you no good to get a good price on a nice person who doesn't understand what you're telling them or what you want them to do.

Where Can You Find Talent for Your Team?

Sources of talent fall into two main categories: online and offline. While there may be overlap between them, this distinction will be relevant when we talk about making the initial contact.

Online Talent Searches

The benefits of the online talent search include:

1. A wider selection of talent to choose from.
2. The ability to target the type of talent you want.
3. The ability to search at any time.
4. The ability to search even when you're not online.

The downsides of online talent search are also significant. I'll offer some suggestions to reduce the risks, but in these types of searches:

1. There could be a lack of personal connection and interaction.
2. The quality of the talent might be harder to verify.

There are dozens of social networks and job services you can use to find talent online, and by the time you read this book, several new ones might have emerged while some of the sites I'm offering might be gone, but this list can be a decent starting point to find both business and creative talent:

1. **Business Talent**
   a. Canva
   b. Facebook
   c. Fiverr
   d. Freelancer
   e. Google
   f. Guru
   g. Indeed
   h. LinkedIn
   i. MeetUp

j.   Upwork

   k.   WeWork

2.   **Creative Talent**

   a.   Comicconart.com

   b.   Comicartcommissions.com

   c.   Deviant Art

   d.   Digital Webbing

   e.   Facebook

   f.   Fiverr

   g.   Google

   h.   Instagram

   i.   MeetUp

   j.   Reddit

Offline Talent Searches

Although we spend much of our lives online now, you can still make connections and build some (or all) of your comic book team through face-to-face contact. As with online searches and many other aspects of this book, this approach resembles Two-Face because there is a good side and a bad side:

The benefits of offline talent searches:

1.   There is more opportunity for personal connection and interaction.
2.   Their skills and talent might be easier to verify if you can see them in action.

The downside of offline searches:

1.   A smaller selection of talent to choose from.
2.   You don't have the same ability to target the type of talent you want.
3.   You can only search when you are out in the world.

Despite the downsides, I would still recommend adding offline searches to your overall plan. The major sources of finding offline talent are comic book conventions and personal referrals from people in your comic book community. Both of these sources require you to interact with strangers in person, but the comic book industry has a social component, even if much of the work is creative and solitary.

When Should You Start Looking for Talent?

Finding the right talent for your team is similar to dating. It might take a considerable amount of time, and you might have to try out multiple people before you connect with the right individuals. That's why you should start as early as possible and accept the idea that you might encounter a few false starts before the right fit comes along.

You need to have some elements of your publishing in place before you start your search because you're going to use them to attract talent and protect yourself. If you've been following the steps of this book, you should have the tools you need:

- The pitch documents to describe what you're looking for.
- The initial investment to pay them.
- The IP registrations and applications to protect your idea from people you don't know yet.

There might also be some value in finding your talent in a certain order. For example, if you're a writer and you find an artist to do at least the character designs and sample pages first, you can add that art to the pitch documents to recruit the rest of the team[215]. This is a good approach if you find the artist first, but don't overlook potential letterers or sales reps if you happen to find them along the way.

How Do You Choose the Talent for Your Team?

Because the members of your team are crucial to the success of your comic book, each potential team member requires some investigation if you don't know them personally. Even if you do know them as friends or colleagues in your secret identity, it pays to conduct a little due diligence on everyone you're thinking about working with.

There is a term in espionage called **single-source intelligence**[216]. This is information you get from one person that is unconfirmed by any other informant. While trying to publish a comic book may not be as important as spying on a foreign government, **you don't want to rely on single-source intelligence to choose the talent for your project**. **Due diligence** can be defined as the care taken to protect property or the research done in preparation for a business transaction[217]. In terms of publishing your independent comic, this means not taking the information on someone's website or social media page at face value.

Conducting your due diligence doesn't have to cost you a lot of time or money. A little digging into their online activity and references from people who know or have worked with your potential team member in the past can help weed out people who don't fit your goals. The most useful information might come from your initial contact with the talent and their reactions to you and your project.

---

[215] Manning p. 165

[216] Culper, S. (2018, April 11). Judging Single Source Intelligence Information. Retrieved May 16, 2020, from https://forwardobserver.com/judging-single-source-intelligence-information/

[217] Due Diligence. (n.d.). Retrieved May 16, 2020, from https://www.merriam-webster.com/dictionary/due diligence

How Do You Make the Initial Contact?

Depending on your personality and your time, **you can take an active, passive, or combined approach to find talent**.

Steps in the *active* approach:

- Spend time looking at different posts and websites of your potential talent, occasionally commenting on their posted work or asking questions about them and their craft.

- Once you find people who are willing to engage with you in a positive way, politely ask them if they would be willing to consider working on your independent comic book project.

- If they're interested, send them the query letter.

- If they want to work on the project, send them the request for proposal to start negotiating the business terms.

Steps in the *passive* approach

- Find groups, forums, and websites appropriate for soliciting comic book publishing work.
- Make a short post that includes:
- A short description of the type of talent you're looking for
- Whether the job is paying or not (you don't have to include the amount here)
- Your pitch
- Your tagline
- The deadline for submissions
- When you get a response from an interested person, send them the request for proposal.
- Select the best talent based on the submissions you get.

Using the combined approach simply means actively looking for talent and passively posting your available positions at the same time, to position potential talent to send a request for proposal.

What is a Request for Proposal?

A **request for proposal** (or RFP) is a document that describes the needs of a project and asks for bids from qualified vendors[218]. To build your team, an RFP will help you compare multiple potential talents so you can pick the best one for the project.

Whether you get interest from the active, passive, or combined approach, if you have a system to compare all the submissions against each other, you're less likely to get confused or overlook an important piece of criteria. Form 4 at the end of this chapter contains sample questions for an independent publishing RFP. As always feel free to tailor it to your own needs.

After your deadline for submissions passes, compare all the RFP's and select the one that best fits the factors you're looking for. Contact the talent and invite them to sign a contract on a small initial project to complete the due diligence process and add them to your team.

---

[218] What is an RFP?: Knowledge Base. (n.d.). Retrieved May 16, 2020, from
https://grantspace.org/resources/knowledge-base/rfps/

Independent Comic Book Publishing
Form 4: **Talent Request for Proposal**

Include the following information in your RFP

1. An explanation of why you're asking for the info concerning your project.

2. The specifications for the role (or roles) that you are looking to fill and what you expect them to do if they get the job.

3. Ask for at least two forms of contact information.

4. Ask what job they're applying for (if you've posted multiple RFPs).

5. Ask what work have they done before in a similar capacity?

6. Where applicable, as for links to their work[219].

7. Ask who they worked with before.

8. Ask for links and contact information.

9. Ask if they will accept the compensation you have set for this position.

10. Ask if they will sign a contract.

11. Ask if they will be available for future work if they don't get this job[220].

12. Ask if they would like to be interested in being considered for other projects[221].

---

[219] Don't have them send you huge files that will clog up your inbox.

[220] This is not a promise of future work. It's just an estimate of their schedule.

[221] In certain circumstances, samples could be used on the website to promote artists even if they're not used on the project.

Creating a mutually beneficial deal requires balancing relationships and interests. Because you're going to be working with the other person for weeks or even months, you don't want that interaction tainted by negative feelings. At the same time, you might not be able to give the other side everything they want just for the sake of the working relationship.

What you can offer any potential business or creative talent will be based on:

1. Your goals.
2. Your budget.
3. Your timetable.
4. Your level of interest in the skills and abilities of the individual.

The offer your potential talent wants to accept is based on:

1. Their professional goals.
2. Their financial needs.
3. Their available time.
4. Their level of interest in your project and you as a publisher.

Because your interests are different, and in some cases in direct opposition to each other, **there is a tendency for each side to try and negotiate a compromise** between the two positions. This is known as positional bargaining[222]. The problem with positional bargaining is that neither side really gets what they want. Depending on the negotiating power of one side over the other, someone might feel they are doing a deal out of coercion or with a certain amount of resentment. This isn't the best way to start a creative relationship.

Fortunately, there is an alternative to positional bargaining. Roger Fisher, William Ury, and other members of the Harvard Negotiation Project developed an alternative negotiation theory known as **interest-based negotiation** in their bestselling books *Getting Past No*[223] and *Getting to Yes*[224]. While it is not a perfect solution to the negotiation process, it does strive to create solutions both sides want, instead of forced concessions.

---

[222] Positional bargaining. (n.d.). Retrieved May 16, 2020, from https://www.pon.harvard.edu/tag/positional-bargaining/

[223] Ury, W. (2007). *Getting past no: Negotiating in difficult situations*. New York, NY: Bantam Books.

[224] Fisher, R., Ury, W., & Patton, B. (2007). *Getting to yes: Negotiating agreement without giving in*. London: Random House Business

How Does Interest Negotiation Work?

Ironically, understanding when it is time to walk away can help bring parties together. One of the primary concepts of interest negotiation is the *Best Alternative to a Negotiated Settlement* or BATNA[225], or what I like to simply refer to as **options**. A BATNA is "the most advantageous course of action someone can take if the contract negotiations fail". For example, if a publisher wanted to hire you as an artist for their comic and your demands were more than they were willing to agree to, their option would be to simply hire someone else.

Most options are not that straightforward. In many instances, options have to be developed. Some negotiators begin by compiling a list of alternatives to the current proposal. At this stage, no alternative is rejected. This is a creative exercise to explore all possibilities to figure out what you want to accomplish with this deal. The most promising opportunities are then singled out and improved upon if possible until the best option to a contract is found. In our example, the publisher might have a list of other artists, or they could learn to do the work themselves, or they could create a novel instead of a comic, or they could sell the idea to another publisher. In the best-case scenario, **you have several different alternatives to achieve your interests**.

The next step in the process involves trying to understand the other side's options in specific detail so you can identify their interests. As an artist, you might want a combination of money, ownership, creative freedom, credit, or other factors that are important to you.

When the time comes for everyone to negotiate, the underlying interests of all parties are used to reach a consensus. Each side understands the interests of the other and expresses their interests to seek a flexible solution. If the goal of the publisher is to keep costs down and the goal of the artist is money, then a possible solution is for the artist to handle the art, inks, lettering, and colors at a reduced page rate than the publisher would have to pay for four different people.

What Are Principled Negotiation Techniques?

While every negotiation scenario is different, some basic principles apply from the perspective of writing the contract.

- Look for a favorable agreement on all sides, not just an acceptable one.
- Create language in the contract on an ongoing basis to record areas of agreement.
- Move gradually towards commitments on both sides.
- Offer tentative commitments until you see the total package.
- Be rigid in the pursuit of your interests, but flexible in terms of solutions.

---

[225] Ibid.

- Do not allow a "bottom line" to blind you from creative solutions.
- Consider being generous near the end but stick to your interests.

How Does Leverage Impact Interest Negotiation?

Different sides often have different levels of power and control in negotiations. **Leverage**[226] is defined as the power one side has over the other side in the pursuit of their interests. Depending on the disparity between the parties, the leverage one side has over the other can undermine the interest negotiation process. For example, if the publisher in our example was Marvel or DC and you were an aspiring artist looking for their first major gig, their options would outweigh your options so much that you might sign whatever deal they put in front of you[227].

The concept of leverage might not strike you as fair, but as attorney and author David Tollen states in his book The Tech Contracts Handbook[228], "*If you focus on what is fair, you might walk away from deals that make economic sense. But that is a poor choice if you can't get better terms from anyone else, and if accepting the terms would be more profitable than dropping the project.*" It makes more sense to **focus on the best option available, rather than fairness**.

Leverage can be abused to the detriment of the more powerful side because the comic book industry is small. Keep the following ideas in mind, especially if you have the leverage:

- Don't damage the relationship.
- Don't damage your reputation.
- Don't overstate your value.
- Don't agree to things that won't work for either side.

Now that you have a basic understanding of how to negotiate, let's take a look at what you should be negotiating for in a talent management situation.

---

[226] Shell, G. R. (2018). *Bargaining for advantage: Negotiation strategies for reasonable people*. NY, NY: Penguin Books.

[227] Hennessy, G. (2016, August 29). David v.s. Goliath: Negotiating Power in Creative Contracts. Retrieved May 16, 2020, from https://www.creativecontractconsulting.com/c3blog/2016/8/29/david-vs-goliath-negotiating-power-in-creative-contracts

[228] Tollen, D. W. (2015). *The tech contracts handbook: Cloud computing agreements, software licenses, and other IT contracts for lawyers and businesspeople*. Chicago, IL: American Bar Association, Section of Intellectual Property Law.

Your idea, your investment, your time, and your energy have a value that deserves legal protection. The potential members of your team have ideas, skills, time, energy, and reputations that they want to safeguard. The art you eventually create will be an asset that can generate substantial money, recognition, and influence, depending on how it is used or exploited. Of course, not every piece of art you create will make billions of dollars, but since you never know when or if your work will become the next big thing, both sides have an incentive to document their contributions to this project with a formal written agreement.

Personal memories are unreliable. Email chains are vague and incomplete. **A signed contract is the best method to protect the rights and specify the responsibilities of everyone involved**. It doesn't matter if you're hiring your best friend to draw your book, or your romantic partner to design the website, or your mom to help you with the accounting. Everyone who is involved with your publishing business needs to sign some kind of contract.

What can happen if you try to publish a comic book without contracts? There is the chance that no one could try to claim ownership of your idea, use your work without your consent, or otherwise take money that could be going to you. However, there is a greater chance of you losing the benefits of your work.

Every creative industry is littered with stories of artists who had their work stolen and wound up making no money at all from their creations. Publishing comics means taking a substantial risk. It doesn't make sense to take a bigger risk by not protecting yourself with written contracts.

Ultimately, **the legal existence of your book, and your level of ownership over it, will largely be defined by the contracts you put in place. Remember, you can't sell what you don't own**[229].

What Is a Contract?

According to the Merriam-Webster Law Dictionary, a **contract** is a "*voluntary promise between two or more parties that can be enforced by the law*"[230]. Most contracts are written, (and in comic book publishing every contract should be written), but as a legal matter, they don't always have to be. A contract can be a simple, one-page document or it can run hundreds of pages.

---

[229] Hennessy, G. (2016, May 24). What is a Contract and Why Do Artists Need Them? Retrieved May 16, 2020, from https://www.creativecontractconsulting.com/c3blog/2016/5/23/what-is-a-contract-and-why-do-artists-need-them

[230] Contract. (n.d.). Retrieved May 16, 2020, from https://www.merriam-webster.com/dictionary/contract

There can be a lot of different elements in a contract, but at a minimum, there needs to be **consideration**, where everyone involved promises to exchange something of value[231]. Written contracts have to be signed by everyone involved to be valid. Everyone who signs has to have the mental capacity to sign and a legal contract can't be made for an unlawful purpose.

What are the Main Elements of a Contract?

Each contract is unique, but many of them share similar terms that I break down into four categories: basic terms, business terms, foundation terms, and housekeeping terms.

- **Basic Terms** are often called the *recitals*. They answer the essential questions about the contract and its participants.
  - Who is involved?
  - What is their relationship to each other?
  - When does the contract begin?
  - Where does each party live (or have an office if it's a company)?
  - Why everyone wants this contract in the first place.

- **Business terms** are usually where the consideration can be found. Many non-attorneys only focus on the hard numbers here, but this part of the contractual agreement also includes:
  - Who has to deliver goods, perform services, or transfer property rights[232].
  - Who has to pay for the goods, services or property, what they have to pay and how they are going to pay[233].
  - If the contract isn't permanent, then how long the agreement lasts. This is also known as the period or the **term**[234].

- **Foundation terms** establish the legal rules covering the business terms. In my experience, this is where lawyers spend more time in contract negotiation, because

---

[231] What is consideration? definition and meaning. (n.d.). Retrieved May 16, 2020, from http://www.businessdictionary.com/definition/consideration.html

[232] Hennessy, G. (2016, August 31). Get What You Give (Rights and Revenue in Comics). Retrieved May 16, 2020, from http://www.creativecontractconsulting.com/c3blog/2016/8/31/get-what-you-give-rights-and-revenue-in-comics

[233] Hennessy, G. (2012, September 26). Your Slice of the Pie Part 1 (Gross and Net Profit Concepts in Creator Owned Deals). Retrieved May 16, 2020, from http://www.creativecontractconsulting.com/c3blog/2012/09/your-slice-of-pie-part-1-gross-and-net.html

[234] Hennessy, G. (2013, June 12). Eternity is a Long Time: License Terms in Comics Contracts. Retrieved May 16, 2020, from http://www.creativecontractconsulting.com/c3blog/2013/06/eternity-is-long-time-license-terms-in.html

depending on how the rules are structured, the business terms might be irrelevant[235]. Foundation terms include language governing:

- The definitions for specific words in the agreement.

- What promises (or warranties) are made by each side.

- Who pays if the contract is broken or anyone is sued because of the contract[236].

- Who can give (or assign) their rights and responsibilities in the contract to a completely different person[237].

- What happens if the contract is breached or terminated.

- What wider body of law (state, federal, or international) will govern any dispute or litigation concerning the contract.

- **Housekeeping terms** (often incorrectly referred to as boilerplate terms) are similar to foundation terms because they define how the business terms will operate. The main difference between foundation and housekeeping terms is that housekeeping terms are normally not the subject of a lot of negotiation. There are exceptions, of course, but by and large, these terms are widely accepted, including:

- How everyone will stay in contact with each other.

- Who benefits from the contract?

- What happens in the event of an unforeseen disaster[238]?

- Confirmation that everyone who signs the contract is over eighteen, read and understood the contract, and received advice from a contract attorney.

Can You Download Any Contract for Your Publishing?

We've talked about the importance of hiring professionals for the legal needs of your project, but now that you know the basic structure, you might be tempted to save some of your investment by simply downloading a generic contract, changing the basic terms and hoping for the best. We've also talked about the considerations you have to take into account if you elect to do everything yourself. But as a

---

[235] Hennessy, G. (2015, August 01). How a Lawyer Beat Darth Vader. Retrieved May 16, 2020, from http://www.creativecontractconsulting.com/c3blog/2015/8/1/how-a-lawyer-beat-darth-vader

[236] Hennessy, G. (2015, February 04). Double Indemnity: Are You Protected? Retrieved May 16, 2020, from http://www.creativecontractconsulting.com/c3blog/2015/2/3/double-indemnity-are-you-protected

[237] Hennessy, G. (2014, October 28). Will You Accept Your Assignment? Retrieved May 16, 2020, from http://www.creativecontractconsulting.com/c3blog/2014/10/27/will-you-accept-your-assignment

[238] Hennessy, G. (2012, November 01). Catastrophe and Contracts (Understanding the "Act of God" Clause). Retrieved May 16, 2020, from http://www.creativecontractconsulting.com/c3blog/2012/11/catastrophe-and-contracts-understanding.html

comic book lawyer, I need to offer two particular warnings against taking the law into your own hands when it comes to your contracts[239].

1. **You probably don't know the laws governing contracts**. While contracts are often supposed to make a deal clear, the underlying legal principles can be confusing. Without training and experience in contract law, your attempts to write your contract can hurt you more than it can help.

2. **You might not understand the meaning or the implications of the words in the contract**. The language used in contracts is often circular, opaque, and dense with words that no one uses anywhere else but in contracts. To complicate the issue, what normal words mean in a specific contract and what you think they mean are often two different things. Without someone there to explain things to you, it is easy to sign something that will hurt you down the line.

This is not an attack on your intelligence. This is a question of training and experience. I'm a writer as well as an attorney, but I don't edit my books or design the covers. I hire professionals to do that. When I get on an airplane, I don't fly the plane. I pay the airline to supply professionals. I could learn editing, cover design, and aircraft piloting, but it saves time and money to bring in a professional.

If you don't hire a lawyer and write the contract yourself, you might save a few hundred dollars upfront, but if you miss something and you lose the rights to your property, you could be looking at a multimillion-dollar loss down the road.

If you hire a lawyer before a deal is signed, it will cost you some of your investment. If you hire one after something goes wrong and you need to go to court, that price can rise exponentially. Court cases can take years and those billable hours pile up fast. For the long-term success of your publishing, it is better to hire a professional early and avoid issues before they happen.

Finally, if you try to create your own contract, you might not know what kind of contract you need. Different contracts exist for different deals and scenarios of comic book publishing. If you use the wrong contract for your deals, you can place yourself in a poor position. For example:

- If you're working with other creators on a book, you'll need an *artist collaboration agreement* for each creator who will own a piece of the underlying intellectual property.

---

[239] Hennessy, G. (2016, May 27). Why Can't You Write the Contracts for Your Freelance Business? Retrieved May 16, 2020, from https://www.creativecontractconsulting.com/c3blog/2016/5/26/why-cant-you-write-the-contracts-for-your-freelance-business

- If you're hiring other freelance artists to work on your project, or if you're working without credit on someone else's material, you need a *work-for-hire agreement*.

- If you hire an accountant, lawyer, or editor, you'll need a *professional services contract* with each one of them.

- If you use someone else's intellectual property you'll need a *license agreement* as we talked about in Chapter 9.

Now that you understand why contracts are important and what goes into a contract, I'm going to focus on the two major types of agreements for comic book publishing talent; collaboration agreements and work-for-hire agreements.

An **artist collaboration agreement** defines the rights and responsibilities between two or more parties who plan to share in the ownership of the overall intellectual property. An artist collaboration agreement is different from a *work-for-hire agreement* (where one party pays another party to work on an intellectual property project for money and not ownership), or a *license agreement* (where one party gives another party the right to use some aspect of the intellectual property in exchange for payment).

When Do You Need a Collaboration Agreement?

You need an artist collaboration agreement when more than one member of the team is going to own a piece of the book. Just like a musical band, each member of the team should know what he or she is getting out of any deal that involves the property they work on. This might not be significant when you are selling a couple hundred books a year on your website and losing money on the cost of production. However, this becomes a huge issue when a property is picked up for a film, TV show, video game, or merchandise deal. It helps to have all the issues squared away before Hollywood starts calling. If you wait too long, anger, resentment, and actual litigation could tear the team apart just when things start to take off. **You need a signed artist collaboration agreement before you start production on the book**.

What are the Main Elements of a Collaboration Agreement?

While an artist collaboration agreement will share some of the same foundation and housekeeping terms found in other comic book contracts, there are several basic and business terms unique to this type of agreement. A well-drafted collaboration agreement will address the following issues:

1. **The Parties** describes who is involved in the contract.

2. **The Work** explains what the Parties are trying to create. This should be described in as much detail as possible, but at a minimum, it should include.

   a. The working title.
   b. A description of what the final product will be: whether it's a webcomic, single print issue, graphic novel, or ongoing series.
   c. The basic elements of the story, including the characters, settings, and other identifiable aspects of the book. If a synopsis and/or character designs of the work are available, they should be included in the contract.

3. **The Copyright**: breaks down the copyright ownership among all the members of the creative team as a percentage.

4. **The Trademarks**: breaks down the trademark ownership among all the members of the creative team as a percentage.

5. **The Compensation**: divides the revenue for all possible uses of the story and characters in the book, including:

    a. Interactive Media
    b. Screenplay Licensing
    c. Premium Cable Licensing
    d. Subscription Television Licensing
    e. Broadcast Television Licensing
    f. Advertising
    g. Emerging Media Licensing
    h. Novelization or Comic Book Publishing:
    i. Merchandising
    j. Trademark Licensing (other than merchandise):
    k. Live Performance Licensing

You might notice that the division of compensation goes far beyond the money you might collect for the initial publication of the comic book. But comic book stories and characters can exist and make money in any form of media. It's better to negotiate the video game rights for your story upfront, even if your book never makes it to Xbox.

6. **The Investment**: Who is contributing the initial investment in the book, how much that investment is going to be, when it will be paid and what mechanism, if any, the collaborator will have to recover their investment.

7. **The Advance Recoupment**: Any and all payments made to any party before revenue is generated and then deducted from the Compensation when revenue is generated. For example, the artist might get a page rate for their work on the book before publication, but that money can get recouped by the rest of the group when the book goes on sale.

8. **The Responsibilities**: lists the business, creative, and administrative responsibilities of each party in the development of the work in terms of both daily management and decision-making authority. It is not uncommon for each member of the team to handle multiple responsibilities including:

    a. Business Management (determining budgets, dealing with contracts, etc.)
    b. Talent Management (hiring work-for-hire artists and professionals)
    c. Creative Production

    i.   Editing

    ii.   Scripts

    iii. Artwork

    iv. Inking

    v.   Lettering

    vi. Coloring

    vii. Design

    viii. Flatting

    ix. Marketing (website maintenance, conventions, and direct market, etc.)

    x.   Advertising (social media, Diamond ads, etc.)

    xi. Distribution (online, printing, shipping)

    xii. Sales (account management, accounts receivable)

    xiii. Finance (accounts payable, taxes)

9. **The Withdrawal**: What happens if one or more members of the team are unwilling or unable to complete the Work before it is completed. Allowances have to be made for several aspects of the deal including

    a. Copyright ownership

    b. Trademark ownership

    c. Compensation

    d. Recoupment (if any)

While the collaboration agreement can be overly complex when dealing with these issues, the best ones are understandable and don't include a large amount of legal gymnastics. At the same time, the elements of a collaboration agreement should not conflict with the terms of any agreement with an outside publisher or licensee of the property. Your legal advisor can review both contracts to ensure there is harmony between them.

A **work-for-hire agreement** leverages the work-for-hire doctrine in copyright law and defines the rights and responsibilities between an owner who commissions a work and the artist who creates that work. Anyone working on the comic book who will not share in the ownership of the intellectual property should sign a work-for-hire agreement. This includes freelance professionals on the business side of publishing like marketers or web designers who are not directly creating the comic book.

What Is the Work-for-Hire Doctrine?

One of the basic concepts in copyright law is the relationship between creation and ownership. In most situations, whoever creates an original work owns that work. The work-for-hire doctrine is an exception to that rule. *"If a work is made for hire, an employer is considered the author even if an employee actually created the work. The employer can be a firm, an organization, or an individual."*[240]

Under copyright law, a work-for-hire is created if it is *"prepared by an employee within the scope of their employment or a work is specially ordered or commissioned for use"* in a variety of situations. One of those situations is *"as a contribution to a collective work"*. Since mainstream comics are by definition a collective work, publishers regularly commission work-for-hire artists using work-for-hire agreements.

What Is the Benefit of a Work-for-Hire Agreement?

While there is plenty of hostility against work-for-hire agreements[241], there are benefits to both the publisher and the work-for-hire artist in the context of comic books. For the work-for-hire artist, there is a short-term financial gain. Many comics do not generate a profit[242], so artists relying on comic book sales to make a living might not be able to sustain themselves. Even if comic sales across the board were healthy enough for artists to survive, the profits for comics don't materialize for months, sometimes years after the work is done and the book is published. Under a standard work-for-hire agreement, the artist is paid upfront, regardless of the sales or profits of the published book.

For publishers, there is long-term profit potential. Published books are a source of revenue, but in the modern entertainment landscape, the intellectual property based on comics drives film, merchandise,

---

[240] United States Copyright Office. (2012). Works Made for Hire. Retrieved from https://www.copyright.gov/circs/circ09.pdf

[241] Fowler, M. (1970, January 01). Cultivating a Healthy Loathing for "Work Made for Hire" Agreements. Retrieved May 16, 2020, from http://www.rightsofwriters.com/2011/05/cultivating-healthy-loathing-for-work.html

[242] MacDonald, H., (2019, July 05). Hold on, some people are actually making money at comics! Retrieved May 16, 2020, from https://www.comicsbeat.com/hold-on-some-people-are-actually-making-money-at-comics/

television, and video games[243]. As an extreme example, the comic book industry as a whole generated two billion dollars in 2017[244]. In 2018, *Avengers: Infinity War* generated a worldwide box office of more than two billion dollars, not counting merchandise or associated advertising[245].

Of course, even in the current age of comic entertainment, only a select few properties crossover into mainstream media and movies might not be a part of your goals, anyway. And almost none of the books that do find their way to various screens and shelves reach the heights of the current MCU, but copyright ownership gives publishers the potential for huge financial success. It is an investment with a substantial risk that the work-for-hire artists don't lose or profit from either way, depending on the agreement.

What are the Main Elements of a Work-for-Hire Agreement?

While a work-for-hire agreement will share some of the same foundation and housekeeping terms found in other comic book contracts, there are several basic and business terms unique to this type of agreement. A well-drafted work-for-hire agreement will address the following issues:

1. The **Owner** of the Work

2. The **Work- for-Hire Artist** for the Work:

3. **The Work** explains what the Owner wants the Artist to do. This should be described in as much detail as possible, but at a minimum, it should include.
   a. The working title.
   b. A description of what the final product will be, whether it's a webcomic, single print issue, graphic novel, or ongoing series.

4. The **Services** the Work-for-Hire Artist is providing.

5. **The Delivery Schedule**: of when the Artist will deliver the Services.

6. **The Compensation**: including page rates, hourly rates, royalties, or any combination of the three. Compensation terms should also include:

---

[243] Hennessy, G. (2018, December 10). Positioning Your Book for the Coming Content War. Retrieved May 16, 2020, from https://www.creativecontractconsulting.com/c3blog/2018/12/10/positioning-your-book-for-the-coming-content-war

[244] Comic Book Sales by Year. (n.d.). Retrieved May 16, 2020, from https://www.comichron.com/yearlycomicssales.html

[245] 21 Marvel Cinematic Universe Movies at the Box Office. (n.d.). Retrieved May 16, 2020, from https://www.imdb.com/imdbpicks/mcu-box-office/ls021825852/

a. The timing of payments

b. Credit in the final product

c. Ownership of the original artwork (if applicable)

d. Use of the Services in their professional portfolio

7. **The Advance Recoupment**: Any and all payments made to any party before revenue is generated and then deducted from any potential royalties when revenue is generated. For example, the artist might get a page rate for their work on the book before publication, but that money can get recouped by the Owner when the book goes on sale.

8. **Missed Deadlines**: any penalties to the Artist for missing the Delivery Schedule.

9. **The Withdrawal**: any penalties if the Artist is unwilling or unable to complete the Work

What Is the Difference Between an Employee and a Work-for-Hire Talent?

When adding work-for-hire talent to your team, you need to be sure that you do not inadvertently create a situation where they become your employee. While the distinction isn't significant in terms of copyright law, it can have a major effect on the taxes you pay[246].

The difference between an employee and work-for-hire talent is based on a variety of factors depending on the state your business operates in[247]. Fortunately, the nature of independent comic book publishing often lends itself to default work-for-hire situations, but it helps to take note of the following distinctions that play a role in the determination[248]:

- An employee often works at the employer's place of business. Work-for-hire talent often works from home or their office.

- An employee has their hours set by the employer. Work-for-hire talent sets their own hours.

- An employee often has their equipment provided by the employer. Work-for-hire talent use equipment they own.

[246] Understanding Employee vs. Contractor Designation. (n.d.). Retrieved May 16, 2020, from https://www.irs.gov/newsroom/understanding-employee-vs-contractor-designation

[247] Cullins, A. (2019, June 19). Hollywood Faces "Devastating" Costs From California Bill Targeting Gig Economy. Retrieved May 16, 2020, from https://www.hollywoodreporter.com/news/hollywood-faces-devastating-costs-state-bill-targeting-uber-1219575?utm_source=Sailthru

[248] Post, J. (2018, September 20). Worker Classification: What You Need to Know about Employee vs. Contractor. Retrieved May 16, 2020, from https://www.businessnewsdaily.com/770-contract-vs-employees-what-you-need-to-know.html

- An employee does continual work. Work-for-hire talent is hired on a project basis.

Drafting, negotiating, and signing the contracts for your creative project might take some time and cost you some money, but if you sign the right contracts upfront, you'll save money in the long-term and put both you and your book in a better position to succeed.

Chapter 24: How Do You Balance Compensation with Performance?

After ownership of the idea, consideration might be the most negotiated aspect of talent management. You need to pay each member of your team the right way depending on their relationship to the project and you need to get everyone on your team to perform their roles on time and in a quality fashion to give your book the best chance for success.

We've touched on both consideration and deliverables in the past three chapters. Now that you have an introduction into general contract concepts and specific comic book related contracts, we need to take a closer look at the relationship between consideration and performance in your agreements.

Can Exposure Be a Form of Consideration?

Like many small business owners, independent comic book publishers try to control costs. One method that persists in this and many creative industries is offering "exposure" to talent instead of actual consideration. There will always be eager novice artists and writers willing to accept this professional abuse, but before we explore legitimate forms of consideration, I'm going to explain why you shouldn't make exposure a part of your pitch to talent at any time.

Exposure is based upon a hypothetical best-case scenario. The publisher has an idea that is a "guaranteed success". Anyone associated with this amazing book will become famous because the book will be famous. Other publishers and creators will then seek out talent from this book to use in their projects, and will pay substantial amounts for the privilege. In essence, talent gives up money now for a chance to "get their name out there" and achieve fame and fortune later.

This scenario falls apart upon casual inspection. First, there are no guaranteed successful ideas in comics or any other form of entertainment. Second, there is no tangible assurance that the work done for exposure will ever lead to later paid work, even if the book is a hit. Third, in the 21st century, every artist, writer, and creative professional can get their name out there using social media. Finally, the talent has financial obligations they are trying to fulfill with their creative work. There is no reason or incentive for them to spend their limited time and resources on the illusion of exposure.

Keep in mind, there is a related form of consideration called **credit**, which does have secondary value to comic book creators. Industry leaders like Jim Lee, Todd McFarlane, Frank Miller, and Mark Millar all leveraged their work for the Big Two into fame and success in their own projects. But the credit came in addition to the page rates and other forms of consideration, not as payment on its own.

Paying talent can be one of the biggest drains on your investment, but your professional reputation and the success of your book will suffer if you attempt to get people to work for free. Exposure by itself is not consideration. You need to offer something more.

What Forms of Consideration Are Used in Collaboration Agreements?

Because creators who sign a collaboration agreement own a portion of the underlying property, there are four major types of consideration they can get, based on the deal negotiated between the parties.

1. **Intellectual Property Ownership**: Collaborators share in the copyrights and/or trademarks associated with the project. This could mean that they get a portion of the revenue generated by uses of the IP not directly related to the publishing, such as the film, TV, and merchandise revenue discussed earlier in Chapter 22. This also means they can have authority over how the IP is developed and what it can and can't be used for. Please note that there is a mathematical limit to IP ownership. You can't offer more than 100% of the property, so pay attention and don't try and give away 130% of your book to various members of the team.

2. **Credit**: Collaborators can get their name on the book and associated properties, as is customary in the industry (i.e. on the cover, in associated advertising, and social media), which can bolster their professional reputation over time.

3. **Revenue sharing**: Collaborators can share in the success of the book by dividing profits between them. For example, if the writer and the artist collaborate on a book that generates $5,000 in profit, and they agreed to split the money evenly, each of them can walk away with $2,500, depending on how revenue is defined. Again, you can't offer more than 100% of the revenue, so be sure to check your math or check with your accountant.

4. **Upfront payment:** Collaborators can negotiate terms where they get a portion of the investment before the collection of revenue in exchange for less initial money when the book starts generating sales. For example, if a writer took $3,000 as his overall page rate in our example above, he wouldn't be able to collect any royalties until the book recouped his page rate from sales.

5. **Copies of the final product**: If you are going to distribute your project in digital or print format, one form of consideration is a specific number of free copies of the book. You can also consider allowing talent to buy additional copies at a discount so they can either give them away as promotional items or sell them on their own. If you decide to use this form of consideration, just be sure to factor this into your print runs. If you have a large team or you offer a large number of copies to each person, you could be cutting too deep into your potential revenue.

How Is Revenue Defined?

Collaborators who decide to share revenue need to be very specific about the definition of revenue if they want to avoid financial disputes[249]. In general, revenue is defined as the income generated from the sale of goods or services[250]. For your project, revenue can come from advertising, book sales, or licensing of the IP. But all revenue is not created equal. **Gross revenue** is all of the money collected from the exploitation of the IP. **Net revenue** is gross revenue minus expenses related to the goods and services being provided[251].

Let's go back to our earlier example to understand the difference between gross and net. If the collaborators made $5,000 in sales from their book and the revenue split is defined as 50% of the gross revenue, then each collaborator is entitled to $2,500. If the book costs $4,000 to produce, print, and ship, then the net revenue is $1,000 ($5,000 - $4,000), so they each are entitled to $500. If the book costs $10,000 to produce, then there is a loss of $5,000 that the collaborators could deduct from their personal income depending on how the underlying business is set up[252].

The majority of collaboration agreements use the net revenue definition, especially when the initial investment doesn't cover production and distribution. We will focus on expenses and profit and loss statements in Chapter 66, but for now, just remember that at least part of the revenue your book makes might have to be used to pay outstanding bills.

What Forms of Consideration Are Used in Work-for-Hire Agreements?

Because creators who sign a work-for-hire agreement do not own a portion of the underlying property, the four major types of consideration they can receive are different from collaborators, based on the deal negotiated between the parties:

1. **Page rate**: Different professions get paid according to different measurements. Lawyers often get paid by the hour. Salespeople get paid based on commissions. Freelance comic book artists get paid a page rate. The basic idea is for every page you're hired to work on, you get a set dollar amount. So, if you get $100 per page and the book is 32 pages, then you get $3,200. A page rate is a base number. It doesn't take into account incentives like royalty pools, recoupment, back end participation, or anything else that could muddy the

---

[249] Hennessy, G. (2012, September 26). Your Slice of the Pie Part 1 (Gross and Net Profit Concepts in Creator Owned Deals). Retrieved May 16, 2020, from https://www.creativecontractconsulting.com/c3blog/2012/09/your-slice-of-pie-part-1-gross-and-net.html

[250] Kenton, W. (2020, January 29). Understanding Revenue. Retrieved May 16, 2020, from https://www.investopedia.com/terms/r/revenue.asp

[251] Id.

[252] Talk to your accountant to determine how the losses from a business apply to you.

waters. It's a straightforward transaction; one page for one price. As long as you know what the price is, everything else is based on that.

2. **Credit**: This is similar to collaborators, where work-for-hire creators can get their name on the book, as is customary in the industry

3. **Revenue sharing**: As an additional financial incentive, some work-for-hire deals include a royalty in addition to, or in place of, a page rate. A **royalty** is defined in comics as a payment based on the revenue generated from a source[253]. For example, you might offer your artist 25% of the net profits from any poster or t-shirt sales that use their artwork. You can also allocate royalties into a *royalty pool*[254] that pays all participants from a shared source of income, but those kinds of financial structures are utilized by larger companies and usually aren't necessary for your initial project[255].

4. **Copies of the final product**: This is a specific number of free copies of the book, similar to the collaboration consideration. The same options exist for free and/or discounted copies, and the same impact on the overall print run needs to be accounted for.

How Do You Determine the Right Page Rates?

Page rates in the comic book industry are not standardized[256], since several factors will go into what a freelance creator will command including:

- Their experience

- Their skill level

- Their established fan base

---

[253] Banton, C. (2020, February 05). How Royalties Work. Retrieved June 27, 2020, from https://www.investopedia.com/terms/r/royalty.asp

[254] Crowell, T. A. (2015). *The pocket lawyer for comic books: A legal toolkit for indie comic book artists and writers.* Burlington, MA: Focal Press.

[255] McMillan, G. (2020, May 16). DC Entertainment Revamps Comic Book Royalty System for Creators. Retrieved May 16, 2020, from https://www.hollywoodreporter.com/heat-vision/dc-entertainment-revamps-comic-book-714656

[256] Hennessy, G. (2016, December 20). How Much Do You Get Paid Per Page? Retrieved May 16, 2020, from https://www.creativecontractconsulting.com/c3blog/2016/12/19/how-much-do-you-get-paid-per-page

While these factors are subjective and based on what you can afford to pay, there are some baselines you should keep in mind. This snapshot of industry page rates is based on information contained on the survey website Fair Page Rates[257]:

1. Writers: $25-$220 per page
2. Cover Artist: $200-$750 per cover
3. Pencils: $100-$250 per page
4. Inks: $75-$200 per page
5. Coloring: $35-$150 per page
6. Flatting: $8-$20 per page
7. Lettering: $10-$50 per page

What Forms of Consideration Are Used in Business Work-for-Hire Agreements?

Business work-for-hire agreements differ from creative work-for-hire agreements in comics because the baseline measurement of a page isn't helpful as a calculation. Besides, each team member has to deliver something different, so you can't use a single standard. Business and creative work-for-hire contracts can be similar if you replace the concept of a page rate with a unique milestone for each role.

A **milestone** is a stage of development in a project that can be used for the measurement of work performance[258]. For in creative work-for-hire agreements, the page serves as the milestone. You can create specific milestones for business work-for-hire agreements. For example, let's suppose you want your book to be available as a printed single issue for comic book shops. The person who takes on the printing role might have the following milestones in their contract. Every milestone can be tied to a date, a payment, or both.

- Create the criteria for printer selection
- Develop a list of potential printers based on printer selection criteria
- Send out RFP to printers
- Collect samples from potential printers
- Evaluate all RFP and assist in the selection of a printer
- Negotiate terms of printing agreement with the selected printer
- Manage the delivery of the final print files to the printer
- Manage the printing of the first issue

---

[257] Fair Page Rates Year in Review, 2016 Survey Results. (2017, February 03). Retrieved May 16, 2020, from https://fairpagerates.com/year-in-review-2016-survey-results/

[258] Milestone. (n.d.). Retrieved May 16, 2020, from http://www.businessdictionary.com/definition/milestone.html

- Ensure the quality of the printing process
- Manage shipment of books from printer to customers
- Confirm accuracy of the invoices received from the printer

Business work-for-hire agreements can also include things like credit in the book and revenue sharing. The important point is to spell out the relationship between milestones and compensation in each contract.

How Can You Define the Relationship Between Consideration and Performance?

The relationship between the consideration you pay your talent and their performance on your project boils down to how you manage your leverage. As an independent publisher, your main source of leverage will come from your consideration.

Managing the timing of your consideration is key. If you pay talent before all the pages or milestones are delivered, then they will have less incentive to perform their role on schedule. If you try to make them finish all the work before you pay them anything, they will probably refuse. Even if they don't, you will have less incentive to pay them if you already have everything you need. This isn't an indictment of anyone's morals on either side. It's simply an observation I have made over the years in my legal practice and my professional life.

The middle ground between everything upfront and everything at the end is a give and take system I refer to as the **tennis method**[259]. The basic process is simple. Each side divides their performance or payment into several stages. One side starts things, normally by making the initial payment. The other side responds by completing part of the performance. This exchange goes back and forth until all the consideration is paid and all the performance is completed. Using our printing manager as an example, consideration and performance can be divided this way:

- Both sides sign the contract: (Publisher pays 5% of the printing consideration)
- Create the criteria for printer selection (Publisher pays 5%)
- Develop a list of potential printers based on printer selection criteria (Publisher pays 10%)
- Send out RFP to all printers (Publisher pays 10%)
- Evaluate all RFP and assist in the selection of a printer (Publisher pays 10%)
- Negotiate terms of printing agreement with a selected printer (Publisher pays 10%)
- Manage the delivery of the final print files to the printer (Publisher pays 10%)

---

[259] Hennessy, G. (2014). *Solving the Payment Problem* [Video file]. Retrieved May 16, 2020, from https://www.youtube.com/watch?v=mmtcKgLrGqg&t=24s

- Manage the printing of the first issue (Publisher pays 10%)
- Ensure the quality of the printing process (Publisher pays 10%)
- Manage shipment of books from printer to customers (Publisher pays 10%)
- Confirm accuracy of the invoices received from the printer (Publisher pays 10%)

This method also applies indirectly to royalties or any kind of consideration based on the performance of the book because the book performance triggers the new payment. For example, if the talent handling your sales gets a bonus if a certain number of issues sell, then the sales milestone triggers the payment.

Whether you are establishing the payment timing for business or creative contracts, remember to pay attention to all the payment dates in relation to each other. Consider both when you'll have investment funds available and how many payments you'll have to make at the same time to avoid draining all your funds at once or failing to pay members of your team.

What Happens If You Don't Pay the Consideration?

The only thing worse than offering exposure is promising to pay your talent and then not paying them. A **breach of contract** is defined as failing to perform a contract obligation without justification[260]. If you sign a contract and then fail to perform (i.e. you don't pay your talent) that can be grounds for a civil lawsuit, arbitration, or mediation which can lead to financial, legal, and professional consequences that far outweigh the money you might save in the short term[261].

- Financial: The penalties for breach of contract often involve the payment of damages, which is the money paid as compensation for the breach[262]. The amount of damages can range from nominal amounts, paying the amounts you owe, or paying a penalty of twice as much as you were supposed to pay in the first place[263].

- Legal: Courts can force you to take a specific action (like pay your talent or not use the work they did for you), transfer your IP to the talent because your breach invalidated the IP ownership clause, or cancel the entire agreement. This might be annoying if your

---

[260] Breach. (2013, January 28). Retrieved May 16, 2020, from https://dictionary.findlaw.com/definition/breach.html

[261] Staff. (2020, April 23). Breach of Contract and Lawsuits. Retrieved May 16, 2020, from https://smallbusiness.findlaw.com/business-contracts-forms/breach-of-contract-and-lawsuits.html

[262] Damage. (2013, January 28). Retrieved May 16, 2020, from https://dictionary.findlaw.com/definition/damage.html

[263] Hennessy, G. (2017, July 12). How to collect an unpaid fee from your client. Retrieved May 16, 2020, from https://blog.freelancersunion.org/2017/06/08/how-to-collect-an-unpaid-fee-from-your-client/

project is just getting off the ground. It could be devastating if you've already sent the books to the printer or if you managed to garner some interest from Netflix for your book.

- <u>Professional</u>: No one wants to work with someone who has a reputation for cheating their business partners. Comic publishing is a small industry. It only takes one lawsuit to define your company in a poor light. So only agree to pay what you can afford to pay and when it's time to pay…pay.

Despite your best efforts, you may face a situation where someone isn't living up to their side of the agreement. They might miss deadlines. The work they deliver doesn't match the standards of their samples. Maybe they just don't get along with you or the other members of the team. For whatever reason, you might need to end some business relationships early for the good of your publishing.

Termination is the ominous and sinister word the legal profession uses for ending a contract earlier than originally anticipated[264]. While termination might make you think of unstoppable cyborg killers from a dystopian future, the reality is usually much less violent. As an independent publisher, you simply have to build contingencies for termination into your contracts from the beginning, look for the red flags that might trigger termination, and then take the appropriate steps to end the contract and move on with your project.

How Is Termination Defined in a Contract?

Termination is one of the foundation terms found in both collaboration and work-for-hire agreements. The termination clause addresses who can terminate the contract and under what circumstances that termination can take place. In general, there are three scenarios where contracts can be terminated[265].

- <u>End of the project or the term</u>: This termination occurs after both sides fulfill their obligations. For example, if you hire a web designer to make your website, they complete the work and you pay them, then the contract is over. Technically, this is completion and not termination. However, depending on how you structure your contracts, this can be the most agreeable way to end a business relationship.

  I suggested earlier that you should consider using small, short term deals as a part of your due diligence. This will allow you to experience the business relationship first hand without a long-term time investment. If your talent does the job but doesn't do it in a way that inspires you to use them again, you can just decide to move in another direction and avoid using them in the future. This can avoid animosity, protecting your reputation in the industry, and leaving you open to working together again in the future if the situation changes.

---

[264] Termination. (n.d.). Retrieved May 16, 2020, from https://legal-dictionary.thefreedictionary.com/termination

[265] Johnson, R. (2019, January 25). 5 Ways to Terminate a Contract. Retrieved May 16, 2020, from https://smallbusiness.chron.com/5-ways-terminate-contract-16020.html

- Termination for cause: This termination occurs after one party fails to perform under the terms of the agreement[266]. For example, if you hired an artist to create covers for your book by a certain date and the covers didn't arrive on time, you may have the right to terminate the agreement based on the missed deadline. Termination for cause is a more stringent type of termination, because you need to articulate why the termination is taking place. Terminations for cause may also include a *cure period*, which gives a party extra time to fulfill their obligations without triggering termination[267].

- Termination without cause: This termination can occur for any reason not related to a failure to perform. For example, if you run out of money, you could terminate the contract to avoid accumulating debts you can't pay. Termination without cause, or at-will termination, is a less stringent type of termination, because you don't need to say why you're ending the agreement or define any specific criteria for termination in the contract. Some talent, especially on the creative side, might want to negotiate a **kill fee** as protection from at-will termination[268].

What Red Flags Should You Look for Prior to Termination?

After the contract is signed and talent is performing their work, there are several traits you need to look out for as they interact with you and the rest of the team. Any one of these issues could trigger termination for or without cause, depending on how the contract is written.

- Late work: Talent misses deadlines. This is a fundamental flaw in talent performance. Comic book publishing adheres to specific deadlines. If one person is late with their work, the whole system can fall apart.

- Unprofessional behavior: Talent behaves in a manner below or contrary to the standards of the profession. Comic book publishing is not a formal or stuffy industry. Everything is fairly laid back. But that doesn't mean you should accept less than professional standards from your team.

- Abrasive or abusive personality: Talent shows little concern for the feelings or perspectives of others. You don't have to be friends with your team and they don't

---

[266] Kokemuller, N. (2017, November 21). Differences Between Termination for Cause and Without Cause. Retrieved May 16, 2020, from https://yourbusiness.azcentral.com/differences-between-termination-cause-cause-25685.html

[267] Cure Period. (n.d.). Retrieved May 16, 2020, from https://www.lawinsider.com/dictionary/cure-period

[268] What is a Kill Fee? (2009, August 11). Retrieved May 16, 2020, from https://www.writersdigest.com/editor-blogs/questions-and-quandaries/legal-questions/what-is-a-kill-fee

necessarily have to like each other. But that doesn't mean anyone should be rude, sexually predatory[269], or create a negative working atmosphere.

- <u>Lack of communication</u>: Talent fails to maintain contact. As the publisher, you need to know what's going on with your project at each of the various stages. Someone who signs a contract, takes an assignment, and then falls off the radar isn't helpful to your publishing or your blood pressure. You might not need to hear from them every day or even every week, but don't be in the dark about what they're doing.

- <u>Work that deviates from samples or requests</u>: Talent isn't producing the work you expect. If their production doesn't match their earlier body of work and that's why you selected them, then that discrepancy might be a reason to terminate. If you make certain requests to your talent, it is normal (and even preferable) for them to inject some of their skill and vision to go beyond your request and make something special. But there are limits to artistic license. If they go so far off message that the work isn't useful anymore, it might be time to terminate.

This list is not definitive or mandatory. Because no one is perfect (even in comics), you need to balance any red flags you see with the ability of the talent in question. There is more than one Eisner-award winning writer in the industry who isn't the nicest person to work with. Some artists will take an idea and come back with amazing work that might not have much to do with the original idea. Under those circumstances, it might be best to take the good with the bad and not terminate.

This caveat does not apply to late work. Don't hold onto anybody who can't hit a deadline and ruins your marketing, production, advertising, and sales schedules.

What is the Formal Process for Termination?

Termination is normally a three-step process:

---

[269] Elbein. A. (2020, July 12). Retrieved July 14, 2020, from Inside the Comic Book Industry's Sexual Misconduct Crisis-and the Ugly, Exploitative History That Got It Here. https://www.thedailybeast.com/warren-ellis-cameron-stewart-and-the-storm-of-sexual-misconduct-allegations-roiling-the-comic-book-industry

1. **Notice**[270]: One party notifies the other that they wish to terminate the contract. This is referred to as notice and is usually done in writing just in case the situation winds up in court and documentation of actions is required.

2. Outstanding disputes resolved: If the termination is hostile or contentious, there is a chance that the legal system might need to get involved to settle any outstanding disputes about ownership, payment, or other factors in the contract. Depending on how the contract was written, legal mechanisms can range from a simple phone call between lawyers on both sides to mediation[271], to arbitration[272], to litigation. Just keep in mind that this type of dispute resolution can be expensive. You want to protect your rights. You might not want to spend your entire investment on legal fees.

3. Termination Date is established: If there is a cure period, then the party that failed to perform gets a limited time to correct the situation before termination is final. If there is no cure period, then termination could be effective as soon as the notice is received (an immediate termination) or within a certain number of days after notice is received.

4. Post-termination obligations begin: There might still be some obligations remaining even after the contract ends. For example, if the talent is still entitled to royalties after termination, those must continue to be paid. Also, there might be confidentiality clauses or warranties that survive after termination.

Your relationships with talent will rise and fall over time if you plan to have a career publishing independent comics. Just remember to treat people as well as you can on your road to your goals and you can gain a reputation in the professional community that's just as impressive as your comic.

---

[270] What is notice? definition and meaning. (n.d.). Retrieved May 16, 2020, from http://www.businessdictionary.com/definition/notice.html

[271] What Is Mediation And How Does It Work? (n.d.). Retrieved May 16, 2020, from https://corporate.findlaw.com/litigation-disputes/what-is-mediation-and-how-does-it-work.html

[272] What is Arbitration? (2016, June 21). Retrieved May 16, 2020, from https://adr.findlaw.com/arbitration/what-is-arbitration-.html

STAGE 1: PRE-PRODUCTION

PART 6: MARKETING

Or Who Is Going to Read Your Comic?

You've made major strides in the development of your book. In the first six steps, you have:

1. Determined your goals for making comics
2. Found an idea that you love and own
3. Conceived how to pay for the comic before it's created
4. Formulated a plan to turn your idea into a comic
5. Created a legal structure to protect both your idea and your investment.
6. Built a team to turn your idea into reality.

Now it's time to find out who you're going to share this reality with.

Marketing is the business process of creating satisfying relationships with customers[273]. As an independent publisher, you need to spend time finding, connecting, and building bonds with the people who are most likely to be interested in your project. Marketing isn't magic, and it doesn't need to be deceptive or sleazy. It does, however, need to tap into collective aspects of human consumption if your book is going to reach the right people.

In the late 1980s, there was a sports fantasy drama called *Field of Dreams*[274]. The tagline for the movie was "If you build it, they will come." This phrase outlasted the popularity of the film and became synonymous with the idea that a great product or service creates its own buzz and audience with little or no effort on the part of the creator[275]. In my experience, a lot of comic book marketing uses the *Field of Dreams* model. In the past, **publishers were spoiled by readers who were more than willing to bear the burden of figuring out what comics they liked, following their favorite titles, keeping track of continuity and recruiting new readers into the hobby. Modern publishers do not have that luxury. I contend that much of the decline in comic book sales over the past forty years can be blamed on this passive and insular approach.**

For example, my experience of getting into comics is a combination of luck and perseverance. It's dated because of my age, but aspects of the story I remember probably resonate with a lot of past and present comic book fans and creators.

---

[273] Drucker, P. (2011). *The Practice of Management*. HarperCollins US.

[274] *Field of Dreams*. (1989, May 05). Retrieved May 16, 2020, from https://www.imdb.com/title/tt0097351/

[275] Chait, D. (2013, August 15). Why the Motto 'If You Build It, They Will Come' is BS. Retrieved May 16, 2020, from https://www.entrepreneur.com/article/227850

At some point, someone gave me a twenty-two-page comic (probably issue #251 of Neal Adams' *Batman*). After enjoying the story (or at least the pictures), I recognized similar comics in spinner racks at newsstands and I began to buy them (or get my parents to buy them) with no knowledge of which comics I might like or what order the story was being told.

Years later, I found my way to a comic shop. That process was relatively easy, since there were a lot of them in New York City when I was growing up. I walked past two on my commute to and from high school. But once in the shop, I had to figure out what to read, where to start, what back issues I had to read, what crossovers I needed to find, and other people who read the same books I did.

My sophistication and tastes expanded over the years by going to conventions, building my collection, and searching out other comic shops. By the time I started working at Marvel Comics, I had enough knowledge of the characters, the products, and the industry to be a professional nerd, but I did the work to add myself to the market. The publishers, newsstands, and comic shops just made the books available. It was my job to become a fan.

A more proactive and effective method of customer interaction comes not from business, but interpersonal relationships. In the best-selling book *The Art of Seduction*[276], Robert Greene describes a system that can be boiled down into five parts:

- Find the right people to connect with
- Understand what they are looking for
- Get their attention
- Offer what they want
- Provide what they want in exchange for what you want

This process isn't limited to dating or winning an election. It can be used to guide your efforts in building the right market for your project. Consider the difference between my experiences in discovering comics over thirty years to my experiences finding out about any action movie released in 2019.

Because I'm in New York, I'm going to see stuff about any particular movie on taxis, buses, and billboards when I'm out in the street. If I look at my phone, it will pop up on social media multiple times per hour. If I look at YouTube, there will be teasers, trailers, interviews, behind-the-scenes material, and speculation. There will be talk show interviews and commercials, magazine spreads, and cross-promotion with various types of merchandise. By the time the movie comes out, it's almost impossible to not know what the movie is about, why you want to see it, and where to get tickets. Based on some

---

[276] Greene, R. (2004). *The Art of Seduction*. London: Gardner's Books.

estimates, the cost to market a feature film can be anywhere from 5-20% of the production budget[277]. The film industry creates excitement designed to put people in seats. When was the last time you heard that kind of buzz generated for any comic ever?

I'm not trying to suggest that you need to buy a billboard in Times Square or get interviewed on the Tonight Show as part of your marketing campaign. I am not asking you to spend twenty percent of your investment on marketing. I am suggesting that **you spend between 5-20% of your time and effort to find the right audience for your project**. There are just too many comics released every month for you to publish and pray that people buy your book.

According to Jim Gibbons[278], editor for Dark Horse and other publishers, there are more than 400 print comics released each month[279] or about 100 per week. Assuming you only rely on comic book shop customers to buy your book (which is a mistake), and all #1 issues are treated equally (and they're not) then you only have about a 1% chance for any random customer to buy your book from any given shop, unless you create a market for your book before it's released. When you factor in variables like well-known publishers, famous characters, media tie-ins, and distributor purchasing incentives, a more realistic chance of a random sale for your book is less than one percentage point.

If you don't market your book, there is a very good chance no one will read it. If you build it, they will come—but part of what you build has to be a positive relationship with the right audience for your book.

So how do you find the right audience? First, let's define the right people and understand what they want.

---

[277] McClintock, P. (2014, July 31). $200 Million and Rising: Hollywood Struggles With Soaring Marketing Costs. Retrieved May 16, 2020, from https://www.hollywoodreporter.com/news/200-million-rising-hollywood-struggles-721818

[278] Make Comics Podcast Episode #169 - Things You Might Not Have Thought About When Marketing Your Comic. (2019, April 23). Retrieved May 16, 2020, from https://www.comicsexperience.com/podcast/169-things-you-might-not-have-thought-about-when-marketing-your-comic/

[279] Harper, D. Are There Too Many Comics Being Published Today? (2015, June 23). Retrieved May 16, 2020, from https://sktchd.com/longform/are-there-too-many-comics/

A **target market** is the specific group of potential customers most likely to buy a company's products or services[280]. The first key to identifying who is in your target market is to understand who *isn't* a potential customer.

Is Everyone in Your Target Market?

Your project can't reach everyone in the world.

Even if you could generate Super-Bowl-ad, Beyoncé-endorsed, viral-cat-video, blockbuster-movie-level exposure, your story would still only appeal to a minuscule portion of that audience. For example, more than one hundred million people watch the Super Bowl every year, making it one of the most-watched programs in the history of television[281]. But if you consider the fact that there are more than three hundred million people in the United States[282], you quickly realize that two out of three people in America don't watch the most popular program in America. If the Super Bowl isn't for everyone, then your book can't be for everyone. **There is no point in wasting your resources trying to tell everyone about your book, because that isn't the way media entertainment is consumed today**.

Wired Magazine editor Chris Anderson described the shift in market composition in his best-selling book *The Long Tail*[283]. According to Anderson, people had fewer choices in the analog era thirty years ago. There were three major television networks and a handful of movie studios, record labels, and major publishers controlling all media consumption. Because there were fewer options to easily select from, most people tended to gravitate towards the same things. Primetime television, Top 40 radio, and the New York Times Best-Seller List dominated media culture. There was always a minority willing to seek out alternative and underground entertainment, but those fans were so scattered that connecting with them wasn't cost-effective for major media producers. Comics shared in this phenomenon. All of the top-selling comic book issues in the modern era were published by the Big Two and all of them were released between 1987 and 1993[284].

---

[280] Target Market Definition - What is Target Market. (n.d.). Retrieved May 16, 2020, from https://www.shopify.com/encyclopedia/target-market

[281] Breech Feb 5, J. (2020, February 05). 2020 Super Bowl ratings revealed: Chiefs-49ers ranks as the 11th most-watched show in TV history. Retrieved June 27, 2020, from https://www.cbssports.com/nfl/news/2020-super-bowl-ratings-revealed-chiefs-49ers-ranks-as-the-11th-most-watched-show-in-tv-history/

[282] U.S. and World Population Clock. (n.d.). Retrieved May 16, 2020, from https://www.census.gov/popclock/

[283] Anderson, C. (2014). *The Long Tail: Why the future of business is selling less of more*. New York: Hachette.

[284] Staff. (2019, May 11). Top 10 Best Selling Comic Books Of The Modern Era - Zap-Kapow Comics. Retrieved May 16, 2020, from https://www.zapkapowcomics.com/top-10-best-selling-comic-books-of-the-modern-era/

Digital production and distribution permanently altered media consumption because it was able to satisfy granular preferences in a cost-effective way. Primetime television lost its importance to niche cable television, on-demand streaming television, and video platforms like YouTube. Record stores vanished with the rise of MP3s, illegal distribution like Napster, and its more legitimate successors like Pandora and Spotify. Amazon crippled bookstore chains. Comics are still clinging to the Wednesday comic shop model, but the number of stores in America has decreased drastically. And the sales of individual comics have followed in this trend. While the top-selling book in 1991 sold more than 7 million copies, the top-selling book of April 2019 didn't reach 200,000[285].

But lower sales at the top of the chart are not necessarily bad news for independent comic book publishers. According to the Long Tail theory, **lower sales at the top are the natural result of more and more people focusing their attention on smaller and smaller niches in the market.** For example, the person who might have listened to Top 40 music twenty years ago because she liked a few hip-hop songs on the list can now focus her time and money on the underground Korean hip hop she really wants to hear. Someone who read best-selling science fiction books in the past can spend all his time reading and writing gay *Serenity* fan fiction now. The teenager in the 1960s who identified with Spider-Man's teenage angst now has an entire category of YA books and comics specific to her race, class, and gender identity to satisfy the same need[286]. Of course, we still have blockbusters in every form of media, but it has never been easier for people to carve out their niche and connect with like-minded people around the world. **We live in a world of niche marketing**[287] now. Director and activist Ava Duvernay once said *"Every creative project has an audience. The key is finding, understanding, and connecting to that audience.*[288]*"*

How do the Long Tail theory and niche marketing apply to your independent comic? Once you strip away all the people who are not in your target market, you'll be able to define and identify all the people who might want to read your book and focus your attention on them.

Are All Comic Book Readers in Your Market?

Trying to define your target market as everyone who reads comics is both too broad and too narrow to be a helpful classification.

---

[285] April 2019 Comic Book Sales to Comics Shops. (n.d.). Retrieved May 16, 2020, from https://www.comichron.com/monthlycomicssales/2019/2019-04.html

[286] 300th-place Comic Books by Month. (n.d.). Retrieved May 16, 2020, from https://www.comichron.com/vitalstatistics/300thplace.html

[287] Niche Market Definition - What is Niche Market. (n.d.). Retrieved May 16, 2020, from https://www.shopify.com/encyclopedia/niche-market

[288] Questlove, & Greenman, B. (2018). *Creative quest.* New York, NY: Ecco, an imprint of HarperCollins.

It is too broad because comic books are not a market. Comics are a narrative medium. It is a way to deliver a story. **An entire medium can't be a defined market**. That would be the logical equivalent of a movie studio trying to release a movie that appeals to everyone who likes movies, or a television network trying to promote a show to everyone who likes to watch television. Comic book buyers are not a single monolithic group[289]. To create a useful definition of your target market, you have to go beyond the medium and focus on the message.

It is also too broad to define your target market as fans of superhero comics. There is a misconception in popular culture that all comics are superhero comics. The reason for this error is obvious, at least in America. The Big Two dominate much of the monthly output of comics, and the vast majority of books they put out are about the adventures of superheroes[290]. The most prominent merchandise, movie, and television shows that take their inspiration from comics focus on the connected universes of DC and Marvel. If a person only knows about comics from mainstream media and never goes into a comic shop, then it's easy for them to think that superhero comics and comics are one and the same.

But **superhero comics are simply one type of comic**. In the same way every movie isn't a summer blockbuster and every television show isn't reality TV, every comic isn't and shouldn't be, about superheroes. If you consider the literary importance that *bandes dessinées* have in France[291], the enormous variety of *manga* genres in Japan[292], or the steady tide of non-superhero work coming out of the independent comic publishers, then you'll realize you can take comic's unique ability to tell any story to create a narrative that is unique to you and your perspective.

Attempting to define your target market as simply comic book readers is also too narrow in the modern comic book marketplace. According to the market and consumer data site Statista, 75% of adults in America have never read a comic book[293]. There are also economic indicators suggesting the overall number of adults buying comics is shrinking[294]. This means that **if you only define your target market as current comic book readers, you're focusing on a small pool that is getting smaller and**

---

[289] Alverson, B. (2017, October 19). NYCC Insider Sessions Powered by ICv2: A Demographic Snapshot of Comics Buyers. Retrieved May 16, 2020, from https://icv2.com/articles/news/view/38709/nycc-insider-sessions-powered-icv2-a-demographic-snapshot-comics-buyers

[290] Comic Book Sales by Year. (n.d.). Retrieved May 16, 2020, from https://www.comichron.com/yearlycomicssales.html

[291] Emina, S. (2019, January 29). In France, Comic Books Are Serious Business. Retrieved May 16, 2020, from https://www.nytimes.com/2019/01/29/books/france-comic-books-angouleme.html

[292] Valentine, E. (2019, May 30). Sales Report Reveals 2019 Best-Selling Manga So Far. Retrieved May 16, 2020, from https://comicbook.com/anime/news/2019-best-selling-manga-one-piece-promised-neverland/

[293] Watson, A. (2019, August 12). Frequency of reading comic books by age U.S. 2018. Retrieved May 16, 2020, from https://www.statista.com/statistics/943127/comic-book-reading-frequency-by-age-us/

[294] Salkowitz, R. (2019, January 18). As Comics' Direct Market Struggles, A Surprising Publisher Rises. Retrieved May 16, 2020, from https://www.forbes.com/sites/robsalkowitz/2019/01/18/as-comics-direct-market-struggles-a-surprising-publisher-rises/

already dominated by two major players. A better approach is to look at a target market that includes a subset of comic book readers, but also identifies a potential group who haven't read comic books yet.

Is Your Market Just Superhero Comic Book Readers?

Even if you are publishing a superhero comic, defining your target market as the readers of all superhero comics is still too broad to be effective.

While the superhero genre is a specific category of narrative characterized by a particular style and form[295], it fits more of Robert McKee's definition of a mega-genre, since it is large and diverse enough to include dozens of sub-genres[296]. There are major differences in narrative content and tone from one superhero story to another. The person who reads *Superman* might not be interested in *The Punisher* or *The Boys*. The same logic applies to other broad categories when considering niche markets. There are multiple variations of comedy, horror, science fiction, and action. For example, Marguerite Bennett's *InSexts* isn't simply a horror title. It can be more accurately described as a historical, lesbian, feminist horror title.

As Seth Godin says *"You are not trying to sell an average story to average people. You are trying to connect your art with the people who will love it. Love takes time and requires a relationship"*[297]. The target market for your book will be defined by the relationship between the content of your book and the particular characteristics of your potential readers. There is an ideal reader for your book that can't be defined by medium or broad genres. Once you identify the nature of your ideal reader, you can figure out how to create satisfying relationships with them.

---

[295] Genre. (n.d.). Retrieved May 16, 2020, from https://www.merriam-webster.com/dictionary/genre

[296] Dercksen, D. (2017, November 13). Genre and genre conventions. Retrieved May 16, 2020, from https://writingstudio.co.za/what-type-of-story-are-you-writing/

[297] Godin, S. (2019). *This is marketing: You can't be seen until you learn to see.* Londres: Penguin Business.

An **ideal reader** is the specific type of person who would enjoy buying and reading your comic. Some writers like Stephen King focus on a specific real-world individual like his wife,[298]. Others use a theoretical profile. This chapter will focus more on the hypothetical idea, since all of us aren't fortunate enough to marry our ideal reader.

Are You the Ideal Reader?

If you are a person who loves comics, and you are in love with the idea for your project, you might think that you are the best template for the ideal reader of your book. This makes a certain amount of sense, but it is only the beginning of the analysis, since several other factors play a role in defining an ideal reader.

First, consider how you chose the comics that you read:

1. How do you find out about them?
2. What are you looking for in a comic?
3. Why do you choose one book over another?
4. Whose opinion do you trust when looking for a comic book recommendation?
5. When do you buy them?
6. Where do you buy them?

Once you understand your current relationship to buying comics, go further, and consider how you first got into comics. Try to remember the context of your early encounters and what factors played a role in your initial relationship with comics as a reader. Then talk to your team about their experiences with comics, both past, and present. Look for common threads and insights that can be applied to your ideal reader. Finally, consider the impact of so-called "cult brands" and how they evolved[299]. There are dozens of examples of pop culture stories taking root in small enthusiastic groups before bursting into the mainstream. Your book and your story are for those small groups, not the masses. The comic industry itself has been a fertile source of **cult brands** since the 1970s, with DC and Marvel building rival cults for almost a century[300] by catering to the qualities of their ideal readers.

---

[298] King, S. (2010). *On writing: A memoir of the craft*. New York: Scribner.

[299] Kenton, W. (2020, January 29). Cult Brand. Retrieved May 16, 2020, from https://www.investopedia.com/terms/c/cult-brand.asp

[300] Reid-Cleveland, K. (2020, April 08). Marvel vs. DC: 4 major differences and the best universe. Retrieved May 16, 2020, from https://www.dailydot.com/parsec/marvel-vs-dc/

What Are the Qualities of the Ideal Reader?

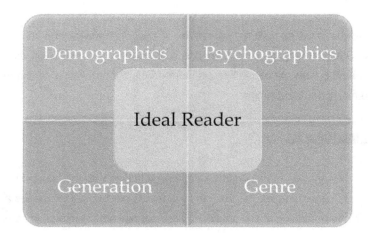

The most basic method to conceptualize your ideal reader is to imagine them based on their **profile**. For our purposes, an ideal reader profile is based on demographics, psychographics, genre, and generation:

- **Demographics** is the statistical characteristics of the human population[301]

- **Psychographics** classifies groups according to psychological variables[302]

- **Genre** is a category of literary composition characterized by a particular style, form, or content[303]

- **Generation** is a group of individuals born and living in the same time period and social context.[304]

The easiest way to differentiate between demographics and psychographics is to look at demographics as a focus on external or physical factors[305], while psychographics focus on internal mental, emotional

---

[301] Demographic. (n.d.). Retrieved May 16, 2020, from https://www.merriam-webster.com/dictionary/demographic

[302] Psychographics. (n.d.) Retrieved May 16, 2020, from https://www.merriam-webster.com/dictionary/psychographics

[303] Genre.(n.d.). Retrieved May 16, 2020, from https://www.merriam-webster.com/dictionary/genre

[304] Generation. (n.d.). Retrieved May 16, 2020, from https://www.merriam-webster.com/dictionary/generation

[305] Walker, B. (n.d.). The Differences Between Psychographics and Demographics. Retrieved May 16, 2020, from https://insights.c2bsolutions.com/blog/the-differences-between-psychographics-and-demographics

factors, and general world view[306]. The combined demographic and psychographic appeal of your book will come from the intersectional positioning of the story.

Intersectionality is the interconnected nature of social categorizations as they apply to a given individual or group[307]. While the term traces its origins in womanist theories of discrimination[308], you can analyze the related components of your story to determine its appeal. For example, a book that appeals to an immigrant, lesbian college student in New York might not appeal to a nationalist, cis-gendered, retired clergyman in Dublin. Neither perspective is wrong in terms of entertainment choices. Everyone is looking for something different. You just need to find the right audience for your book.

Intersectional elements exist in your characters and their impact on the story. Kevin Feige, film producer and architect of the Marvel Cinematic Universe stated in an interview that *"people want to see themselves in the stories they watch"*[309]. If the characters you create and the stories you tell give prominence to the psychographic and demographic perspectives of the reader, you have a better chance of appealing to them, especially if no one else is telling their story[310]. If your plot and theme resonate with conflicts your ideal reader can recognize, they will identify with your book[311]. For example, consider the role of the following elements in these books:

- Gender (*InSexts*)
- Race (*X-Men, Black Panther*)
- Income (*Spider-Man)*
- Religion (*Ms. Marvel*)
- Traditions (*Lone Wolf & Cub*)
- Personal History (*Maus*)
- Orientation (*Bingo Love*)
- Sexuality (*Sunstone*)

When you sit down to determine the demographics of your book, look at any applicable features of your characters and their world. Basic characteristics like race, religion, education, gender identity, sexual orientation, and income will be some of the factors that influence your ideal reader.

---

[306] Nastos, M. (2011). *Comic Book Marketing 101*. Nifty Entertainment

[307] Meaning of Intersectionality. (n.d.). Retrieved May 16, 2020, from https://en.oxforddictionaries.com/definition/intersectionality

[308] Id

[309] 'Black Panther' Represents "Real Hopes & Dreams" Says Producer Kevin Feige [Interview by The Hollywood Reporter]. (2018, November 2).

[310] Osajyfo, K. (2017). *New York Comic Con Marketing Panel*. Lecture presented in New York Comic Con, New York

[311] Manning, Write or Wrong, p. 25

As part of the psychographic analysis, think about what news sources your ideal reader might use, what websites they visit, what subgroups they belong to in social media, what pronouns they use, what they eat, what they wear, what movies, television, books they read and who they trust for news. One exercise you can consider is to pretend you are your ideal reader and look online for people like you. As you search, look at the ads and suggestions Google, YouTube, and other outlets offer in association with your potential ideal reader. This can give you some insight into what might be important to them, at least from a marketing perspective.

Of course, your story is more than a clinical dissection of demographics and psychographics. Almost every narrative falls within, or is a combination of, story **genres** that shape the content and conventions of a story in ways that appeal to some groups more than others. We touched upon the superhero genre as a major element of modern American comics, but McKee developed this list of the major genres that apply to all forms of narrative media[312]:

1. Action Adventure
2. Avant-Garde
3. Biography
4. Comedy
5. Coming of Age
6. Crime
7. Disaster
8. Drama
9. Epic
10. Erotic
11. Family Life
12. Fantasy
13. Historical
14. Horror
15. Martial Arts
16. Mystery
17. Religious
18. Romance
19. Science Fiction
20. Slice of Life
21. Sports
22. Superhero
23. Thriller
24. Tragedy
25. War
26. Western

At first glance, this list might seem short. Keep in mind that each major genre contains multiple sub-genres. For example, cyberpunk and alien invasion stories are just two of the many science fiction sub-genres. Spy thrillers and medical thrillers are both forms of thriller. More expansively, stories can combine conventions from multiple genres to create an unlimited number of hybrids.

- *The Shadow* combines historical with action-adventure and crime.

---

[312] Dercksen, D. (2017, November 13). Genre and genre conventions. Retrieved May 16, 2020, from https://writingstudio.co.za/what-type-of-story-are-you-writing/

- *Alien Legion* uses science fiction and war.

- *Lone Wolf and Cub* mixes the historical with martial arts.

- *The Walking Dead* combines dystopian science fiction (which is its own sub-genre) with horror and drama.

- *Star Wars* is a combination of space opera, action-adventure, and war.

- The superhero genre, as it has been shaped by the Big Two and emulated by others, might be the largest mashup genre of them all, since almost all of the genres listed have been thrown into the superhero stew at one point or another.

Your ideal reader seeks out specific sub-genres and combinations of sub-genres when they seek out entertainment. For example, the person looking for romantic comedy might not want dystopian horror. Again, no individual perspective is wrong, and I'm not trying to say people can't expand their horizons and try new things. But before you try to convince the general public to love your work, make sure you appeal to the genre preferences of your ideal readers.

To find the sub-genres of your story, look at the creative influences that inspired your ideas. Art critic and author Jerry Saltz advised creators to "make a list of your interests, every major book, movie, television show, video game, and website"[313]. This list will help you position your story in the overall universe of narrative art and identify relationship connections with your ideal reader beyond comics.

Your story also exists in a broader social and historical context of your **generation** that can be pivotal to the appeal of your book[314]. Major fiction categories, like children or young adult, use generation as the major appeal of their work[315]. Marketers identify six major generations currently consuming media in America[316]:

1. New readers (2010-present)
2. Young adult (1990's- 2010)

---

[313] Ritter, J., Orellana, M., & New York Magazine. (2018, November 27). Jerry Saltz's 33 Rules for Being an Artist. Retrieved May 16, 2020, from https://www.vulture.com/2018/11/jerry-saltz-how-to-be-an-artist.html

[314] Greene, R. (2019). *The Laws of Human Nature*. S.l.: Profile Books., p. 518

[315] Peterson, V. (2018, December 16). Young Adult Book Market Facts and Figures. Retrieved May 19, 2020, from https://www.thebalancecareers.com/the-young-adult-book-market-2799954

[316] Friesner, T. (2019, June 29). The Six Living Generations In America. Retrieved May 16, 2020, from http://www.marketingteacher.com/the-six-living-generations-in-america/

3. Millennials (1980s-1990s)
4. Generation X (1965-1979)
5. Baby Boomers (1946-1964)
6. Silent Generation (1925-1945)

Generation also has an impact because every story is influenced by the era when it was created. *Superman* was an answer to the Depression[317]. *Captain America* was a response to WWII[318]. The various anti-heroes of the '90s were a reaction to rampant urban crime. Today's stories have to serve the needs of today's audience. *Harry Potter, Game of Thrones, Walking Dead*, and the MCU struck a chord for this generation. What's next? How does your story appeal to the audience of 2020? Your story needs to resonate with today's ideal reader and not try to recreate a past era. Your publishing company can't be the "next Marvel"[319], but you can respond to the generational zeitgeist and give your ideal reader what they're looking for.

When you sit down to define your ideal reader, you can use Form 5 to get a handle on the concept. As always, feel free to modify this form to suit your needs. You don't need to fill in every category if it doesn't apply to your project. Again, you don't need to personally fit the definition of your ideal reader. Lee and Kirby developed *Black Panther*. Whedon created *Buffy* and he wasn't a teenage girl. Identifying with your ideal reader can certainly help, but it isn't a necessity.

---

[317] Cantu, A. (2016, October 21). Into the Comic World: Superman and American Anxieties in the Great Depression. Retrieved June 27, 2020, from https://stmuhistorymedia.org/into-the-comic-world/

[318] Spiegelman, A. (2019, August 17). Art Spiegelman: Golden age superheroes were shaped by the rise of fascism. Retrieved May 16, 2020, from https://www.theguardian.com/books/2019/aug/17/art-spiegelman-golden-age-superheroes-were-shaped-by-the-rise-of-fascism

[319] McMillan, G. (2020, April 18). The Myth of Comic Book Startups as the "Next Marvel". Retrieved May 16, 2020, from https://www.hollywoodreporter.com/heat-vision/myth-comic-book-start-ups-as-next-marvel-1202516

Independent Comic Book Publishing

Form 5: Ideal Reader Profile Analysis

- What **demographics** are relevant to this book?
  - Gender
    - Male
    - Female
    - Non-Binary
    - Trans
  - Sexual orientation
    - LGBTQA
    - Straight
  - Race: _____
  - Residence
    - Urban
    - Suburban
    - Rural
  - Education
    - Grade School
    - High School
    - College
    - Masters
  - Religion
    - Atheism
    - Buddhism
    - Christianity
    - Hinduism
    - Islam
    - Judaism
    - Non-religious
    - Spiritual
  - Relationship status
    - Divorced
    - Married
    - Significant Other

- Single
- Widowed
- Family status
  - With children
  - Without children
- Disabilities: _____
- Income
  - Low
  - Middle
  - Upper

- What **psychographics** are relevant to this book?
  - Values
  - Attitudes
  - Interests
  - Lifestyles
  - Motivations
  - Priorities
  - Influences

- What are the **genres and sub-genres** of your story?
  - Action Adventure
  - Avant-Garde
  - Biography
  - Comedy
  - Coming of Age
  - Crime
  - Disaster
  - Drama
  - Epic
  - Erotic
  - Family Life
  - Fantasy
  - Historical
  - Horror
  - Martial Arts
  - Mystery
  - Religious
  - Romance
  - Science Fiction
  - Slice of Life
  - Sports
  - Superhero
  - Thriller
  - Tragedy
  - War
  - Western

- What **generation** will this book appeal to?
  - New Readers (2010-present)
  - Young Adult (1990's- 2010)
  - Millennials (1980s-1990s)
  - Generation X (1965-1979)
  - Baby Boomers (1946-1964)
  - Silent Generation (1925-1945)

- What are the major entertainment, literary, or media influences for this book?

- How does the current social and political context impact the book?

Your idea is unique and original, but it doesn't exist in a vacuum. There are probably similar elements in other narratives that appeal to your ideal reader profile no matter what your story is about. Understanding what's already out there and the characteristics of your competition can provide valuable information in both creating relationships with your reader and producing a better book.

Competition is the effort of two or more parties acting independently and adversely to each other to secure the business of a third party[320]. For an independent comic book publisher, competition is defined as all media that can appeal to the ideal reader profile. Because readers do not have unlimited time or money, they have to make choices about what narratives they consume. For our purposes, we are going to consider competition beyond just comics, since the modern ideal reader can choose from books, comics, movies, television, the theater, and video games to get the stories that interest them. Expanding your concept of competition offers more information about the world your ideal reader lives in.

How Do You Find Your Competition?

Because your story isn't targeting everyone, you're not in direct competition with every comic book and movie ever created. The good news is **you only have to compete with the media that appeals to your ideal readers**.

If you created a high concept, then there is a good chance the existing media you used could be your competition. If you filled out the ideal reader profile form, then you already have a handle on the other media influences that helped shape your idea. There is a good chance that some of those stories will be your future competitors, too. For a more comprehensive look at potential competition, there are several painless research options available both inside and outside of comics. I'm going to provide five research options in addition to a basic Google search, but keep in mind this is current as of 2020. They may be irrelevant or replaced by the time you read this book.

For the sake of this exercise, we'll need some keywords. **Keywords** are any words used to classify or organize digital content or to facilitate an online search for information[321]. Let's imagine that you have a story called *Blood Bond* about an organized crime family who happen to be a group of vampires. The key genres are vampire horror and organized crime. For our search, we'll keep it simple and just use "vampire crime" and look at the following search options.

---

[320] Competition. (n.d.). Retrieved May 16, 2020, from https://www.merriam-webster.com/dictionary/competition

[321] Keyword. (n.d.). Retrieved May 16, 2020, from https://www.dictionary.com/browse/keyword

- **Amazon** is one of the largest e-commerce retailers on the planet[322]. In addition to owning Comixology and hundreds of other companies, it is also the most used search engine for product search, even bigger than Google[323]. A search for "vampire crime" here reveals not only graphic novels, but long-running book series from both J.R. Rain and Laurell K. Hamilton, games like *Vampire: Bloodlines*, and *Vampyr*, as well as several TV series including *NOS4R2, True Blood,* and *Vampire Prosecutor*

- **Comichron** is a resource for comic book research[324]. It tracks monthly and annual sales for both comic books and graphic novels since 1991. It also has a Google custom search engine. If you type in "vampire crime", you'll get dozens of hits. The titles that will stand out as the most relevant will probably be *American Vampire*, *Anita Blake, Vampire Hunter*, *Bite Club*, and *Buffy the Vampire Slayer.*

- **Comixology** is a digital comic book distributor owned by Amazon[325]. It sells individual comics, graphic novels, and subscription services. It also has a genre page as part of its browsing features. If you use the "Browse" drop-down menu, you'll see a selection for "genre". Both crime and vampires have their own selections. Searching through them will reveal new possible competitors including *Angel*, *Blade*, *Spike*, and *Vamps.*

- **The Grand Comics Database** is a user-generated database attempting to catalog every comic, graphic novel, manga, creator, and character ever created[326]. It also has a search function. A search for "vampire crime" reveals not only specific titles that might compete with your book, including *Fray* and *The Vault of Horror*, it also lists specific characters who match those keywords including Bloodscream and Nico Minoru. This can be helpful to ensure that your characters and concepts don't inadvertently infringe on pre-existing copyrights.

- **Goodreads** is a social media network dedicated to books and reading owned by Amazon[327]. In addition to an internal search engine, it also has user-maintained lists of books and graphic novels in a variety of subgenres and configurations. A search for "vampire crime" here confirms some of the usual suspects, but it also reveals titles like *Vampire, PA,* and *Crimes of Vampires.*

---

[322] Amazon (company). (2020, May 14). Retrieved May 16, 2020, from https://en.wikipedia.org/wiki/Amazon_(company)

[323] Alaimo, D. (2018, September 07). Amazon now dominates Google in product search. Retrieved May 16, 2020, from https://www.retaildive.com/news/amazon-now-dominates-google-in-product-search/531822/

[324] A Resource for Comics Research. (n.d.). Retrieved May 16, 2020, from https://www.comichron.com/

[325] Digital Comics - Comics by comiXology. (n.d.). Retrieved May 16, 2020, from https://www.comixology.com/

[326] Grand Comics Database. (n.d.). Retrieved May 16, 2020, from https://www.comics.org/

[327] Goodreads. (2020, May 13). Retrieved May 16, 2020, from https://en.wikipedia.org/wiki/Goodreads

- **Kickstarter** is a public benefit corporation that maintains a global crowdfunding platform[328]. Comics are one of the major categories of projects funded on Kickstarter. A search in their database pulls up both successful and unsuccessful projects including *Rush* and *Nocturna*.

- **Tapas** is a webtoon syndicate launched in 2012[329]. A search for vampire crime in its search engine reveals several potential competitors including *S.C.A.R. Unit*, *Vampire and Single*, and *Stripper and the Vampire King*.

- **Webtoons** is a creator-owned webtoon syndicate[330]. Typing "vampire and crime" into their search engine will show you titles including *Acursian*, *Identity Crisis,* and *Overflow*.

- **Wikipedia** is a free online encyclopedia that was launched in 2001[331]. It maintains a category of comics by genre[332], which includes one hundred and eighty-four crime titles[333] and sixty vampire titles[334]. Not only can these pages be useful to find new competitors, but they can also provide detailed descriptions of characters and plotlines for competitors you've already found.

How Do You Compare Your Competition?

All competition is not created equal. While your story idea might share genre characteristics with the competitors you found, there will be points of difference you can use to appeal to your ideal reader. **Using a comparative analysis of your ideal reader profile and SWOT will reveal the whitespace your book can fill for the target market**. Let's explore both concepts to see how they work with my *Blood Bond* example.

To conduct an **ideal reader profile comparison**, look at the demographic, psychographic, genre, and generational aspects of each competitor in relation to your story. Consider the following questions:

---

[328] Kickstarter. (2020, May 15). Retrieved May 16, 2020, from https://en.wikipedia.org/wiki/Kickstarter

[329] Burszan, D. (2013, December 05). Interview with Chang Kim, CEO and Founder of Tapastic. Retrieved June 28, 2020, from https://www.denofgeek.com/culture/interview-with-chang-kim-ceo-and-founder-of-tapastic/

[330] Webtoon. (n.d.). Retrieved June 28, 2020, from https://www.webtoons.com/en/

[331] Wikipedia. (2020, May 14). Retrieved May 16, 2020, from https://en.wikipedia.org/wiki/Wikipedia

[332] Category: Comics by genre. (2019, January 09). Retrieved May 16, 2020, from https://en.wikipedia.org/wiki/Category:Comics_by_genre

[333] Category: Crime comics. (2019, August 10). Retrieved May 16, 2020, from https://en.wikipedia.org/wiki/Category:Crime_comics

[334] Category: Vampires in comics. (2014, March 28). Retrieved May 16, 2020, from https://en.wikipedia.org/wiki/Category:Vampires_in_comics

- What demographic aspects of your story are similar to each competitor?

- Which ones are different?

- What psychographic values does your book share with the competitor?

- In what ways do they deviate?

- How much sub-genre overlap exists?

- How many unique sub-genres does your book have?

- What generation does the competitor speak to?

- What message does it support?

- What generation does your book speak to?

- How is the message different?

If the profile of your competitors and your book are identical, it might be time to consider altering aspects of your story to give it a fresh perspective. I'm not advocating changing essential elements of a story just for the sake of change, especially if you love the story. I'm simply pointing out that it will be hard to compete with an established competitor if you are both fighting for the same readers with a similar story,

SWOT is an acronym that stands for Strengths, Weaknesses, Opportunities, and Threats[335]. It is a framework for evaluating the competitive position of a company, product, or service. While SWOT can be used for various aspects of your business, in this context you want to compare your book to the competition in terms of appeal to your ideal reader. This comparison is done not only for the elements of your story, but for broader factors including the relative popularity of the characters, creative teams, and publishers for each book. Your SWOT analysis can help you adjust your marketing based on your conclusions.

Taking *Blood Bond* as an example, a possible strength could be that my story has more generational relevance than the competitors, or maybe my specific genre mix is underrepresented in the market. Possible weaknesses could be similar plot points or more popular characters that prevent my story from standing out. My opportunities could come from the fact that the last new competitor was published several years ago, creating whitespace that needs to be filled. My weaknesses could come from the announcement of a new book in the same space.

Of course, the best way to understand your competition is to read every book your target market might read. This will help you understand what they do well, the pitfalls you want to avoid, and the qualities that are missing from the market. This isn't an exercise in denigrating your rivals or ego gratification. In many instances, your competitors might be masters of their craft who have created classics in the medium. Use them as goals to achieve and teachers to learn from.

---

[335] Grant, M. (2020, March 02). How SWOT (Strength, Weakness, Opportunity, and Threat) Analysis Works. Retrieved May 16, 2020, from https://www.investopedia.com/terms/s/swot.asp

You can use the following form to understand your competition and give you the context to connect with your target market. There is a good chance you will find more than three competitors for your book, so feel free to add additional entries as needed.

You can use what's already in the market to help you connect with the right people and you can differentiate yourself from the competition before your book is created because you know what they offer. You can also wrap your head around just how big the target market is and what steps you can take to make it bigger.

Independent Comic Book Publishing
Form 6: Ideal Reader Comparison and SWOT Analysis Template

(For all competitor's published within the last three years. Add additional competitors as necessary)

1. **Potential Competitor 1**
   a. Title
   b. Ideal Reader Comparison
      i. Demographic
      ii. Psychographic
      iii. Genre
      iv. Generation
      v. Distribution Channel
   c. SWOT Analysis
      i. Strength
      ii. Weakness
      iii. Opportunity
      iv. Threat

2. **Potential Competitor 2**
   a. Title
   b. Ideal Reader Comparison
      i. Demographic
      ii. Psychographic
      iii. Genre
      iv. Generation
      v. Distribution Channel
   c. SWOT Analysis
      i. Strength
      ii. Weakness
      iii. Opportunity
      iv. Threat

3. **Potential Competitor 3**
   a. Title
   b. Ideal Reader Comparison
      i. Demographic
      ii. Psychographic
      iii. Genre
      iv. Generation

The size of your target market defines various aspects of your project. A narrow-focused market will require different marketing, distribution, advertising, and sales strategies than a larger group of ideal readers. Your market size can influence what type of book you create. Depending on your goals and your resources, it might even lead to altering the definition of your ideal reader or story idea. Again, don't chase a market when you develop your story. The key is to fill a niche that is small enough for you to focus on, and large enough to make the effort worthwhile.

How Do You Measure the Size of Your Target Market?

Measuring market size for an independent comic is as much art as it is science. The psychographics and genre appeal of any story to any individual reader is emotional and subjective. It can fluctuate at will, and there's no way to track that shift unless you're Charles Xavier. At the same time, statistical analysis and historical sales figures can only estimate current demand or potential interest in any given story. There are two main methods of calculating market size, but for our purposes, neither is sufficient.

A **Bottom-Up Analysis** involves determining how many retail locations will sell your product and how many units each one typically sells[336]. This type of analysis makes sense for other products, but for independent comics, it creates a challenge in terms of data. As we'll see when we talk about distribution methods, it is difficult to determine in advance which comic shops, book stores, libraries, alternative outlets, or online retailers will carry your book before it is produced. Amazon will carry most projects, but that single data point might not be enough to justify bottom-up analysis, even if they are the 80,000-pound gorilla.

A **Top-Down Analysis** involves determining the overall size of the market and then establishing a realistic estimate of the market share that you can capture[337]. This would be a better option for an independent publisher, since you already have access to the competitors in your niche market from the last chapter. The problem is the lack of reliable data. Direct market sales count units sold to comic shops, not sales to actual readers[338]. Digital distribution channels like Comixology don't share their sales numbers with the public[339]. There is no mechanism to track sales at conventions and other transactions between publishers and

---

[336] Zhuo, T. (2016, March 07). 5 Strategies to Effectively Determine Your Market Size. Retrieved May 16, 2020, from https://www.entrepreneur.com/article/270853

[337] Cremades, A. (2018, September 23). How to Effectively Determine Your Market Size. Retrieved May 16, 2020, from https://www.forbes.com/sites/alejandrocremades/2018/09/23/how-to-effectively-determine-your-market-size/

[338] Comic Book Sales by Year. (n.d.). Retrieved May 16, 2020, from https://www.comichron.com/yearlycomicssales.html

[339] Allen, T., & Allen. (2018, January 22). Comparing Comixology Sales Ranks With Print Sales – A Tangled Web Emerges. Retrieved May 16, 2020, from https://www.comicsbeat.com/comparing-comixology-sales-ranks-with-print-sales-a-tangled-web-emerges/

readers. Finally, there are organizations like NPD Bookscan[340] and Ibisworld[341] that can provide data on the bookstore market, but I'm working under the assumption you don't want to spend a thousand dollars on those kinds of services.

My less than optimal third solution involves creating a theoretical sales model for each competitor based on the available information online. The method is as follows:

1. Determine which distribution channels a competitor uses
2. Determine the sales number of each competing book ("S") through direct market sales every month using a database like Comichron
3. Estimate the sales in other relevant channels
4. Determine total sales
5. Repeat for each competitor

This estimation can work because according to ICV2, digital comic sales add about 20% to the direct market of any given comic. Book channel sales add an additional 90%, and all other channels add an additional 3%[342]. So, if we only know the direct market sales for a competitor, we can create a simple formula:

- Direct market sales (DM) can be represented as S
- Digital comic sales (DS) can be estimated as S x .2
- Book channel sales (BC) can be estimated as S x .9
- Other channel sales (OC) can be estimated as S x .03
- The total estimated sales for a competitor can then be calculated as DM + DS + BC + OC

So let's suppose there is a competitor to *Blood Bond* called *Night Moves* that is available in comic shops, online and in bookstores. If the total annual sales were 3,000 copies (DM), then the total estimated sales for this competitor would be as follows:

- DM = 3000 copies
- DS = DM x .2 or 600 copies
- BC = DM x .9 or 2,700 copies
- OC = DM x .03 or 90 copies
- Total sales = DM + DS + BC + OC or 3,000 + 600 + 2,700 + 90 or 6390 copies

[340] NPD Bookscan. (n.d.). Retrieved May 16, 2020, from https://www.ecpa.org/page/npdbundle

[341] Industry Market Research, Reports, and Statistics. (n.d.). Retrieved May 16, 2020, from https://www.ibisworld.com/industry-trends/specialized-market-research-reports/consumer-goods-services/book-publishing-broadcasting/comic-book-publishing.html

[342] Comics and Graphic Novel Sales Hit New High in 2018: Image 3. (n.d.). Retrieved May 16, 2020, from https://icv2.com/gallery/43106/3

As you work through this exercise for each competitor, keep three things in mind:

1. These numbers are only educated estimates. The actual sales for each competitor may vary considerably and because of the way the industry is currently structured, there is no way to confirm these numbers.

2. These estimates include all standard formats but don't account for webtoon syndicates, emerging distribution models, subscriptions or other distribution not measured by ICV2

3. The estimates only cover units sold. It doesn't take into account how much each copy cost, or how much revenue or profit was generated.

Once you get an idea of how many copies each competitor might be selling, you can estimate how many copies you might sell. Let's continue to use *Blood Bond* in this thought experiment and keep the numbers simple. If I found ten competitors for *Blood Bond* and the total number of single-issue sales in December of 2018 was 20,000 units, how much could I expect to capture with the first issue of my book?

If the market was divided evenly, then each competitor sold 2,000 copies (20,000 divided by 10) because they each had 10% of the market. If I came in and also captured an equal share of the market, then I would be trying to capture about 9% of the market, or 1,800 copies.

In reality, capturing market share is not that easy, especially for new products. Several analysts in the startup space advise new businesses to assume they can grab no more than 1-5% to start with[343], no matter how many competitors are in the market[344].

How Do You Measure the Dollar Value of Your Target Market?

It's one thing to know how many copies you can sell to your target market. It is another thing to understand how much money that market can generate. **Market value is the amount of revenue a market generates over a given period**[345]. For example, if the average price of a monthly comic is $3.99, then the monthly market value of the *Blood Bond* niche is around $80,000.

---

[343] Cremades, A. (2018, September 23). How To Effectively Determine Your Market Size. Retrieved May 16, 2020, from https://www.forbes.com/sites/alejandrocremades/2018/09/23/how-to-effectively-determine-your-market-size/

[344] As a point of reference, the title that sold the lowest amount in December of 2018 (#500 on the list) was an independent first issue that sold 461 copies December 2018 Comic Book Sales to Comics Shops. (n.d.). Retrieved May 16, 2020, from https://www.comichron.com/monthlycomicssales/2018/2018-12.html

[345] Cremades, A. (2018, September 23). How To Effectively Determine Your Market Size. Retrieved May 16, 2020, from https://www.forbes.com/sites/alejandrocremades/2018/09/23/how-to-effectively-determine-your-market-size/

There are three things you need to remember when looking at market value for independent comics because like market size, market value isn't an exact science.

- The numbers are going to be gross—not net—so the payments to both the retailer and the distributor will be deducted from what the publishers ultimately receive.

- The numbers are based on the average cost of each comic. It doesn't include discounts, premium sales, or subscription sales.

- This example only takes into account single issue sales. A similar analysis would have to be done for graphic novels, trade paperbacks, digital sales, or any other distribution model you plan to use[346].

How Do You Measure the Growth Rate of Your Market?

Market size isn't a fixed number. Every month and every year, the market size can change, especially for discretionary entertainment like comics. As an independent publisher, it would help you to know if your market size was growing or shrinking before you make your book.

Fortunately, sites like Comichron track monthly and annual sales trends. Once you determine how big your target market is now, go back between six months to two years and see if you can see any trends.

- Did the number of competitors go up or down?
- Did the overall market grow or shrink?
- What do the past trends suggest about the future?

This last question is mostly speculation, since there is no definitive way for you to know what the market will look like two or three years from now. But if you see numbers that are continuously dropping month after month, you might want to take that into consideration.

---

[346] We'll discuss distribution methods in Part 7 of this book

How Do You Determine the Patterns of Your Market?

In the same way, there are trends in terms of rising and falling, there can also be a predictable sequence of events in comic book sales. Check the monthly sales number to see if you can spot them for your niche.

- Do more books get sold during convention season or the holidays?
- Is there a dry spell every year when no one is releasing new content?
- Do sales of new issues fall off a cliff the month after release, or do the sales from month to month appear stable?

Understanding the specific patterns of your target market can help you decide when and how to release your book and give it the best chance to succeed.

Knowing the size and characteristics of your existing market is a helpful tool for building a foundation with your customers. But if you are a new independent publisher trying to fight for the same ideal readers as all of your competitors, you will be fighting a battle that most will lose. It is vital for your project—and for the industry as a whole—to expand the target market to that vast untapped population that has never read a comic before.

If you want more people to read your comic, you need to convince more new people to read comics.

This is not a simple challenge. The bad news is that the comic book industry faces several substantial barriers to growth that you'll have to consider and overcome if you want to avoid fighting for scraps. The good news is that comics have a substantial amount of growth potential, so if you can develop marketing that expands beyond the current comic book market, you can succeed while your competition struggles.

What Factors Limit the Growth in Comics?

As an entertainment medium, comics have six major factors that make it difficult to expand the market:

- Barriers to Entry: Comics have inherent cultural roadblocks that discourage the uninitiated from reading them. If you have spent years immersed in the subculture, walking into a shop or scanning titles online might be second nature to you because of your comic book literacy, but there are fundamental questions facing a new reader, including:

  - Who are the best creators of the type of story I like?
  - What types of comics are available besides superhero comics?
  - Where can I buy comics?
  - When are comics released?
  - Why should I read comics instead of watching comic content on TV?
  - How do you even read a comic book page?

  If you don't take the time to reduce or remove these barriers, you'll lose your potential reader.

- Competition from other media: Your ideal reader potentially consumes stories from several different sources, including:

  - Books
  - Film
  - Social Media
  - Television (and other forms of streaming media)
  - Video Games

In addition to the competition of unique narratives coming from these distribution channels, the growth of comic-related media[347] could theoretically cannibalize readers who might otherwise consider spending time and money on comics.

- Higher prices for comic consumption: Your ideal reader can arguably get more entertainment value for a lower cost by choosing other forms of media over comics because economies of scale drive down the cost of a mass-market product[348].

  Let's think about the ideal reader who might be interested in an urban crime superhero story like *Daredevil*. In 2019, a premium subscription to Netflix costs $13[349]. With that monthly payment, your ideal reader can currently get thirty-six episodes of *Daredevil*, plus dozens of hours of related Marvel Netflix shows, plus hundreds of hours of comic-related entertainment, as well as thousands of hours of additional viewing options[350]. By contrast, that same $13 will get your ideal reader 3 single issues of the current *Daredevil* 22-page comic.

  If you consider the relationship between film and comics, consider the relationship between the movie *Avengers: Infinity War* and *Infinity War* the graphic novel. As of 2019, your ideal reader can buy the film for $14. The graphic novel is available on Amazon for $21[351]

  It can be argued that the stories and experiences in each of my examples aren't the same and can't be used as a meaningful comparison. You might also think that your story is too unique to be subject to market cannibalization from Chris Evans, Chris Hemsworth, and Chris Pratt, but keep in mind that narratives don't have to be identical to face competition from other media. And even if your story isn't a superhero epic, you probably found competitors to your story in other media that is cheaper than your average comic.

---

[347] Wilding, J. (2018, November 28). Every Confirmed (And Rumored) Comic Book Movie Being Released In 2020. Retrieved May 16, 2020, from https://www.comicbookmovie.com/birds_of_prey/every-confirmed-and-rumored-comic-book-movie-being-released-in-2020-a164974

[348] Kenton, W. (2020, January 29). What You Need to Know About Economies of Scale. Retrieved May 16, 2020, from https://www.investopedia.com/terms/e/economiesofscale.asp

[349] Levenson, J. (2020, April 28). How Much Does Netflix Cost? A Breakdown of the Plans. Retrieved May 16, 2020, from https://www.digitaltrends.com/movies/netflix-cost-pricing-plan-breakdown/

[350] There are additional embedded costs for having a television, and internet access but those systemic costs are basic to modern American life, so your ideal reader would probably absorb those costs regardless of what type of entertainment they choose.

[351] Starlin, J., Lim, R., Milgrom, A., Scheele, M., & Morelli, J. (2017). *The Infinity War*. New York: Marvel Worldwide.

- Isolated Distribution: The distribution of content in the comic book industry is a topic that deserves in-depth analysis, but an overview of the history of getting comics into the hands of readers will help you understand the context for your book.

  In the early days, multiple retail outlets carried comics. Newsstands, candy stores, drug stores, and book stores all had metal spinner racks stuffed with books from various major publishers[352]. The fairly low price per book (for years a single-issue comic cost less than twenty-five cents[353]) and the ubiquitous availability of comics made it easy to reach everyone.

  In the 1980s, shops dedicated to comics started becoming a dominant distribution channel for the industry[354]. By the '90s, there were comic shops in every major city in every state of the country. The combination of newsstand distribution and comic shops created a dynamic similar to a gateway drug scenario. A person could stumble onto comics at a newsstand, graduate to their local comic shop and become a lifelong comic book collector. It was a pipeline that led to a significant expansion of the market.

  Since then, the pipeline has collapsed for several reasons. First, comic book publishers abandoned the newsstand market to focus almost exclusively on the comic shops[355]. What little newsstand distribution remained became irrelevant when high-speed internet made news available on-demand online, shutting many newsstands down[356]. The comic shop industry suffered from a combination of speculation[357], overdependence on specific publishers[358], and insular sexist culture that created unnecessary barriers to entry[359]. The collapse of this pipeline, combined with the other challenges, conspired to make comics harder to buy than they had been in the past.

---

[352] Accampo, D. (2017, October 24). My (Not So) Secret History with the Comics Spinner Rack. Retrieved May 16, 2020, from https://bookriot.com/2014/11/30/my-not-so-secret-history-with-the-comics-spinner-rack/

[353] Median Comic Book Cover Prices by Year. (n.d.). Retrieved May 16, 2020, from https://www.comichron.com/vitalstatistics/mediancoverprices.html

[354] Gearino, D., & Spurgeon, T. (2019). Comic shop: The retail mavericks who gave us a new geek culture. Athens, OH: Swallow Press, Ohio University Press.

[355] Newsstand Editions History and Newsstand Pricing Policies. (2018). Retrieved May 16, 2020, from http://milehighcomics.com/newsletter/031513.html

[356] Knolle, S. (2019, May 23). Death of L.A. Newsstands. Retrieved May 16, 2020, from https://www.laweekly.com/death-of-l-a-newsstands/

[357] Last, J. (2011, June 04). The Comic Book Crash of 1993. Retrieved May 16, 2020, from https://www.weeklystandard.com/jonathan-v-last/the-crash-of-1993

[358] Elbein, A. (2017, May 25). The Real Reasons for Marvel Comics' Woes. Retrieved May 16, 2020, from https://www.theatlantic.com/entertainment/archive/2017/05/the-real-reasons-for-marvel-comics-woes/527127/

[359] Ahlin, C. (2016, January 22). 10 Struggles All Female Comic Book Fans Understand. Retrieved May 16, 2020, from https://www.bustle.com/articles/136980-10-struggles-all-female-comic-book-fans-understand

Keep in mind, other channels of distribution exist that make it *easier* to access comics than before. Bookstore, library, and digital distribution give potential readers painless ways to get comics. Up to twenty percent of new readers now discover comics online, and two-thirds of those readers go on to patronize comic shops,[360] but the pipeline from stumbling onto a comic to becoming a regular reader isn't as universal as it had been in the past.

- Perception Stigma: Unlike movies, television, and books, comics suffer from the inaccurate historical image of being a medium primarily for children or losers[361]. Although the success of comic book related media has reduced this falsehood in recent years[362], the narrow image of comics is a barrier to growth.

  This issue has its origins in the religious and anti-communism movements of the 1950s[363]. Before that period, comics had been popular with children and adults throughout the history of the medium, with specific titles published for everyone from toddlers to soldiers on the frontlines of World War II[364]. But in 1954, a psychiatrist named Dr. Henry Wertham published a book titled *Seduction of the Innocent*[365]. The premise of this work accused comic books of everything from criminality to homosexuality[366]. Wertham's work sparked public backlash to the point that Congress held hearings on the dangers of comics to American morality[367]. In response to this public relations disaster, the comic book industry imposed a code of conduct on itself and developed an organization called the **Comics Code Authority**[368] to review the content of every published comic from the publishers who signed onto this code.

---

[360] Allen, T. W., & Waid, M. (2014). *Economics of digital comics*. United States of America: p. 152

[361] Dumay, J., & Puccetti, G. (2018, October 02). Comics are for Losers. Retrieved May 16, 2020, from https://wp.nyu.edu/fogdv2/2018/10/02/comics-are-for-losers/

[362] Salkowitz, R. (2018, December 26). How Superhero Movies Dominated The Box Office in 2018. Retrieved May 16, 2020, from https://www.forbes.com/sites/robsalkowitz/2018/12/26/how-superhero-movies-dominated-the-box-office-in-2018/

[363] Lopes, P. D. (2009). *Demanding Respect*. Temple University Press.

[364] Lauren, B. (2017, June 22). The Powerful Popularity Of Superhero Comics During World War II. Retrieved May 16, 2020, from https://www.bleedingcool.com/2017/06/22/popularity-superhero-comics-world-war-ii/

[365] Wertham, F. M. (1954). *Seduction of the Innocent*. Place of publication not identified: Amereon.

[366] Wilson, M. (2016, April 19). Comics Bogeyman: A Look Back At 'Seduction of the Innocent'. Retrieved May 16, 2020, from https://comicsalliance.com/history-fredric-wertham-seduction-of-the-innocent/

[367] Ibid.

[368] Ibid.

The Code stunted the growth of comics as a creative medium by forcing every book to be acceptable and appropriate for a child to read[369]. Imagine the creative state of movies, television, theater, and novels today if every story had to be designed for a ten-year-old to see. Imagine how hard it would be to convince adults to engage with any of these media if the content didn't evolve with their growing mental and emotional sophistication[370]. This is the situation the comics industry found itself in after *Seduction of the Innocent* and the Comics Code. Although Wertham's work was eventually discredited[371], the damage was already done. Comic books became perceived as a medium for children, unworthy of attention from any other group.

Eventually, the comic book industry moved away from and rejected the Comics Code[372]. Books like *The Dark Knight Returns*, imprints like Vertigo and Marvel Knights, and Wildstorm sought to appeal to older readers with darker themes and more adult content[373]. While this did act as a counterbalance to some degree, the overemphasis on sexism in the female portrayals and gratuitous violence created a negative backlash of its own[374].

Today, there is a mainstream disconnect between comic book stories and comic books themselves. While comics are the source of successful media franchises across the board, that hasn't translated into an explosion of comic book sales[375]. The popularity of the stories isn't surprising. Mike Marts, editor of AfterShock Comics (and this book) articulated this point well: *"There's something classic about comic stories that resonate with people. What matters is the type of journeys these characters take and that's never going to go away, so I don't think there is going to be any significant drop off of fantastic movies and TV shows made based on comic books."*[376]

---

[369] Abad-Santos, A. (2014, December 15). The insane history of how American paranoia ruined and censored comic books. Retrieved May 16, 2020, from https://www.vox.com/2014/12/15/7326605/comic-book-censorship

[370] Miller, L. (2019, October 08). 10 Crazy Rules The Comics Code Authority Made Creators Follow. Retrieved May 16, 2020, from https://www.cbr.com/comics-code-authority-crazy-rules-comic-book-superheroes/

[371] Tilley, C. (2012, November 10). Seducing the Innocent: Fredric Wertham and the Falsifications That Helped Condemn Comics. Retrieved May 16, 2020, from http://muse.jhu.edu/article/490073

[372] Wolk, D. (2011, January 24). R.I.P.: The Comics Code Authority. Retrieved May 16, 2020, from http://techland.time.com/2011/01/24/r-i-p-the-comics-code-authority/

[373] Knight, R. (2018). How Marvel Knights Changed the Face and Fate of Marvel Comics. Retrieved May 16, 2020, from https://nerdist.com/article/marvel-knights-history-importance-punisher-black-panther

[374] Ca-Staff. (2011, August 29). The Problem Of Women In Comics: Where They Are (and Aren't) [Opinion]. Retrieved May 16, 2020, from https://comicsalliance.com/superhero-comics-women-sexism/

[375] Barnett, D. (2019, April 26). Why are comics shops closing as superheroes make a mint? Retrieved May 16, 2020, from https://www.theguardian.com/books/2019/apr/26/why-are-comics-shops-closing-superheroes-avengers-endgame

[376] Gregoire, W., & Luo, B. (2016, May 11). Marvel and DC's Ex-Executive Editor Reveals Why We'll Never Hate Superhero Stories. Retrieved May 16, 2020, from http://nextshark.com/mike-marts-aftershock-comics-interview/

But the divide between the success of comic content presents a confusing challenge, even when you consider niche markets. It is as if millions of people decided that they loved wine, but didn't like grapes. The fact that the stories resonate outside the medium suggests that the problem isn't with comic book stories, but the way people see comic books.

- Established Patterns: Most of America does not currently read comics on a regular basis. The people who do read comics already have their favorites. Also, most of America is used to having potential entertainment pushed at them in a dozen different directions. They don't have to go and hunt for it. They don't have to order most of their entertainment in advance and then show up to a specific place on Wednesday to get it. When you ask people to change their behavior to consume your story both in terms of buying and consuming, you make it easier for them to just avoid your work completely and stick to their established pattern[377].

What is the Impact of the Lack of Growth in Comics?

The combination of barriers to entry, media competition, comparative value, isolated distribution, and negative perception create an environment that suppresses growth in the market. In fact, **there are economic indicators that suggest the size of the single-issue comic book market is shrinking.**

According to a 2018 study, only 4% of Americans read comics on a regular basis[378]. If there are 330 million people in the US[379], that's just 13 million people overall. Industry analysis and comic shop owners claim the Big Two are pursuing tactics that attempt to squeeze more and more money from a limited group of devoted fans while their corporate owners only look to sell their content to the mainstream market in other media[380]. At the same time, fundamental flaws in the direct market distribution model have plagued the industry for decades[381] creating a closed system where the majority of growth comes from variant covers, crossover events, and narrative reboots that don't fundamentally change the industry dynamics[382].

---

[377] Godin, This is Marketing

[378] Watson, A. (2019, August 12). Frequency of reading comic books U.S. 2018. Retrieved May 16, 2020, from https://www.statista.com/statistics/943111/comic-book-reading-frequency-us/

[379] U.S. and World Population Clock. (n.d.). Retrieved May 16, 2020, from https://www.census.gov/popclock/

[380] Staff (2019, July 05). Tilting at Windmills #270: Pondering Whether to Close A Comic Shop. Retrieved May 16, 2020, from https://www.comicsbeat.com/tilting-at-windmills-270-pondering-whether-to-close-a-comic-shop/

[381] Salkowitz, R. (2017). Marvel's Problem Isn't Diversity -- It's Much Bigger (And It's Not Just Marvel's Problem). Retrieved May 16, 2020, from https://icv2.com/articles/columns/view/37177/marvels-problem-isnt-diversity-its-much-bigger-and-its-not-just-marvels-problem

[382] Pulliam-Moore, C. (2017, July 23). DC Has an Epic Plan To Save Itself From the Comics Apocalypse It Helped Create. Retrieved May 16, 2020, from https://io9.gizmodo.com/dc-has-an-epic-plan-to-save-itself-from-the-comics-apoc-1797174893

But comic book sales are not limited to comic book shops. In the same way prices in the real estate market rise and fall depending on what city you're in and what part of the city you're in, different elements of the comic book market are growing. The library market is increasing[383]. The manga market is increasing[384]. Graphic novel sales overall are increasing relative to single issues[385]. The growth in other comic sectors and the popularity of comic ideas outside of the comic medium show that there is a potential audience hungry for your story, as long as you are willing to find them and build a relationship with them. You can't rely on the growth of a particular sector to sell your book. The answer isn't to just avoid comic shops or make graphic novels. You need to go out and build a market.

Where Does the Growth in the Target Market Come From?

Because you have limited resources, you need to focus on those groups of people who will be more open to your message and ignore those who won't read your book no matter what you do. As both Greene[386] and Godin[387] say, you can't win over everyone. For our purposes, **we can divide the world into four distinct groups in relation to your book**. Each group will have qualities that make them more or less probable to join your market and enjoy your work based on their relationship to your medium and your message.

- The Core Market: This is your main focus in terms of marketing.
  - Positive: They fit your ideal reader profile and enjoy the medium of comics.
  - Negative: They are going to be the smallest group and depending on your ideal reader profile, the size of this group might be getting smaller.
  - Negative: There may be several different existing books competing for their attention.

- The Potential Market: This is your largest source of new readers.
  - Positive: They fit your ideal reader profile.
  - Positive: They are not reading your competition
  - Negative: They are ignorant of or resistant to the medium of comics.

---

[383] MacDonald, H. (2017). Comics, the King of Libraries. Retrieved May 16, 2020, from https://www.publishersweekly.com/pw/by-topic/industry-news/libraries/article/73599-comics-the-king-of-libraries.html

[384] Peters, M. (2019, May 29). New Report Breaks Down Manga's Booming 2018 Sales. Retrieved May 16, 2020, from https://comicbook.com/anime/2019/05/29/manga-sales-2018-north-america-increasing-popular/

[385] Schedeen, J. (2019, May 06). Comic Book and Graphic Novel Sales Reached New High in 2018. Retrieved May 16, 2020, from https://www.ign.com/articles/2019/05/06/comic-book-and-graphic-novel-sales-reached-new-high-in-2018

[386] Greene, The Art of Seduction

[387] Godin, This is Marketing

- The False Market: This group offers the illusion of growth but lacks real potential. They include the overall comic book market, other comic creators, and your family and friends who do not fit the ideal reader profile.
  - Positive: They are interested in either reading comics or you as an individual. They may support your work out of courtesy or obligation, but not actual enthusiasm.
  - Negative: They do not fit your ideal reader profile.
  - Negative: They drain on your attention and resources without growing your market. They can also create emotional stress if you feel they are rejecting your creative project.

- The Non-Market: This group is outside of your direct influence.
  - Positive: This is the largest group of people because it can include the entire population of wherever you distribute your book.
  - Negative: They do not fit your ideal reader profile and they are ignorant of or resistant to the medium of comics.
  - Negative: They are the most expensive group to reach.

Once we divide the world into these four groups, it becomes easy to see where you should direct your efforts. **Cultivate and nurture the core market and then reach out to engage the potential market for growth**. Your core market and your potential market will make up your overall **target market.** Avoid both the false market and the non-market to conserve your time, energy, and money by not wasting them on fruitless efforts.

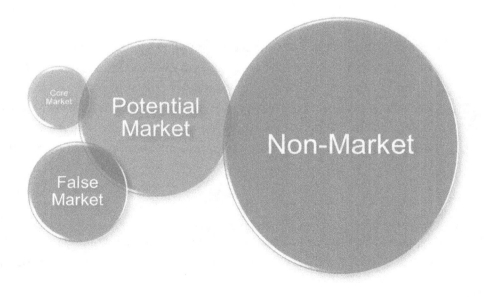

What Tactics Can Be Used to Increase the Size of the Target Market?

Tapping into the potential market involves looking at both the way you connect with people and the way you interact with them. Remember, you're not trying to change the reality of entertainment consumption with your book. You're trying to build a satisfying relationship with those people who are interested in what you have to say. If only one percent of your potential market joins your target market, you can still create a significant increase in sales. There are ways to counteract each of the challenges we identified before and spur growth in the readers of your book.

- Barriers to Entry: If you can help your potential market gain comic book literacy, they could be more likely to join your target market. You can provide this assistance in several ways. You can become an educational resource by reviewing old and new comics to explain who you think the best creators are, what the difference is between comics and other media, when comics come out and where to get them. You could host introductory events or post videos on how to read comics, how to start a comic collection, or how to find comics you love. You can use this educational process to expose your potential readers to independent comics, and then mention your book when the time is right.

- Media Competition: The relationship between comics and other media can be complementary instead of combative. The increased popularity of comic stories is raising the profile of the medium overall. While there hasn't been a proportional increase in comic book sales, awareness of comics is creating the potential for a new wave of fandom[388]. If you position your book to ride the wave of this new awareness through your high concept or other forms of association, you can use the success of other media to your advantage.

- Comparative Pricing: While other publishers use pricing models that make it harder to compete on price, the price of your book doesn't have to follow the same formula[389]. There are options for you to distribute your book at a lower price (or in some cases at no cost to the ideal reader) and reduce the impact of price disparity[390]. Of course, publishing your book still requires costs that need to be covered and all the different alternative distribution methods and economies of scale might not apply to your book, but you're not necessarily locked into one pricing model that may not be sustainable over time[391].

---

[388] Grebey, J. (2016, July 15). Comic Books are selling better than they have in 20 years -- here's why they're so popular. Retrieved May 16, 2020, from https://www.businessinsider.com.au/comic-books-are-popular-again-heres-why-2016-7

[389] Terror, J. (2020, January 01). As We Head Into the Next Decade, Is It Time to Rethink Digital Comics? Retrieved June 07, 2020, from https://www.bleedingcool.com/2020/01/01/as-we-head-into-the-next-decade-is-it-time-to-rethink-digital-comics/

[390] We'll explore different distribution and pricing options in chapter 70.

[391] Griepp, M. (2019). ICv2 Interview: Image's Eric Stephenson. Retrieved May 16, 2020, from https://icv2.com/articles/news/view/43847/icv2-interview-images-eric-stephenson

- Isolated Distribution: New gateway drugs and sales pipelines have replaced the historical models. You can use them to connect with your readers and give them alternative ways to find you. Whether you take advantage of the keyword algorithms of Amazon's "also liked" functions, or Facebook groups, or social media hashtags, or Google analytics to isolate your potential market, there are opportunities to get your book in front of the right people and avoid the false and non-markets[392]. If you focus on the growing number of independent book stores[393], book fairs, and other specific retail opportunities, you can diversify your distribution options[394]. If you utilize in-app advertising, tie your story to emerging mobile and independent games, or even prominent YouTube micro stars, you can leverage emerging fan bases who share your ideal reader profile. The new distribution opportunities have a lot more potential than the spinner racks of the past.

- Negative Perception: As an independent comic book publisher, you can help change the image of comics by becoming an advocate for the medium. This goes beyond acting as a spokesperson for your comic and becoming a champion for comics in general. You can engage in discussions with your potential market that comics are not just for children or even for a certain type of adult. You can educate people that comics are simply another way to tell a story, using aspects of their ideal reader profile to capture their attention. You can expand their definition of comics beyond superheroes to all the other types of stories comics have to offer[395]. You can show people that if they can read a meme, which is essentially images and text used to deliver a message, they can understand a comic. You can even buy comics for your friends and family based on the types of stories you know they like and deduct the cost of the books as a marketing expense for your business[396].

- Established Patterns: People can alter their routines if you provide enough incentive. If you make the pleasure of experiencing your story greater than the pain of trying something new, then you can achieve what's called a **pattern interrupt**[397]. A good example of this can be

[392] Find your book's target audience in 3 easy steps. (2020, May 01). Retrieved May 16, 2020, from https://blog.reedsy.com/3-steps-reaching-target-audience/

[393] Schlesinger, J. (2018, November 23). Small bookstores are booming after nearly being wiped out. Retrieved May 16, 2020, from https://www.cbsnews.com/news/small-bookstores-are-booming-after-nearly-being-wiped-out-small-business-saturday/

[394] DiChristopher, T. (2016, January 25). Three publishers changing the comic book industry. Retrieved May 16, 2020, from https://www.cnbc.com/2016/01/24/comic-book-publishers-thrive-in-the-industry.html

[395] Reber, C. (2016, September 14). Children's Graphic Novels: The Push for Mainstream Recognition. Retrieved May 16, 2020, from https://bookriot.com/2016/09/13/childrens-graphic-novels-push-mainstream-recognition/

[396] Are Marketing Expenses Tax Deductible?- A 2020 Update. (2020, February 13). Retrieved May 16, 2020, from https://www.voxpopbranding.com/tax-deductible-marketing-expenses/

[397] Simple NLP solutions for entrepreneurs and solopreneurs. (2020, May 15). Retrieved May 16, 2020, from https://dailynlp.com/pattern-interrupt/

found in the world of video games where flagship exclusive video game franchises like *Halo, Mario Kart* and *God of War* are so popular that people are willing to spend five to ten times more than the cost of the game to buy the console to play it on[398].

Expanding the market for your comic isn't easy. There is no quick fix to overcoming decades of inertia and systemic issues within the industry. You'll have to engage and re-engage with your potential market, trying different methods in a variety of situations over an extended period to build that relationship[399]. It might take years to increase your market, but since it might also take years to generate the investment and produce your book, many of these actions can happen at the same time. But the reward is worth the effort. A larger target market means more people reading your comic and more potential revenue for your publishing. If your story can build relationships with people who don't read comics yet, you can succeed where other publishers have failed.

[398] Loveridge, S., & Wald, H. (2020, April 17). The 20 best PS4 exclusives that you need to play. Retrieved May 16, 2020, from https://www.gamesradar.com/best-ps4-exclusives/

[399] Phillip, A. (2017, September 22). Selling Comics To Comic Readers... The Beginning... Retrieved May 16, 2020, from https://unknown-comics.com/selling-comics-to-comic-readers/

Now that you have a detailed understanding of who your ideal reader is, how many of them might exist, and the importance of finding more of them, we can move to the second aspect of Greene's formula. Understanding what your ideal reader wants will help you establish the connection that can lead to a long-term relationship between them and your book.

What Does Your Target Market Want?

The most basic thing to understand is that your ideal reader does not want to read your book. They do not want books in your genre. In fact, they don't want any book at all. This is the same for anything they buy or consume. When you reduce human motivation to its philosophical core, you realize that people want the things that their various purchases and products can do for them. **They want the feelings that these intermediate goods and services generate**, not the things themselves[400].

If you are hungry, it is difficult for you to relive that hunger without the intermediate process of eating something. As a meta example, you didn't buy this book just to give me money. You want to publish comics. You came to the conclusion that reading this book is an intermediate step you need to take to accomplish your goal. As an independent comic book publisher understand that your book is a delivery mechanism for your story, and your story needs to be a source of the feeling that your ideal reader is looking for. Realize what is important to the reader and you can relate to them in a way that works.

This means the first step in building a relationship with the ideal readers in your target market is to **define what feeling your story is supposed to induce in them and then continue to communicate that feeling** in all your messages and interactions. At a basic level, if you have a horror story, then focus on the type of fear your ideal reader wants, whether it's the campy jump scares of teen slasher movies or the nauseous squirming of splatter films. On a more profound level, consider the way Stan Lee related to Marvel readers when he was editor-in-chief. Everything he did, from the friendly style of Stan's Soapbox, to the Bullpen Bulletins, to his rebellious rivalry with the Distinguished Competition[401] connected with readers in ways that went beyond comics that earned him almost universal praise when he died at 95[402]. When you think about building relationships with your target market, Lee is the gold standard.

---

[400] Godin, This is Marketing

[401] Batchelor, B. (2017). *Stan Lee - The Man Behind Marvel*. Rowman & Littlefield.

[402] Nickolai, N. (2018, November 13). Robert Downey Jr., Chris Evans, Ryan Reynolds and More Pay Tribute to Comic Book Legend Stan Lee. Retrieved May 16, 2020, from https://variety.com/2018/film/news/chris-evans-ryan-reynolds-kevin-feige-tribute-stan-lee-1203026258/

The second step in building this relationship involves **combining your story and what you know about your ideal reader to create a hook that will transform your ideal readers into true fans** online and offline. Let's take a look at what a hook and a true fan are before we try to apply this idea to concrete marketing actions.

What is a Hook?

For our purposes, a **hook** is an aspect of your story designed to attract and hold the attention of your ideal reader. It is a promise that your story will deliver the desired feeling[403]. It is similar to how a successful trailer can give you the tone and flavor of a two-hour movie in two minutes of video and create enough excitement to inspire you to go buy a ticket. The reason that I don't suggest developing the hook during the initial creation of the Idea Structure is that a hook requires knowledge of the ideal reader profile that you didn't have when you were first dreaming up your story. Now that you have both components for a hook, you can incorporate it not only when you're connecting with your market but in the actual development of the book, as well.

Because comics combine images and text to deliver their message, a hook can be visual, verbal, or both. A classic visual example of a hook can be found in *Captain America #1*. The book offered readers a chance to feel powerful and patriotic during the dark days of World War II, so the cover promised all those things by showing a muscular male character wrapped in the American flag punching Hitler right in the jaw[404].

Verbal hooks can be just as powerful. Lee's greeting of "Hey, True Believer!" in the Soapbox[405] gave the comic book reader more than a story. It suggested this was a modern mythology and invited readers to become acolytes. The powerful imagery of the new, colorful *X-Men* charging through a washed-out poster of the old team combined with the words "*Deadly Genesis*" is an example of words and images promising a narrative revolution that has become iconic[406]. When you can understand your story and its potential appeal, you can create a hook that will convert an ideal reader into a true fan.

---

[403] Hook. (n.d.). Retrieved May 16, 2020, from https://dictionary.cambridge.org/us/dictionary/english/hook

[404] Kirby, J. (1940). Captain America Comics #1. Retrieved May 16, 2020, from https://www.comics.org/issue/1313/

[405] Bullpen Bulletins. (2019, September 27). Retrieved May 16, 2020, from https://en.wikipedia.org/wiki/Bullpen_Bulletins

[406] Giant-Size X-Men #1 (Homages #38). (n.d.). Retrieved May 16, 2020, from https://comicvine.gamespot.com/profile/cbishop/lists/giant-size-x-men-1-homages/64200/

What is a True Fan?

The concept of a **true fan** was developed in 2008 by *Wired Magazine* editor Kevin Kelly[407]. The basic premise is that creators of all types do not need millions of customers or millions of dollars or millions of anything to profit from their creations. Instead, he promoted the idea that **if you can create a situation where a small number of people are willing to buy everything you create, then you can make a decent living.**

The original essay focused on 1,000 true fans for a musician but that number fluctuates depending on what you create and what people are willing to pay for it. For example, if you're a painter and your work sells for $1,000 each, then you might only need 100 true fans. If you're an author and your books sell for $10, then you might need 10,000 true fans[408].

As an independent publisher, the idea of the true fan is similar to your definition of the ideal reader since your book can't, and isn't designed to, appeal to everyone. The difference between an ideal reader and a true fan is that the ideal reader is a theoretical construct you created based on your book while the true fan is a specific person. In other words, **an ideal reader is the type of person you look for. The true fan is the people that you find and build relationships with** because they respond to your hook and identify with you.

How Can Ideal Readers Identify with Your Book?

Imagine you're walking down the street and a total stranger steps into your path pushing you to buy a book you've never heard of that has nothing to do with you or the things you like, but is supposed to be the Best Book Ever! Now imagine you're walking down the street with a friend. You know she shares a lot of your tastes and you look forward to your conversations with her. When she offers to tell you a story about topics you enjoy and characters you relate to, there's a good chance your response to her will be different than your reaction to the stranger.

This thought experiment illustrates a core marketing principle. **People interact with and buy from companies they like and identify with.** If they like you or something about you, then they'll be more likely to buy from you. If they see you as just a salesman with a gimmick, then they are less likely to buy from you[409].

---

[407] Kelly, K. (2008). The Technium: 1,000 True Fans. Retrieved May 16, 2020, from https://kk.org/thetechnium/1000-true-fans/

[408] Id.

[409] Port, M. (2018). *Book yourself solid: The fastest, easiest, and most reliable system for getting more clients than you can handle even if you hate marketing and selling.* Hoboken, NJ: Wiley.

This type of **identification often has more to do with the relationship between the ideal reader and their image of themselves and less to do with your book**[410]. You can consider many famous marketing campaigns to understand this point. The ads for Calvin Klein, Dos Equis, Mercedes, and Apple don't talk much about their products. They spend more time showing images of specific types of people enjoying different types of activities. The subliminal message is constant: People like these use products like this. If you're this type of person, or you want to be, then you need to buy this stuff[411]. Identification creates a sense of belonging that motivates consistent action.

Gimmicks and trends tend to reduce this kind of identification. A **gimmick** is a trick or device used to attract short term business[412]. It can create attention and excitement, but over time it loses its novelty. For comics, gimmicks have little or no relevance to the characters or story, and are often used purely as shock value or to attract speculation. Temporary superhero deaths are a long-standing gimmick, as are variant covers, "reboots" to issue #1 and cameos from more popular characters[413].

A **trend** is a related concept because it is an idea that simply follows the popular taste at a given time[414] and may have little or no relationship to your original story or your ideal reader. As an independent publisher, there are three distinct reasons to avoid trends and focus all your attention on your target market.

- Trends change without warning. What might be popular today might be passé tomorrow. Because independent publishing often takes more time than mainstream comic book publishing, the risk of missing the trend is even greater. At the same time, you don't know what the next big trend will be, so it's difficult to anticipate the Next Big Thing and publish a book in time to capture the zeitgeist[415].

- Trends make it harder to stand out from the competition. Because a trend is popular by definition, there will be more competitors fighting for that share of the market. If you copy a trend, you'll have to pull eyeballs away from established properties, big-name creators, and

---

[410] Godin, This is Marketing

[411] Id.

[412] Gimmick. (n.d.). Retrieved May 16, 2020, from https://www.merriam-webster.com/dictionary/gimmick

[413] Bennett, S. (2019, June 5). Confessions of a Comic Book Guy - Death in Comics. Retrieved May 16, 2020, from https://icv2.com/articles/columns/view/43352/confessions-comic-book-guy-death-comics

[414] Trend. (n.d.). Retrieved May 16, 2020, from https://www.vocabulary.com/dictionary/trend

[415] Magnett, C. (2019, August 22). 8 Takeaways from Eric Stephenson's ICv2 Interview. Retrieved May 16, 2020, from https://comicbook.com/comics/2019/08/22/eric-stephensons-interview-image-comics-analysis/

market dominance[416]. For every *Teenage Mutant Ninja Turtles* that makes it big, there will be dozens of *Adolescent Radioactive Black Belt Hamsters* that don't last over time[417].

- Trends may not inspire you in the long term. As we learned earlier, loving your story is an important motivator for independent publishing because it gives you the resolve to overcome the inevitable setbacks and stumbles. If you don't love the trend, you might not finish the book. Even if you do get the book out the door, your lack of enthusiasm will show and alienate the ideal readers. As Stan Lee said before his death, "*You have to write stories that are interesting to you and then find an audience for them*[418]".

You can find your audience because you know the type of person who will enjoy your book. You can build a relationship with them because you understand what they want and how to identify with them. Now your book is ready to implement the final two elements of Greene's formula. You can use your theoretical analysis of your target market, captured in the following form, to take concrete steps to get their attention and offer them the feelings they want. In the modern world, there are two avenues of marketing activity: online and offline. We're going to start with online activity, since it is easier to both start and expand out into your offline efforts.

---

[416] Manning, Write or Wrong p. 135

[417] Adolescent Radioactive Black Belt Hamsters (1986) 1A FN. Retrieved May 16, 2020, from https://www.mycomicshop.com/search?TID=114031

[418] Lee, S. (2014). Stan Lee: Advice for Comic Book Writers and Other Artists [Interview]. Retrieved May 16, 2020, from https://www.youtube.com/watch?v=Bjb05OurpBc

Independent Comic Book Publishing

Form 7: Marketing Template

- What potential keywords can you use to find your target market?
  - Demographic
  - Psychographic
  - Genre
  - Generation
  - Competition

- Which social media platforms appeal most to your target market?
  - Which groups and subgroups in each social media platform contain a significant number of ideal readers?

- What key dates or seasons are important to your target market?
  - Events
  - Holidays
  - Conventions
  - Festivals

- What is the hook for this comic?

- How can you use your marketing message to overcome limiting factors?
  - Barriers to entry
  - Competition from other media
  - Higher prices for consumption
  - Isolated distribution
  - Perception stigma
  - Established patterns of behavior

Chapter 33: How Can a Website Help Your Marketing?

Your website is the base of operations for all your marketing efforts. While your book might be sold in various online platforms and your interactions with true fans might happen in multiple forums and social media threads, your website will create the core experience for everyone from readers to the press to potential partners. It is your virtual flagship store[419]. Everything you do online should revolve around this site.

While it is possible to publish a book without a dedicated website, placing all your online marketing efforts at the mercy of other companies is an unnecessary risk. **Digital sharecropping**[420] is the term used for displaying all of your online content on a website you don't own. It is feasible to have all your marketing on Facebook or Twitter, distribute books through Comixology and WebToons, and avoid the time and money it takes to build your website. But if you find yourself in Facebook Jail[421], or if WebToons shuts down or changes their terms of service, you can suddenly find yourself without a way to connect with your true fans online. It makes more sense to build your own site and connect it to the wider web. That way, if you can't use any third-party site for any reason, you can still use your website to maintain those relationships. Losing the ability to sell on Amazon will still be a challenge, but it won't cripple your business.

Because you need to connect with your market before your book is published, your website needs to go online as early as possible. It might not be a fully functioning, multi-page monster on launch day, but websites evolve and you can add content over time as your marketing and your book develop.

Today, anyone can build, launch, and maintain a website. It can be as complex or as simple as your talent and investment dictates. You and your team can build the site, or you can hire a web designer, or you can use a combination of the two methods. The theory and practice of website construction and maintenance is an industry that has generated hundreds of books and tutorials. I'm only going to offer some general considerations about the design and content of the site and its relationship to your marketing research.

---

[419] Flagship store definition and meaning: Collins English Dictionary. (n.d.). Retrieved May 16, 2020, from https://www.collinsdictionary.com/us/dictionary/english/flagship-store

[420] Nick, Ross, P., Phil, Carr, N., Brad, & Carr, N. (2016, August 26). Digital sharecropping. Retrieved May 16, 2020, from http://www.roughtype.com/?p=634

[421] Skaf, E., & Postcron.com. (2018, June 06). 10 Tips to Avoid Facebook Jail or Being Blocked by Facebook. Retrieved May 16, 2020, from https://postcron.com/en/blog/how-to-avoid-being-blocked-by-facebook-jail/

What are the Major Design Considerations for Your Website?

Website design includes several different components, including graphic design, interface design, user experience, and search engine optimization[422]. As an independent publisher, you need to consider six elements of design as your flagship store is being constructed.

1) *User Experience*: Since your site is going to be the basis for your online relationship with your true fan, the way they feel about the site has a fundamental importance. All their interactions with the site need to reinforce your hook, motivate them to visit the site on a regular basis, and inspire them to take whatever action you design for your true fans.

   When thinking about the look and feel of your site, research what your competition is doing on their sites. Take inspiration from the better aspects of what they're doing and avoid the things that wouldn't appeal to your market. Consider other sites you enjoy and see what elements might also work for your site. Just don't copy the actual images or underlying code of your inspiration, because that can constitute infringement[423]. Finally, to the extent that you have logos, colors, and other creative elements of the book already established, use those to influence the web design and create an integrated feel between the site and the book.

2) *Platform Selection*: As of the writing of this book, there are twelve major services you can use to build and host your site[424]. Each one has good and bad aspects, and the right one for your book will depend on your overall goals and resources. The two main selection criteria will be the price and ease of use. While website costs can be deductible expenses for your publishing company[425], you don't want to drain too much of your investment on a costly website solution. Because your website needs regular updates if it is going to be effective and your team needs to focus most of its available time and attention on creating the actual book, you don't want a service that is difficult to learn or use.

---

[422] Web Design. (n.d.). Retrieved May 16, 2020, from https://techterms.com/definition/web_design

[423] Thomas, V., Chapman, A., Pat, & Artem. (2020, May 15). The Legalities of Copying a Website Design. Retrieved May 16, 2020, from https://thomasdigital.com/the-legalities-of-copying-a-website-design/

[424] Balkhi, S. (2020, May 08). How to Choose the Best Website Builder in 2020 (Compared). Retrieved May 16, 2020, from https://www.wpbeginner.com/beginners-guide/how-to-choose-the-best-website-builder/

[425] Warnes, B. (2017). How to Deduct the Cost of Web Development: Bench Accounting. Retrieved May 16, 2020, from https://bench.co/blog/tax-tips/web-development/

3) *Domain Name*: The name of your website or the domain name[426] is one of the main online elements that will drive traffic to your site, so it pays to take some time and find the right fit[427]. In general, there are three keys to domain name selection[428]:

a. Make it easy to type.
b. Keep it short.
c. Avoid numbers and hyphens.

When considering the specific domain name for your book, you have several unique ways to tie the website to the story. Your domain name could be:

d. The title of the book.
e. The tagline of the book (as long as it's short).
f. A major character in the book.

There are several services you can use to research which domains are available and purchase the best option[429]. Depending on the nature of your domain, the potential for competition, and your long-term goals, it might make sense to purchase variations of the name (.com, .net., .tv, etc).

4) *Site Usability*: If the site isn't fast, it won't make a difference what content you put on it. If the site is difficult to navigate, your ideal reader will go somewhere else. If they don't feel comfortable or respected on your site, they will reject you and your story. Therefore, the following tips will help enhance the user experience on your site.

a. Test your site to ensure all images and text load on-screen within three seconds or less to prevent people from clicking somewhere else[430].

---

[426] Beal, V. (n.d.). Domain Name. Retrieved May 16, 2020, from https://www.webopedia.com/TERM/D/domain_name.html

[427] Wampler, D. (2015). *Selling Your Comic Book Concept: A Step-by-Step Guide for Creators.* Amazon.com Services LLC. Retrieved May 16, 2020, from https://www.amazon.com/Selling-Comic-Concept-Step-Step-ebook/dp/B011M3I4XS/ref=sr_1_1?

[428] Rowland, A. (2019, December 17). How to Choose a Domain Name [10 Tips] - GoDaddy. Retrieved May 16, 2020, from https://www.godaddy.com/garage/10-tips-for-choosing-the-perfect-domain-name/

[429] Glenn, Jamie, Okita, Paul, Dietrich, Firoz, Hulett Gross. (2020, April 04). The Best Domain Registrars 2020 - the Good, the Bad and the Ugly - 2020 Guide. Retrieved May 16, 2020, from https://makeawebsitehub.com/reviews/domain-registrars/

[430] Dotcom Tools. (2018, June 22). How Fast Should My Website Load? Dotcom-Monitor Tools Blog. Retrieved May 16, 2020, from https://www.dotcom-tools.com/blog/how-fast-should-my-website-load/

      b.   Use responsive design to ensure the site layout is functional and pleasing on computer screens, laptops, tablets, and phones[431].

      c.   Develop terms of use and privacy policies that protect user privacy and discourage abusive behavior.

      d.   Create a navigation button to help users find the basic pages on your site:

          i.   Home

          ii.   About the Story

          iii.   About the Team

          iv.   Online Store

          v.   Mailing List

          vi.   Contact Us

5)   *Search Engine Optimization*: One of the major benefits of online marketing is that time and distance are not barriers to relationship building. Ideal readers can find your content and become true fans when you're not online. They can find you when they are ready to connect with you, but only if your site is easy to find. Search engine optimization (or SEO) is the name given to the strategies, techniques, and tactics used to increase the number of visitors to a website by obtaining a high-ranking placement in the search results page of a search engine[432]. The goal of SEO is to place a website on the first page of a relevant search, because people rarely click beyond the first page in their online searches[433]. SEO is an industry in its own right, with several books and advisors willing to offer tips, and major search engines like Google have tools you can use to optimize every page of your site[434]. As an independent publisher, your SEO will be based on keywords, and your keywords will come from your title, your pitch, your tagline, your competition, and the characteristics of your ideal reader. If you can determine the words your ideal reader will use, they can discover you and visit your site.

6)   *Shareability*: Your website does not exist in isolation. It is only useful to the extent it can attract ideal readers and give them ways to interact with your story. Shareability is the likelihood of any content on a social media website or application[435]. You want to ensure that the pages of

---

[431] Rouse, M. (2012, January 26). What is responsive design? - Definition from WhatIs.com. Retrieved May 17, 2020, from https://whatis.techtarget.com/definition/responsive-design

[432] Beal, V. (n.d.). SEO - search engine optimization. Retrieved May 17, 2020, from https://www.webopedia.com/TERM/S/SEO.html

[433] Chris, A.,(2020, May 04). What Is SEO (Search Engine Optimization) And Why Is It Important. Retrieved May 17, 2020, from https://www.reliablesoft.net/what-is-search-engine-optimization-and-why-is-it-important/

[434] Choose the Right Keywords with Our Research Tools. (n.d.). Retrieved May 17, 2020, from https://ads.google.com/home/tools/keyword-planner/

[435] Shareability. (n.d.). Retrieved May 17, 2020, from https://www.lexico.com/en/definition/shareability

your site include plugins[436] to most if not all of the major social media platforms and search engines. Conversely, you also want to ensure that content you post on other websites drives traffic back to your website.

What are the Major Content Considerations for Your Website?

The design of your website will not transform ideal readers into true fans. Your content will. The form your content takes will be a function of your goals, your story, and the unique characteristics of your ideal reader, but in general, your site should include consistent updates, a mailing list, and an online store. I'll devote an entire chapter to mailing lists in Chapter 35, so let's focus on content updates and the store here.

1) *Updates*: If your site never changes, ideal readers might visit once, but they won't revisit the site consistently enough to build a strong relationship. If your site is static, your SEO will suffer. New content, whether it's in the form of updates, blog posts, or other current information related to your story, will help maintain your marketing relationships over time. Updates can come in several different varieties.

   a. The most obvious are posts about the development of the book. This could be character designs visitors can vote on, samples of the unfinished art, background information on your characters and world, or behind the scenes lessons that you learn in the process of publishing your book.

   b. You can spotlight the work that your team has done in the past or even other work they are currently involved in (as long as there are no confidentiality issues with those posts).

   c. You can update your readers on convention and comic shop appearances of you and your team.

   d. You can offer free or **freemium**[437] content in the form of artwork, screensavers, or wallpapers.

   e. You can also offer your opinion on other books and media in the genre or topics of interest to the ideal reader.

---

[436] Plug-In: Definition in the Cambridge English Dictionary. (n.d.). Retrieved May 17, 2020, from https://dictionary.cambridge.org/us/dictionary/english/plug-in

[437] What is freemium? definition and meaning. (n.d.). Retrieved May 17, 2020, from http://www.businessdictionary.com/definition/freemium.html

The key to updates is maintaining an interesting stream of connection to fortify the sense of identification your ideal reader has with your story. The more they bring you into their regular life, the more willing they will be to buy from you.

2) *Online Store*: If you are going to sell your book in a print or digital format, then your website should have some sort of e-commerce page. This could be a solution provided by your platform, or it could be a third-party solution like Amazon, but whichever route you use, there are elements you can include in your store to enhance the buying experience.

    a.   Ensure that the financial data of you and your customers are as secure as possible. Nothing will damage your reputation faster than an ideal reader who has money stolen from their account because they bought your book.

    b.   Make the shopping process pleasurable. If looking at your books is work, your ideal reader will go to a competitor. Provide relevant information on every title including:
        i.   A cover image thumbnail large enough to be seen on various devices
        ii.   The release date
        iii.   The tagline
        iv.   The pitch
        v.   The hook
        vi.   The creative team
        vii.   The purchase button

    c.   Make the buying process easy to use. The more complicated the checkout or payment process, the fewer sales you'll make.

A well designed and maintained website can be a pivotal tool in your online marketing. You have more control over your content than on any other site. You can tailor the design and the content to appeal directly to your ideal reader and use it to build relationships that will create true fans. But you can achieve more results from your online marketing if you combine your website development with the power of social media to create a continuing conversation with your target market.

There are several benefits to **social media**[438] in terms of marketing your story. It's usually cheap. It's easy to use. It gives you the ability to connect with large groups of people simultaneously regardless of time or place. It also has inherent tribal divisions that allow you to tune out the non-market and focus on your ideal readers.

There are also several detriments to marketing with social media. Because anyone can use it, there is a constant potentially numbing barrage of noise clogging up everyone's timeline as people fight for attention. The remote and disconnected nature of online interactions often encourages the most abusive and asocial behavior. It also has the addictive ability to suck up all of your time and energy, leaving you little or no time to actually publish a book.

Because social media is an almost universal phenomenon, I'm not going to waste time explaining the basics of how it works. Instead, this chapter will highlight how to choose a social media platform for your story, as well as tips for what to do and what to avoid when you're out there. But before we dive into deep water, remember the reasons you're marketing on social media:

- You want to find, establish, and maintain a connection to your target market.
- You want to drive traffic back to your website.
- You want to provide information about your team and your story.
- You want to open a line of communication with your potential partners, buyers, and readers.
- You want to stay informed about your competition.

All these tasks take time and attention to manage, but keep in mind that marketing is only 5-20% of your publishing efforts, and social media marketing is only one aspect of your marketing. Finding the right balance is a key aspect of time management in the life cycle of your book[439].

How Do You Choose the Right Social Media Platform for your Story?

Meredith Nudo, comic book editor, and social media manager[440] has advised independent publishers to stick to the social media platforms they're already comfortable with, because the benefits you might gain from

---

[438] Social Media. (n.d.). Retrieved May 17, 2020, from https://www.merriam-webster.com/dictionary/social_media

[439] Rivera, C. L. (2015, June 26). Marketing In The Goldilocks Zone: How Do You Know When You've Got It 'Just Right'? Retrieved May 17, 2020, from https://www.websearchsocial.com/marketing-in-the-goldilocks-zone-how-do-you-know-when-youve-got-it-just-right/

[440] Meredith Nudo. (2020, January 23). Retrieved May 17, 2020, from https://www.comicsexperience.com/staff/meredith-nudo/

using a platform you dislike isn't worth the added time and stress[441]. In addition to personal preference, the visual nature of the platform should be taken into account because comics rely heavily on art to tell stories. Also, you should consider what types of posts you're likely to be using and how easy they will be to post and share on each platform. As I write this book, most platforms are agnostic in terms of the ability to display promo pieces, videos, contests, surveys, and other content, but you might find some platforms work better than others. Finally, and perhaps most importantly, you need to take your social media message where your target market is most likely to see it. It makes no sense to spend all your time on Twitter if your ideal reader loves Goodreads.

How Should You Market Your Book on Social Media?

Your social media marketing style will be unique to you and your story. It will evolve as you build connections with your target market. The following recommendations are guidelines to help you develop your approach.

- *Take advantage of keywords* to filter out the non-market: Most platforms have mechanisms to help you focus on a specific group. Whether it's the subgroups of Facebook, the hashtags on Twitter, or the keyword search functions of other platforms, use them to isolate your target market and maximize your efforts.

- *Post regularly*: You don't have to post, comment, or share all day every day, but developing a regular schedule will give your market incentives to connect with you and provide a way for you to manage your time online.

- *Keep your secret identity separate* from your independent publishing: Because your friends and family might not be a part of your target market, they might not be interested in your antagonist character design survey. At the same time, your target market might not want to see your foodie posts or your vacation photos. Social media profiles are free, so it only costs you a bit of extra time to maintain different pages for your work and your life. Separating the two can be beneficial both for your book and for your privacy.

- *Be consistent across all platforms*: Social media marketing is more effective if you maintain a consistent voice[442]. The various aspects of your pages and posts, from the name of the page, to the look and feel of the posts should be recognizable as coming from

---

[441] Make Comics Podcast Episode #139 - Social Media 101 with Meredith Nudo. (2019, April 23). Retrieved May 17, 2020, from https://www.comicsexperience.com/podcast/episode-139-social-media-101-meredith-nudo/

[442] Dibenedetto, M. (2018, November 07). 5 Steps To Maintaining a Consistent Brand Voice On Social Media. Retrieved May 17, 2020, from https://medium.com/@moondustagency/5-steps-to-maintaining-a-consistent-brand-voice-on-social-media-7030300bb2e1

the same source. There should also be a recognizable relationship between your social media pages and your website to the extent that it's possible.

- *Build connections and relationships*: This is social media. It's not selling media. Your job here isn't to constantly ask people to buy your book. Your job is to find, establish and maintain a connection to your target market. This means engaging with potential readers, potential retailers, other creators, and critics. You should attempt to connect with people from every aspect of independent publishing, from accountants to web designers. Try to interact with people from every discipline in the industry to broaden your network and get a better understanding of the whole process[443].

- *Be courteous and professional*: As we discussed in the Talent Management section, comics is a small industry, and reputations matter. So, no matter who you are dealing with, don't sabotage your book or your career by creating a negative image[444]. This is especially true, and harder to accomplish when dealing with criticism[445]. If you put a lot of time, money, and effort into a story that you love, it's not farfetched for you to feel defensive when someone attacks it. But you don't win anything from a social media outburst. It's more likely that you're creating enemies and chasing ideal readers away[446].

- *Think before you post*: Social media posts are forever[447]. Even if you take down an embarrassing post, someone will almost always be able to find it. This means you need to consider what you post before pressing enter because you won't be able to take it back. This is especially important when responding to someone online, since your reactions to negative statements might be more emotional and heated than your planned professional messaging.

- *Be open to legitimate critiques*: Not everyone online is a troll. There will be instances when a reader, retailer, or other critics will point out areas of your work that could use improvement. In these cases, it is even more important to be thoughtful and courteous. No book is perfect. Different perspectives could make your story better. Never chase away or dismiss someone engaged enough with your project to give you sincere feedback. If someone goes so far as to publicly reject your work, let them know it's not for them and

---

[443] Questlove, Creative Quest

[444] Scalera, B. (2017, June 11). Don't Be a Jerk - Professionalism in Comics. Retrieved May 17, 2020, from http://www.comicbookschool.com/dont-jerk/

[445] Penn, J., Swann, L., Shannon, S., McKenna, S., Beth, & Eve, C. (2018, April 18). Writing And The Fear Of Judgment. Retrieved May 17, 2020, from https://www.thecreativepenn.com/2018/04/18/writing-and-the-fear-of-judgment/

[446] Greene, The 48 Laws of Power

[447] Fineman, M. (2014, November 24). What We Post Online Is Forever, and We Need a Reminder. Retrieved May 17, 2020, from https://www.inc.com/meredith-fineman/what-we-post-online-is-forever-and-we-need-a-reminder.html

give them the name of one of your competitors. It probably won't change the mind of your critic, but it shows your target market your generosity, your knowledge of the market, and your desire for people to enjoy comics.

- *Be political*: The great author Toni Morrison once said, "*The best art is political and you ought to be able to make it unquestionably political and irrevocably beautiful at the same time.*[448]" As an art form, comics have also promoted or rejected strong political positions[449]. Just as in the imagery of Captain America, the anti-racist position Stan Lee fostered in the Soapbox[450] or Art Spiegelman focused on in Maus[451], or the political foundations of **Comicsgate**[452], your book will have a political position simply because it will have a specific perspective and a specific focus. It makes no sense to shy away from that in your story or your marketing. I'm not suggesting that you need to abuse, vilify or denigrate anyone to market your book, but part of the reason your ideal reader will identify with you will be based on the politics of your book, so it makes sense to lean into that.

- *Consider the potential backlash* your book/team/ marketing could create. In the current social environment, any story can be seen as offensive to one group or another. Because your story will inevitably stand for something, it is likely to stand against something else and the people who support that "something else" can quickly undermine or overwhelm your marketing efforts. While you can't predict every possible attack on your book, it is possible to get a sense of who might have a problem with it by creating a "nemesis reader" profile (reversing the ideal reader into a Joker/ Batman dichotomy). As you are building your marketing efforts and your book, think about how things could go wrong in a public arena from the following perspectives and try to anticipate and prepare for the potential backlash with professional poise. If you lash out, you can make a bad situation worse:

[448] Nance, K. (2018, February 23). The Spirit and the Strength: A Profile of Toni Morrison. Retrieved May 17, 2020, from https://www.pw.org/content/the_spirit_and_the_strength_a_profile_of_toni_morrison

[449] Magnett, C. (2019, July 08). Marvel and DC Get Political. Retrieved May 17, 2020, from https://comicbook.com/comics/2019/07/08/marvel-dc-comics-politics-political/

[450] Butler, B. (2018, November 12). Stan Lee used his platform to call out racism in the 1960s - and he never stopped. Retrieved May 17, 2020, from https://www.washingtonpost.com/arts-entertainment/2018/11/12/stan-lee-used-his-platform-call-out-racism-s-he-never-stopped/?noredirect=on

[451] Spiegelman, A. (1997). *Maus: A survivor's tale*. New York: Pantheon Books.

[452] Jancelewicz, C. (2018, October 08). Comicsgate: What is it, exactly, and what's going on? Retrieved May 17, 2020, from https://globalnews.ca/news/4421411/comicsgate-what-is-it/

- Legal: You need to avoid libel[453], slander[454], and defamation[455]
- Personal: You don't want your independent publishing to harm your secret identity
- Publishing: You don't want to do or say anything to injure your relationship with your target market. You don't have to worry as much about the nemesis reader in the non-market because you weren't going to attract them anyway.

- *Be witty*: While anger in social media can damage your reputation, sarcasm can be a useful tool in your arsenal. While it can be overused and misinterpreted online[456], a prudent use of sarcasm can take the sting out of negative comments or turn a tense exchange into something more pleasant. Several major brands from Charmin to Old Spice to Wendy's have made it a focus of their social media marketing[457]. The key is to use it on competitors and critics at or above your level and never use it to attack colleagues, readers, or retailers[458].

- *Be a publisher and a fan*: Comic readers identify with other comic readers. Your potential readers who don't read comics might be more interested in the medium if they see people they identify with reading comics. Your social media marketing needs to convey not just your enthusiasm for your book, but for your genre and comics as an art form. You can promote and review other books (especially your competition), comment on the work of other creators you enjoy, or discuss aspects of comics that interest you. Let your love of comics act to counter the perceived inferiority complex it struggles with in America[459].

- *Share your work*: As your project develops and moves closer to completion, share your milestones with your target market to help them feel included in the process, and identify with the story. Strive to tell stories instead of selling a book[460]. Encourage comments and

---

[453] Libel. (n.d.). Retrieved May 17, 2020, from https://dictionary.law.com/Default.aspx?selected=1153

[454] Slander. (n.d.). Retrieved May 17, 2020, from https://dictionary.law.com/Default.aspx?selected=1969

[455] Defamation.(n.d.). Retrieved May 17, 2020, from https://dictionary.law.com/Default.aspx?selected=458

[456] Gino, F. (2015, November 17). The Surprising Benefits of Sarcasm. Retrieved May 17, 2020, from https://www.scientificamerican.com/article/the-surprising-benefits-of-sarcasm/

[457] Kolowich, L. (n.d.). Funny Tweets & Social Media Examples From 17 Real Brands. Retrieved May 17, 2020, from https://blog.hubspot.com/marketing/funny-brands-social-media

[458] Make Comics Podcast Episode #139 - Social Media 101 with Meredith Nudo. (2019, April 23). Retrieved May 17, 2020, from https://www.comicsexperience.com/podcast/episode-139-social-media-101-meredith-nudo/

[459] McLauchlin, J. (n.d.). Does Comics Culture Have an Inferiority Complex? Retrieved May 17, 2020, from https://www.wired.com/story/comics-inferiority-complex/

[460] Nastos, M. (2011). *Comic Book Marketing 101*. Nifty Entertainment.

invite people to share the posts they enjoy. Give your ideal readers the incentive to become true fans and part of the community you are building.

- *Ask everyone on the team to share with their networks*: The job of building marketing connections shouldn't be limited to one member of the team. If possible, everyone working on the book should be encouraged to leverage their professional comic book social media to help in the marketing effort. It doesn't matter if they are working in a collaboration or work-for-hire capacity, since everyone will benefit if the book does well. Of course, freelance business and creative team members may need more incentive to add social media marketing to their work. You might need to offer an additional incentive in the contract to access all their followers.

- *Guest Blog or Vlog* (if you have time): One of the easiest ways to reach your target market is to tap into pre-existing audiences. Guest blogging or writing a blog post on another published blog as a temporary featured author[461] can save time for a blog always in search of content and give you access to a wealth of ideal readers. This process involves several steps and should only be pursued as part of your long-term marketing schedule if you have the time.

  - Find blogs that focus on your genre or ideal reader profile or check out the relevant guest blogging opportunities available[462] to find appropriate target blogs.
  - Understand the type of content your target blogs post on a regular basis
  - Link to current posts on the blog to drive traffic to them.
  - Post relevant comments on posts on your target blog to become a part of the conversation.
  - Ask to pitch a guest post once you get the positive attention of the blogger.
  - Pitch your guest post according to their guidelines. Explain what you want to write about, why their readers would want to read it, and why you're the best person to write it.
  - Write a post that is relevant to the readers, not an advertisement for your project.
  - End post with an invitation to join your social network
  - Make sure you deliver the post on time and error-free.
  - Promote the post on your network and your website.

- *Tie your physical marketing to your social media*: Your online and offline marketing are two connected parts of your overall relationship building. To the extent you're going to

---

[461] What is Guest Blogging? - Definition & Information. (2018, December 31). Retrieved May 17, 2020, from https://www.marketingterms.com/dictionary/guest_blogging/

[462] Patel, N. (2020, January 24). The Ultimate Guide to Guest Blogging. Retrieved May 17, 2020, from https://neilpatel.com/blog/guide-to-guest-blogging/

employ advertising, business cards, or print physical copies of your book, include your social media links wherever possible and practical. You want to add people to the conversation wherever they encounter your work and prominent physical links are a useful addition to an online posting[463].

- *Follow up offline meetings with social media connections*: In the same way you leverage your real-world marketing, turning isolated face to face meetings into extended social media relationships can also enhance your marketing. You might meet people at comic shops, conventions, or other meetups. Try to invite those people to connect with you on social media or your mailing list[464].

- *Track your results*: It will be difficult to determine how many people your marketing efforts are reaching if you don't track your performance over time. Most social media platforms will show you some sort of statistics on your reach (the number of people who saw your post[465]) and level of engagement (the public likes, shares, and comments on a particular post[466]). There are also various short links or UTM codes[467] that will let you know how many people clicked on any particular post you create[468]. This kind of tracking doesn't translate directly into true fans or sales, so use them to guide your efforts, but like social media marketing in general, don't obsess over these numbers when you should be publishing your book.

What Activity Should You Avoid on Social Media?

There are a lot of things you can do on social media to market your book. There are a few things you should not do if you want to give your book the best chance to succeed. This isn't as easy as it sounds. Every year,

---

[463] 5 Offline Marketing Tactics That Boost Social Media Engagement. (2016, September 15). Retrieved May 17, 2020, from https://www.cision.com/us/2016/09/5-offline-marketing-tactics-that-boost-social-media-engagement/

[464] Fullan, R. (2017, November 01). Developing a Social Media Plan. Retrieved May 17, 2020, from http://www.meetings-conventions.com/Resources/Planner-Basics/Checklist/social-media/

[465] Loomer, J. (2015, September 09). 3 Facebook Metrics That Don't Mean What You Think They Mean. Retrieved May 17, 2020, from https://www.jonloomer.com/2013/10/07/facebook-metrics-meaning-confused/

[466] What is social media engagement? (2020, May 15). Retrieved May 17, 2020, from https://www.bigcommerce.com/ecommerce-answers/what-is-social-media-engagement/

[467] Kranz, J. (2020, June 22). What Is a UTM Code? The Complete Guide Everyone Can Love. Retrieved June 28, 2020, from https://buffer.com/library/utm-guide/

[468] Guz, D. (2020, February 26). 8 Best Free URL Shortener APIs for Creating Your Short Links. Retrieved May 17, 2020, from https://blog.rebrandly.com/8-best-free-url-shortener-apis-for-creating-your-short-links/

dozens of companies and brands stumble on social media in ways that damage their image[469]. While no one is perfect, these six concepts can add to the previous list of tips to help keep you out of trouble.

1. *Avoid Targeting the Non-Market*: You have a specific story to tell to a specific group. Everyone outside that group isn't ready for, or interested in, that message. While you need to reach out to ideal readers outside of comics, pushing your book on friends, family, and the general public will only lead to frustration and fatigue.

2. *Avoid Overselling*: Remember the analogy of the aggressive stranger and your friend with a story. Think about your own time on social media and the way you feel when you see the same people pop up on your feed every day with a different version of "Buy My Stuff!!!" This isn't the way to build connections. According to social media experts, 30% of your posts should be your original content like status updates about the book, blog posts, and opinion pieces. 60% should be content you curate from other sources, like reviews of similar books, articles about the genre, and the work of other creators in the industry. The remaining 10% is reserved for the promotion of your book and invitations to your website[470]. It is a longer process than constant selling, but it can lead to better results in the end.

3. *Avoid Errors*: Your words are the main vehicle for connection in social media. Misspelling distracts from your message. Inaccurate statements damage your credibility. Certain platforms like Twitter have subverted traditional grammar and spelling rules, but you want your posts to be remembered for their content, not for their spelling mistakes[471]. False stories, opinions presented as facts, and blatant falsehoods are common on social media[472], but building connections with your target market based on lies isn't a winning strategy in the long run. The only fiction you need to promote is your story. Leave the fake news to others.

4. *Don't Feed the Trolls*: A **troll** is a person who antagonizes others online by deliberately posting irrelevant or offensive comments[473]. Social media is a breeding ground for trolls and your marketing efforts will invariably attract them at some point. There will always be people who have a desperate need to attack you, or your book, or comics, or the comics industry, or people who read comics or anything you might post. There are several reasons people decide

---

[469] Griffith, E. (2018, April 17). 19 Massive Corporate Social Media Horror Stories. Retrieved May 17, 2020, from https://www.pcmag.com/feature/335422/19-massive-corporate-social-media-horror-stories

[470] Duran, S. (2016, June 01). Social Media's 30/60/10 Principle-Not Too Hot, Not Too Cold. Retrieved May 17, 2020, from https://medium.com/@stevenduran_96808/social-medias-30-60-10-principle-not-too-hot-not-too-cold-b04d8cc45d21

[471] DeMers, J. (2014, July 21). Is Bad Grammar Killing Your Brand? Retrieved May 17, 2020, from https://www.forbes.com/sites/jaysondemers/2014/07/15/is-bad-grammar-killing-your-brand/

[472] Fox, M. (2018, March 09). Fake News: Lies spread faster on social media than truth does. Retrieved May 17, 2020, from https://www.nbcnews.com/health/health-news/fake-news-lies-spread-faster-social-media-truth-does-n854896

[473] Troll. (n.d.). Retrieved May 17, 2020, from https://www.merriam-webster.com/dictionary/troll

to troll[474], but in the end, their motivations don't matter to your marketing. If your goal is to make connections with your ideal reader, spending time and energy on a troll is counter-productive. Let professional courtesy be your shield and sarcasm be your sword, but don't get dragged into long engagements. The best alternative might simply be to block them and move on.

5. *Don't Attack the Wrong People*: It is generally not advisable to attack anyone on social media, since it goes against the principles of professional courtesy and prudent posting, but politics is war by other means, so the inherent political position of your art will inevitably criticize some institution, movement or standard. There isn't anything inherently wrong with that, as long as your marketing and your story don't cause unintended collateral damage or create accidental enemies. Don't offend the wrong people[475], or your marketing efforts will be focused on damage control instead of building relationships.

6. *Don't Buy Followers*: Several services claim to be able to deliver large numbers of followers for a fee. In most cases, these are not real people, but bots or automated programs that mimic human activity on the internet[476]. These bots can inflate your social media numbers, but they damage your marketing efforts for several reasons[477]:

    a.   Bots can get you banned from some platforms
    b.   Bots dilute the accuracy of your tracking
    c.   Bots waste your investment money
    d.   Bots can't buy comics.

Social media takes effort, but it is a key component of your online marketing. It can connect you to your target market at a financial cost that can be close to free. When used in coordination with your website, it can foster the growth of true fans. But for all its potential, it is not the most effective form of online marketing.

That title is reserved for the mailing list.

---

[474] Fox, J. (2014, August 12). Why the Online Trolls Troll. Retrieved May 17, 2020, from https://www.psychologytoday.com/us/blog/better-living-technology/201408/why-the-online-trolls-troll

[475] Robert Greene, The 48 Laws of Power

[476] Bot. (n.d.). Retrieved May 17, 2020, from https://techterms.com/definition/bot

[477] Lips, A. (2018, September 18). 5 Reasons Why You Shouldn't Buy Fake Followers. Retrieved May 17, 2020, from https://socialmediaweek.org/blog/2018/09/5-reasons-why-you-shouldnt-buy-fake-followers/

Social media can be a powerful tool for your marketing, but in the end, it is still digital sharecropping. Algorithms are constantly changing[478], so the level of activity and interaction that you have one day might disappear the next. Your account can be blocked on a temporary or permanent basis, especially if you engage in conduct that violates the principles we outlined in the last chapter, or if you violate a platform's terms of use[479]. At the end of the day, the pages on social media aren't yours and the connections you make are indirect because they always have to go through someone else's service.

Email marketing or the use of email to promote products and services[480] can give you direct access to your target market in ways that social media can't. When used in combination with your website and your social media accounts, a consistent and focused email campaign can be the best way to interact with your true fans before, during, and after the publication of your book.

What Are the Advantages of Email?

According to email marketing expert Cara Wilson[481] and author Tim Grahl[482], there are several benefits to email marketing for independent publishers.

- *Permission*: Because subscribers make an active choice to join your email list, you're more likely to get or retain their attention than in other forms of marketing. This type of permission-based marketing[483] is far more valuable than forced marketing because it implies an actual interest in the message.

- *Target audience*: Depending on a variety of factors, your social media post might not be seen by your target market. They might miss the message because they aren't looking at their feed

---

[478] Prodan, D. (2018, December 27). The Biggest Changes to Social Media in 2018 and What They Mean For Marketers. Retrieved May 17, 2020, from https://www.skyword.com/contentstandard/marketing/the-biggest-changes-to-social-media-in-2018-and-what-they-mean-for-marketers/

[479] Parrack, D. (2013, February 06). How To Get Banned From Social Networks. Retrieved May 17, 2020, from https://www.makeuseof.com/tag/how-to-get-banned-from-social-networks/

[480] Ward, S. (2020, January 20). Why Email Marketing Is Still the Best Thing Since Sliced Bread. Retrieved May 17, 2020, from https://www.thebalancesmb.com/email-marketing-2948346

[481] 10 benefits of email marketing. (2020, February 9). Retrieved May 17, 2020, from https://www.pure360.com/10-benefits-of-email-marketing/

[482] Grahl, T. (2013). *Your first 1000 copies: The step-by-step guide to marketing your book*. Lynchburg, VA: Out:think Group.

[483] Godin, S. (2018, May 30). Permission Marketing. Retrieved May 17, 2020, from https://seths.blog/2008/01/permission-mark/

at the right time or because the platform is limiting the reach of your message. With email, you have a much better chance of getting your message in front of your target audience.

- *Sales*: When your true fan is ready to buy your book, an email with a link to your online store can create a frictionless buying experience.

- *Use*: Email marketing software is designed to have you up and running in less than an hour. It might take some time to design your initial template and add the content for your ongoing email campaigns, but it consumes less of your time than social media.

- *Measurement*: It can be difficult to tell how many people read your post based on the number of social media likes. It can be hard to know who is responding to your message based on the comments. E-mail marketing software, however, can tell you who opened your email and who clicked on the links. This can be a stronger indicator of who your true fans are and what messages resonate with them most.

- *Shareability*: Your true fans probably know people you don't know who like what they like. Because it takes no effort for them to forward your email to other people, they can spread your message and build your tribe on their own. This kind of **social proof**[484] can be the most powerful, and the most elusive type of marketing connection.

- *High Return on Investment*: A **conversion rate** is the percentage of people who complete a desired action based on a marketing message[485]. For example, if you have 1,000 Twitter followers and 10 of them visited your website after you posted something, then the conversion rate for that post is 1%. According to author Mat Nastos[486] and the Data & Marketing Association, conversion rates for email are ten times higher than for social media[487]. For an independent publisher with limited time and resources, email can make the most difference with the least amount of resources.

---

[484] Rouse, M. (2017, January 28). What is social proof? - Definition from WhatIs.com. Retrieved May 17, 2020, from https://whatis.techtarget.com/definition/social-proof

[485] Vaughan, P. (n.d.). Your Complete Guide to Measuring Email Marketing Success. Retrieved May 17, 2020, from https://blog.hubspot.com/blog/tabid/6307/bid/29510/your-complete-guide-to-measuring-email-marketing-success.aspx

[486] Nastos, M. (2011). *Comic Book Marketing 101*. Nifty Entertainment.

[487] Chutich, A., (2018, September 21). Email is the Most Effective Digital Marketing Channel. Retrieved May 17, 2020, from https://thinkbigfish.com/email-digital-marketing-channel/

What Are the Disadvantages of Email?

Email marketing is similar to the Death Star. For all its power and potential, there are still thermal exhaust ports you need to worry about[488]. While these shortcomings can be reduced, ignoring them could lead to significant setbacks in your plans to bring order to the galaxy.

- *Cost*: If you don't buy ads on social media, then using those platforms are free in terms of financial investment. Email marketing has a cost. While these costs aren't exorbitant, and they are deductible as a business expense, it can be another drain on your investment, however small it might turn out to be.

- *Spam*: People get an average of 70-90 emails per day[489]. Many of them are never opened or read. In addition, people can have their email filters set in such a way that your message goes straight to their spam folder without ever being seen. Many email marketing programs attempt to get around this problem, but no solution is guaranteed.

- *Legal Violations*: The Federal Trade Commission enforces a law known as the CAN-SPAM Act[490]. This law sets out guidelines for regulating commercial email. Failure to adhere to these guidelines can lead to penalties of more than $42,000, so you need to ensure your marketing email:

  - Doesn't use misleading header information
  - Doesn't use deceptive subject lines
  - Identifies the message as a marketing message
  - Provides your physical address
  - Gives recipients the ability to opt-out of receiving future messages
  - Removes people who decide to opt-out

- *Inconsistent appearance*: People read emails on various types of devices with different screen sizes using different email programs. This means that your cover thumbnail might look beautiful on a laptop but appear deformed on a desktop or not appear at all on a tablet. Again, some of the major email services give you the ability to work around this problem, but even if you test every email, you can still run into issues.

---

[488] Forneris, J. (2017, November 21). The Disadvantages of Email Marketing. Retrieved May 17, 2020, from https://smallbusiness.chron.com/disadvantages-email-marketing-3472.html

[489] Leibowitz, G. (2017, May 19). 6 Annoying Email Habits That Ruin Productivity and Destroy Trust. Retrieved May 17, 2020, from https://www.inc.com/glenn-leibowitz/270-billion-email-messages-are-sent-every-day-heres-whats-wrong-with-many-of-the.html

[490] CAN-SPAM Act: A Compliance Guide for Business. (2020, January 22). Retrieved May 17, 2020, from https://www.ftc.gov/tips-advice/business-center/guidance/can-spam-act-compliance-guide-business

How Do You Choose an Email Marketing Program?

Email marketing software is similar to other online business services. New options are being offered constantly and established brands alter their offerings to keep pace with the competition. There are dozens of reviews published every year[491], so you just need to be aware of what you're looking for when it's time to make your selection. The major criterion for independent publishers tends to be:

- Price
- Ease of Use
- Template options
- Reporting
- Customer support
- Social media integration

How Do You Get People to Join Your Email List?

The first thing to understand about building your email list is that **people have to choose to join**. You decrease the advantages of email marketing and increase the disadvantages if you buy email lists, import your personal contacts folder, or otherwise send people email without their permission[492]. You need to build an email list of ideal readers over time by offering them what they want. Since we know that your ideal readers want to feel certain emotions, your invitations should convey that message.

The invitation to join your mailing list can help create a seamless relationship between your other marketing efforts. Your website can have a page where people can join your mailing list. When it's time to promote yourself on social media, part of that call to action can be a link to your website mailing list sign up form. Each email you send out can include links to both your website and your social media to complete the circle.

There are also opportunities in the real world to get people to join your list. Creating a sign-up sheet for people at conventions and comic shops can be a way to turn an in-person meeting into ongoing communication. It often helps to give away some kind of content or prize when requesting email addresses, so people feel like they're getting something in exchange for access to their inbox[493].

---

[491] The Best Email Marketing Software for 2020. (n.d.). Retrieved May 17, 2020, from https://www.pcmag.com/roundup/320693/the-best-email-marketing-software

[492] Wainwright, C. (n.d.). Why Buying Email Lists Is Always a Bad Idea (And How to Build Yours for Free). Retrieved May 17, 2020, from https://blog.hubspot.com/blog/tabid/6307/bid/32892/why-purchasing-email-lists-is-always-a-bad-idea.aspx

[493] (2017). *New York Comic Con Marketing Panel*. Lecture presented in New York Comic Con, New York.

How Do You Create the Right Email Marketing Messages?

The form and content of your email messages depend on your ideal reader and the emotions they want to feel, but there are principles that email marketers have found effective. Ariel Hyatt, a crowdfunding expert who integrates email marketing into her campaigns divides successful emails into three parts: Greeting, Guts, and Getting[494].

- *Greeting*: is a personalized statement to connect with the reader. It could be a behind-the-scenes update of your process, someone on the team, or an observation about a topic relevant to the ideal reader.

- *Guts*: is the core of the email. This could be anything from an official update, like the release of the book or your attendance at a convention. It could be a review of a competitor's media, a how-to video on something relevant to the ideal reader, or a special offer for some artwork or content you want to share.

- *Getting*: is your call to action[495] where you encourage the reader to do something, whether it's sharing the email with friends, joining you on social media, visiting your website, or buying your book. If this portion is compelling, easy to accomplish, and readers feel they are getting something for their effort, your chances of conversion increase.

In addition to the core elements of your email, there are several other elements to consider in your overall email campaigns:

- *Be consistent*: Send your emails on a regular basis, whether it's once a month or whatever frequency makes sense for your project. Have them arrive on the same day and time. Give them a similar look and feel that matches the style of the website and social media pages.

- *Make the list members feel special*: Offer them something that isn't available on social media and you create a powerful motivator for people to make the leap from social media to your mailing list.

- *Identify what's in it for the reader*: People don't join your mailing list because they want to hear from you. They join because they want to get some benefit for their attention.

---

[494] Hyatt, A. (2016). *Crowd start: The ultimate guide to a powerful & profitable crowdfunding campaign*. New York: Hunter Cat Press.

[495] Call to Action: Definition in the Cambridge English Dictionary. (n.d.). Retrieved May 17, 2020, from https://dictionary.cambridge.org/us/dictionary/english/call-to-action

- *Provide a way to unsubscribe*: The taste and interest of people change over time. Your message might not give people what they're looking for. When that happens, give them the ability to unsubscribe from your list to avoid hostility and comply with the CAN-SPAM Act.

How Do You Measure Success?

Conversion rates are the ultimate measure of an email marketing campaign, but there are other benchmarks to quantify the level of connection you're creating. An **open rate** is the percentage of people who opened your email[496]. A **click rate** is the percentage of people who clicked on any link in the email[497]. When you look at the results of your email campaign, don't expect one hundred percent rates because no marketing message gets through to everyone, even when you have an engaged and targeted audience. According to MailChimp, open rates hover around 22% for publishing and 21% for art-related emails. Click rates for these categories are between 3 and 4%[498].

The combination of your website, social media, and email marketing makes up your online marketing efforts. The next section will take a look at options for marketing your comic in the real world and making direct contact with your ideal readers

---

[496] About Open and Click Rates. (n.d.). Retrieved May 17, 2020, from https://mailchimp.com/help/about-open-and-click-rates/

[497] Id.

[498] Email Marketing Benchmarks. (n.d.). Retrieved May 17, 2020, from https://mailchimp.com/resources/email-marketing-benchmarks/

All marketing is not created equal. One type can reach people all over the world at any time of day while you're wearing your pajamas or not actively engaging with your ideal readers at all. The other type is limited to where you can travel and only works when you are actively engaged and wearing clothing of some type.

Based on this description, you might think that offline marketing isn't worth the time or investment. That line of thinking overlooks a powerful method of connecting with your target market. What offline marketing lacks in reach and convenience it makes up for in its ability to enhance your online efforts and convert ideal readers into true fans.

Understanding the difference in the impact of the two tactics requires distinguishing between direct marketing and brand marketing. **Direct marketing** is an activity that seeks to motivate action in a target market[499] with a specific call to action. This can be anything from clicking on a link to buying a product or service. According to Seth Godin, direct marketing is also the type of activity that can be measured[500]. Whether you're looking at click rates, or likes, or comments, you can get some idea of the impact of each and every marketing message creates. Much of the online activity we explored in the previous chapters qualifies as direct marketing.

Brand marketing is creating an identity that differentiates you from your competition[501]. It creates subliminal, subconscious associations but it can't be measured in a meaningful way[502]. Consider this: companies spend millions of dollars for thirty seconds of advertising every Super Bowl[503], but there is limited data on how many people go out and buy Coke, Doritos, or Budweiser based on those spots in the following days, months or years. However, sustained brand marketing can define and dominate an idea. When you think of Mercedes, Nike, and Starbucks, you probably don't just think about a generic car, sneaker, or cup of coffee. There is a distinct personality in each of those words that you either relate to or you don't.

Brand marketing can go deeper than name recognition. It can define an entire category of products. When I was growing up 500 years ago, Pampers was synonymous with diapers, even though they were only one

---

[499] Campos, B., & Cyberclick. (n.d.). What is Direct Marketing? Benefits, Steps and Examples on How to Start a Campaign. Retrieved May 17, 2020, from https://www.cyberclick.es/numericalblogen/what-is-direct-marketing-benefits-and-steps-to-campaign

[500] Godin, This is Marketing

[501] Sorensen, M., Kohler, M., & Soccolich, A. (n.d.). Branding Definition. Retrieved May 17, 2020, from https://www.entrepreneur.com/encyclopedia/branding

[502] Godin, This is Marketing

[503] Nittle, N. (2019, January 25). What makes a Super Bowl ad successful? An ad exec explains. Retrieved May 17, 2020, from https://www.vox.com/the-goods/2019/1/25/18197609/super-bowl-ads-commercials-doritos-sprint-skittles

brand out of several[504]. The same was true for Xerox with photocopiers and Kleenex with facial tissues. As we have already discussed, superhero comics have dominated the popular culture so much that most of America associate comics with superheroes, no matter how many *Sabrinas* and *Smiles* might be published. On the level of individual creators, people like Stan Lee, Stephen King, James Patterson, and J.K Rowling all attract a particular group based on their name recognition that is eager to engage with their work.

But that level of cultural influence takes time, consistency, and engagement to create. You might not be able to build it hiding in your studio posting to social media. At some point and in some fashion, you might need to get out there and physically meet your ideal reader before they decide to become your true fan. Direct marketing is easier to develop online, but brand marketing can have more impact offline.

What Are the Goals of Brand Marketing?

Because a significant portion of offline marketing generates more brand results than direct ones, your mindset when deciding which opportunities to pursue can't be guided by the same evaluations or motivations. All your marketing is designed to create a positive relationship, but the hierarchy of brand marketing needs to focus on different goals than your online efforts, because as we said, you can't directly measure the impact of this work. Here are a few offline goals in order of importance:

1. Make connections with readers and retailers that differentiate you from the competition in a positive manner.

2. Collect email addresses whenever possible and practical to continue building connections online (as long as this activity doesn't undermine item one)

3. Provide the ideal reader with some physical takeaway to reinforce the encounter, whether that item is free or for sale.

4. Use brand marketing events (like appearance announcements, pictures, and interviews) as potential content for your direct marketing online.

---

[504] What is the difference between Diaper and Pamper? (n.d.). Retrieved May 17, 2020, from https://www.quora.com/What-is-the-difference-between-Diaper-and-Pamper

What are the Offline Locations for Brand Marketing?

You don't have to stand on a random street corner trying to market your comic or comics in general. You have a specific ideal reader and that person can be found in certain geographic locations. The next three chapters will go in-depth into the comic shop, the convention, and the potential market location so you can pick the best avenue to focus your offline marketing efforts.

You might consider **direct market comic shops** as the main way to sell physical copies across the country. This could be true for your book, but there is more potential for comic book stores beyond serving as retail locations. There is also more opportunity for you to find local success if you can create mutual benefits for you and the shop.

Unlocking this potential involves looking at your local comic shops from a marketing perspective rather than a sales opportunity. As we will see in Chapter 44, creating a positive relationship with the store is just as important as creating connections with your ideal readers if you want to sell certain types of books. Since we already know giving people what they want is a key marketing concept, let's think about what a store owner and the potential reader might want and then figure out how you can provide it.

We've already seen that your potential reader wants a positive emotional experience, not any particular product or book. They might be interested in stories like the one you plan to tell, but they might not even know where to find comics[505]. If they do happen to know where the shop is, they might avoid going in because of either the negative stigma attached to comics that we discussed in Chapter 31, or the pervasive stereotypes associated with comic book shops[506]. Finally, your potential reader could simply have never had an incentive to step beyond the threshold of a comic shop to see what's inside.

But if you could provide them with knowledge, comfort, and support then they might be willing to take a chance on the experience you're offering. If you promise them something fun and related to what they find interesting, you can tap into their need to know more. If you fulfill that promise and give them the feelings they're looking for, you can transform ideal readers into true fans.

Like the potential reader, the owner of the shop doesn't necessarily want your independent book. They don't want another title with no track record taking up limited space on the shelves and costing money they could put into a more profitable title. They probably love comics and they might even have a special place in their heart and in their store for independents, but the economic realities don't change. They need to sell books to keep the lights on, and there's no guarantee that your book is going to sell.

But the shop owner needs something else besides popular books to have a successful store. They need people coming into the store who might be interested in buying books. In business terms, they need **foot**

---

[505] Owens, H., R., R., Eyestone, K., Van, T., & Chris. (2019, October 07). Where Can I Buy Comic Books and Graphic Novels? " How To Love Comics. Retrieved May 17, 2020, from https://www.howtolovecomics.com/2013/01/24/where-can-i-buy-comic-books/

[506] Narcisse, E. (2018). A Snapshot of How Comic Book Shops and Fandom Keep Changing Each Other - io9. Retrieved May 17, 2020, from https://io9.gizmodo.com/a-snapshot-of-how-comic-book-shops-and-fandom-keep-chan-1825205065

traffic[507] from people who like what they are selling. A store could have the best selection of comics in the world—but if no one comes into their store, it doesn't matter.

This is where you can create a benefit. If you transform the shop into a community meeting place, you can bring potential readers into the store[508]. Once they're inside, they can see all the cool stuff the store has to offer. If the staff does their part, they can turn casual customers into frequent shoppers. If you are the catalyst for this increased revenue, the owner of the shop will be more likely to support the marketing efforts for your book.

What I am proposing is marketing your book by becoming the link between your potential readers and your local comic shop. This kind of brand activity can benefit both parties and put you in a better position in the mind of your target market than your competition.

How Do You Convince Comic Shops to Help Your Marketing?

The first step in linking comic shops and potential readers is finding a store willing to work with you. If you love comics and have a favorite local shop, this might be the best place to start. If you're planning to work with a new shop, then it might make sense to patronize it for a few months and talk to the staff about comics and their business before you offer your proposal. This way, you're a little more of a known quantity and not just someone off the street. Also, this will give you some time to see how the store operates and what kind of customers they usually attract.

In the initial stages, it's probably best to focus on only those comic book shops that are easily accessible to you and your team. Because comic book shop marketing can be time and labor-intensive, it doesn't make sense to try and pull off your first few offers in places where distance is a hindrance. Also, I refer to "comic book shops" in this chapter, but if there isn't a suitable direct market location near you, these ideas are also suitable for bookstores and libraries[509].

When you figure out who is the best person in the store to approach, frame your offer in terms of the benefits to the shop, not the benefit to you. It is natural for someone to be more open to a proposal when their upside is clear[510]. They will probably understand the benefit to you both as a comics fan and a comic creator, so make sure they see what's in it for them.

---

[507] What is foot traffic? definition and meaning. (n.d.). Retrieved May 17, 2020, from http://www.businessdictionary.com/definition/foot-traffic.html

[508] "Perch" (Producer). (2020). *Doing Well? Doing Bad? The In Between World of Comic Shops* [Video file]. Retrieved May 17, 2020, from https://www.youtube.com/watch?v=9Y7BZz_oSDk&feature=youtu.be

[509] Rutkowska, A. (2018, July 13). Publishing Tips for Indie Authors: How to Get Your Book Into Libraries. Retrieved May 17, 2020, from https://www.writersdigest.com/editor-blogs/there-are-no-rules/marketing-self-promotion/indie-authors-how-to-get-your-book-into-libraries-indie-publishing-tips

[510] Greene, The 48 Laws of Power

Your offer is to attract more potential readers to the store with some sort of event or series of events, but the exact form of that offer will vary. It will be based on the nature of the store, your ideal reader, and the investment and time you can put into it[511]. Many of these ideas are inspired by comic convention events on a smaller scale, but some examples include:

- **Cosplay contests**[512] where players can dress up as characters in your genre (or if you already have a following, characters from your story)

- Debates, discussions and trivia contests about characters, books or trends in your genre

- Educational classes on comic art, how to read comics, cosplay, or topics of interest to your target market[513]

- Family events for children in the target market to get kids introduced to the stories and the genre itself

- Game nights related to your target market. These could be tabletop games, traditional role-playing games or video games

- Holiday events: including Back-to-school, Halloween, Christmas, or any other event relevant to your target market

- Launch parties (or watch parties) for comic book related films, games, or television shows in your genre

- Panel discussions with comic creators or other personalities of interest to the target market

- Comic Book Reading Clubs[514]: that meet in the store periodically

You can probably think of more examples that fit your ideal reader. The key is to create something that brings potential readers together and gets them interested in your genre of comics. It needs to be something

[511] Griepp, M. (2019). Exclusive: AfterShock Deploys First Nine Direct Market Ambassadors. Retrieved May 17, 2020, from https://icv2.com/articles/news/view/44267/exclusive-aftershock-deploys-first-nine-direct-market-ambassadors

[512] Sergienko, O. (2018). How to Organize a Cosplay Contest. Retrieved May 17, 2020, from https://www.judgify.me/l/blog/how-to-organise-a-cosplay-contest/

[513] Candelieri, D. (2019, August 22). New York City comic shop allows kids to learn, create, sell own comics. Retrieved May 17, 2020, from https://abc7ny.com/society/nyc-comic-shop-allows-kids-to-learn-create-sell-own-comics/5463175/

[514] Caffrey, A. (2012). Starting a Comic Reading Club. Retrieved May 17, 2020, from http://www.thereadingclub.co.uk/starting-comic-reading-club.html

that you can organize and promote beforehand, manage during the big day, and help clean up after it's done. While it shouldn't simply be a "comic book sale", because that doesn't create the incentive or engagement you're trying to create, there are sales opportunities for the store.

- They could alter their display or their sales to coincide with the nature of the event.

- They could set up a raffle for anyone who signs up for the mailing list, opens a pull account, or joins the discount program.

- Taken a step further, you could offer some quality artwork from your story as the incentive and take the strain off their inventory.

The only thing you might want to avoid is charging a fee for entry in most circumstances. Selling tickets creates a barrier to entry and since this event is designed to remove barriers to entry, you don't want to cannibalize your efforts to attract potential readers.

The other practical consideration to keep in mind with these events is that you want to **disrupt the normal business of the store as little as possible**. You don't want your comic book shop to lose money because of your marketing. This means common-sense steps like not trying to schedule an event on a Monday, Tuesday, or Wednesday if the shop relies on weekly single-issue sales. It means not creating any event that is going to damage the store or its merchandise. It also means complying with any building codes, health codes, ordinances, or local laws for meetings or retail properties that affect your shop. There can be other specific considerations that will factor into your events, but creating a good working relationship with your shop can help navigate through them.

Finally, keep in mind that you might need to manage several events before the store sees a significant increase in regular customers. A potential patron often needs to visit the shop multiple times before they "stick" as a regular customer[515], so your events might need to keep them coming back a few times to have a real impact.

How Do You Convince Ideal Readers to Attend Your Event?

Announcing your event to your target market is a three-part process. The first part is taking advantage of your existing online marketing. Posting an announcement about your event on your website, social media, and to your email list for a few weeks before is a good use of your resources. The second step is taking advantage of apps like Eventbrite, Facebook Events, or Meetup to manage and coordinate information flow and attendance. Finally, utilizing local resources specific to your target market like fliers, signs, and local press releases can get the word out to people who are most likely to be in the area.

---

[515] "Perch" (Producer). (2019). *Organizing Comics For New Customers* [Video file]. Retrieved May 17, 2020, from https://www.youtube.com/watch?v=BhOmRoDcjlk&feature=youtu.be

Design your announcement to attract your target market into the comic shop. Your message should contain three elements:

- A clear call to action (Go to this thing)

- All the information they need to get there clearly spelled out (date, time, location, etc.)

- A compelling reason to alter their routine, which could be the people who are attending or what you're offering, but it has to be relevant enough to your target market to disrupt their existing patterns.

During and after the event, you should also coordinate posting with your social media to maintain momentum and let everyone else know what they missed out on.

How Do You Manage the Event?

Managing an event shares some similarities with talent management. The best events are often the result of a certain balance between planning and flexibility[516].

- *Before the event*, determine all the different tasks that need to be handled and assign a specific person or people to those tasks. These people could be members of your team who are helping out as part of their contract, members of the comic book shop staff, or gig-based services like Task Rabbit. Whoever you use, take the time to explain what you need them to do or the job might not be done well.

- *During the event*, do what you can to remain flexible and friendly while you make yourself useful. Things might come up that you didn't prepare for. Manage them without undermining your attempt to connect the potential readers and the store. Before the event is over, you might become hangry, stressed, or tired. But remember the importance of reputation in independent comics. You don't want to sabotage your book with a bad attitude in front of your target market.

- *After the event*, be sure to wrap things up in the store, post to social media, and review what went right and what went wrong with your team. Touch base with the store (and perhaps invite them to lunch or coffee as a token of your appreciation) to understand what went right or wrong from their perspective, too.

---

[516] Top 10 Tips for Successful Event Management. (n.d.). Retrieved May 17, 2020, from
https://www.brightonsbm.com/news/top-10-tips-successful-event-management/

Comic shop marketing events, like all brand marketing, is labor-intensive and difficult to measure[517]. It requires consistent effort over time, a certain amount of extroverted activity, and can be a drain on the limited resources available for your book. It also explicitly isn't about your book the way the Macy's Thanksgiving Day Parade isn't about selling clothes and Mercedes Benz Fashion Week isn't about cars. It also doesn't guarantee the success of a shop, since there are several other concerns they have to manage as a brick and mortar establishment in an increasingly online world[518]. But if you decide to utilize local comic book shops as a marketing opportunity you can position your book ahead of your competition. It can also help prepare you for the larger marketing possibilities that come with conventions.

---

[517] Godin, This is Marketing

[518] "Perch" (Director). (2019). *The Hard Details of Running a Shop* [Video file]. Retrieved May 17, 2020, from https://www.youtube.com/watch?v=klcwxzbJg-Y&feature=youtu.be

Comic book conventions (or cons) are events with a primary focus on the business and culture of comics[519]. They offer unique in-person marketing opportunities for independent publishers because they provide a venue where you can directly interact with an enthusiastic target market in ways that are often problematic for the film, theater, and television industries. At the same time, conventions give you a chance to:

- Connect with potential talent
- Experience comics as a fan
- Find out about industry trends
- Get inspiration from the latest releases
- Increase your professional intelligence
- Learn more about your competitors and your genre
- Network with other publishers and professionals from other media
- Sell your comics
- Test your ideas

In my experience, conventions can be a whirlwind of activity that often leave participants exhausted in an afterglow of emotions[520]. They are also a reminder of why we love comics in the first place. As an independent publisher, making the most of your convention experience requires planning upfront, time management during the event, and efficient follow up in the days and weeks after. This chapter will primarily examine conventions from a marketing angle, but we'll also explore the other potential benefits of adding convention attendance to your publishing plans.

Which Conventions Should You Attend?

The website Convention Scene maintains an ongoing list of pop culture conventions in various parts of the world. The following was taken from their comic book convention list for Summer 2019- Summer 2020 for the US and Canada.[521]

---

[519] Comic book convention. (2020, April 23). Retrieved May 17, 2020, from https://en.wikipedia.org/wiki/Comic_book_convention

[520] Carson, E. (2018, July 17). How to survive your first Comic-Con experience. Retrieved May 17, 2020, from https://www.cnet.com/news/how-to-survive-your-first-comic-con-experience/

[521] Comic Book Conventions. (2020, May 07). Retrieved May 17, 2020, from https://www.conventionscene.com/schedules/comicbookconventions/ © Convention Scene, All Rights Reserved

Date(s)	City	Event
08/02/19 - 08/04/19	Tampa, FL	Tampa Bay Comic Convention
08/02/19 - 08/04/19	Honolulu, HI	Comic-Con Honolulu
08/03/19 - 08/04/19	Roanoke, VA	Big Lick Comic-Con
08/03/19 - 08/04/19	Belton, TX	Bell County Comic-Con
08/04/19	North Olmsted, OH	NEO Comic-Con
08/09/19 - 08/11/19	Uncasville, CT	TERRIFICon
08/10/19	East Ridge, TN	FarleyCon
08/10/19	Rahway, NJ	Rah-Con
08/10/19 - 08/11/19	Lewisville, TX	Dallas Comic Show: Fantasy Festival
08/10/19 - 08/11/19	Rochester, MN	Nerdinout Con
08/10/19 - 08/11/19	Springfield, IL	Springfield Comic Expo
08/11/19	Essington, PA	Philadelphia Comic-Con!
08/16/19 - 08/18/19	San Jose, CA	Silicon Valley Comic-Con
08/16/19 - 08/18/19	Detroit, MI	Michigan Comic Convention
08/17/19 - 08/18/19	New York, NY	FlameCon
08/17/19 - 08/18/19	Albuquerque, NM	New Mexico Comic Expo
08/18/19	McLean, VA	Shoff Promotions Comic Book Show
08/23/19 - 08/25/19	Atlanta, GA	ONYXCON
08/23/19 - 08/25/19	Colorado Springs, CO	Colorado Springs Comic-Con
08/23/19 - 08/25/19	Philadelphia, PA	Keystone Comic-Con
08/23/19 - 08/25/19	San Mateo, CA	ToyXpo Comic and Fan Experience
08/24/19 - 08/25/19	Chantilly, VA	Fairfax Comic-Con
08/24/19 - 08/25/19	Kissimmee, FL	Infinity Toy and Comic-Con

08/24/19 - 08/25/19	Boise, ID	Boise Comic Arts Festival
08/30/19 - 09/01/19	Indianapolis, IN	Indiana Comic-Con
08/31/19	Harrisburg, IL	Burg Comics Con
09/05/19 - 09/07/19	Salt Lake City, UT	FanX® Salt Lake Comic Convention™
09/07/19 - 09/08/19	Cocoa, FL	Space Coast Comic-Con
09/07/19 - 09/08/19	Little Rock, AR	Arkansas Comic-Con
09/07/19 - 09/08/19	Elkhart, IN	Hall of Heroes Comic-Con
09/08/19	Laurel, MD	Comic Book and More Show
09/13/19 - 09/15/19	Portland, OR	Rose City Comic-Con
09/14/19	Merced, CA	California Republic Comic-Con
09/14/19	Alsip, IL	Southside Comic Book Show
09/14/19	Monroe, MI	Monroe Pop Fest
09/14/19 - 09/15/19	Manchester, NH	Granite State Comicon
09/14/19 - 09/15/19	Bethesda, MD	Small Press Expo (SPX)
09/14/19 - 09/15/19	Saskatoon, SK	Saskatchewan Entertainment Expo
09/16/19	San Mateo, CA	South City Comic-Con
09/20/19 - 09/22/19	Cincinnati, OH	Cincinnati Comic Expo
09/20/19 - 09/22/19	San Antonio, TX	Big Texas Comicon
09/21/19	Florence, SC	Power Comicon
09/21/19	Walla Walla, WA	Adam West Day
09/21/19	Somerville, MA	LadiesCon
09/21/19	Wildwood, NJ	Wild Con
09/21/19 - 09/22/19	Plattsburgh, NY	Plattsburgh Comic-Con
09/22/19	Annandale, VA	Shoff Promotions Comic Book and Card Show
09/26/19 - 09/29/19	Columbus, OH	Cartoon Crossroads

09/28/19	Madison Heights, MI	Great Lakes Comic Expo
09/29/19	Essington, PA	Philadelphia Comic-Con!
10/03/19 - 10/06/19	New York, NY	New York Comic-Con
10/04/19 - 10/06/19	Dothan, AL	Alabama Fanaticon
10/05/19 - 10/06/19	London, ON	London Comic-Con
10/06/19	Westlake, OH	Cleveland Comic Book and Nostalgia Festival
10/11/19 - 10/13/19	Los Angeles, CA	Los Angeles Comic Con
10/12/19 - 10/13/19	Austin, TX	STAPLE! Independent Media Expo
10/18/19 - 10/20/19	Baltimore, MD	Baltimore Comic-Con
10/18/19 - 10/20/19	Houston, TX	Fandemic Tour Houston
10/19/19	Ocala, FL	Brick City Comic and Toy Show
10/19/19	North Charleston, SC	CharlestonCon
10/19/19 - 10/20/19	Memphis, TN	Memphis Comic Expo
10/19/19 - 10/20/19	Mount Hope, ON	Hamilton Comic-Con
10/21/19	Sacramento, CA	Sac-Con
10/26/19	Nashua, NH	SNH Comic Bash
10/26/19 - 10/27/19	Maui, HI	Maui Comic-Con
11/01/19 - 11/03/19	New Orleans, LA	Big Easy Con
11/01/19 - 11/03/19	Providence, RI	Rhode Island Comic-Con
11/01/19 - 11/03/19	Adelaide	Supanova Comic Con & Gaming
11/03/19	Daytona Beach, FL	Daytona Beach Comic-Con
11/08/19- 11/10/19	Brisbane	Supanova Comic Con & Gaming
11/08/19 - 11/10/19	Reno, NV	Reno Pop Culture Con
11/11/19	Modesto, CA	Central Valley Con
11/16/19 - 11/17/19	Framingham, MA	New England Super Megafest Comic-Con

11/17/19	Frederick, MD	Shoff Promotions Frederick Maryland Comic-Con
11/17/19 - 11/18/19	Bakersfield, CA	Bakersfield Comic-Con
11/22/19 - 11/24/19	New York, NY	New York Winter Con
11/23/19	Fort Myers, FL	SW-FloridaCon
11/23/19 - 11/24/19	Richardson, TX	Dallas Comic Show: Holiday Special
11/24/19	Columbus, OH	Buckeye Comic-Con
11/29/19 - 12/01/19	Boxborough, MA	NorthEast Comic-Con
11/30/19 - 12/01/19	St Charles, IL	Chicago Pop Culture Con
12/07/19	Roanoke, VA	Roanoke Valley Comicon
12/08/19	Laurel, MD	Comic Book and More Show
12/14/19	Madison Heights, MI	Great Lakes Comic Expo
12/29/19	Essington, PA	Philadelphia Comic-Con!
01/04/20 - 01/05/20	St. Charles, IL	Cosmic Comic-Con
01/17/20 - 01/19/20	Albuquerque, NM	Albuquerque Comic Con
02/28/20 - 03/01/20	Pensacola, FL	Pensacon
03/12/20 - 03/15/20	Seattle, WA	Emerald City Comicon
03/20/20 - 03/22/20	Kansas City, MO	Planet Comicon, Kansas City
04/04/20	Salem, VA	Roanoke Valley Comicon
05/16/20 - 05/17/20	Cernobbio	Lake Como Comic Art Festival
05/30/20 - 05/31/20	Homestead, PA	3 Rivers Comicon
06/19/20 - 06/21/20	Charlotte, NC	HeroesCon

© Convention Scene

One look at this list and you'll quickly realize that **you do not have the time or the resources to attend all of the cons**. It wouldn't make sense to hit every show even if you could, because you're only trying to connect with your target market, not every fan of comics or comic adjacent material.

The key is to develop a set of criteria to allow you to pick and choose the right con for your publishing goals. Different cons have different sizes, areas of emphasis, and uses for independent publishers. Depending on what your goals are, the time and money you have available, what stage your team is in the development of the book, and your other marketing efforts, some shows will be a better fit than others.

In the beginning, starting small and building your way up is a valid tactic[522]. It does you no good to try and fight your way into San Diego Comic-Con before you get your feet wet in smaller shows. I recommend trying a couple of comic shop-related events first, then going to local cons if there's one in your area. That way the cost tends to be lower, with less logistical challenges and a stronger potential to continue to connect with local fans. Once you've mastered the local shows, then you can level up into regional, national, international, interplanetary, and interdimensional events.

Another type of convention to consider is one that focuses more on your potential market, even if it is not a traditional comic con. There are cons for many different types of fans. If your goal is to connect with readers that your competition might miss, or to encourage new people to read comics, then why not take your space opera book to a science fiction con[523], or your historical serial killer graphic novel to a horror con[524]? You can expand your vision by targeting a specialized book festival[525], or target niche-specific shows like Flame Con[526] for LGBTQ readers or Wakanda-Con[527] for Afrofuturism fans. Film, television, and video games use comic cons on a regular basis to market their stories[528]. You can also use the large number and variety of conventions to pick and choose the best events for your book.

---

[522] James, T. (2012). Tabling at Your First Comic Convention. Retrieved May 17, 2020, from http://www.comixtribe.com/2012/03/26/tabling-at-your-first-comic-convention/

[523] Science Fiction Conventions: List of Upcoming Sci-Fi Cons. (n.d.). Retrieved May 17, 2020, from https://www.upcomingcons.com/science-fiction-conventions

[524] Horror Conventions: List of Upcoming Horror Cons. (n.d.). Retrieved May 17, 2020, from https://www.upcomingcons.com/horror-conventions

[525] Lemay, J. (2019). Select Book Conferences, Festivals, and Fairs in 2019. Retrieved May 17, 2020, from https://www.publishersweekly.com/pw/by-topic/industry-news/trade-shows-events/article/78933-select-book-conferences-festivals-and-fairs-in-2019.html

[526] The World's Largest Queer Comic Con. (n.d.). Retrieved May 17, 2020, from https://www.flamecon.org/

[527] Gibbs, A. (2019, July 24). 'Come Find Your Tribe': WakandaCon Takes Over Chicago And 'Black Panther' Fans Rejoice. Retrieved May 17, 2020, from https://www.forbes.com/sites/adriennegibbs/2019/07/24/come-find-your-tribe-wakandacon-takes-over-chicago-and-black-panther-fans-rejoice/

[528] Hunt, J. (2019, July 17). Comic-Con 2019: All The Movie & TV Trailers To Expect. Retrieved May 17, 2020, from https://screenrant.com/comic-con-2019-movie-tv-trailers-prediction-sdcc/

Do You Need to Get a Table?

Tabling, or getting a table at a con means renting a small area of real estate in the convention venue for your independent publishing company[529]. While it is not mandatory for an independent publisher to rent space at a con, the decision to get a table will define much of your experience before, during, and after the show. I suggest visiting several cons during the pre-production and production phases of your first book to collect information and get a feel for the process, but we'll cover the positives and negatives of both methods to provide a complete picture.

- Mobile Attendance:

  - Advantages: A nomadic independent publisher at a convention can take advantage of increased time and lower costs.

    - Time: Because you aren't spending hours working at your booth, you're free to attend panels, meet with comic shop owners and potential talent, or check out what the competition is doing. You can also take in the show as a fan, buy cool stuff, connect with friends, and take pictures with cosplayers when you're not working your hustle.

    - Costs: Renting a table costs money. Printing books or manufacturing merch costs money. Shipping the stuff to the venue costs money. Shipping the unsold inventory back costs money. Paying labor costs money. Having a table means you might also be paying for electricity, Wi-Fi, taxes, and insurance. If you get a table, you're going to spend money marketing your project[530]. If you don't get a table, more of your investment can go into other aspects of your publishing.

  - Disadvantages: If you decide to spend the con walking the show floor, you have to deal with invisibility and lost sales:

    - Invisibility: When you have a table, you have an established presence at the show, however small it might be. Without one, people may not know where to find you. Potential fans can't stumble onto your amazing artwork. The perceived legitimacy of being an active comic book publisher is harder to attain. You don't have a stable place to relax, store your swag, or meet your market. For the duration of the show, you're a drifter with no place to hang your hat.

---

[529] Table Space and Badges. (2014, September 08). Retrieved May 17, 2020, from https://www.newyorkcomiccon.com/Industry-Info/Exhibitors/Already-An-Exhibitor/Artist-Alley-Manual/Table-Space-and-Badges/

[530] Altemus. (2018, August 19). Costs & Info for Exhibiting at NYCC. Retrieved May 17, 2020, from https://argentstarr.com/costs-info-on-exhibiting-at-new-york-comic-con-2014/

- **Lost Sales**: Without a table, it is difficult to sell any meaningful quantity of product for several reasons. First, some cons may have formal or informal rules against commercial activity without a table, because they have to protect all the exhibitors who do pay. Second, unless you're taking pre-orders, you can only sell what you can carry. Unless you're Professor Hulk, you won't be able to sell a ton of books from your bag. Third, handling cash and/or credit card transactions on the move can create a series of problems. Finally, even if there is no rule against non-table sales, and you can sell decent quantities out of your backpack, and you can keep track of your money, the potential loss of reputation might not be worth the money you have coming in. It only takes a couple of other independent creators who paid for space to see you selling mobile and getting upset. The potential blowback in the professional community could be far worse than the cost of a table.

- **Best Situation for Mobile Attendance**: If you don't have the upfront investment to pay for a table or if you don't have anything to sell, then it makes sense to stay mobile and use the convention for the other benefits it has to offer.

- Stationary Attendance:

  - **Advantages**: Tabling at a con provides the reverse benefits to mobile attendance, namely visibility and potential sales

    - **Visibility**: Your table is your spot on the convention show map, your popup shop, and your temporary flag in the comic industry ecosystem. Competitors, fans, potential partners, and the press can see you and what you're doing, which is critical for your marketing. On a simpler level, a table gives you a port in the storm of convention madness. While everyone else might be on their feet for ten hours, dragging around their stuff and eating trail mix, you at least can have a place to sit.

    - **Potential Sales**: The main point of getting a table at a con is to sell your stuff. Depending on how well you do and how much you control expenses, this distribution model can more than cover the costs of attending the show[531]. I've had clients who use conventions sales as their primary method of distribution, because they can cut out the middlemen and keep more of the revenue for themselves as profit.

  - **Disadvantages**: Tying yourself to a table means lost time and money.

---

[528] How Much Did Indie Exhibitor Earn at Comic Cons. (2014). Retrieved May 17, 2020, from https://comicsbeat.com/wp-content/uploads/2015/01/convention-survey-zine-2014.pdf

- Time: Comic creators and independent publishers who table often miss the other events of the show because they spend most of their time stuck peddling their wares like a shopkeeper in a fantasy RPG. In certain extreme cases, you might not have time to eat, go to the bathroom, or do anything else besides table for 8-10 hours at a time[532]. Conventions allow you to experience several benefits for your business, but only if you can get away from the booth.

- Money: The various costs of tabling at a con can run between a few hundred to a few thousand dollars. While certain convention expenses are deductible if you set up a company[533],[534] and the revenue you make from the table can exceed the costs[535], there is no guarantee you'll make a profit from attending the show[536]. You can lose money marketing your project at a convention just as easily as you can make it.

- Best Situation for Stationary Attendance: If you have the investment to spend, a product to sell, and multiple people who can staff your table, then you can establish your presence and make some money without feeling trapped for the entire weekend.

How Do You Manage Convention Expenses?

Whether you get a table or not, you need to understand how much of your investment you're likely to spend to attend a con. In many cases, you might want to reduce or eliminate certain costs. As we said before, even though you can make money at the con and the costs can be tax-deductible, you still don't want to spend money like Bruce Wayne.

- Building a Convention Spreadsheet: All the costs for attending a con can be listed on a simple spreadsheet. Adding up all the different costs will give you a rough idea of your overall convention costs. Keep in mind that some prices will have a range and not a fixed number based on the city you're going to and the available options. In those cases, it's safer to assume the higher cost and be pleasantly surprised by a lower cost than to hope for a low price and get hit with a higher bill. Also, some costs will cover all the people from your team attending the show. Other costs will be

---

[532] Warren, K. (2018, October 05). A day in the life of a Comic Con Retrieved May 17, 2020, from https://www.businessinsider.com/day-in-the-life-of-a-comic-con-vendor-new-york-photos-2018-10

[533] Topic No. 511 Business Travel Expenses. (n.d.). Retrieved May 17, 2020, from https://www.irs.gov/taxtopics/tc511

[534] Murray, J. (2019, July 31). Deducting Advertising Expenses on Your Business Tax Return. Retrieved May 17, 2020, from https://www.thebalancesmb.com/what-business-advertising-expenses-are-deductible-398945

[535] How Much Did Indie Exhibitor Earn at Comic Cons. (2014)

[536] Wheeler, Z. (2020, May 09). An Author's Guide to Comic Cons. Retrieved May 17, 2020, from http://www.zachrywheeler.com/an-authors-guide-to-comic-cons/

per person in your group. I've created a sample budget on the next page. Feel free to tailor it for your own purposes.

- Convention Item: is the tickets, good or service you need to attend the show
- Cost: is the amount of your investment you are spending
- Payment Due Date: keeps track of payment deadlines and will help you control your cash flow. Plus, you'll know when you'll have cash walking out the door.

Name of Convention:

Convention Location:

Dates of Convention:

Convention Item	Cost	Payment Due Date
Convention Badges (per person, per day)		
Table, Booth or Exhibition Fees		
Transportation to Convention City		
Transportation in Convention City		
Hotel Accommodations		
Printing or Manufacturing Inventory		
Shipping Inventory to Convention		
Shipping Inventory from Convention		
Signage for Table		
Electricity for Table		
Wi-Fi for Table		
Labor Costs		
Meals		
Barcon[537]		
Press Releases		
Taxes		
Merchandise and Research Purchases		
Other Fees		
Total Costs		n/a

---

[537] Barcon will be explained in the Section on convention attendance

- <u>Reducing Attendance Costs</u>: Attending any convention requires money, but there are several ways an independent publisher can reduce costs:

  - <u>Going Mobile</u>: For the reasons we listed above, going to the con and not getting a table eliminates exhibition fees, printing/shipping costs, signage, electricity, Wi-Fi, labor costs, and taxes. There are downsides to not getting a table, but the money saved could be worth it depending on your circumstances.

  - <u>Stay local</u>: If you attend shows close to where you or members of your team live, then you can eliminate the costs of travel to the convention and hotel accommodations and possibly reduce the costs of meals and Barcon because you can take advantage of native knowledge of the local cuisine.

  - <u>Friends and Family</u>: If you attend shows close to where someone close to you lives, you can eliminate the costs of hotel accommodations. Just be sure to not overstay your welcome, because this is essentially a gift investment that we talked about in Chapter 13.

  - <u>Team Participation</u>: If multiple members of the publishing team can attend the con, you can save on labor costs. Whoever is in charge of marketing should attend the shows whenever possible, but it's a good idea to include convention participation as an element of both collaboration and work-for-hire contracts.

  - <u>Convention Partnerships</u>: If you share convention expenses with other comic creators, independent publishers, or local comic shops, you can reduce the costs each partner pays. The concerns here are choosing partners that you're comfortable with and making sure there is a written agreement between each partner covering the financial terms of the partnership. You don't want to work under the assumption that you're going to split the costs for a show and then find out you're getting stuck paying for everything.

How Do You Attend a Convention?

Attending a comic con as an independent publisher can be divided into our basic framework of pre-production, production, and post-production. Different members of your team might be responsible for different elements of this list, because it might be too much for one person to deal with. Let's walk through the steps of getting a table at a con because it's a more involved process. If you decide to go mobile, you'll be able to skip some of the steps.

- **Pre-Production** (Getting Ready for the Con)

  - <u>Registration</u>: Most cons have applications that need to be filled out by a specific date if you want to reserve space at a show. Space is always limited, so the bigger the show, the harder it will be to secure a spot[538]. You need to reserve space at some cons a year or more in advance[539]. If you miss the deadline without getting a spot, some cons have a waitlist[540], but the costs can be higher, and space isn't guaranteed.

As you're filling out the application form, keep in mind that it is essentially a contract between your company and the event organizers. Most of the forms will have terms and conditions limiting the liability of the con if something goes wrong or property is damaged[541]. Take some time to read over those terms and if anything doesn't make sense or seems odd, talk to your attorney before you send in the form and pay your money.

- Travel/ Lodging: Once you know you can get into the show, you need to decide how you're going to get there. Price and availability are based on timing, so again, earlier is often better. Getting to the convention city and finding a place to sleep are the major considerations, but don't forget to make arrangements for travel within the city for you, your team, your booth items, and your inventory. Trying to cram four people, signage, and multiple boxes of books into an Uber the morning of the show isn't a recipe for success.

- Pre-Show Marketing: When you attend a con as an independent publisher, everyone in your target market needs to know about it. It should appear on your website, be a prominent aspect of your social media self-promotion, and appear in your marketing e-mail. If you have relationships with local comic shops, it might make sense to let them know too, especially if they will have a presence there. In many cases, this doesn't have to be done as early as registration, so making the pre-show announcements about a month before the show gives people enough time to find out without giving them too much time to forget.

- Booth Items: Your table is going to be competing with hundreds if not thousands of others for the attention of convention fans. If you're going to catch the eye of your target market, your table has to appeal to their aesthetic. There are basic universal items like a table skirt, pricing signs, and a sign-up sheet for your mailing list[542], but you can also

---

[538] Salkowitz, R. (2012). *Comic-con and the business of pop culture: What the world's wildest trade show can tell us about the future of entertainment*. New York: McGraw-Hill Professional.

[539] Exhibitors. (2019, August 06). Retrieved May 17, 2020, from https://www.comic-con.org/cci/2019/exhibitors

[540] Artist Alley Table Request. (2014, June 17). Retrieved May 17, 2020, from https://www.newyorkcomiccon.com/Industry-Info/Artist-Alley-Table-Request-2020/

[541] *Application for Exhibit Space Comic-Con International 2020* [PDF]. (2019). San Diego: San Diego Comic Con.

[542] Childers, M. (2020, February 18). Convention Tabling - A Beginners Guide. Retrieved May 17, 2020, from http://www.matthewchilders.com/convention-tabling-beginners-guide/

incorporate banners, easels, photo backdrops, and other visual aids depending on the rules of your con. However, you decide to dress up your table, make sure it's mobile, reusable, affordable, and easy to work with[543]. You don't want to buy a new display for every show and you don't want to spend several hours setting up or breaking down your table every day.

Beyond the visual stage, you are creating for your audience, there are also several backstage items you'll find helpful. Pascual Productions has some suggestions every independent publisher should consider including [544]:

- Storage bins
- Battery packs for electronics
- A lockbox or fanny pack for the cash
- Several denominations of currency for those who pay cash (singles, fives, etc.)
- A card reader for people who pay with credit cards
- A wi-fi hotspot just in case the venue's wi-fi isn't reliable
- An extension cord for faraway outlets
- Emergency supplies and first aid kit
- Water
- Snacks
- A hand truck to move everything

- Inventory: If you are going to be selling books or merchandise, you need to get the material made, deliver it to the venue on time in good condition, and be prepared to remove the unsold material from the venue when the show is over. The lead time on the printing will depend on where it's being produced and how many units you're getting made, but keep in mind most of the printers who specialize in comics and graphic novels might be busy before major conventions, so check to make sure they can deliver the product on time.

When trying to determine how many books to bring to the show, remember to keep it small[545]. You want to have enough copies to create an appealing visual display, but don't print too much. It's rare for any publisher to sell out of their entire inventory[546], and there's

---

[543] Blaylock, J. (2006). *How to self-publish comics not just create them*. Chicago: Devil's due.

[544] Pascual, J. (2019, May 29). A Beginner's Guide To Artist Alley: What To Bring. Retrieved May 17, 2020, from https://www.pascualproductions.com/blog/2018/1/24/a-beginners-guide-to-artist-alley-what-to-bring-to-artist-alley

[545] Guide to Comic Cons. Retrieved May 17, 2020, from http://www.zachrywheeler.com/an-authors-guide-to-comic-cons/

[546] Telvin, T. (2019, October 16). Prepping for your first convention – Prints and Banners. Retrieved May 17, 2020, from https://toddtevlin.com/prepping-first-convention-prints-banners/

no point in printing and shipping a bunch of books that you're just going to have to ship back when the show is over. Of course, you can get one set of books printed and then burn through that inventory slowly over the course of several shows, as long as you have a cheap and reliable way to transport them and you plan to exhibit at more than one show.

- Scheduling: If one of your goals is networking with other comic professionals and you know you're going to have some time away from the booth, it makes sense to try and schedule meetings before you get to the show. You can meet with anyone from comic shop owners, creators, distributors, press, printers, and fans depending on your goals and the development stage of your book. This might not be feasible in the early stages of your publishing career if you don't know many people, but as your publishing program grows and you work the con circuit over the years you'll run into the same cast of characters and build relationships with them. It's always fun to bump into an acquaintance on the show floor, but you're probably going to be running somewhere and they're going to invariably be running in a different direction. So, if you need to sit down and discuss business, reach out to them a month or so before the show and carve out some time to get together.

- Set-Up: Most con organizers will give you access to the show floor to set up your table before the show starts, ranging from a couple of hours to a full day. This means planning to get into the city and into the venue early, with all your booth items and inventory ready to go. If you've forgotten anything or something goes wrong, this is the last chance you'll have to fix it before the doors open. If everything goes according to plan, you can enjoy the quiet in preparation for the coming storm, roam the show floor to see what the other exhibitors are showing off, or just read some comics.

- **Production** (Time Management in the Con)

- Booth Time: The time you spend behind your table is critical to your offline marketing because you may never have a better chance at direct interaction with a potential reader. Because most publishers who get a table are selling their book and because marketing and selling have a symbiotic relationship at cons, we'll focus more on the process of selling in Chapter 47, but the fundamental marketing concept is to use your time at the booth to attract and engage your target market.

Valiant editor and Comics Experience instructor Heather Antos has another tip for working your table[547]. When you're not talking to people at your exhibition space, take a moment to

---

[547] Make Comics Podcast Episode #170 - The Pros & Cons of Tabling Versus Walking Around at Cons. (2019, April 23). Retrieved May 17, 2020, from https://www.comicsexperience.com/podcast/170-the-pros-cons-of-tabling-versus-walking-around-at-cons/

watch your neighbors and check out the way they engage with potential readers. Are they using a lot of free giveaways or some other swag to draw people in, or is it something else about their table? How long do they take before they acknowledge each person? Are they introverted or extroverted? Are they making a lot of sales or do most people walk away? Over time, you can learn and adapt the techniques that work and use them in your interactions. Part of attending cons is learning from others, whether you're at your table or attending a panel.

- Panels: a **panel** is a group of people who discuss a topic of interest in front of an audience[548]. At a comic con, panels cover a variety of topics from showing teachers and librarians how to use comics in the classroom, to how-to guides for cosplay, to triple-A video game announcements, to blockbuster movie trailer reveals and cast interviews. As a fan of comics, the options for attending panels can often be overwhelming. As an independent publisher, there are three types of panels that can offer the best use of your time. Check the con schedule before the show and try to pick out panels that fit these categories.

- General publishing-related panels: Cons often have panels for people who are interested in the business side of comics. Topics can range from how to break into comics, the best techniques for crowdfunding, the current status of the direct market, or tips for scripting and layouts. Comics is an industry that is always in transition. This book tries to be comprehensive, but the day it is published, something in the business will change. Attending panels is a good way to stay on top of those developments. That's why I make time to attend and speak in panels at most cons I visit[549].

- Genre related panels: If you're going to compete in a specific market, then it will help you to stay on top of the new releases and developments in your genre. If there is a panel related to a comic, game, movie, or television show that appeals to your target market, it should be on your radar.

- Competitor panels: Based on your competition analysis, you know which books have market share within your target market. With a little digging, you can find out who works on each book from both a business and creative standpoint. If any of them are speaking in panels at the show you're attending, it might make sense to be in the room when the announcement is made. This isn't a nefarious attempt to spy on your rivals. It is an example of **competitive intelligence**, or the collection and analysis of information for the purpose of creating more

---

[548] Panel. (n.d.). Retrieved May 17, 2020, from https://www.merriam-webster.com/dictionary/panel

[549] Hennessy, G. (2019, June 26). Comic Book Attorney and Author Gamal Hennessy to Speak At Four Upcoming Industry Events. Retrieved May 17, 2020, from https://www.creativecontractconsulting.com/c3blog/2019/6/25/comic-book-attorney-and-author-gamal-hennessy-to-speak-at-four-upcoming-industry-events

effective business strategies[550]. If your competitor is planning something that could impact your SWOT analysis or your publishing plans, the sooner you know about it, the better off you'll be.

- Meetings: Comics are often planned, created, and published in isolation. Creative teams working together for years might never meet in person[551]. Business associates scattered across the country might only be an email address or a website in your mind. But face-to-face meetings provide benefits that can't be replicated over email or social media[552]. Cons give you the chance to sit down and meet with the people who are important to your business. Many conventions also have an Artist's Alley where you can roam around and find potential business or creative partners. So, whenever possible, make time to sit down with members of your team, competitors, comic shop owners, the press, printers, and fans to establish those stronger relationships. Because there is so much else going on, you might not always have time to meet during the convention day. Fortunately, business-related meetings also occur after hours at many cons in a semi-formal ritual known as Bar Con.

  - **Bar Con** is the unofficial collective term for the dinners, drinking, parties, and other events that take place after the convention day ends[553]. Bar Con could range from an official event organized by a distributor or publisher, to an informal gathering of friends, or something in between. The importance of Bar Con for an independent publisher is the opportunity to relax and make connections with your peers. The industry is small. The process is isolated. Many professionals, myself included, have been able to connect with colleagues, form friendships, and survive the insanity of the business partially because of Bar Con. If you have the energy, it often pays to make this a part of your agenda.

    As an independent publisher, there are four things to keep in mind when it comes to Bar Con.

    1. Make sure you count your money and secure your inventory before you go out, because you might not have the energy or the intellectual capacity to deal with it later[554].

---

[550] Bloomenthal, A. (2020, February 03). Competitive Intelligence: Eyeing Your Business Rivals. Retrieved May 17, 2020, from https://www.investopedia.com/terms/c/competitive-intelligence.asp

[551] Nicholson, H., Ali, N., & Coover, C. (2019). *Pros and comic cons*. Milwaukie, OR: Dark Horse Books. p. 101

[552] Sellouk, M. (2019, April 26). Why You Should Be Having Face-to-Face Meetings. Retrieved May 17, 2020, from https://www.business.com/articles/benefits-of-in-person-meetings/

[553] Nicholson, H., Ali, N., & Coover, C. (2019). *Pros and comic cons*. p. 103

[554] Blaylock, J. (2006). *How to self-publish comics not just create them*. Chicago: Devil's due.

2. Although Bar Con is an informal celebration, remember this is still a professional setting. Any social blunder, criminal act, or personal embarrassment can have negative repercussions on your reputation and your company[555].

3. Whether you consume alcohol or not, remember to pace yourself both in terms of consumption and how late you stay out. If you have to be friendly and engaging at your table at 10:00 am, it might not make sense to get back to your hotel room from the after-party at 7:00 am.

4. There is a lot of potential for new creative ideas, business plans, and other opportunities in the warm camaraderie of Bar Con. In some instances, Bar Con is the only chance you might have to meet a potential partner or make a special deal. Just make sure to follow up on anything you want to pursue after the con is over and always get a contract for whatever multi-million-dollar earth-shattering shared universe handshake you had outside the bar when the sun was coming up.

- **Post-Production** (Follow Up After the Show)

  - Post Show Marketing: After you get yourself and all your inventory back home, sharing your experience with your true fans closes the loop on the marketing aspect of your weekend. You can use your social media network to share pictures from the show floor, blog posts about your experiences or announcements that will appeal to your ideal reader. The idea is to combine your offline and online marketing into a single ongoing conversation between you and the target market.

  - Professional Follow-Up: If you made any industry connections during the show, solidify that link with an email follow-up during the following week. If you made any deals during Bar Con, confirm them as soon as possible and start the process for getting whatever contracts you need to be completed. If you found out any information vital to an aspect of your business, touch base with the member of your team responsible for that and discuss how it might impact your books. If necessary, modify your plans to take advantage of your competitive intelligence.

  - Cost Analysis: Figure out how much you actually spent and compare it to the budget we created earlier in the chapter. Determine if you are over or under your budget and why. Figure out how much money you made from selling your stuff. Make sure you didn't lose any inventory without getting paid for it. Collect all the receipts and records you might need for your deductible expenses and deliver them to your accountant before it slips your mind.

---

[555] Jackson, M. (2020, June 26). Major comics creators pledge to do better amid new allegations of sexual misconduct. Retrieved July 04, 2020, from https://www.syfy.com/syfywire/major-comics-creators-pledge-do-better-allegations-sexual-misconduct

- <u>Lessons Learned</u>: The Prussian general Helmuth von Moltke is famous for the quote "No plan survives contact with reality.[556]" You will probably experience this firsthand when you look back at the time you spent at the con. Things will happen that you didn't anticipate. Opportunities will reveal themselves. You'll be able to modify how you prep, or how you interact with fans, or how you manage time, if you take a breath when it's all over and figure out what worked, what didn't work and what you want to try next time.

- <u>Prep for the Next Show</u>: As an independent publisher with limited time and resources, you can't spend all your free time at cons, no matter how much fun you have or how important it is for your marketing. But you can't do everything in one show, so whether your next con is in a month or a year, it makes sense to start your preparations as early as possible...especially if your next con isn't a comic con at all.

---

[556] Daniel J. Hughes and Harry Bell (1993) *Moltke on the Art of War: Selected Writings*

Comic shops and comic cons have positive marketing potential for independent publishers, but they are still limited when it comes to connecting with the potential market. Both opportunities suffer from **self-selection bias**, meaning that the people you encounter have, for one reason or another, chosen to come to that shop or attend that con[557]. Connecting with a self-selecting group is vital for marketing to your ideal reader, but if you want to expand your reach to more members of the potential market, you have to leave the safety of comic venues and reach into the wider world.

If you have any success in the other aspects of your marketing, you won't have to do this alone. **Word of mouth** is an oral or written recommendation by a satisfied customer to other potential readers[558]. When you connect with and inspire true fans, especially in comics, they become some of your most active spokespeople, online or offline. When they share your posts, write reviews for your book, or otherwise broadcast their enthusiasm for your story, it creates a form of social proof that you can't create on your own[559]. Who do you think potential readers are more likely to believe more when they hear about your book, the people they know and trust[560], or the person with a financial interest in the book (i.e. you)?

The problem with word-of-mouth marketing and social proof is that they can't be directly controlled unless you're Killgrave. While you can't make people run out into the streets singing your praises, you can facilitate the process. Social media marketers have boiled down the process into something called the **Three E's**[561], but independent publishers can use the process both online and offline. Many aspects of this process are by-products of your main marketing efforts, but this describes the ripple effect that work can have.

- Engage: means interacting with your true fans on a consistent basis to generate the positive connection they want to share.

- Equip: means giving them reasons to talk about you, whether it's your story, your events, or the information you provide about the genre.

---

[557] Self-select. (n.d.). Retrieved May 19, 2020, from https://www.merriam-webster.com/dictionary/self-select

[558] What is word of mouth marketing? definition and meaning. (n.d.). Retrieved May 19, 2020, from http://www.businessdictionary.com/definition/word-of-mouth-marketing.html

[559] Cole, S. (2014, May 05). How To Use the Psychology Of Social Proof To Your Advantage. Retrieved May 19, 2020, from https://www.fastcompany.com/3030044/how-to-use-the-psychology-of-social-proof-to-your-advantage

[560] Leadem, R. (2018, September 15). Why Word-of-Mouth Marketing Matters (Infographic). Retrieved May 19, 2020, from https://www.entrepreneur.com/article/320097

[561] Whitler, K. (2019, September 09). Why Word Of Mouth Marketing Is The Most Important Social Media. Retrieved May 19, 2020, from https://www.forbes.com/sites/kimberlywhitler/2014/07/17/why-word-of-mouth-marketing-is-the-most-important-social-media/

- Empower: means giving them the ability to share how they feel about your story. This can be something as simple as making the posts on your site shareable to having cool t-shirts your fans can wear to spark conversations.

I would add a fourth element to this process in the form of **exposure**. If you only go where comic book fans go, you can only reach comic book fans. But if you expose your message to the potential market, you can reach those people who might enjoy your message but be unfamiliar with your medium.

This means attending conventions not directly related to comics, as I mentioned before. But it also means attending events that aren't specifically book or entertainment related. I've seen Afrofuturism comics sold at music festivals like Afropunk, so if your book is set in a martial arts tournament, why not try to sell it at a real martial arts tournament? If your book goes in-depth on military hardware, what's stopping you from tabling at a gun show? If your story is rooted in Irish mythology, why not do something related to St. Patrick's Day? If your main character is a hacker, why not attend the hacker Meetups? If your story is similar to the latest movie or video game release, why not use that synergy to raise the profile of your project[562]?

Remember, if you are marketing at these events, the goal is connecting with the potential market, not selling stuff to them. It might make sense to connect with the organizers of the event and give them some free books. You could have flyers and maybe even some books to raffle off to attendees. Whatever you can do to bridge the gap between their interest and your book should be considered, as long as it fits within your marketing budget. You won't be able to hit every meeting related to your book and you may only win over a few people with this effort, but every new true fan can become an influencer for your book.

Influencers are people who have the power to affect purchase decisions because of some elevated standing they have within a niche group[563]. They can impact word-of-mouth marketing on a higher level of magnitude because they can leverage their pre-existing audiences to help you find true fans. There are influencers for every type of interest from Acid House to zombies[564] and the number of people they can affect can range from a few hundred to several million[565]. Where a true fan can share your book with their social circle, an influencer has the potential, in theory, to turn your book into a best seller.

---

[562] Harper, M. (2020, March 30). Pop into our Pop Up Comic Shop: National News. Retrieved May 19, 2020, from https://drafthouse.com/news/pop-into-our-pop-up-comic-shop

[563] What are influencers? definition and meaning. (n.d.). Retrieved May 19, 2020, from http://www.businessdictionary.com/definition/influencers.html

[564] Influence.co. (n.d.). Empowering the influence generation. Retrieved May 19, 2020, from https://influence.co/category/a

[565] Roose, K. (2019, July 16). Don't Scoff at Influencers. They're Taking Over the World. Retrieved May 19, 2020, from https://www.nytimes.com/2019/07/16/technology/vidcon-social-media-influencers.html

Influencer marketing isn't as organic as other forms of social proof, but you still need to build a relationship with a person before you can expect them to share your story with their followers[566].

- Find one who fits your potential reader and follow them to see if they're message matches with the feeling you want to generate with your reader.

- Try to interact with them on their platform of choice, both to connect with them and to increase your exposure.

- When you find a potential fit, only then should you reach out to them and discuss a deal including compensation and creative control.

- Decide when the best time to launch your influencer campaign, based on the release schedule of your book.

- Finally, because this is an activity governed by the Federal Trade Commission, be sure to conform to all the relevant rules about social media influence[567] and consult with your attorney if you have questions.

Like other forms of marketing, influence marketing isn't a Mother Box. There is no guarantee that the campaign will work and even in the best-case scenario, you might only attract less than one percent of the influencer's followers to take an interest in your story.

There are no guarantees in any aspect of independent comic book marketing. There are no quick, straightforward solutions. Like any relationship, marketing connections can fail, end abruptly or last for dozens of years. But the reward is worth the risk if you want your book to succeed. The right number of true fans eager to read your book will make all the effort worthwhile, as long as you figure out the right way to get your story into their hungry little hands.

You found the ideal reader for your comic. You understand what they're looking for and how to get their attention. The next step in Greene's formula is offering your true fans what they want. In the next section, we'll explore the different options for distribution so you can deliver the right type of book to the right type of reader when they are ready to explore your story.

---

[566] Newberry, C. (2020, March 05). Influencer Marketing in 2019: How to Work With Social Media Influencers. Retrieved May 19, 2020, from https://blog.hootsuite.com/influencer-marketing/

[567] The FTC's Endorsement Guides: What People Are Asking. (2019, May 15). Retrieved May 19, 2020, from https://www.ftc.gov/tips-advice/business-center/guidance/ftcs-endorsement-guides-what-people-are-asking

STAGE 1: PRE-PRODUCTION

PART 7: DISTRIBUTION

Or How Will Readers Get Your Comic?

I know you're probably itching to start creating your comic, but there is one more aspect of the pre-production process we need to cover before you make magic. Most of the fundamental building blocks are in place now because you have:

1.   Determined your goals for making comics
2.   Found an idea that you love and own
3.   Conceived how to pay for the comic before it's created
4.   Formulated a plan to turn your idea into a comic
5.   Created a legal structure to protect both your idea and your investment
6.   Built a team to turn your vision into reality
7.   Connected with a target market eager to explore your story

The final step in the pre-production process involves understanding how you can deliver your story to your target market.

Distribution is the movement of goods from their source to the final consumer, and the reciprocal movement of payment from the consumer to the source of the goods[568]. As an independent publisher, this means finding ways to get the pages of your comic in front of readers in a way that generates revenue. We're going to devote an entire segment of this book to collecting money (See Section 11). This section will focus on the various distribution channels available to you today and in the near future.

A **distribution channel** is the journey your comic makes to get from you to the reader[569]. The path of your book may be direct (a one-step transaction between you and the reader on your website) or it can include printers, distributors, retailers, and other intermediaries. As we explore the different channels, keep in mind that **wider distribution systems can give you more reach in the market, but they often have more requirements and can be more expensive,** as each intermediary takes a cut of the revenue.

Selecting the right distribution channels for your book will depend on four main factors:

1.   <u>Your available investment</u>: Different distribution channels require different levels of upfront investment, so your selection may be limited by the money you have to spend.

---

[568] What is distribution? definition and meaning. (n.d.). Retrieved May 19, 2020, from http://www.businessdictionary.com/definition/distribution.html

[569] Kenton, W. (2020, February 19). How Distribution Channels Work. Retrieved May 19, 2020, from https://www.investopedia.com/terms/d/distribution-channel.asp

2. <u>Your target market</u>: Different ideal readers frequent different retail locations, so your book needs to be available where they like to shop.

3. <u>Your resources</u>: Different types of distribution create different constraints of time and expertise, so you have to match your output with what your team can realistically accomplish.

4. <u>Your story</u>: Some content is not acceptable or suitable for some distribution channels, so you have to release your book in a manner that considers those sensitivities.

Ultimately, the combination of distribution channels you select has to be tailored for your book. As publisher Hope Nicholson has said. "There is no one path, there are a billion different paths and you have to figure out what's best for your product.[570]." The goal is to figure out which of the major channels fits the unique elements of your book.

What Are the Major Distribution Channels for Independent Comics?

According to ICV2 and Comichron, the comic book market has six major distribution channels[571] which accounted for an estimated $1.1 to 1.34 billion dollars in sales in 2018:

1.	The direct market (mainly comic shops):	$510 million
2.	The book trade: (bookstores and libraries):	$465 million
3.	Subscriptions (Digital subscriptions)	$245 million[572]
4.	Digital sales: (Websites and apps)	$100 million
5.	Newsstand sales (mostly retail outlets)	$ 10 million
6.	Crowdfunding (Kickstarter and others)	$ 10 million[573]

Distribution numbers by format also indicate where the money is being spent in comics[574]:

---

[570] Kazden, N., & Destito, D. (2019, August 16). SDCC '19: "The Business of Comics" in an ever-changing landscape. Retrieved May 19, 2020, from https://www.comicsbeat.com/sdcc-19-business-of-comics-panel/

[571] Comics and graphic novel sales hit new high in 2018. (n.d.). Retrieved May 19, 2020, from https://www.comichron.com/yearlycomicssales/industrywide/2018-industrywide.html

[572] Unlimited online subscription services don't provide hard numbers, but estimates suggest 3.5 million subscribers who pay approximately $70 per year or $245 million dollars Clark, T. (2018, November 09). Amazon's Comixology has provoked a fierce debate in the comic-book world, but creators say it could help revitalize the industry. Retrieved May 19, 2020, from https://www.businessinsider.com/amazons-comixology-could-revitalize-comic-books-creators-say-2018-11

[573] Other sources state crowdfunding has generated more than $16 million in funding, so this number isn't exact. Arrant, C. (2019). Kickstarter Boasts $16m Comics Funding in 2018, Wants More Marginalized Creators. Retrieved May 19, 2020, from https://www.newsarama.com/43590-kickstarter-boasts-16m-in-comics-funding-in-2018.html

[574] Comics and graphic novel sales hit new high in 2018. (n.d.). Retrieved May 19, 2020, from https://www.comichron.com/yearlycomicssales/industrywide/2018-industrywide.html

1. Graphic Novels (including trade paperbacks) $635 million
2. Single Issues $300 million
3. Digital Comics $100 million

As we will see in the following chapters, these numbers are not hard and fast and subject to interpretation[575]. Keep this in mind as we go into detail on each of the major online and offline distribution channels as well as the emerging alternatives.

---

[575] FAQ: Monthly Comic Shop Market Distributor Sales Charts. (n.d.). Retrieved May 19, 2020, from https://www.comichron.com/faq/directmarketsalesdata.html

A **webcomic** is a comic published exclusively on an internet page or app[576]. They are slightly different from digital comics which are traditional print comics formatted for digital distribution. They began in the 1990s when creators began to use the internet as a way to circumvent the gatekeepers of newspaper syndication[577]. Webcomics can be one panel or several comic pages long. They can be distributed on your website, email blasts, or visual-based social media sites like Instagram and Tumblr, but as we discussed earlier independent publishers should avoid digital sharecropping whenever possible.

What Are the Benefits of Webcomics Distribution?

The four benefits of webcomics come from the open nature of the digital medium.

1. The startup and maintenance costs of webcomics tend to be lower than other forms of print distribution.

2. Webcomics allow for more diverse formats and genres than other forms of comics, because in many cases there are no gatekeepers or censors to limit the content or style of the work[578].

3. Webcomics can theoretically be available forever, as long as the server containing information is operational and the website where the webcomic lives can be accessed.

4. Webcomics have viral potential because they can be instantly shared across a variety of social media systems.

What are the Downsides of Webcomics Distribution?

Some of the upsides of webcomic distribution create challenges for the independent publisher. Because it is relatively easy to publish webcomics compared to other forms of distribution, there can be a lot of competition in your niche. Because revenue streams in webcomics tend to be indirect and/or

---

[576] Webcomic. (n.d.). Retrieved May 19, 2020, from https://www.dictionary.com/browse/webcomic

[577] Ferguson, C. (2019, April 05). Webcomics: An oral history. Retrieved May 19, 2020, from https://www.theverge.com/2019/4/5/18295369/webcomics-xkcd-questionable-content-dinosaur-comics-90s-internet-social-media

[578] Dorchak, S. (2011). Pioneering the Page, The Gauntlet. Retrieved May 19, 2020, from http://www.archive.thegauntlet.ca/story/pioneering-page?qt-latest_and_most_popular=0

microtransactions[579], it may take 5-10 years of consistent publication for the webcomic to be profitable, and those profits may never rise to a level where you can give up your secret identity[580].

How Can You Generate Revenue with Webcomics?

Many webcomics generate revenue from multiple direct and indirect sources[581]. Direct revenue comes from selling goods directly related to your comic. This could be selling the comic itself as a Patreon subscription or selling merchandise related to the comic. **Indirect revenue** is income that isn't directly related to your comic[582]. This could be advertising revenue you collect when readers visit your page or commissions you get from readers who want personalized images of your characters. Diverse sources of revenue can offset the small amount of money coming from any one source.

Webcomics can also generate income over the long term as a stepping stone into other forms of distribution. In some cases, the webcomic can be used as a form of marketing to build a group of true fans. Successful books like *Cyanide and Happiness* and *Smile* began as webcomics before branching out into print and merchandise[583], but veteran webcomics publishers suggest finding your 10,000 fans before you risk diving into more expensive distribution models[584].

How Can You Submit Your Webcomics to Established Syndicates?

A **webcomics syndicate** is a company that aggregates webcomics on a single website or app and distributes revenue to comic publishers based on traffic, ads, or other criteria[585]. Some of these companies are digital versions of the newspaper syndicates that webcomics publishers first tried to avoid. Others are

---

[579] Colagrossi, M. (2020, March 24). How Microtransactions Impact the Economics of Gaming. Retrieved May 19, 2020, from https://www.investopedia.com/articles/investing/022216/how-microtransactions-are-evolving-economics-gaming.asp

[580] Davis, L. (2015, December 15). The Biggest Mistakes People Make When They Start A Webcomic. Retrieved May 19, 2020, from https://io9.gizmodo.com/the-biggest-mistakes-people-make-when-they-start-a-webc-1614779817

[581] Dale, B. (2015, November 16). The Webcomics Business Is Moving on From Webcomics. Retrieved May 19, 2020, from https://observer.com/2015/11/webcomics-changing-business-model/

[582] Kennan, M. (2016, October 26). Indirect Revenue Definition. Retrieved May 19, 2020, from https://smallbusiness.chron.com/indirect-revenue-definition-65745.html

[583] Rudulph, H. (2019, October 24). Get That Life: How I Became a Best-Selling Graphic Novelist. Retrieved May 19, 2020, from https://www.cosmopolitan.com/career/a63918/raina-telgemeier-graphic-novelist-get-that-life/

[584] Davis, L. (2015, December 15). The Biggest Mistakes People Make When They Start A Webcomic. Retrieved May 19, 2020, from https://io9.gizmodo.com/the-biggest-mistakes-people-make-when-they-start-a-webc-1614779817

[585] List of comic strip syndicates. (2020, March 07). Retrieved May 19, 2020, from https://en.wikipedia.org/wiki/List_of_comic_strip_syndicates

new companies that focus only on digital. In theory, syndication can give your comic wider reach and increased revenue[586], but it won't be a substitute for marketing on your part.

Each of these companies has their guidelines for submissions, including Andrews McMeel[587], King Features[588] and Webtoons[589]. Because the individual players in this industry will change, consolidate, and shift, it doesn't make sense to try and provide comprehensive submission advice here. There are a few general concepts to keep in mind if you want to consider syndication.

- <u>Understand the legal terms</u>: Every relationship between your company and the syndicate will be governed by the terms of a contract. It will be up to you to understand the terms of that contract and how it affects the intellectual property in your comic. Before you agree to any syndication, review that agreement and go over it with your attorney if any aspect of it is unclear to you.

- <u>Understand the payments</u>: Syndication is helpful because it can produce revenue for your company. But if you don't understand how the syndicate makes money and more importantly, how you make money from the syndicate, it might not make sense to post your comics there. Again, your attorney and your accountant can be useful resources if you don't understand the business terms.

- <u>Avoid digital sharecropping</u>: It may be faster and easier to post your work in a syndicate rather than maintaining your own website, but this isn't a wise long-term move. Syndicates can go out of business, change their terms, or otherwise become unavailable to you and your readers. It might be a hassle to redirect your true fans to your website if the syndicate goes down. It will be more painful if the syndicate is your only distribution channel and it suddenly vanishes.

---

[586] Reid, C. (2019). Webtoon Builds an Audience for Webcomics. Retrieved May 19, 2020, from https://www.publishersweekly.com/pw/by-topic/industry-news/comics/article/81073-webtoon-builds-an-audience-for-webcomics.html

[587] Submitting Features to Andrews McMeel Syndication. (n.d.). Retrieved May 19, 2020, from http://syndication.andrewsmcmeel.com/help/faq-submissions

[588] Submission Guidelines. (2019, March 27). Retrieved May 19, 2020, from http://kingfeatures.com/contact-us/submission-guidelines/

[589] Webtoons: Resources for Creators. (n.d.). Retrieved May 19, 2020, from https://www.webtoons.com/en/creator101/wanted

What Are the Best Practices for Webcomics Distribution?

If you decide to pursue webcomics distribution, the Kone Foundation in Finland published a guide called *Making Money from Webcomics*[590]. While it's helpful to read in its entirety, it can be boiled down into a few helpful tips:

- Give your webcomic time to find a market. Overnight success is almost non-existent, so don't expect a quick return on your investment.

- Make sure you and your team have the time and the stamina to publish over the long-term. Because it takes time for a market to grow, you need to know the people working on your comic can commit to the process and balance their secret identities.

- Publish on a consistent schedule. Whether you publish daily, weekly, or monthly, establish a pattern your readers can expect to rely on. Erratic publication is a good way to lose readers.

- Create a substantial amount of inventory before you begin publishing. If you produce 2-6 months of content before you begin publishing, you can maintain a consistent publishing schedule without stress on you and your team, avoiding any disruptions to your publishing schedule.

Webcomics may not be the most profitable form of distribution, but it does offer a relatively low risk, low-cost method of delivering content to your market. As an independent publisher, consider webcomics before you explore digital alternatives like Comixology and other apps.

---

[590] H-P Lehkonen (2019, January 18). Making Money from Webcomics – An Illustrated Guide. Retrieved May 19, 2020, from http://www.creatorresource.com/making-money-from-webcomics-an-illustrated-guide/

As we discussed earlier, **Comixology** is a digital comic book distribution app owned by Amazon[591] that sells individual comics, graphic novels, and subscription services. It started in 2007 as an alternative to webcomics and PDF delivery[592]. Today, **Comixology is one of the major digital distribution platforms** for comics, with more than seven million people downloading the app between 2014 and 2018[593]. While it is **not the only app available to independent publishers,** this chapter will focus on Comixology as the primary alternative for digital distribution.

What Are the Benefits of Comixology Distribution?

Independent publishers can benefit from distribution on an app like Comixology because the system is designed to be streamlined for both the publisher and the reader.

The reader who decides to read comics on an app has instant access to their entire digital library of comics on any device wherever they are. They do not have to dedicate space in their home to store comics or drag their books along with them when they're away. If they are collectors, they don't have to risk damaging the precious physical copy to read the contents of the book. New readers unfamiliar with the conventions of reading a comic book page can take advantage of Comixology's Guided View technology that divides each page into the proper reading sequence[594]. Finally, free introductory books and monthly sales provide a financial incentive for readers to try new titles[595].

The publisher who decides to distribute comics on an app gains access to a platform that many core readers trust and already use[596]. Space on the digital shelf is infinite compared to a physical comic shop, so if you get accepted, you'll still be able to sell your books no matter how many titles the Big Two release. Apps can be used as a gateway method to attract new readers who might be unwilling or unable to find a local comic shop because phones and computers are universally available among many target market groups. The

---

[591] Digital Comics - Comics by comiXology. (n.d.). Retrieved May 19, 2020, from https://www.comixology.com/

[592] Comixology Press Release (2013, March 06). ComiXology Launches "ComiXology Submit" Self-Publishing Platform. Retrieved May 19, 2020, from https://www.cbr.com/comixology-launches-comixology-submit-self-publishing-platform/

[593] Clark, T. (2018, November 09). Amazon's Comixology has provoked a fierce debate in the comic-book world, but creators say it could help revitalize the industry. Retrieved May 19, 2020, from https://www.businessinsider.com/amazons-comixology-could-revitalize-comic-books-creators-say-2018-11

[594] Comixology Press Release (2013, March 06).

[595] Allen, T., & Destito, D. (2018, April 12). Comixology Drops Marvel 99¢ Sale, But Amazon Keeps It – Split Decision? Retrieved May 19, 2020, from https://www.comicsbeat.com/comixology-drops-marvel-99%C2%A2-sale-but-amazon-keeps-it-split-decision/

[596] Clark, T. (2018, November 09)

submission process is open to everyone[597], there is no cost to submit[598], and the potential revenue generated for each comic sold is competitive compared to other distribution models[599]

What Are the Downsides of Comixology?

Independent publishers may hesitate to distribute through Comixology for both practical and philosophical reasons.

- **Practical Issues**

    - The fact that Comixology has the right to approve your submission makes them a gatekeeper that can restrict the type of content you can sell through them based on unspecified criteria[600].

    - The submission process itself can take several months[601], making it difficult to predict when you can announce the digital release to your target market or coordinate your digital release with your print release or convention schedule.

    - Approval can be difficult to obtain both for technical and content-related reasons[602]

- **Philosophical Issues**

    - Because Comixology is a cloud-based system, your readers are paying to access your comic, not to own it[603]. If and when they delete or lose their Comixology account, they lose

---

[597] McCracken, H. (2014, March 14). Submit: ComiXology Helps Independent Comics Publishers Go Digital. Retrieved May 19, 2020, from https://time.com/25373/comixology-is-helping-indie-comics-publishers-go-digital/

[598] What is required for a submission to comiXology Submit? Retrieved May 19, 2020, from https://support.comixology.com/hc/en-us/articles/360042720894-What-is-required-for-a-submission-to-comiXology-Submit-

[599] What percentage of the sales will I earn? Retrieved May 19, 2020, from https://support.comixology.com/hc/en-us/articles/360043193693-What-percentage-of-the-sales-will-I-earn-

[600] How did you determine what kinds of content to put in the age rating levels? Retrieved May 19, 2020, from https://support.comixology.com/hc/en-us/articles/360043193593-How-did-you-determine-what-kinds-of-content-to-put-in-the-age-rating-levels-

[601] How quickly will I be notified if my comic is accepted? Retrieved May 19, 2020, from https://support.comixology.com/hc/en-us/articles/360042722254-How-quickly-will-I-be-notified-if-my-comic-is-accepted-

[602] White Fire Comics, & Admin. (2019, April 13). My Experience with publishing digital comics... so far... Part 1: Comixology. Retrieved May 19, 2020, from http://whitefirecomics.com/wordpress/2019/04/12/my-experience-with-digital-comics-part-1-comixology/

[603] Polo, S. (2018, December 26). The best ways to buy and read digital comics right now. Retrieved May 19, 2020, from https://www.polygon.com/comics/2018/12/26/18104852/where-to-buy-read-download-digital-comics-apps-subscription-services

access to their comics. This situation can be avoided with the DRM free backup option[604], but this isn't universal.

- Amazon as a company has a negative reputation for employee abuse[605], tax avoidance[606], residential gentrification[607], dangerous delivery conditions[608] , and other social and economic issues. While none of these situations is directly related to comic distribution, some companies may be more sensitive to this than others[609].

- Amazon also has a history of reducing or eliminating competition in different markets[610], and there were concerns that their acquisition of Comixology could create a bottleneck in distribution similar to what recently existed in the direct market with Diamond[611], creating a monopoly that limits distribution options in the long term. There are still alternatives to Comixology, but their size and market share could force other companies to shut down.

---

[604] DRM-Free Backups Now Available on Comixology. (n.d.). Retrieved May 19, 2020, from https://www.comixology.com/drm-free-backup

[605] Ghosh, S. (2018, May 05). Peeing in trash cans, constant surveillance, and asthma attacks on the job: Amazon workers tell us their warehouse horror stories. Retrieved May 19, 2020, from https://www.businessinsider.com/amazon-warehouse-workers-share-their-horror-stories-2018-4

[606] Isidore, C. (2019, February 15). Despite record profits, Amazon didn't pay any federal income tax in 2017 or 2018. Here's why. Retrieved May 19, 2020, from https://www.cnn.com/2019/02/15/tech/amazon-federal-income-tax/index.html

[607] Goodman, J. (2019, February 14). Amazon Pulls Out of Planned New York City Headquarters. Retrieved May 19, 2020, from https://www.nytimes.com/2019/02/14/nyregion/amazon-hq2-queens.html

[608] Callahan, P. (2019, September 05). Amazon Pushes Fast Shipping but Avoids Responsibility for the Human Cost. Retrieved May 19, 2020, from https://www.nytimes.com/2019/09/05/us/amazon-delivery-drivers-accidents.html

[609] MacDonald, H. (2019, September 09). Indie creators call on comics festivals to cut ties with Amazon sponsorships. Retrieved May 19, 2020, from https://www.comicsbeat.com/cartoonists-against-amazon-release-statement/

[610] González, Á. (2017, August 09). How big is too big? Amazon sparks antitrust concerns. Retrieved May 19, 2020, from https://www.seattletimes.com/business/amazon/how-big-is-too-big-amazon-sparks-antitrust-concerns/

[611] Allen, T. W., & Waid, M. (2014). *Economics of digital comics*. United States of America pages 35 and 132.

What Are the Alternatives to Comixology?

Independent publishers should consider all the available digital options for their comics regardless of their position on Comixology since Amazon doesn't require exclusive distribution rights[612] and digital sharecropping applies to digital distribution just as much as it does to online marketing.

There are several major digital comic distributors in 2019[613]. While they might not have the popularity or reach of Comixology, if you are driving your target market to the distribution channel then you don't need to rely on a large undefined reader base to stumble onto your book. Each app will have their own submission guidelines, revenue models, and contractual terms that you need to explore and possibly discuss with your accountant and attorney.

- Global Comix[614]
- Google Play Books[615]
- Hoopla[616]
- Humble Bundle[617]
- iBooks[618]
- Kobo[619]
- SmashWords[620]

---

[612] Can I sell my comic elsewhere? (n.d.). Retrieved May 19, 2020, from https://support.comixology.com/hc/en-us/articles/360043193913-Can-I-sell-my-comic-elsewhere-

[613] Lindley, N. (n.d.). Nate Lindley, Making Indie Comics Tips: The Adventures of Self-Publishing. Retrieved May 19, 2020, from https://www.ashcancomicspub.com/nate-lindley-making-indie-comic-books-tips-self-publishing.html

[614] Professional Comics Publishing with Global Comix. Retrieved May 19, 2020, from https://globalcomix.com/

[615] Books on Google Play. (n.d.). Retrieved May 19, 2020, from https://play.google.com/store/books

[616] Hoopla Publishers. (n.d.). Retrieved May 19, 2020, from http://hub.hoopladigital.com/publishers

[617] Humble Bundle. (n.d.). Retrieved May 19, 2020, from https://www.humblebundle.com/

[618] IBooks Author. (n.d.). Retrieved May 19, 2020, from https://www.apple.com/ibooks-author/

[619] Kobo Graphic Novels. (n.d.). Retrieved May 19, 2020, from https://www.kobo.com/us/en/ebooks/comics-graphic-novels

[620] How to Publish and Distribute Ebooks with Smashwords. (n.d.). Retrieved May 19, 2020, from https://www.smashwords.com/about/how_to_publish_on_smashwords

How Do You Generate Revenue with Comixology?

Independent publishers make money from Comixology and similar apps through direct revenue. As of 2019, you will get 50% of the gross sales for every copy of a book that a reader pays for, minus mobile distributor fees and credit card fees[621]. Payments are made 45 days after the end of each quarter[622].

How Do You Submit to Comixology?

Submission guidelines for your cover art, comic, company logo, and team photos can all be submitted to Comixology online via their website[623].

Comixology and other related apps are the standard for digital distribution, but they are not the Final Frontier. New technologies are constantly being developed and repurposed for the comics industry. Independent publishers can and should take advantage of emerging distribution formats if they can help reach their target market.

---

[621] What percentage of the sales will I earn?. (n.d.). Retrieved May 19, 2020, from https://support.comixology.com/hc/en-us/articles/360043193693-What-percentage-of-the-sales-will-I-earn-

[622] How will I get paid and how often? (n.d.). Retrieved May 19, 2020, from https://support.comixology.com/hc/en-us/articles/360042721674-How-will-I-get-paid-and-how-often-

[623] What is required for a submission to comiXology Submit? (n.d.). Retrieved May 19, 2020, from https://support.comixology.com/hc/en-us/articles/360042720894-What-is-required-for-a-submission-to-comiXology-Submit

One of the many unique qualities of comics is their ability to adapt to a different technology. Since the first comics featured Superman and Batman in the 1930s, comic stories have found their way into radio, television, video games, and digital apps in a process referred to as **concomitant culture**[624]. The only limits to the ways narrative content can be delivered to the market are cost and ease of use. As an independent publisher, your comic doesn't have to be limited to the current distribution channels, but you need to consider your options before you waste valuable resources chasing every distribution trend.

What are the Benefits of Emerging Distribution Channels?

A new system for delivering your book to your market can disrupt current industry standards and alter the relationship between you, your competition, existing distributors, and readers. If you can get your books into a new publishing platform, some of the potential advantages include:

- Avoiding competition who are only using present distribution methods
- Avoiding gatekeepers who can block you from accessing certain markets
- Capturing early adopters who enjoy new technology as much as they enjoy new content[625]
- A greater chance for casual viewing based on low content volume, especially when the new service is in its infancy
- Increased marketing potential because you're connected to the "next new thing"

What are the Downsides to Emerging Distribution?

Pursuing any new course of action involves a certain degree of risk. Humans are creatures of habit[626], and your target market is no different. Publishing an independent comic based on a new or unproven IP is an uncertain proposition. **Using a new or unproven distribution method increases the challenge** when you consider the following factors:

- Acquisition: New distribution companies are often startups looking to raise cash or be acquired by a larger company, so your new distributor could change hands or disappear at any time the way it did with Comixology or Comic Blitz[627].

---

[624] Lopes, *Demanding Respect*

[625] Godin, *This is Marketing*

[626] Greene: *The Laws of Human Nature*

[627] McMillan, G. (2020, May 19). Digital Comics Platform ComicBlitz Acquired by Cinedigm. Retrieved May 19, 2020, from https://www.hollywoodreporter.com/heat-vision/comicblitz-acquired-by-cinedigm-1164495

- Cost: There may be a higher cost to consumers if they have to purchase a new device or application to read your comic.

- Functionality: The new service might not work on a technical level or gain traction with consumers

- Impact: A shiny new distribution model can't replace the development of a target market based on ideal readers.

- Revenue: The pricing model might be undefined or not designed to reward publishers for their content[628].

What are the Different Types of Emerging Channels?

New methods and variations of print and digital distribution are constantly being developed. **The channels I list in this book today can easily be old by the time you read this**, and other more radical concepts might still be a dream in the mind of some entrepreneur. These companies have tried to shake up the system over the past few years. Use them as a starting point for your exploration.

- Eefio is trying to recreate the Netflix DVD, Rent-the-Runway type of home delivery rental model for comics[629].

- eOneBook is a Japanese variant digital comics reader that captures the feel of holding paper while offering the convenience of digital storage[630].

- Motion Books is an app that displays artwork in 3D for a more immersive experience[631]

- Virtual Reality Comics like Project Hikari, Magnetique VR, and Mixed reality comics each try to create first-person 360-degree comic art that can be used with devices like Oculus[632]

---

[628] Terror, J. (2019, September 06). Eefio Wants to be the Netflix of Comics... Netflix Circa 2000, That Is. Retrieved May 19, 2020, from https://www.bleedingcool.com/2019/09/06/eefio-wants-to-be-the-netflix-of-comics-netflix-circa-2000-that-is/

[629] Ibid

[630] Press Release. (2017, September 20). E Ink Partners with Progress Technologies to Deliver a New Comic Book Experience. Retrieved May 19, 2020, from https://www.businesswire.com/news/home/20170920005325/en/Ink-Partners-Progress-Technologies-Deliver-New-Comic

[631] Hayden, S. (2019, February 04). Madefire Releases 3D Comics App for Magic Leap One. Retrieved May 19, 2020, from https://www.roadtovr.com/madefire-releases-3d-comics-app-magic-leap-one/

[632] Pitre, V. (2017, December 22). Virtual Reality (VR) is the Next Big Medium for Comic Books. Retrieved May 19, 2020, from http://www.vudream.com/virtual-reality-vr-next-big-medium-comic-books-graphic-novels/

- Visual Novels[633] are interactive narratives using Digital Novel Markup Language (DNML)[634] popular in Japan, that focus primarily on using static images and text to tell a story in a linear fashion on game consoles.

How Should You Choose an Emerging Channel?

There are common questions to answer when you analyze each new distribution model. While you might not find a perfect fit for your independent publishing, some tech will make more sense for you than others.

- Does it appeal to your target market? Why get involved with a new technology if your ideal reader can't or won't embrace the change?

- Is it an exclusive deal? Why tie yourself to an unproven distribution model and limit your options for reaching your market?

- Does it require more work than it's worth? Your team probably has their hands full with doing everything required to get your book out the door and maintaining their secret identities. Can they absorb more work to get on this platform?

- Does it fit with your story? If your IP doesn't benefit from a slick new delivery system, why pull readers out of the story?

- Do you understand the legal relationship? Are you and your attorney certain that you'll retain ownership and control of your IP if you sign onto this system?

- Do you understand the revenue model? Can your potential distribution partner explain how you'll make money?

Emerging media can disrupt the market and give you an edge against your competition, but you can't count on them to replace traditional distribution channels. Even established services like Comixology only represent a fifth of all comic sales in North America. Digital comics might be the wave of the future, but many ideal readers in your target market want the feeling of paper in their hands. To satisfy that desire, you need to consider printing and distributing your book in the real world.

---

[633] Visual novel. (2020, May 16). Retrieved May 19, 2020, from https://en.wikipedia.org/wiki/Visual_novel

[634] Digital Novel Markup Language. (n.d.). Retrieved May 19, 2020, from https://enacademic.com/dic.nsf/enwiki/10982777

I've mentioned comic shops throughout this book, but a book on the business of comics publishing isn't complete without a chapter dedicated to this unique channel of distribution. Independent publishers need to understand the dynamics of the direct market and its impact on the industry, even if they don't dream of seeing their book on the shelf of their local comic shop (LCS).

The **direct market** is the name given to the network of independent retail outlets that specialize in comics and comics-related merchandise[635]. The shops developed in the early 1980s, when a comic collector named Phil Seuling transitioned from organizing comic cons to creating a specific market for comic book collectors to solve the problems of comic book readers during that period[636].

What is the History of the Direct Market?

Before the direct market, newsstands and smoke shops were the primary retail outlet for comics[637]. Magazine distributors handled the comic book business, but it wasn't a priority for them because glossy magazines made more money and had more prestige than the twenty-two-page floppies still suffering under the narrative limitations of the Comics Code Authority. Their second-class status often meant comics arrived at the newsstands late, the inventory was random from one month to the next, the discounts the newsstand received were low compared to the magazines, and the books were returnable to the publishers if they didn't sell.

This state of affairs was detrimental to everyone[638]. The newsstand owners didn't know when the books were coming, or which books they would get, and the cost of carrying the books wasn't as attractive as the latest fashion magazine. The readers couldn't know which comics they could buy from their local newsstand from one month to the next, which forced them to conventions and flea markets to track down their favorite characters in long boxes. The publishers had to expect a significant amount of returns, which limited their overall revenue. Even the writers of comics in that period were limited in the length of stories they could commercially sell, because a multi-issue epic was less viable in this environment. The newsstand distribution model worked for almost 50 years and was influential in the creation of the first comic cons, but **Seuling came up with a model that solved all the negative elements of newsstand comics.**

---

[635] Allen, p. 10

[636] Schelly, W. (2010). *Founders of comic fandom: Profiles of 90 publishers, dealers, collectors, writers, artists and other luminaries of the 1950s and 1960s.* Jefferson, NC: McFarland.

[637] Smith, G. (2018, January 17). Finding Personality in the Ephemeral Comic Shop. Retrieved May 19, 2020, from https://www.popmatters.com/finding-personality-in-the-ephemeral-comic-shop-2519184383.html

[638] Gearino, D., & Spurgeon, T. (2019). *Comic shop: The retail mavericks who gave us a new geek culture.* Athens, OH: Swallow Press, Ohio University Press.

If newsstands were Bruce Banner, the direct market shops were designed to be the Hulk. Instead of being delivered late, comic shops would get books two to three months early. Instead of being forced to sell a random collection of books, comic shop owners had to order exactly the books they wanted to sell or their customers pre-ordered. Instead of a low discount, direct market shops could buy books at up to 60% off the cover price. Finally, the books were non-returnable, giving shops the incentive to build collections of **back issues** (comics released in prior months) that could increase in value as collector's items[639].

Throughout the 1980s and 1990s, several new distributors used Seuling's model to distribute comics[640]. Long time comic book fans and collectors opened up shops all over the country, and at the height of the direct market, there were close to 10,000 comic book shops in the United States[641]. This was also the golden age of the newsstand to the comic shop to convention pipeline for readers who now had several ways to get their old or new comics. Sales began to rise, top-level creators began to gain prominence, and comics were seen as an alternative investment to those more interested in the price of the comics than the story.

The direct market model also created negative unintended consequences. The community of comic shop owners who began as fans and collectors often opened shops that were more private clubhouses than retail outlets[642]. The open universal atmosphere of the newsstand was replaced by a largely white heterosexual male, often alienating setting[643]. The "comic shop guy" became a negative pop culture stereotype[644]. From a financial standpoint, investment speculation created boom and bust cycles[645]. Prices were artificially inflated based on perceived value, only to come crashing down when publishers flooded the market with hundreds of thousands of copies of a "valuable book[646]." LCS that played in this market were often forced to close when they found themselves stuck with hundreds of copies of a non-returnable book

---

[639] Gearino, Comic Shop

[640] Pulfer, R. (2020, April 13). Just What is the Direct Market in Comics and Where Did It Come From? Retrieved May 19, 2020, from https://screenrant.com/direct-market-comic-book-industry/

[641] Allen, p. 12

[642] MacDonald, H., (2019, July 05). Breaking: A comic shop in this day and age is staffed by customer-repelling losers. Retrieved May 19, 2020, from https://www.comicsbeat.com/breaking-a-comic-shop-in-this-day-and-age-is-staffed-by-customer-repelling-losers/

[643] Id.

[644] Kennedy, P. (2019, December 18). Real Comics Shop Folk Dish On "Comic Book Guy". Retrieved May 19, 2020, from https://monkeysfightingrobots.co/real-comics-shop-folk-dish-on-comic-book-guy/

[645] Gearino, Comic Shop

[646] Id

that no one wanted[647]. The number of comic distributors also decreased, and until recently only one national distributor remained, Diamond Distributors[648].

Outside forces had an adverse effect on comic book shops too. As we have seen, the rise of the video game industry, cable television, and high-speed internet access all began to compete with comics for the attention and money of readers. Digital comics and the rise of bookstore and library distribution also reduced the number of visitors to the LCS[649]. The combination of internal and external forces has placed the industry in a precarious position[650]. At the height of the industry in 1992, there were nearly 10,000 LCS. Today, that number hovers around 2,000[651].

What Are the Benefits of Comic Shop Distribution?

Despite the popular perception of the comic shop as a collapsing market[652], there are signs of strength in comic retail[653]. If independent publishers decide to distribute print comics on a national scale, they can capitalize on several benefits:

1.   There are only a few companies that handle comic shop distribution in the United States, so you don't have to deal with dozens of companies to get your book into most of the shops in the country.

2.   Because the LCS exists to sell comics, there is no inherent bias against the medium from the staff or among the customers.

3.   The physical location is designed to display and preserve different formats of print comics in ways that other retail outlets are not.

---

[647] Pulfer, R. (2020, April 13). Just What is the Direct Market in Comics and Where Did It Come From? Retrieved May 19, 2020, from https://screenrant.com/direct-market-comic-book-industry/

[648] Diamond Timeline Chronicles 30 Years of Service & Success. (n.d.). Retrieved May 19, 2020, from https://www.diamondcomics.com/Home/1/1/3/597?articleID=117735

[649] Gearino, Comic Shop

[650] O'Leary, S. (2019). Comics Is a Market in Transition. Retrieved May 19, 2020, from https://www.publishersweekly.com/pw/by-topic/industry-news/comics/article/79292-comics-is-a-market-in-transition.html

[651] Griepp, M. (2019). GFE CRO Chris Powell Responds on Diamond Data Leak. Retrieved May 19, 2020, from https://icv2.com/articles/news/view/44778/diamond-comic-distributors-store-count-revealed

[652] Johnston, R. (2019, March 08). Who's to Blame For Falling Comics Sales? And What's to be Done? Brian Hibbs at ComicsPRO. Retrieved May 19, 2020, from https://www.bleedingcool.com/2019/02/28/blame-falling-comics-sales-brian-hibbs-comicspro/

[653] Rogers, V. (2017). Can Comic Books Last? Publishers' Views on Future of Serialized Comics. Retrieved May 19, 2020, from https://www.newsarama.com/33362-can-comic-books-last-publishers-views-on-future-of-serialized-comics.html

4. Because comic shop owners and employees are often fans of the medium. They can become expert influencers at the point of sale. Several independent comics like *Elfquest*, *Scott Pilgrim*, and *Princeless*[654] enjoyed wider success and sales because comic shop owners promoted the book to their ideal reader customers.

What Are the Downsides of Comic Shop Distribution?

There is no shortage of opinions on the struggles of comic shop distribution that have existed since the shops opened[655]. For the independent publisher, this channel is an even bigger challenge because of inherent biases built into the system.

Bill Jemas, former EIC of Marvel and Chairman of AWA said it most succinctly: "*The direct market is not a place for independents to be successful*[656]." The historical numbers support this statement. According to certain statistics, 75% of all independent comics are purchased by only 300 comic shops, or 15% of the total number of all direct market retailers[657]. In addition, title saturation from the Big Two takes up most of the available shelf space and budgets of most comic shops[658]. This means that **if you are an independent publisher, the vast majority of LCS won't even consider buying your book**.

Vocal comic industry veterans claim this situation is by design. For example, Diamond has been described as "*a single point of failure in the comic book industry, dependent on the superhero genre and the Big Two*[659]. Tony Panaccio, formerly of Crossgen, claimed that Diamond's primary business model is to "*shrink the comics industry down to its lowest common denominator and squeeze out any potential competition to its premier publishers*[660]". Chuck Rozanski, owner of the venerable Mile High Comics in Colorado echoes this sentiment from the retailer's perspective. "*Almost every part of the current issue economic model is bad. The key to success is don't open up a shop just to be a Diamond Previews catalog outlet store*[661]."

[654] Smith, G. (2018, January 17). Finding Personality in the Ephemeral Comic Shop. Retrieved May 21, 2020, from https://www.popmatters.com/finding-personality-in-the-ephemeral-comic-shop-2519184383.html

[655] Eskey, N. & Kaplan, A. (2018, April 26). SD Comic Fest '18: The 'What's Wrong with Comics?' Panel Explores the Many Missteps of the Comic Book Industry. Retrieved May 21, 2020, from https://www.comicsbeat.com/sd-comic-fest-18-the-whats-wrong-with-comics-panel-explores-the-many-missteps-of-the-comic-book-industry/

[656] Allen, p. 21

[657] Allen p. 26

[658] Rogers, V. (n.d.). Is Comic Industry Being Over-Saturated? Retailers, Publishers Weigh In On 2017 State of the Business. Retrieved May 21, 2020, from https://www.newsarama.com/32778-is-comic-industry-being-oversaturated-retailers-publishers-weigh-in-on-2017-state-of-the-business.html

[659] Allen p. 33

[660] Allen p. 18

[661] McLauchlin, J. (2019). Business 3x3 Special Edition: Chuck Rozanski of Mile High Comics. Retrieved May 21, 2020, from https://icv2.com/articles/columns/view/43436/business-3x3-special-edition-chuck-rozanski-mile-high-comics

But Diamond is not the only source of difficulty for independents trying to sell their books in comic shops. Some LCS still cling to unappealing store design and hostile attitude that drives new business away[662]. Some retailers and creators place the burden of maintaining the comic shop industry on comic book readers, as if it is somehow the consumer's responsibility to go against their self-interest for the sake of a comic shop[663]. Finally, the economic model that Seuling put into place almost fifty years ago forces independents into a financial situation that Jemas warns against.

How Do You Make Money with Comic Shop Distribution?

Diamond buys comics and graphic novels from publishers at 60% off the cover price[664]. If you price your book at $4, then you make $1.60 from every book ordered through Diamond. Printing and shipping costs are based on volume, so the more copies you sell the lower cost you'll pay for each copy sold. Depending on your creative, marketing, printing, and shipping costs, it can cost you anywhere from $.60-$2.77 per single issue to distribute in the direct market[665]. This means many publishers need to sell between 7,000 and 10,000 copies to **breakeven** (make as much money as you spent)[666] or make a profit. As a point of reference, 279 of the top 505 comics sold in August 2019 sold less than 7,000 copies[667]. This doesn't necessarily mean that all these comics lost money, but it does indicate that selling comics in the direct market requires a publisher to control costs while they try to fight for limited space on store shelves. According to Diamond, new publishers can expect their initial sales of single-issue comics to be between 1,000 and 2,000 copies and graphic novels to be between 100-300 copies[668].

If you do decide to brave the waters of the direct market, you'll have to navigate around two major gatekeepers. The first hurdle is distributors like Diamond. The second is LCS owners.

---

[662] Fritz, M. (2017). The Life And Death Of The American Comic Book Shop: How A Distributor Monopoly Is Killing It Retrieved May 21, 2020, from http://m.benzinga.com/article/9622653

[663] Terror, J. (2019, August 27). Fanboy Rampage: Whose Job Is It To Sell Comics, Anyway? Retrieved May 21, 2020, from https://www.bleedingcool.com/2019/08/27/fanboy-rampage-whose-job-is-it-to-sell-comics-anyway/

[664] *Submission Guide for New Publishers* [PDF]. (2018). Diamond Comics Distributors. Retrieved May 21, 2020, from https://www.diamondcomics.com/SiteData/Downloads/Submitting_to_Diamond_11-2016.pdf

[665] Allen, T. W., & Waid, M. (2014). *Economics of digital comics*. United States of America

[666] What is breakeven? (n.d.). Retrieved May 21, 2020, from http://www.businessdictionary.com/definition/breakeven.html

[667] August 2019 Comic Book Sales to Comics Shops. (n.d.). Retrieved May 21, 2020, from https://www.comichron.com/monthlycomicssales/2019/2019-08.html

[668] *Submission Guide for New Publishers* [PDF]. (2018). Diamond Comics Distributors. Retrieved May 21, 2020, from https://www.diamondcomics.com/SiteData/Downloads/Submitting_to_Diamond_11-2016.pdf

How Do You Get Diamond to Distribute Your Books?

If you want to distribute through a distributor like Diamond there is a formal submission process for comic book publishers[669], which includes sending a submission package via snail mail. The submission package has four components:

1. A product sample of either the finished book or the cover and interior pages stapled together if the book hasn't been printed yet.

2. A cover letter introducing your company and your book.

3. A completed product info sheet for each book you're submitting[670]

4. A marketing plan for your book[671].

Keep in mind that if you developed your idea from Part 2 of ICP and developed a marketing plan based on Part 6, then your submission package can simply be a compilation of information you've already collected.

Once Diamond gets your submission in the mail, it can take up to six weeks to get a response, so keep this in mind when you're planning your publication schedule. You don't want to tie your entire launch plan for your horror title in Halloween only for the book to hit the LCS in time for Thanksgiving.

After you mail in your submission package, but before your book can ship, you need to acquire some kind of barcode[672] for your book. A **barcode** is an image made up of black and white lines that retailers can scan to keep track of their inventory[673]. Comics require a **universal product code** or UPC that you can acquire from GS1 US or a UPC resale site[674]. Graphic novels require an **international standard book number** or ISBN from the US ISBN agency[675]. The cost of getting a barcode varies depending on the type of book you are publishing.

---

[669] Id

[670] Id

[671] Id

[672] Id

[673] Liberto, D. (2020, March 31). Barcode Definition. Retrieved May 21, 2020, from https://www.investopedia.com/terms/b/barcode.asp

[674] How to Get UPC Barcodes for Your Products. (n.d.). Retrieved May 21, 2020, from https://guides.wsj.com/small-business/starting-a-business/how-to-get-upc-codes-for-your-products-2/

[675] Welcome to the U.S. ISBN Agency! (n.d.). Retrieved May 21, 2020, from http://www.isbn.org/

If your submission is accepted, you'll have to sign a contract with Diamond to distribute your book. In most cases, this will be a **consignment agreement**, which means you sell your books to Diamond based on orders from the direct market, and Diamond pays you when those books are sold[676]. Diamond then sells your books to the direct market.

As with any contract, there are basic terms, business terms, foundation terms, and housekeeping terms you'll need to understand before you sign. Your attorney should review your specific contract, but I've seen these basic terms in the Diamond contracts I've reviewed for my clients in the past.

- Rights: Diamond gets exclusive worldwide English language distribution rights to your book. This exclusive covers the direct market and can also include Amazon, bookstores, and retail outlets. Your website and your convention sales are not covered by this exclusivity.

- Discount: Diamond normally buys books from you at 60% off the retail price

- Payment Terms: After your book is released, Diamond pays weekly, minus any reserves or damages

- Risk of Loss: If Diamond stores copies of your book in their warehouses, they are not responsible for the damage or theft of that inventory.

After the contracts are signed, the book will be listed in **Previews**, Diamond's monthly direct market catalog and you will receive a Diamond order code specific to your book[677]. LCS owners will typically have three weeks to complete their orders and then Diamond will send the print order to you. It is then your job to get your printer to print and ship the books to Diamond according to their terms of sale[678] which you and your attorney should read and understand before your book appears in Previews.

---

[676] Consignment Sale (n.d.). Retrieved May 21, 2020, from http://www.businessdictionary.com/definition/consignment-sale.html

[677] *Submission Guide for New Publishers* [PDF]. (2018). Diamond Comics Distributors. Retrieved May 21, 2020, from https://www.diamondcomics.com/SiteData/Downloads/Submitting_to_Diamond_11-2016.pdf

[678] Id

How Do You Get Comic Shops to Order Your Books?

Just because your book is advertised in Previews doesn't mean comic shop owners will order it. In fact, many LCS have specific incentives not to buy independent comics. We touched on the importance of building a marketing relationship with your LCS in relation to your ideal readers. Now let's look at marketing your book to the comic shop itself.

In the direct market, it is the LCS and not the reader who buys your comic[679]. Because the books are usually non-returnable, the shop will own every copy that they cannot sell to a reader. This means that **store owners take a financial risk with every book they order**[680] because the money they spend on your book is lost if they can't sell it.

This gamble is increased due to a lack of information. If the first issue of your comic comes out in January, the LCS has to order it in November of the prior year. If the second issue comes out in February, the LCS has to order it in December, before they know the actual sales of the first issue. If you have a third issue, it will be ordered in January and the shop might have some data on the performance of issue one, but it might not be enough data to make an accurate order. Over ordering, under ordering, or ordering pre-order books that are never picked up can be one of the fastest ways to kill a store[681].

A typical LCS will attempt to reduce this risk by hedging their bets. First, they will order books that have a proven track record, well-known characters, and established creative teams. That is one of the reasons 80% of sales go to the top five publishers. Second, because books come out on Wednesday, the sales from that day need to cover the entire cost of their order. Sales from the rest of the week are allocated to operating costs and profit[682]. Third, orders for subsequent issues are often reduced to anticipate reduced demand. This means the order for issue two will be half of issue one, and issue three might be a third of issue 2[683].

As an independent publisher, your marketing job is to create a positive relationship between your book and as many LCS as possible. Part of this task is associating your book with the feeling owners want to feel, namely the satisfaction of happy customers and more money in their bank accounts. From an ordering

[679] Mayo, J. (2017, April 13). Why Is Batman the Benchmark? Comic Book Sales Data, Explained. Retrieved May 21, 2020, from https://www.cbr.com/comic-book-sales-data-explained/

[680] Johnston, R. (2019, June 24). Comic Store in Your Future - "Ordering from Marvel Is Like Playing Russian Roulette". Retrieved May 21, 2020, from https://www.bleedingcool.com/2019/06/24/comic-store-in-your-future-ordering-marvel-russian-roulette/

[681] Desiato, A. (2017). My Comic Shop History Episode 3.1: Aw Yeah Comics. Retrieved May 21, 2020, from https://www.podomatic.com/podcasts/flatsquirrelproductions/episodes/2017-06-20T21_11_56-07_00

[682] Id.

[683] Gearino, Comic Shop

standpoint, this means **taking steps to reduce the risk of buying your book** and increasing their confidence in selling the book to readers if they decide to buy it[684].

The first step in reducing risk is focusing on the right LCS. Like comic book readers, comic book shops are not a single monolithic stereotype. Different stores in different markets have unique traits, customer bases, and inventory needs[685]. Many shops carry a general stock of current issues, but others specialize in serving families with children, or collectors, or independent publishers[686]. It doesn't make sense to try and convince a shop that only carries vintage back issues from the '60s to buy your cutting edge, experimental graphic novel. It will take some research to look through comic shop databases like Find a Comic Shop[687] or Diamond's Comic Shop Locator[688], but the time you spend here can save you frustration later.

The second step is providing the right information to the right shops to help them make their ordering bets. A **sell-sheet** is a one-page collection of information designed to increase interest in a product[689]. Your sell sheet can contain a combination of details on your book and your target market, including;

- Your cover
- Your distributor order code
- Your pitch
- Your tagline
- Your target market (both the core market and the potential market)
- Your relationship to your competition
- Your marketing efforts designed to increase their sales

Once your book is in Previews, you can send your sell sheet to prospective LCS owners and offer to answer any questions they might have about the book[690]. You can send the sell sheet via email, set up meetings with shop owners at conventions, or visit the shops that you can reach without a hassle. It doesn't make sense to cold call with this information, because the staff at a store is busy during operating hours and the

[684] Newsarama 2020 Staff. (2020). Boom! Studios: Too Many Comics in Direct Market, 'Publishers Need to Earn' Space on Shelves. Retrieved May 21, 2020, from https://www.newsarama.com/49124-boom-says-too-many-comics-in-direct-market-publishers-need-to-earn-space-on-shelves.html

[685] Gearino, Comic Shop

[686] Desiato, A. (2017). My Comic Shop History Episode 3.1: Aw Yeah Comics.

[687] The most complete directory of Comic Book, Graphic Novel and Pop-culture Shops Near You! (n.d.). Retrieved May 21, 2020, from https://findacomicshop.com/

[688] Home Page- Comic Shop Locator. (n.d.). Retrieved May 21, 2020, from https://www.comicshoplocator.com/

[689] Balle, L. (2017, November 21). What Is a Product Sell Sheet? Retrieved May 21, 2020, from https://smallbusiness.chron.com/product-sell-sheet-23659.html

[690] Hendrick2016, J. (2016). How to Sell Your Comic: A Retailer's Perspective. Retrieved May 21, 2020, from https://sktchd.com/longform/how-to-sell-your-comic-a-retailers-perspective/

sell sheet has too much information for them to retain or write down[691]. Like with most marketing efforts, don't expect a majority of LCS to respond to your email, but be sure to answer every email you get from a comic shop. If they take the time to email, they are more likely to order.

The third step is taking concrete actions to reduce LCS risk. This can be anything from the marketing events we discussed in Chapter 37 to get your true fans to pre-order the book from specific LCS once it appears in Previews. From an operational perspective, you might consider publishing quarterly instead of monthly to give LCS owners time to evaluate the sales of prior issues before they have to order the next issue[692], or offering returns so they inherent risk of the books is eliminated[693].

Whatever actions you decide to take to increase direct market confidence in your book, the one thing you cannot do is ship books late. Late books can cripple both LCS and your reputation as a publisher. Even major publishers like Image[694] and Marvel[695] take a financial hit when their books are late. Your book might not be able to recover from that kind of stumble, so **make sure you print and ship your books out on time**.

What Are the Alternatives to Diamond Distribution?

Diamond is the single largest access point to the direct market, but it is not your only option. New distributors are changing the direct market landscape[696]. Many LCS are looking for alternatives to the Big Two to diversify their market and decrease their dependence on Diamond even if the move is incremental[697]. If you give them the incentive to champion your book outside the direct market system, you can find some success.

You still have the option to market to LCS directly even if you don't have an account at Diamond. Because your time is limited, you might not be able to contact every LCS, so it makes sense to start small, build relationships one store at a time and build momentum. You might have to educate some owners on the

[691] Ibid

[692] Newsarama Staff. (2019). Aftershock Rolls Out New Plans Aimed at Retailers. Retrieved May 21, 2020, from https://www.newsarama.com/47996-aftershock-rolls-out-new-plans-aimed-at-retailers.html

[693] AfterShock Comics Offers Retailers Returns on Remaining 2018 First Issues. (2018). Retrieved May 21, 2020, from https://icv2.com/articles/news/view/41142/aftershock-comics-offers-retailers-returns-remaining-2018-first-issues

[694] "Wizard Magazine, Market Watch". Wizard (22). June 1993. pp. 134–5.

[695] Johnston, R. (2015, June 09). More On Secret Wars Lateness. Retrieved May 21, 2020, from https://www.bleedingcool.com/2015/06/08/more-on-secret-wars-lateness/

[696] Schedeen, J. (2020, June 17). How DC Just Broke Up the Most Powerful Monopoly in Comics. Retrieved June 20, 2020, from https://www.ign.com/articles/dc-diamond-comics-distributor-wars-monopoly-marvel

[697] Gearino, Comic Shop

process of buying directly from you[698]. You might need to leverage in-store events, sponsorship swaps, or other tactics to reduce the risk to the LCS. You might have to provide free samples and you're going to need to have individual sales agreements with each shop, whether it's on a consignment or straight sales basis[699]. You might even have to lose some money when you're getting started. The key is to calculate whether it is better to go through Diamond or go it alone.

Alternative print distribution methods are not as common as digital, but they do exist in one form or another. Regional distributors like Emerald Comics Distribution are trying to offer an alternative to Diamond's monopoly[700]. Companies like Sitcomics offer a type of "sell through distribution" to leverage binge consumption[701]. The League of Comic Geeks and even Diamond themselves are testing digital services to allow readers to manage their orders directly[702]. There are companies offering to place comic book vending machines in high traffic areas to forego the direct market and capture more of the potential market[703]. There is even a proposal to set up a comic book cart or kiosk in malls or other consumer areas as a mobile substitute for the LCS[704]. As with emerging digital distribution, independent publishers need to investigate each potential company and weigh the pros and cons of the alternatives.

What Is the Future of the Direct Market?

The direct market has always been volatile, so it is difficult to predict the future of this distribution model[705]. Some experts predict the emergence of a more niche LCS that is less focused on the superhero genre and provides more space for other types of comics[706]. Some see the rise of Comixology, their aggressive sales, and their lower distribution costs as a direct threat to the future of the comic shop[707]. In my travels, I've seen

---

[698] Becker, D. (2019, April 03). Comics Pros and Cons: Episode 145: Travis McIntire at C2E2. Retrieved May 21, 2020, from https://player.fm/series/comic-pros-cons/episode-145-travis-mcintire-at-c2e2

[699] Johnston, R. (2017, March 12). The Fine Art of Getting Your Book into Store Shelves. Retrieved May 21, 2020, from https://www.bleedingcool.com/2017/03/12/fine-art-getting-book-store-shelves/

[700] Arrant, C. (2017). A New Comic Book Distributor with Big Ambitions Launches. Retrieved May 21, 2020, from https://www.newsarama.com/33568-a-new-distributor-comes-to-challenge-diamond.html

[701] Terror, J. (2017, December 28). Darin Henry's Sitcomics Wants to Disrupt Comics Industry With Sell-Through Distribution, Binge Books. Retrieved May 21, 2020, from https://www.bleedingcool.com/2017/12/28/henry-sitcomics-disrupt-comics-industry/

[702] Terror, J. (2018, April 04). League of Comic Geeks Launches Competing Pull List Service Ahead of Diamond's Pullbox Launch. Retrieved May 21, 2020, from https://www.bleedingcool.com/2018/04/04/league-comic-geeks-pull-list-service/

[703] Samax. (1970, January 01). 9 Places to Make Money with a Comic Book Vending Machine. Retrieved May 21, 2020, from https://ghettomanga.blogspot.com/2018/05/8-places-to-make-money-with-comic-book.html?m=1

[704] Wampler, D. Selling Your Comic Book Concept (2015)

[705] Johnston, R. (2020, April 16). Comic Book Retailers Plans to Fix the Direct Market When It Returns. Retrieved May 21, 2020, from https://bleedingcool.com/comics/comic-book-retailers-plans-to-fix-the-direct-market-when-it-returns/

[706] Allen, p. 40

[707] Johnston, R. (2018, April 07). Brian Hibbs Issues Open Letter to Marvel over ComiXology Discounts. Retrieved May 21, 2020, from https://www.bleedingcool.com/2018/04/07/brian-hibbs-letter-marvel-execs-comixology-discounts/

comic shops place less emphasis on single issues and back issues to provide more shelf space to merchandise, toys, games, and coffee.

Independent publishers have a vested interest in preserving and promoting the direct market because they provide an oasis to the comic book community. Many traditional businesses have been replaced by online services, including large books and record store chains, and video rental stores. At the same time, other businesses like bars, clubs, and restaurants have survived and thrived, even though the goods and services they offer are also available online and often for a cheaper price. **I believe the difference between Blockbuster and your local bar is community**. The businesses that endure offer the opportunity for personal connections in addition to whatever goods or services might be on sale[708]. The direct market can be a gathering place that happens to sell stories, in the same manner as a local book store or library.

---

[708] "Perch" (Producer). (2020). *Are We Looking At The End Of Comic Book Shops?* [Video file]. Retrieved May 21, 2020, from https://www.youtube.com/watch?v=4Gcmxfqq-_I&feature=youtu.be

The relationship between comics and bookstores over the past thirty years is a study in contrasts. When the major book retailers had megastores in every major city, comics were often regulated to spinner racks or a minor space in the magazine section. In an effort to develop alternative distribution channels, major publishers began to experiment with more consistent graphic novel and trade paperback additions to their catalogs. During my time at Marvel, I worked on a deal to bring the Masterworks to Barnes and Noble[709]. But then Amazon decimated the megastores, forcing Borders and Waldenbooks to shut down[710] and reducing Barnes and Noble to an acquisition target for a hedge fund[711]. Pundits predicted the end of the brick and mortar bookstore[712] just as comics were becoming a staple on the shelves.

But the fall of the megastores did not lead to the fall of bookstores in general or comic distribution in particular. Small independent bookstores have increased in numbers in recent years[713]. Sales of comics in the book channel have also experienced growth while the direct market struggles[714]. **Navigating this distribution channel continues to be a challenge for independent publishers**, but depending on your comic, this might be a better distribution option for you than the direct market.

As we look at the viability of bookstores for independent publishers, one important caveat to keep in mind is that while most of the focus will be on physical bookstores, for this discussion, Amazon is part of this distribution channel. It started by selling physical books[715], it is one of the largest distributors of books in the world[716] and it has dozens of physical bookstores in America[717]. As an independent publisher, it doesn't

---

[709] Shooter, J. (2020, April 15). Marvel Masterworks: The Avengers Vol. 20: Retrieved May 23, 2020, from https://www.barnesandnoble.com/w/marvel-masterworks-jim-shooter/1133030534

[710] Borders to close 200 Waldenbooks, cut jobs. (2009, November 06). Retrieved May 23, 2020, from http://www.nbcnews.com/id/33690100/ns/business-retail/t/borders-close-waldenbooks-cut-jobs/

[711] Alter, A., & Hsu, T. (2019, June 07). Barnes & Noble Is Sold to Hedge Fund After a Tumultuous Year. Retrieved May 23, 2020, from https://www.nytimes.com/2019/06/07/books/barnes-noble-sale.html

[712] Crowe, A. (2016, July 15). Is Borders' Bankruptcy the End of Brick and Mortar Stores? Retrieved May 23, 2020, from https://www.aol.com/2011/03/01/is-borders-bankruptcy-the-end-of-brick-and-mortar-stores/

[713] Schlesinger, J. (2018, November 23). Small bookstores are booming after nearly being wiped out. Retrieved May 23, 2020, from https://www.cbsnews.com/news/small-bookstores-are-booming-after-nearly-being-wiped-out-small-business-saturday/

[714] Salkowitz, R. (2019, October 08). Surprising New Data Shows Comic Readers Are Leaving Superheroes Behind. Retrieved May 23, 2020, from https://www.forbes.com/sites/robsalkowitz/2019/10/08/surprising-new-data-shows-comic-readers-are-leaving-superheroes-behind/

[715] DePillis, L., & Sherman, I. (2019, July 05). Amazon's extraordinary 25-year evolution. Retrieved May 23, 2020, from https://www.cnn.com/interactive/2018/10/business/amazon-history-timeline/index.html

[716] Easter, M. (2017, November 20). Remember when Amazon only sold books? Retrieved May 23, 2020, from https://www.latimes.com/business/la-fi-amazon-history-20170618-htmlstory.html

[717] Riecks, D. (n.d.). Amazon Physical Store Locations. Retrieved May 23, 2020, from https://www.amazon.com/find-your-store/b/?node=17608448011

make sense to ignore Amazon when trying to reach your target market with your printed books. There are other print booksellers online[718], but I'm going to focus most of my attention on Amazon when talking about online print sales.

What Are the Benefits of Bookstore Distribution?

The benefits of bookstore distribution become evident when you compare it to the direct market[719]:

- There is more organic foot traffic in bookstores.

- There is a more diverse population of consumers in bookstores[720], who are interested in buying a wider range of titles[721]

- There is no inherent stigma against going into a bookstore.

- Bookstores generate more backlist sales than comic book shops because the store does not retain the inventory the way it does in the direct market.

These benefits become more pronounced when you consider online print sales, which are "open" twenty-four hours a day and can potentially reach your target market anywhere in the world.

What Are the Downsides of Bookstore Distribution?

The detrimental aspects of bookstores can also be understood in relation to comic shop distribution[722]:

- Bookstores can return books, which can severely cut into your revenue stream.

- The payment cycle in the bookstore channel can be anywhere from six to twelve months.

---

[718] Zhukova, A. (2017, April 17). The 7 Best Alternatives to Amazon for Buying Books. Retrieved May 23, 2020, from https://www.makeuseof.com/tag/amazon-alternatives-buying-books/

[719] Blaylock p. 25

[720] Reid, C. (2017). Comics Shops Fight Bookstores In the Race to Sell Graphic Novels. Retrieved May 23, 2020, from https://www.publishersweekly.com/pw/by-topic/industry-news/comics/article/75086-comics-shops-fight-bookstores-in-the-race-to-sell-graphic-novels.html

[721] Salkowitz, R. (2019, October 08). Surprising New Data Shows Comic Readers Are Leaving Superheroes Behind. Retrieved May 23, 2020, from https://www.forbes.com/sites/robsalkowitz/2019/10/08/surprising-new-data-shows-comic-readers-are-leaving-superheroes-behind/

[722] Allen p. 52

- The physical environment of a bookstore is conducive to anthologies, graphic novels, and trade paperbacks, but not single-issue comics.

- The potential for an influencer at the point of sale is reduced because comics are only one type of book competing with everything else the retailer sells.

These issues are not a factor when dealing with Amazon[723], but some publishers may want to consider the negative considerations of dealing with them that we mentioned earlier when we discussed Comixology.

How Do You Make Money with Bookstore Distribution?

Different book distributors and retailers demand different wholesale discounts which will impact the amount of money you can generate in this channel. The **discounts range from 60%-70% of the list price** when you add up the percentages taken by the distributor, wholesaler, and the retail store[724]. These discounts don't include creative, marketing, or printing costs, so keep that in mind when you look at three of the major book distributors for comics.

- Amazon Advantage: Publisher earns 45% of the list price, not counting the annual fee[725]

- Diamond: Publisher earns 40% of the cover price[726]

- Ingram Spark: Publisher earns 45% of the cover price, not counting the set-up fee[727]

Again, you also have to be prepared for returns when dealing with the book market. When I worked for CPM and Marvel, many of our contracts included a **reserve for returns**[728], or money set aside to payback possible returned items during a given period. It is difficult to predict the future in this situation, especially when investment funds are limited[729]. Companies like First Comics couldn't survive a wave of returns before it shut down[730], so talk to your accountant to determine the best way to prepare for and deal with returns.

---

[723] Amazon Advantage - Frequently asked Questions. (2011). Retrieved May 23, 2020, from https://www.amazon.com/gp/seller-account/mm-product-page.html?topic=200329770

[724] Allen p. 52

[725] Amazon Advantage - Frequently asked Questions. (2011)

[726] *Submission Guide for New Publishers* [PDF]. (2018). Diamond Comics Distributors.

[727] Ingram Content Group. (n.d.). How to Self-Publish a Book: What you Need to Self-Publish with IngramSpark. Retrieved May 23, 2020, from https://www.ingramspark.com/how-it-works?utm_referrer=https%3A%2F%2Fwww.ingramspark.com%2F

[728] Bragg, S. (2018, November 24). Reserve for product returns. Retrieved May 23, 2020, from https://www.accountingtools.com/articles/2017/5/5/reserve-for-product-returns

[729] Allen p. 53

[730] First Closes Offices," The Comics Journal #148 (February 1992), p. 27.

How Do You Get Distributors to Carry Your Books?

There are dozens of book distributors available to independent publishers[731] and each one has its pros and cons in terms of reach, price, and level of service. They will all require you to own the distribution rights to your book (something you should have already secured in your idea management) as well as an ISBN for each title[732]. As distributors, most of them will be exclusive[733] and many will claim to find sales opportunities for your book[734], but they won't replace marketing on your part. I'm going to focus on the three examples I used earlier, to give you an idea, but don't feel like you can't explore other options.

- Amazon Advantage is a program that enables publishers to list and sell their products on Amazon.com right alongside products that have massive marketing and distribution[735]. Publishers apply online, pay a $99 annual fee, and ship a small number of books to Amazon on a consignment basis. As copies are sold, Amazon pays you monthly for any month where you earn more than $100. Amazon will order more copies when their initial inventory runs low.

- Diamond Books is a book channel program from Diamond Distributors[736] that is similar to its direct market program[737] discussed earlier.

- Ingram Spark is the distribution arm of Ingram designed for independent publishers[738]. It is one of the major sources of books for chain stores, libraries, and universities. Graphic novels printed with Ingram for a set-up fee of $49 and a print fee determined by your design can get access to 40,000 retail and educational outlets[739].

---

[731] 40+ Best Print Book Distributors in 2019: The Ultimate Guide. (2020, May 06). Retrieved May 23, 2020, from https://blog.reedsy.com/list-of-print-book-distributors/

[732] James, T. (2013). Barcodes, ISBNs, UPCs, Oh My! Retrieved May 23, 2020, from http://www.comixtribe.com/2013/07/10/barcodes-isbns-upcs-oh-my/

[733] IBPA: Distributors and Wholesalers. (n.d.). Retrieved May 23, 2020, from https://www.ibpa-online.org/page/distributors

[734] 40+ Best Print Book Distributors in 2019: The Ultimate Guide.

[735] Amazon Advantage - Frequently asked Questions. (2011)

[736] About Diamond Book Distributors. (n.d.). Retrieved May 23, 2020, from http://www.diamondbookdistributors.com/default.asp

[737] *Submission Guide for New Publishers* [PDF]. (2018). Diamond Comics Distributors.

[738] Ingram Content Group. (n.d.). Global Book Distribution with IngramSpark: Access 40K+ Retailers & Libraries. Retrieved May 23, 2020, from https://www.ingramspark.com/how-it-works/distribute

[739] Ingram Content Group. (n.d.). Plan Your Book: Self-Publish a Print & Ebook with IngramSpark. Retrieved May 23, 2020, from https://www.ingramspark.com/plan-your-book

How Do You Get Bookstores to Order Your Books?

Just as with a comic book shop, the fact that a bookstore can order your book doesn't mean that they will order it without a good reason. Unlike a comic book shop, bookstores don't face the same inherent financial risk because the books are returnable. This means that your job as an independent publisher is less about reducing risk for the bookstore and more about raising awareness.

Many of the ideas we explored in the comic shop chapter apply here as well. Researching lists of bookstores[740] and understanding which stores are more likely to carry graphic novels[741] or cater to your target market will save you time and effort. Starting small and contacting local bookstores will allow you to create a one on one relationship to benefit your book. Sell sheets with all the relevant information will give the store all the information they need to make a decision on your book. Organizing activities and events to attract people into the store can improve the chances of them carrying your book[742].

There are two additional steps to remember when dealing with the book market. First, don't emphasize any relationship you have with Amazon or how well your book is doing on the site. Many bookstores consider Amazon their natural enemy and will be less interested in taking any actions that may benefit that specific competitor[743]. Also, you might want to consider getting your book reviewed by an established service, because many bookstores use companies like Kirkus and Publisher's Weekly to make their purchases, just like libraries do.

---

[740] NewPages Guide to Bookstores in the U.S. and Canada. (2018, July 31). Retrieved May 23, 2020, from https://www.newpages.com/independent-bookstores

[741] Bookstores Specializing in Graphic Novels. (n.d.). Retrieved May 23, 2020, from https://www.biblio.com/bookstores/graphic-novels/3446

[742] About Diamond Book Distributors.

[743] Staff, I. (n.d.). How to Sell Your Self-Published Book to Bookstores. Retrieved May 23, 2020, from https://www.ingramspark.com/blog/how-to-sell-your-book-to-bookstores

Comics were not always accepted in American public libraries. The residual stigma of *Seduction of the Innocent* and a general perception of comics as lowbrow entertainment[744] tainted the medium in the eyes of most librarians[745].

This perception began to change in 1986 with the publication of *Maus* and accelerated after 2009 when the MCU raised the profile of comic[746] entertainment to mainstream audiences. Today, libraries are constantly looking for ways to bring readers through the door. Comics is a growth area, so more and more librarians are looking for ways to add comics to their collections[747]. National associations of librarians are focusing on graphic novels[748] and major conventions are dedicating significant portions of their panels to helping librarians increase their expertise with comics[749]. **Independent publishers who add libraries to their distribution model can tap into a market that isn't available to comic shops, if they learn the particular needs of this environment.**

What Are the Benefits of Library Distribution?

Some publishers might wonder how relevant libraries are in the 21st century, when most people have twenty-four-hour access to the internet in their pockets. But libraries are a public service for their communities. They serve to educate and entertain populations that may not have the resources to access other distribution channels. They exist as a public good, not as a profit center[750]. For independent publishers, they can help you reach your target market because:

---

[744] MacPherson, K. (2020, February 27). Perspective | Don't be afraid to let children read graphic novels. They're real books. Retrieved May 23, 2020, from https://www.washingtonpost.com/entertainment/books/dont-be-afraid-to-let-children-read-graphic-novels-theyre-real-books/2020/02/27/ed374b92-4dd7-11ea-9b5c-eac5b16dafaa_story.html

[745] Pyles, C. (2013). It's No Joke: Comics and Collection Development. Retrieved May 23, 2020, from http://publiclibrariesonline.org/2013/02/its-no-joke-comics-and-collection-development/

[746] Id.

[747] MacDonald, H. (2017). Comics, the King of Libraries. Retrieved May 23, 2020, from https://www.publishersweekly.com/pw/by-topic/industry-news/libraries/article/73599-comics-the-king-of-libraries.html

[748] MacDonald, H. (2019). The ALA Is Ready to Shake Things Up...With Comics. Retrieved May 23, 2020, from https://www.publishersweekly.com/pw/by-topic/industry-news/comics/article/80398-the-ala-is-ready-to-shake-things-up-with-comics.html

[749] The New York Public Library Events at New York Comic Con. (2019, September 12). Retrieved May 23, 2020, from https://www.newyorkcomiccon.com/Explore/NYPL/

[750] Grady, C. (2018, July 24). Why public libraries are still essential in 2018. Retrieved May 23, 2020, from https://www.vox.com/culture/2018/7/24/17603692/public-libraries-essential-forbes-amazon

1. There are more than 120,000 libraries in the United States, compared to 2,000 active comic book shops[751].

2. Some potential readers who visit libraries regularly never patronize comic shops[752], especially younger demographics[753].

3. More libraries are actively looking to expand their comic collections to include independent comics[754].

4. Libraries often purchased the same title multiple times. Because each book is loaned out to a borrower, the quality of the book degrades over time due to normal wear and tear. The number of times a book can be borrowed is known as it's "**circ**". Once the circ threshold is passed, the book is unusable and another copy needs to be purchased. Graphic novels have an average circ of 20, which is seen as a good value for a library[755]. Circ also applies to digital copies, since publishers allow libraries to loan out e-books a specific number of times before they have to buy another copy[756].

What Are the Downsides of Library Distribution?

For all their potential as a distribution channel, libraries represent a significant distribution challenge due to the fragmented and public nature of their activity.

1. There is no one agency or service managing library collections across the country, so independent publishers don't have a one-stop-shop like Diamond[757].

[751] Langley, R., DuLaney, J., & Storey, B. (2018, November 27). How To Get Libraries To Buy Your Book. Retrieved May 23, 2020, from https://www.standoutbooks.com/libraries-buy-book/

[752] MacDonald, H. (2017). Comics, the King of Libraries

[753] Na, K., & Simmons, E. (2019, June 12). Book Marketing: How To Get Your Book Into Libraries. Retrieved May 23, 2020, from https://www.thecreativepenn.com/2019/06/12/book-marketing-how-to-get-your-book-into-libraries/

[754] EBSCO Information Services, Inc. (2017). Supply and Demand - Build the Graphic Novel Collection Your Students Are Waiting For. Retrieved May 23, 2020, from https://www.ebsco.com/blog/article/supply-and-demand-build-a-graphic-novel-collection

[755] Q. What are the differences between circulating, reference, and reserve materials? (n.d.). Retrieved May 23, 2020, from http://libanswers.nvcc.edu/faq/135647

[756] Kelly, H. (2019, November 26). E-books at libraries are a huge hit, leading to long waits, reader hacks and worried publishers. Retrieved May 23, 2020, from https://www.washingtonpost.com/technology/2019/11/26/e-books-libraries-are-huge-hit-leading-long-waits-reader-hacks-worried-publishers/?arc404=true

[757] LibGuides: Marketing to Libraries: Basics. (n.d.). Retrieved May 23, 2020, from https://libguides.ala.org/marketing-to-libraries

2. Librarians manage dozens, if not hundreds of different collections in their libraries, so they may not have the time or the focus to dedicate to comics on a regular basis.

3. Many libraries have procurement guidelines that require a comic to display a certain threshold of quality or validation that isn't required in other distribution channels[758].

4. Because libraries serve the public, it is easier for members of the public to create controversy over the content of a comic and attempt to get that book banned[759].

How Do You Make Money with Libraries?

Revenue from libraries is often indirect. Because they have to buy thousands of books every year, it's not practical for them to buy directly from every publisher they want to carry. Most libraries order from established book distributors and comics fall into this pattern as well. This means that if a particular library orders from their local comic shop[760], that revenue will be captured at the direct market level because comic shop revenue is only counted at the retailer level, not by the person, or in this case institution, that buys it. If the library buys the book from a book distributor, then that revenue will be captured in the book channel in the manner we discussed in the last chapter.

How Do You Get Libraries to Carry Your Book?

While you might not see the results of library distribution from a revenue standpoint, **you still need to market your book to libraries if you want to make the most of this channel**. The same pattern of targeting, raising awareness and building relationships applicable to LCS and bookstores also applies to libraries, with certain caveats specific to this public institution.

1. Targeting: Different libraries serve different communities and order different books. While some have extensive comic collections, others might not have any. At the same time, your local libraries will be easier to build a relationship with than distant institutions. LibWeb maintains a website of all public libraries divided by state[761]. Select as many local and specialty libraries that you think will appeal to your target market, review their submission guidelines to determine if your book qualifies[762] and then rely on the snowball effect to expand

---

[758] MacDonald, H. (2017). Comics, the King of Libraries

[759] Ibid

[760] Shop Assistance: How to Work with Your Local Comic Shop. (n.d.). Retrieved May 23, 2020, from https://www.diamondbookshelf.com/Home/1/1/20/823?articleID=142933

[761] List of Public Libraries in the US. (n.d.). Retrieved May 23, 2020, from https://www.lib-web.org/united-states/public-libraries/

[762] Langley, R., DuLaney, J., & Storey, B. (2018, November 27). How To Get Libraries To Buy Your Book. Retrieved May 23, 2020, from https://www.standoutbooks.com/libraries-buy-book/

the reach of your book as other libraries follow the lead of your early adopters and order additional copies[763].

2. <u>Raising Awareness</u>: Thousands of books are published every month. Librarians have various methods and services to sift through all the potential products, so if you want to get on their radar, you need to consider these methods.

3. <u>Reviews</u>: Libraries use professional book review services to evaluate titles. Each one has a cost and/or submission guidelines of their own, but they have the potential to get you in front of thousands of librarians at once.

    a. Booklist[764]
    b. Choice[765]
    c. Kirkus[766]
    d. Kirkus Indie[767]
    e. Library Journal[768]
    f. Midwest Book Review[769]
    g. Net Galley[770]
    h. Publisher's Weekly[771]
    i. School Library Journal[772]
    j. Self-e[773]

---

[763] Palmer, A. (2015). How to Get Self-Published Books into Stores and Libraries. Retrieved May 23, 2020, from https://www.publishersweekly.com/pw/by-topic/authors/pw-select/article/68467-how-to-get-self-published-books-into-stores-and-libraries.html

[764] Booklist Online. (n.d.). Access to Booklist Online. Retrieved May 23, 2020, from https://www.booklistonline.com/get-reviewed

[765] Choice: A Publishing Unit of ACRL. (n.d.). Retrieved June 07, 2020, from http://www.ala.org/acrl/choice/

[766] Kirkus Reviews. (n.d.). Retrieved May 23, 2020, from https://www.kirkusreviews.com/

[767] Get Reviewed. Get Discovered. (n.d.). Retrieved May 23, 2020, from https://www.kirkusreviews.com/indie-reviews/

[768] Graphic Novel Reviews+. (n.d.). Retrieved May 23, 2020, from https://www.libraryjournal.com/?page=Review-Submissions

[769] MBR Review Copy Submission Guidelines (Get a Book Reviewed). (n.d.). Retrieved May 23, 2020, from http://www.midwestbookreview.com/get_rev.htm

[770] Net Galley: We Help Books Succeed: Retrieved June 15, 2020 from https://www.netgalley.com/

[771] Book Reviews, Bestselling Books & Publishing Business News: Publishers Weekly. (n.d.). Retrieved May 23, 2020, from https://booklife.com/

[772] School Library Journal Reviews+. (n.d.). Retrieved May 23, 2020, from https://www.slj.com/?subpage=Reviews%2B%2CBooks%2CGraphic+Novels

[773] Connecting Indie Books, Libraries and Readers. (n.d.). Retrieved May 23, 2020, from https://self-e.libraryjournal.com/

4. Ordering: Learning about your book isn't going to be helpful to librarians if they can't order the book easily. Since some libraries order from comic shops and some order from book distributors like Createspace or Baker and Taylor, be sure to have your book available in multiple channels and convey the ordering information to librarians whenever practical[774]. Keep in mind that while graphic novels and trade paperbacks are natural formats for libraries, some of them also stock single issues and digital versions of comics[775].

5. Promotional Services: Some libraries use book promotional services as an adjunct to book reviews. You can use something free and easy like Amazon's Author Central service or one of the paid services online, but in the end, you'll probably get a better return on your investment if you create a personal relationship with the library you want to carry your book.

6. Building Relationships: Like comic shops and bookstores, library distribution benefits from a personal connection. Setting up a meeting with the head of acquisitions at your local library with a preview copy can have more impact than a promotional email[776]. Offering to host an event at the library to attract your target market[777] can have even more impact because you're helping bring people in the door who might patronize the library in the future[778]. Libraries already invested in comics may already be conducting in house library cons that you can participate in or even help organize[779] or you could table at artists alleys available in some library conventions[780]. The higher your interaction with your libraries, the more likely they will be to order your book.

Working with extended distribution channels like bookstores and libraries can connect you to a wider audience, but there is no more direct and personal distribution experience than when you sell your book to

[774] Rutkowska, A. (2018, July 13). Publishing Tips for Indie Authors: How to Get Your Book Into Libraries. Retrieved May 17, 2020, from https://www.writersdigest.com/editor-blogs/there-are-no-rules/marketing-self-promotion/indie-authors-how-to-get-your-book-into-libraries-indie-publishing-tips

[775] Johnston, R. (2019, October 14). CBLDF Launches Free Webinars for Comic Book Retailers - Including Dealing With Schools, Libraries, the Law and Media. Retrieved May 23, 2020, from https://www.bleedingcool.com/2019/10/14/cbldf-webinars-schools-libraries-law-media/

[776] Palmer, A. (2015). How to Get Self-Published Books into Stores and Libraries.

[777] Rutkowska, A. (2018, July 13). Publishing Tips for Indie Authors: How to Get Your Book Into Libraries.

[778] Zeman, M. (2015). Authors For Libraries. Retrieved May 23, 2020, from http://publiclibrariesonline.org/2015/05/authors-for-libraries/

[779] MacDonald, H. (2014). How to Throw a Comic Con at Your Library. Retrieved May 23, 2020, from https://www.publishersweekly.com/pw/by-topic/industry-news/comics/article/61940-how-to-throw-a-comic-con-at-your-library.html

[780] Adair, T., (2020, February 24). American Library Association opens applications to their Artist Alley in June. Retrieved May 23, 2020, from https://www.comicsbeat.com/american-library-association-opens-applications-to-their-artist-alley-in-june/

your ideal reader without a middleman. We discussed comic conventions from a marketing perspective in an earlier chapter. Now let's go back and look at the con as a pure distribution model.

There is a substantial amount of overlap between marketing to ideal readers and selling comics to them at a convention. In the best-case scenario, the process is seamless. Readers who have connected with you online might go out of their way to buy your book at a particular show. You might have been charming enough on a panel to inspire people to visit your table. But taking advantage of conventions as a distribution channel requires planning before the show and efficient use of time at your booth. We won't revisit the pre-show preparations from Chapter 38. Instead, this chapter will focus on using conventions and other target market events to deliver books to readers.

What are the Advantages of Convention Distribution?

When you distribute books at a con, you remove the middle man from the equation. This creates several benefits:

1. No gatekeepers between you and the market: You can distribute any book you want as long as you abide by whatever guidelines the individual con has in terms of content.

2. No discounts to third parties: In convention distribution, no distributor or retailer takes a cut of your revenue. Whatever price you charge your customers you get to keep. You might reduce your price to attract more sales, but that is optional.

3. No returns: Sales at cons are final. You don't have to worry about maintaining reserves against your returns when you sell directly to a customer.

4. Superior advocacy for your book: No one knows more about your book than you. No one is more invested in the success of your book than you. While you might not be the best salesperson or the most extroverted, you might be the best advocate to sell your book.

5. Superior connection to readers: Because marketing and sales occur together at cons, the opportunity exists to build relationships with your readers during the sales process. A quick chat about their favorite character from your story or the direction of the genre can turn a reader into a true fan. A signature on the book they just bought or some free swag can have a powerful impact on a reader that Amazon and Diamond can't easily replicate.

What Are the Downsides to Convention Distribution?

The hands-on nature of convention distribution creates specific challenges for publishers with limited resources:

1. Attendance: There are dozens of conventions every year, but your resources and your secret identity will limit the number of shows you can attend, if you can attend them at all.

2. Inventory: When you are the final distributor, you are responsible for shipping the books to the show, managing the inventory during the show, and returning any books that didn't sell.

3. Cost: Attending conventions costs money. Your revenue will be reduced by the amount you have to spend to get to, participate in, and get home from the show.

4. Time: As we discussed in Chapter 38, time spent selling at your table reduces your ability to schedule meetings, attend panels, or otherwise enjoy convention activities.

How Do You Make Money with Convention Distribution?

Generating profit at a convention boils down to selling a number of books that exceed the cost of attending the show. For example, if the cost to attend your local con is $1,000 (once you factor in the costs of the table, printing and shipping the books and Bar Con) and your graphic novel costs $20, then you need to sell more than 50 books to make a profit.

The more you can keep costs down, the easier it will be to generate a profit. Building a convention spreadsheet and the other methods we discussed in the convention marketing chapter are equally applicable here. Maximizing the number of books you sell involves choosing the convention that has the best chance of exposing your work to your target market and capitalizing on your physical presence to convince readers to give your book a chance.

How Do You Convince Readers to Buy Your Book?

The time you spend behind your table is critical to your convention distribution because you may never have a better chance at direct interaction with a potential reader. Based on the experience of creators who have worked cons for years, the key is to balance personal engagement with stamina[781]. Conventions are often crowded and hectic, so you won't have much time with each person. Try to keep it short and sweet. Use the fundamental marketing realities as a guide to your conversation:

1. **People buy from publishers they like, so give them reasons to like you** with a friendly welcome. Following up with a question about what they like, how they're enjoying the show or a comment about what they've already bought can help make them comfortable and give you an idea of how close they might be to an ideal reader.

---

[781] Nasser, N. (2017, May 07). Artists: How to Sell Your Work at a Convention. Retrieved May 23, 2020, from https://medium.com/@nolannasser/artists-how-to-sell-your-work-at-a-convention-85f5e1bdc4bb

2. **People don't want your book, they want the feeling your book offers**, so if it makes sense, try to leverage whatever you can tell about them (what they're wearing, what they said they liked, or the book on your table that they're glancing at) with a hook for your book. Your pitches from Chapter 5 can be useful tools if they hint at an experience that they might be interested in. If you can't describe your book in under ten seconds, you're going to lose them.

3. **People buy things they identify with, so they might not instantly buy your book if it doesn't speak to them in the moment**. If they give a positive response to your pitch, offer to ring it up for them. If they hesitate, don't be afraid to invite them to join your mailing list or if you have free promotional items, hand it to them with a smile. The potential reader who doesn't buy today could still become a true fan later after they've had a chance to identify with you and your message online.

4. **Your book can't be for everyone, so don't get discouraged when people decide they're not your ideal reader**. Rejection isn't fun on any level, but every time you greet someone at your table you get a chance to practice and refine your technique. You'll also get to be around people who love comics, and there are worse ways to spend the day.

Whether you are distributing your comic through a one on one sale or a major retail chain, the process is more than simply uploading a file or shipping books to a warehouse. It is building a system that connects your work to your readers and gives you a return on your investment of time and money. Choosing the right combination of distribution systems can be the difference between successful publishing and a frustrating experience.

One of the most crucial components of your print distribution will be getting the books printed and shipped. We've mentioned printing in relation to the direct market, bookstores, and conventions. Now it's time to take a deeper look at choosing a printer and working with them to complete the distribution process.

Even in the age of online everything, dozens of comic book apps, and emerging comic formats, the comic book industry is still dominated by printed books. Print comics outsell digital comics by a ratio of four to one[782]. You can't take advantage of the direct market, book channel, library, or convention distribution if you don't print your book. There is also a level of personal and professional legitimacy that comes from seeing the physical manifestation of your ideas on the shelf. Independent publishers need to embrace print if they want to maximize the potential of their books in the market.

But printing comics is a complex endeavor with dozens of variables to choose from. Each choice, or combination of choices, can impact the cost, quality, and timely delivery of your comic to the market. That's why it is important to wrap your head around the printing process before you dive into making your book.

What Pre-Production Factors Will Impact Your Printing Choice?

While there is a wealth of options to choose from when you decide to print your comic, those choices will be influenced by plans and resources you've already put in place. The final shape of your physical comic will be based on:

1. Your goals on where and how you want your story to be experienced.

2. Your budget and the level of investment available for printing

3. Your target market and their preferences for consuming comics

4. Your talent and who is managing the printing process[783]

5. The schedule you've developed to deliver the books to your distribution channels

6. The space you have available as storage for books on a long-term basis.

---

[782] Comics and Graphic Novel Sales Hit New High in 2018: Image 2. (2019). Retrieved May 23, 2020, from https://icv2.com/gallery/43106/2

[783] As we noted in chapter 18, the role of print manager needs to be spelled out in a contract and compensated in some manner.

How Much Does It Cost to Print Your Comic?

Comic book printing costs are similar to page rates because there is no one standard price to cover all the different variables in the process of securing a print quote[784], and each one of those variables can change over time. Understanding the pros and cons of each of the major considerations below will give you the foundation you need to determine the most viable cost for your book:

1. The type of paper you choose

2. The type of printing you choose

3. The geographic location of your printer

4. The shipping costs of your book

5. The storage costs (if any) for your book

What Are the Elements of Comic Book Paper?

Printed comics are categorized by their interior **paper stock**[785], cover stock, physical dimensions, and binding.

1. Interior paper stock (or text stock) comes in a variety of combinations based on five characteristics:

   a. **Thickness** is the measure of how many sheets of a particular paper it takes to make an inch of that paper[786]. This is measured in pages per inch (PPI). For example, paper with a PPI of 600 is half as thick as paper with a PPI of 300[787]. This consideration is important in determining both how wide the book might be on the shelf and in the shipping boxes.

[784] Comic Printing UK. (2019, March 27). How much does it cost to print a comic? Retrieved May 23, 2020, from http://www.creatorresource.com/how-much-does-it-cost-to-print-a-comic/

[785] In this context, paper stock is simply and industry term for the type of paper being used. Paper Stock. (n.d.). Retrieved May 23, 2020, from https://www.merriam-webster.com/dictionary/paper stock

[786] JAM Paper & Envelope Paper Weight Chart. (n.d.). Retrieved May 23, 2020, from https://www.jampaper.com/paper-weight-chart.asp

[787] Interview with Stephen Pakula Associate Director, Publishing Operations, Penguin Random House [Personal interview]. (2019, October 18).

b. **Weight** is the measure of the durability of each sheet of paper. This is measured in pounds (lbs)[788]. For example, 24 lb. paper is common for office usage, while 110 lb. paper is common in manila folders. The choice of paper weight impacts how much of the printing on one page will be visible when the reader turns the page to read the other side[789].

c. **Color** is the shade of paper before having any image printed on it[790]. There are a variety of colors to choose from, and even "white" paper has white/blue and cream variations[791]. The color of paper can have an impact on the way your final artwork catches the eye of the reader.

d. **Coating** is the additional surface placed on paper to alter the look and feel of the pages[792]. Matte paper is slightly reflective. Gloss coating is brighter. Uncoated paper is the most basic and economical[793].

e. **Availability** is the amount of inventory of any particular type of paper at any given time[794]. Depending on the timing of your book, this could be the most critical aspect of printing. Many printers will have a certain amount of stock on hand, which eliminates the need to order it from a paper mill. In these cases, options may be limited. However, any printer can order any stock direct from the mill, and will typically have samples for review by request, but it might take more time for your book to be printed. More frequently used stock may be cheaper than something that is rarely used[795].

2. **Cover Stock** is the type of material used on book covers[796]. Variations on cover stock can range from paper similar to text stock, or it can be rigid cardboard for hardcover titles. Like text

---

[788] About Paper Weights. (n.d.). Retrieved May 23, 2020, from https://paperworks.com/about-paper-weights

[789] Pakula Interview

[790] Pakula Interview

[791] Pakula Interview

[792] Baner, G. (n.d.). Understand Paper Weight, Different Types and Grades of Paper. Retrieved May 23, 2020, from https://www.colorcopiesusa.com/all-about-color-printing/printing-paper.htm

[793] Chilli Printing. (2020, April 21). Self-Publishing: How to Print Comic Books and Graphic Novels. Retrieved May 23, 2020, from https://www.chilliprinting.com/Online-Printing-Blog/self-publishing-how-to-print-comic-books-graphic-novels/

[794] Pakula Interview

[795] Pakula Interview

[796] Paper Weight Comparisons. (2020, April 23). Retrieved May 23, 2020, from https://printninja.com/printing-resource-center/printing-options/book-services/paper/weight

stock, cover stock can be coated to create specific effects. Unlike interior stock, cover stock is sometimes measured in points, with average comic cover stock ranging from 10-14 points[797].

a. <u>Physical Dimensions</u> are the length, width, and depth of your book. The depth (also referred to as the spine size or the spine width) will be influenced by the number of pages and the thickness of the text stock. The length and width are influenced by where you plan to distribute the book and how much you are willing to pay. Standard sized books are easier to fit on comic shop racks and bookshelves. Unique formats can help your book stand out, but they can increase the price. Standard sizes for single-issue comics and graphic novels are 6 5/8 inches in width and 10 3/16 inches in height[798] but there is some variation in the graphic novel dimensions. For example, the Dark Horse line of *Lone Wolf and Cub* trades were a smaller 7 ½ x 5, while the hardcover edition of The *Killing Joke* was slightly larger than the standard graphic novel.

b. <u>Binding</u> is the process that holds the pages of the book together. In comics, there are two main types of binding:

    i. **Saddle-stitched** books have the folded sheets held together by wire staples[799]. This is the common form of binding for single issues.

    ii. **Perfect bound** books are held together by glue on the spine of the book. This is the common form of binding for trade paperbacks and graphic novels. This type of binding also allows printing on the book's spine[800].

How Do You Select the Paper for Your Book?

Between the four main variables for paper, there are potentially thousands of permutations for printing your book. But your time and resources are limited. You don't want to reinvent comic book printing. Fortunately, there is a two-step process you can use to cut through the noise and spotlight the type of printed comic you want to publish.

1. <u>Personal preference</u>: Choose a comic from your collection (or the collection of one of your team members) that matches the look and feel of the type of comic you envision publishing. As an exercise, every member of the team can offer up a personal favorite and the group can

---

[797] Id.

[798] Chilli Printing. (2020, April 21). Self-Publishing: How to Print Comic Books and Graphic Novels.

[799] Beaty, K. (2013, October 22). Formax Printing Solutions. Retrieved May 23, 2020, from https://www.formaxprinting.com/blog/2013/10/six-things-to-consider-when-printing-a-comic-book-or-graphic-novel/

[800] Id.

weigh the pros and cons of each one. The winner of this process can be used as a sample in terms of all four variables.

2. <u>Competitive preference</u>: Pick up a copy of each of your competitors and select the best one to emulate. In the alternative, you can look at all your competitors together and try to determine if there are common elements you'd like to follow or deviate from. Going with the pack might help you fit in, but it might make it harder for you to stand out. Choosing a radically different printing template will have the opposite effect. Consider the options in terms of both ease of distribution and the preferences of your target market. Again, the winner of this process can be used as a sample book.

These two selection methods are not mutually exclusive. You can compare and contrast your personal favorites with the competition and select the best option from both categories.

What Are the Major Types of Comic Book Printing?

In addition to the physical aspects of your printed book, you also need to decide the process of printing. Comic book printing can be broken down into two major types: digital and offset[801].

1. **Digital printing** (often referred to as print on demand or POD) uses computers to deliver files to inkjet, laser, or thermal printers[802].

   a. <u>Benefits</u>:
      i. Faster turnaround time due to shorter set up times
      ii. Smaller print runs from 1 to 500 units are common
      iii. Modifications are easier to implement on the digital file if there is a problem

   b. <u>Downsides</u>:
      i. Costs are higher per unit than for offset printing
      ii. Limited size because digital printers might not be able to accommodate unique sizes

---

[801] Schiff, A. (2016). Offset Printing Versus Print-on-Demand. Retrieved May 23, 2020, from https://www.publishersweekly.com/pw/by-topic/authors/pw-select/article/63094-offset-printing-versus-print-on-demand.html

[802] Chilli Printing. (2020, April 21). Digital vs Offset Printing: The Ultimate Guide To Printing Methods. Retrieved May 23, 2020, from https://www.chilliprinting.com/Online-Printing-Blog/digital-vs-offset-printing-ultimate-guide-printing-methods/

        iii.   Colors limited to grayscale[803] and CMYK[804]

  2. **Offset Printing** uses ink transferred from a metal plate onto a rubber sheet which is then rolled onto paper fed through a press[805]. The large rolls are then cut into book shape and bound.

    a. Benefits[806]
        i.   Costs are often lower per unit than digital printing
        ii.   Increased number of options for sizes and materials
        iii.   Increased number of options for color palettes

    b. Downsides[807]
        i.   Longer set up times
        ii.   Larger print runs required

Why Does the Printer's Location Matter?

The physical location of your printer can impact the price and delivery time of your book. There are three major options each with their own benefits and downsides:

  1. **Local printers** are easily accessible to the residence of someone on your team.

    a. Benefits
        i.   You can establish a personal working relationship with printers who you can meet face to face.
        ii.   You have the option of being able to pick up the books yourself, saving on shipping costs[808].

---

[803] Grayscale is the collection or the range of monochromic (gray) shades, ranging from pure white on the lightest end to pure black on the opposite end. What is Grayscale? (n.d.). Retrieved May 23, 2020, from https://www.techopedia.com/definition/7468/grayscale

[804] CMYK stands for "Cyan Magenta Yellow Black." These are the four basic colors used for printing color images. CMYK. (n.d.). Retrieved May 23, 2020, from https://techterms.com/definition/cmyk

[805] Schiff, A. (2016). Offset Printing Versus Print-on-Demand. Retrieved August 16, 2020, from https://www.publishersweekly.com/pw/by-topic/authors/pw-select/article/63094-offset-printing-versus-print-on-demand.html

[806] Chilli Printing. (2020, April 21). Digital vs Offset Printing: The Ultimate Guide to Printing Methods.

[807] Ibid

[808] This benefit won't apply to orders from Diamond or other distributors

        iii.   You can be available to deal with any issues as they arise with the printing process[809].

    b.   <u>Downsides</u>
        i.   Local printers might not have any experience or skill printing comics
        ii.   Local printers may have limited options in terms of paper on hand
        iii.   Local printers may have limited options in terms of printing methods

2.   **National printers** are located in the publisher's home country, but might not be easily accessible by the team

    a.   <u>Benefits</u>
        i.   Easier to find experienced comics printers because you're casting a wider net
        ii.   Easier to find printers with access to the paper you want
        iii.   Easier to find printers with the printing method you want

    b.   <u>Downsides</u>
        i.   Business relationships are often remote
        ii.   Shipping costs can be higher

3.   **International printers** are located outside the publisher's home country

    a.   <u>Benefits</u>
        i.   Easier to find experienced comics printers because you're casting a wider net
        ii.   Potentially lower prices compared to domestic printers

    b.   <u>Downsides</u>
        i.   Business relationships are remote
        ii.   Shipping costs can be higher
        iii.   Shipping times can be longer because books have to travel by ship for 6-8 weeks[810]
        iv.   Customs, trade tariffs and other international trade regulations can increase the cost and delivery time of your book[811]

---

[809] Beatty, G. S. (Producer). (2016). *Publishing Comics Blog, Ep. 3, with Gary Scott Beatty: Choosing a Printer* [Video file]. Retrieved May 23, 2020, from https://www.youtube.com/watch?v=8VHpa-3CXs8&list=WL&index=6&t=0s

[810] Allen p. 51

[811] Tan, T. (2019). Taking a Closer Look at the Hong Kong and China Printing Industry. Retrieved May 23, 2020, from https://www.publishersweekly.com/pw/by-topic/industry-news/manufacturing/article/81031-taking-a-closer-look-at-the-hong-kong-and-china-printing-industry.html

Keep in mind that it might not always be readily apparent where your book is being printed based on the company you work with. Local printers might subcontract the job to a national printer and international printers can have offices in the United States to work with local clients. If the location of the printer matters to you, it helps to determine where the book is actually being printed as part of your selection process.

How Do You Select a Printer?

Once you have a firm grasp of what you want and how you want it printed, you'll be in a better position to evaluate each potential printer.

The easiest option is to go with a large national POD operation. Comixology recently announced a POD option[812] to coincide with their Createspace service and there are several other web-based print options available[813] including Alterna[814], Kablam[815], Mixam[816], Lightning Source[817], Print Ninja[818], and RA Comics Direct[819]. Some of these printers also offer distribution services, which can be helpful to coordinate delivery. Just keep in mind that many of these companies only offer limited options when it comes to text, cover stock, and dimensions, and their terms are often non-negotiable.

Publishers who want a more custom book need to secure a print quote from the sales reps of several different printers and evaluate them like the talent RFP we discussed earlier. The sample books you selected should be used as part of the initial discussion to make sure everyone understands what you're looking for. In this situation, the factors that should be considered include:

1. References (do they have experience printing and shipping comics?)

2. Samples they can deliver for your review

3. Availability in terms of both paper and the printing service itself

---

[812] Terror, J. (2018, June 01). ComiXology Introduces Amazon Print-on-Demand - The Future of Comics? Retrieved May 23, 2020, from https://www.bleedingcool.com/2018/06/01/comixology-introduces-amazon-print-on-demand-the-future-of-comics/

[813] King, B. (2018, July 16). The 4 Best Online Print-on-Demand Book Services for Self-Publishers. Retrieved May 23, 2020, from https://www.makeuseof.com/tag/top-4-online-selfpublishers-book-write/

[814] Alterna Printing Partnership Program. (n.d.). Retrieved May 23, 2020, from https://www.alternacomics.com/ppp

[815] Ka-Blam Digital Printing: Comics, Paperbacks, Manga and more since 2005. (n.d.). Retrieved May 23, 2020, from http://ka-blam.com/main/

[816] Comic Book Printing - The Best Price & Quality. (n.d.). Retrieved May 23, 2020, from https://mixam.com/comicbooks

[817] Print-On-Demand. (n.d.). Retrieved May 23, 2020, from https://www.ingramcontent.com/publishers/print/print-on-demand

[818] Comic Book Printer: PrintNinja makes offset printing affordable. (2019, January 30). Retrieved May 23, 2020, from https://printninja.com/printing-products/comic-book-printing

[819] RA Comics Direct. (n.d.). Retrieved May 23, 2020, from https://www.racomicsdirect.com/racomicsdirect/

4. Pricing for printing, shipping and if necessary, storage

5. Timing of delivery

6. Process for delivering print files

7. Contractual terms between your company and the printer

The print quotes from each sales reps can then be evaluated relative to your pre-production factors to narrow down your search for the right printer.

How Do You Work with Your Printer?

Once you select a printer, it is your job as a publisher to maintain an efficient working relationship. You have to ensure at least one person on your team is the main point of contact for the printer, and that person needs to understand the specific process with that printer to avoid costly mistakes and delays[820].

Every printer has slightly different delivery requirements, so your team's print manager needs to both understand the trim, bleed, safe areas, and file specs and relay that information to the creative team[821].

Prior to actual printing, many printers will offer digital or physical **proofs**[822] or a preliminary version of a printed book for review and approval. These proofs are often the last opportunity a publisher will have to correct any mistakes in the creative elements or errors in the printing, so multiple members of the team should review the proofs wherever possible. Multiple sets of fresh eyes are an asset here.

Timing is also an issue that will affect creative scheduling and distribution timing. Depending on the printer and method of distribution, final print-ready files may need to be delivered anywhere from 4-10 weeks before the scheduled on-sale date. For international printing, you may need to add 6-8 more weeks to account for ship transportation and customs[823].

---

[820] Manning p. 101

[821] Smith, A. (2019, April 13). Comic Printing 101: Understanding the Basics of Comic Book File Setup. Retrieved May 23, 2020, from https://cxcbuzz.com/comic-printing-101-understanding-the-basics-of-file-setup/

[822] Beaty, K. (2011, June 09). Printing Lingo: What is a Proof? Retrieved May 23, 2020, from https://www.formaxprinting.com/blog/2011/06/printing-lingo-what-is-a-proof/

[823] Paukla Interview

How Much Should You Print?

Overprinting[824] is an easy way for independent publishers to lose money. To reduce the per-unit cost by offset printing, some publishers will print hundreds, or perhaps thousands of copies more than they need for any given period. This creates two potential problems. First, you could burn through your limited investment by increasing the print run when you could be using that money for other aspects of your business. Second, you might create an additional cost to store the unused books somewhere if your secret identity doesn't have ready access to suitable storage space.

Whenever possible, I suggest offset printing as little as possible to satisfy your target market. Make sure your print run can cover whatever Diamond orders you get, plus whatever you think you might need for conventions, sample copies, and local distribution. When printing overseas, you might want to print a few extra so you don't have to wait two months or more for new books to come in. Of course, you can solve the overprinting problem with POD, as long as the higher per-unit costs make sense for your business.

Congratulations. You now know what story you're going to publish, how you're going to pay for it, who is going to make it, who is going to read it, and how you're going to deliver it. It's time to take the next major step in independent publishing.

It's time to make your comics.

---

[824] Overprint. (n.d.). Retrieved May 23, 2020, from https://www.dictionary.com/browse/overprint

STAGE 2: PRODUCTION

Or "How Are You Going to Create Your Comic?
"

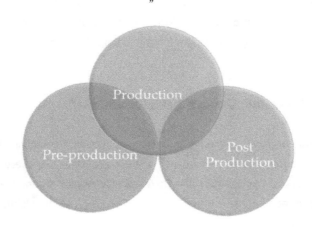

Creative skill is central to the production of narrative sequential art. While a prudent business professional can build the structure to finance, produce, and distribute comics, it takes inspired artists to translate the formal copyrights into stories readers care about. An independent publisher can always engage creative talent to create their comics, but there are concrete benefits to also learning and developing your creativity for your book.

But the conventions and techniques of sequential art are not innate. No one is born knowing how to make comics. Professional comic creators take years learning and honing their craft. It might take a decade or more for them to develop a distinctive style. I wrote the pre-production section of ICP under the premise that you could assume any or all of the roles required to make comics. Your options for acquiring creative skills are the subject of this chapter.

If you don't already possess the creative skill to make comics, **there are three general methods you can use to improve your abilities; formal, informal, and practical**. These methods are not mutually exclusive. During your career, it might make sense for you to utilize any and all of these options to improve your narrative storytelling ability.

What Formal Education Options Exist for Comics?

Independent publishers who aspire to be artists can acquire a certificate, bachelor's, or master's degrees in comics, graphic novels, and sequential art[825]. These programs are offered in schools created for comic arts like the Kubert School[826] or SCAD[827] the Savannah College of Art and Design, general visual arts colleges like SVA or FIT, or at prestigious universities like Carnegie Mellon, Columbia or UCLA[828].

---

[825] Sequential Art College and Program Information. (2019). Retrieved May 23, 2020, from https://study.com/articles/Sequential_Art_College_and_Program_Information.html

[826] The Kubert School. (n.d.). Retrieved May 23, 2020, from http://www.kubertschool.edu/

[827] Sequential art at SCAD. (n.d.). Retrieved May 23, 2020, from https://www.scad.edu/academics/programs/sequential-art

[828] Sequential Art College and Program Information. (2019)

Emerging writers can earn a degree with a specific focus on comics from institutions like the California College of the Arts[829], the International School of Comics[830], or the New York Film Academy[831]. They can also study at any college or university for a Masters of Fine Arts in writing[832].

There is also a school of thought emphasizing the importance of a business education to succeed in comics[833]. The argument here is that while artistic skill and creative voice can be developed through other means, understanding marketing, advertising, sales, and overall business management require more traditional learning. If you decide to go this route, there are hundreds of business schools across America to choose from[834].

Consider both time and costs before you enroll in a degree program for comics. This type of formal education can run from 6 months to 4 years on a part-time or full-time basis and can require just as much study and homework as other fields of study whether you do it online or in person. The costs of these programs can run between $10,000 and $55,000 depending on the institution and related costs for the degree.

Why would an independent publisher spend years of their lives and thousands of dollars to get a formal education in comics? The main reasons boil down to managing the resources of time and money. A publisher with a high-risk tolerance at the beginning of their professional career might decide to make comics their secret identity and make a living from the art form[835]. Formal education can provide a springboard into that career that will only enhance their ability as an independent publisher. At the same time, it might take several years to stumble on the perfect idea, secure enough investment, find the right team, and establish a substantial market. If you can devote your secret identity to learning the craft of comics while you're in pre-production, you'll be in a better position to capitalize on your ideas.

Of course, not everyone has the time or the inclination to get a degree in comics. For them, an informal education might make more sense.

---

[829] The Best Masters of Fine Arts (MFA) Degrees. (n.d.). Retrieved May 23, 2020, from https://www.collegechoice.net/rankings/best-master-of-fine-arts-degrees/

[830] International School of Comics Chicago. (n.d.). Retrieved May 23, 2020, from http://www.schoolofcomics.us/

[831] 15-Week Online Writing For Comic Books Workshop. (n.d.). Retrieved May 23, 2020, from https://www.nyfa.edu/online-screenwriting/workshops/15-week-online-writing-for-comic-books.php

[832] MFA Programs Database. (n.d.). Retrieved May 23, 2020, from https://www.pw.org/mfa

[833] "Perch" (Producer). (2019). *Breaking into Comics? What's the Best College Degree to Have?* [Video file]. Retrieved May 23, 2020, from https://www.youtube.com/watch?v=VSOd6AqzUIE&feature=youtu.be

[834] The Best MBA Programs in America, Ranked. (n.d.). Retrieved May 23, 2020, from https://www.usnews.com/best-graduate-schools/top-business-schools/mba-rankings

[835] Become a Comic Book Artist: Education and Career Roadmap. (2020). Retrieved May 23, 2020, from https://study.com/articles/Become_a_Comic_Book_Artist_Education_and_Career_Roadmap.html

What Informal Education Options Exist for Comics?

Creating comics is not like being a lawyer or driving a car. **There are no official requirements or licenses you need to be an accepted part of the profession**. While comic degrees may be helpful in your comics career, they are not essential or even necessary[836]. Having said that, learning the craft of comics from professionals who can help you find your voice and navigate the pitfalls can be beneficial to your independent publishing.

Informal learning differs from formal programs in cost, time, and recognized certification. Where a formal education might cost tens of thousands of dollars, informal classes normally don't cost more than a few hundred. Earning a formal degree might take years. Finishing an informal course might take months. Reading a book on comics might take a couple of weeks. Attending a university can earn you a degree. An online class can't. Deciding which is better depends on your goals, your resources, and your position in life.

The two main types of informal learning are specialized training and informal study. Specialized training can come from established online services like Comics Experience[837], Sequential Arts Workshop[838], or the Cartoonist Academy[839]. You might also be able to find someone willing to train you on a one on one basis. Just make sure that you do your due diligence on whatever program you are considering. You want to avoid wasting money with people who don't have any real knowledge of the craft or experience in the business.

There are also several well-made books about drawing and writing for comics. Some of these books are classics in the industry, others are more recent and technical, but both types belong in the library of any independent publisher:

- *The Complete Guide to Self-Publishing Comics* by Comfort Love and Adam Withers[840]

- *Creating Comics from Start to Finish* by Buddy Scalera and Chris Eliopoulos[841]

---

[836] Blaylock, J. (2006). *How to self-publish comics not just create them*. Chicago: Devil's due.

[837] Schmidt, A. (2014, July 12). Comics Experience Courses and Community. Retrieved May 23, 2020, from https://www.comicsexperience.com/

[838] Drummond, B., Eby, J., & Antunes, K. (n.d.). Courses in Comics and Graphic Novels by SAW's Top Educators. Retrieved May 23, 2020, from https://learn.sawcomics.org/

[839] The Cartoonist Academy. (n.d.). Retrieved May 23, 2020, from https://www.thecartoonistacademy.com/available-online

[840] Love, C., & Withers, A. (2015). *The complete guide to self-publishing comics: How to create and sell your comic books, manga, and webcomics*. Berkeley: Watson-Guptill.

[841] Scalera, B. (2011). *Creating comics from start to finish: Top pros reveal the complete creative process*. Cincinnati, OH: IMPACT Books.

- *The DC Guide to Creating Comics*[842]

- *How to Draw Comics the Marvel Way* by Stan Lee and John Buscema[843]

- *The Insider's Guide to Creating Comics and Graphic Novels* by Andy Schmidt[844]

- *Making Comics* by Scott McCloud[845]

- *Story* by Robert McKee[846]

- *Words for Pictures* by Brian Michael Bendis[847]

- *Writing for Comics* by Alan Moore and Jacen Burrows[848]

There are also several online tutorials explaining details on the craft of creating comics. Channels like Strip Panel Naked[849] on YouTube deconstruct the techniques of well-known artists and writers that you can learn from in your books.

What Practical Education Options Exist for Comics?

Whether you decide to pursue a formal or informal education on the creation of comics, at some point you're going to have to spread your wings and make a comic of your own. **Ultimately, the best way to learn how to make comics is to make comics.** On a larger scale, the entire premise of this book is for you to publish a comic as a method for understanding the comic book industry as a whole.

As with any education process, mistakes and failures are inevitable. Your first comic will probably not be your best comic. This is why **starting small is usually the best course of action**. If you start by focusing on a one-page story first, you can build your confidence without being overwhelmed. If you level up to a

---

[842] Potts, C., & Lee, J. (2013). *The DC Comics guide to creating comics: Inside the art of visual storytelling*. New York: Watson-Guptill Publications.

[843] Lee, S., & Buscema, J. (1984). *How to draw comics the Marvel way*. New York: Fireside.

[844] Schmidt, A. (2009). *The insider's guide to creating comics and graphic novels*. Cincinnati, OH: Impact.

[845] McCloud, S. (2008). *Making comics storytelling secrets of comics, manga and graphic novels*. New York, NY: Harper.

[846] MacKee, R. (2010). *Story: Substance, structure, style, and the principles of screenwriting*. New York, NY: ItBooks.

[847] Bendis, B. M. (2014). *Words for pictures: The art and business of writing comics and graphic novels*. Berkeley, CA: Watson-Guptill.

[848] Moore, A., & Burrows, J. (2010). *Alan Moore's writing for comics*. Rantoul, IL: Avatar Press.

[849] Strip Panel Naked (Producer). (n.d.). *Strip Panel Naked* [Video file]. Retrieved May 23, 2020, from https://www.youtube.com/channel/UCYJAToPH5GSGShP7Yoc3jsA/about

three-page story, then a five-page story, you can play with ideas you are considering for your final book. By the time you are ready to tell your full story, you can gain several benefits from a gradual approach:

- Idea Management: You can ensure that you can tell a coherent and interesting story in a short amount of time. You can also experiment with radical ideas without feeling compelled to publish them before they are ready.

- Investment: Your overall costs will be lower if you start with fewer pages.

- Talent Management: You can test out different members of your team and a combination of team members without burning through your budget.

- Marketing: Your creative and developmental process can be shared with your target market as a way of building a connection with them.

This book can't teach you the art of making comics. That's not my background and there are too many other quality sources of experience and knowledge for you to choose from. What I can do is lay out the options you have when it comes to production for you to make the most of your resources for publishing your comic. After you gain the skills to make a comic, the first major production decision you need to make is the specific form your comic will take.

Chapter 50: How Do You Select the Form of Your Comics?

We've used the terms "comic", "book" and "project" to describe your publishing content up to this point. But in the same way the word "car" can be used to refer to a Honda, Mercedes or Lamborghini, comic is a generic term. We're now at the point where we need to be specific about the form your story will take and how you go about selecting it.

The format you choose shouldn't be selected in a vacuum. Like every other aspect of the production and post-production process, the form you choose will be influenced, if not determined, by the decisions and resources you collected in pre-production. Specifically, the form of your book will be based on:

- Your goals for the book
- The nature of your story
- Your budget
- The capabilities of you and your team
- The preferences of your target market
- The characteristics of your distribution channels
- Your time table for release

There is a direct relationship between each of these factors individually and collectively when it comes to the form of your story. In the simplest terms, **your format needs to fit your story**. Industry veterans don't choose a format and then treat it as a container that they have to "fill" with a story[850]. They only use the format that fits the story and the market.

For example, it doesn't make sense to decide to do an ongoing series of single-issue comics if your story can't sustain momentum for more than four issues. It might make more sense to choose a limited series or a graphic novel in that case and save yourself the pain of watching your story fizzle out of existence or sputter along after the magic is gone.

---

[850] Make Comics Podcast Episode #171 - What Streaming TV Can Teach Us About Story Formats. (2019, April 23). Retrieved May 23, 2020, from https://www.comicsexperience.com/podcast/171-what-streaming-tv-can-teach-us-about-story-formats/

What Are the Major Comic Book Formats?

Let's agree on a couple of basic definitions before we examine each comic book format. These definitions are not universal or set in stone[851], but we can use them to establish a common terminology and work from there.

- A **panel** is a single comic book image, with or without text, often bordered by four black lines known as the gutter[852]. This is the foundation of all comic book formats[853].

  There are also many non-traditional panel styles that are limited only by the creativity of your team and the capabilities of your technology. For example, Matt Wagner's *Grendel: Devil by the Deed* used a series of art deco style frames in overlapping sequences instead of gutters. The pages of David Mack's *Kabuki* often had no panels but instead offered stream of consciousness like musings that would guide the reader's eye from one image or block of text to another.

- A **page** is a collection of panels that can all be viewed on a single surface. In printed formats, it is one side of a sheet of paper from the fold in the middle out to one edge[854]. In digital formats, it is one PDF image.

  Page Variations: There are several basic variations to a page to keep in mind when thinking about this definition. These variations have a long history in printed comics, but depending on the device your target market uses, they might not be as effective.

  A **splash page** is an entire page covered by a single panel[855].

  A **double-page** spread is two facing pages joined by an overlapping element (often a single image) and intended to be read across the fold of a printed book[856].

---

[851] Weldon, G. (2016, November 17). The Term 'Graphic Novel' Has Had A Good Run. We Don't Need It Anymore. Retrieved May 23, 2020, from https://www.npr.org/2016/11/17/502422829/the-term-graphic-novel-has-had-a-good-run-we-dont-need-it-anymore

[852] Love, C., & Withers, A. (2015). *The complete guide to self-publishing comics: How to create and sell your comic books, manga, and webcomics*. Berkeley: Watson-Guptill p. 60

[853] Love and Withers, p.59

[854] Schmidt, A. (2009). *The insider's guide to creating comics and graphic novels*. Cincinnati, OH: Impact. P. 7

[855] Love and Withers, p. 61

[856] Schmidt p. 6

Now that we can agree on the basic building blocks of comics, we can use these definitions to establish the main comic book formats and the factors you use to select the best one for you. Keep in mind that we are not focusing on the content of the comics here. Any format of comic can support any genre of story. The consideration of format simply defines the structure used to distribute the story.

- A **webcomic** is a comic published online[857]. They can be composed of a single panel, or they can be comprised of several comic book pages.

- A **single issue** is what we refer to as a generic "comic". It can be published as a digital comic [858] on a service like Comixology or as a traditional printed comic (sometimes called a "floppy"). Single issues are often published as part of an ongoing series, but this is not always the case since "one-shot" comics are fairly common[859]. The length of a traditional printed comic has varied over time[860], but the average comic book length today is between 20 and 32 pages[861]. with the story running between 20 and 24 pages and the overall printed length running between 28 and 32 pages

- A **mini-series** or a limited series is a finite number of single issues ostensibly used to tell a defined story[862]. Typical mini-series contain 3-12 issues.

- A **trade paperback** (also known as a trade or abbreviated as TPB) is a collection of single issues perfect bound together and sold as a single unit. The single issues are often released first, either as an ongoing series or as a mini-series. The norm hovers between 3 and 7 issues for a normal trade or considerably more issues for an omnibus edition[863].

- A **graphic novel** (also known as a GN or an OGN for original graphic novel) is a comic that is perfect bound and contains a complete story. For my purposes, a graphic novel differs from a trade because a graphic novel is not released in prior single issues. Some use graphic novel to describe any comic that is book-length[864], but since there is no standard for the length of a

[857] Webcomic. (n.d.). Retrieved May 25, 2020, from https://www.dictionary.com/browse/webcomic

[858] Digital comic. (2020, May 20). Retrieved May 25, 2020, from https://en.wikipedia.org/wiki/Digital_comic

[859] Carven, D., Zyn, Van, T., (2019, August 01). Glossary of Comic Book Terms. Retrieved May 25, 2020, from https://www.howtolovecomics.com/comic-book-glossary-of-terms/

[860] Cronin, B. (2017, August 14). How Many Pages Long Have Marvel Comic Stories Been Over the Years? Retrieved May 25, 2020, from https://www.cbr.com/marvel-comics-how-many-pages-long/

[861] Id

[862] Mini-Series (Concept). (n.d.). Retrieved May 25, 2020, from https://comicvine.gamespot.com/mini-series/4015-56281/

[863] Trade Paperback (Concept). (n.d.). Retrieved May 25, 2020, from https://comicvine.gamespot.com/trade-paperback/4015-44515/

[864] A Glossary of Basic Comics Terms. (2016, February 11). Retrieved May 25, 2020, from https://bookriot.com/2016/02/11/glossary-basic-comics-terms/

book, this definition can be vague. Graphic novels can be as short as several dozen pages or as long as several hundred pages.

- An **anthology** is a collection of comics, often involving different characters and/or creative teams[865]. They may contain webcomics or comic strips too short for standalone publication[866], or they might be a compilation of single issues. To the best of my knowledge, there is no theoretical limit to the length of an anthology.

What Are the Differences Between Formats?

We looked at some of the main formats as part of our analysis of distribution, but since many formats are native to multiple distribution channels, it pays to examine the characteristics of each one from a production standpoint, based on the factors we listed at the beginning of the chapter. As you review each format, keep in mind that the "budget" is only the creative costs, and doesn't cover overhead, printing, or shipping. This amount is measured as a range between $10-$100 per page because as we saw earlier, page rates can vary wildly from one publisher to another.

- **Webcomics**
    - Goals: Publishers who want an immediate and direct connection to their market should consider webcomics

    - Stories:
        - Webcomics can be extremely current and timely because the production cycle is the shortest in the industry.
        - Webcomics work well for both humor, pop culture, and political genres[867]
        - Webcomics also translate well into merchandise and viral content because a small number of images can migrate to social media memes as easily as they can appear on t-shirts.

    - Budget: $10-$100 per issue. If the number of pages is less than 1, then the cost per issue is based on whatever you pay for that one page.

    - Team Capabilities:

---

[865] Anthology (Concept). (n.d.). Retrieved May 25, 2020, from https://comicvine.gamespot.com/anthology/4015-49312/

[866] Comics anthology. (2019, November 11). Retrieved May 25, 2020, from https://en.wikipedia.org/wiki/Comics_anthology

[867] Allen, p. 74

- The time commitment for each comic might be relatively small based on the amount of content required for each issue, but since it might take 3 years or more to gain market traction[868], the team needs to be willing to stick with the project.
- Many webcomics are sometimes created by solo creators.

- Market Preferences: Webcomics are good for audiences that do not frequent the book channel, conventions, the direct market, or libraries

- Distribution Channels:
  - Digital distribution (including social media)
  - Compilations of webcomics can often be collected into print anthologies at a later date

- Time Table: Frequency is set by the publisher, but consistency is key to maintaining the audience[869]

- Other Considerations: The rapid nature of webcomics can create a situation where inadvertent errors, legal complications like slander and infringement, or social media faux pas slip out because the content is being delivered faster than the publisher can review for those types of issues. An editorial review is recommended to avoid these problems.

- Example: Safely Endangered[870]

- **Single Issues**
  - Goals: Publishers with an ongoing story who want to create consistent novelty in the traditional comic book markets should consider single issue comics.

  - Stories: Single issues lend themselves towards episodic stories that have major **cliffhangers**[871] (or suspenseful endpoints) spread throughout the narrative.

  - Budget: $200-$3,200 per issue. If the number of pages is between 20 and 32, then the cost per issue is based on whatever you pay per page and the total number of pages.

---

[868] Allen, p. 101

[869] Allen p. 101

[870] McCoy, C. (2019, July 31). Safely Endangered. Retrieved May 25, 2020, from https://www.safelyendangered.com/

[871] Cliffhanger. (n.d.). Retrieved May 25, 2020, from https://www.dictionary.com/browse/cliffhanger

- Team Capabilities: The team needs to be able to work together to both finish the creative aspects of the book and handle the business responsibilities of each issue for as long as the series runs

- Market Preferences: Single issues work well for markets who consume content in the direct market, online, and conventions

- Distribution Channels: conventions, digital distribution, direct market

- Time Table: Comixology approvals, Diamond acceptance and solicitations, printing, and shipping all need to be taken into account.

- Other Considerations:
  - According to some analysts, single-issue sales make most of their money from initial orders and there is usually very little reorder activity[872].
  - Momentum is important in single-issue sales. If your books are late or published too far apart, you risk losing the interest of the direct market[873].
  - Some experienced comics readers engage in a practice referred to as "**trade waiting**" where they read the first issue of a series and then wait for the TPB[874]. This can directly impact the financial viability of your single issues depending on how long you plan to publish your series.
  - According to ICV2, 72% of the purchases in comic shops are male with 71% white, 12% Hispanic, 10% Black, and 8% Asian[875]

- Example: *Cerberus the Aardvark*[876]

- **Limited Series**
  - Goals: Publishers with a finite story to tell but would still like to take advantage of the potential single-issue revenue should consider a limited series

---

[872] Allen, P. 50

[873] Wampler, D. (2015). *Selling Your Comic Book Concept: A Step-by-Step Guide for Creators.* Amazon.com Services LLC. Retrieved May 16, 2020, from https://www.amazon.com/Selling-Comic-Concept-Step-Step-ebook/dp/B011M3I4XS/ref=sr_1_1?

[874] Van, T., (2019, September 27). The Advantages and Disadvantages of Trade Waiting " How To Love Comics. Retrieved May 25, 2020, from https://www.howtolovecomics.com/2013/12/10/trade-waiting-advantages-disadvantages/

[875] Alverson, B. (2017). NYCC Insider Sessions Powered by ICv2: A Demographic Snapshot of Comics Buyers. Retrieved May 25, 2020, from https://icv2.com/articles/news/view/38709/nycc-insider-sessions-powered-icv2-a-demographic-snapshot-comics-buyers

[876] Cerebus. (n.d.). Retrieved May 25, 2020, from https://comicvine.gamespot.com/cerebus/4005-24391/

- Stories: Limited series follow the same pattern as an ongoing single-issue story.

- Budget: $600-$38,400. If the number of issues is between 3 and 12, then the cost per issue is based on whatever you pay per page and the total number of pages.

- Team Capabilities: The team needs to be able to work together to both finish the creative aspects of the book and handle the business responsibilities of each issue for the length of the series.

- Market Preferences: Limited series work well for markets who consume content in the direct market, online, and conventions

- Distribution Channels: conventions, digital distribution, direct market

- Time Table: Comixology approvals, Diamond acceptance and solicitations, printing, and shipping all need to be taken into account.

- Other Considerations: Limited series lend themselves to trade paperback releases after the series is over, but trade waiting can have a major impact on limited series sales.

- Example: Last Days of American Crime[877]

- **Trade Paperback (TPB)**
    - Goals: Publishers with a collection of single issues who want to take advantage of expanded distribution channels should consider a TPB

    - Stories: Limited series follow the same pattern as an ongoing single-issue story.

    - Budget: $0. If the creative costs were absorbed in the single-issue sales, then there is no creative cost to the trade other than a design cost. While there may be additional costs for a designer, proofreader, and printing of the new editions, if there are any outstanding creative costs that haven't been recovered in the single issues, the publisher may be able to recover some of those costs by releasing a trade

    - Team Capabilities: The publication of the trade is more of a responsibility of the business team, unless there is new creative material added to the trade to entice single issue readers to buy the story again.

---

[877] Remender, R., & Tocchini, G. (2010). *The last days of American crime*. Los Angeles, CA: Radical.

- **Market Preferences**: Trades work well for markets who consume content in the direct market, online, conventions, book channel, and libraries

- **Distribution Channels**: book channel, conventions, digital distribution, direct market, libraries

- **Time Table**: Comixology approvals, Diamond acceptance, and solicitations, book channel solicitations, printing, and shipping all need to be taken into account.

- **Other Considerations**: Trades can physically survive in retail environments like bookstores and libraries better than single-issue comics

- **Example**: Dark Ark[878]

- **Graphic Novel (GN)**
  - **Goals**: Publishers with a finite story who want to focus on the bookstore and library markets should consider graphic novels

  - **Stories**: Graphic novels lend themselves to closed narratives. They are similar to novels because they can use recurring characters and settings, but unlike single issues or trades, they don't typically have a potentially perpetual existence

  - **Budget**: $480- $20,000+. The GN cost is based on the amount you pay per page multiplied by the total number of pages.

  - **Team Capabilities**:
    - The team needs to be able to work together to both finish the creative aspects of the book and handle the business responsibilities of each issue without any incremental income or other milestones in the creative process
    - GN are sometimes created by solo publishers.

  - **Market Preferences**: Trades work well for markets who consume content in the direct market, online, conventions, book channel, and libraries

  - **Distribution Channels**: book channel, conventions, digital distribution, direct market, libraries

---

[878] Bunn, C., Doe, J., Hill, R., & Sharpe, D. (2017). *Dark ark*. Sherman Oaks, CA: AfterShock Comics.

- Time Table: Comixology approvals, Diamond acceptance, and solicitations, book channel solicitations, printing, and shipping all need to be taken into account.

- Other Considerations:
  - GN can physically survive in retail environments like bookstores and libraries better than comics
  - There is anecdotal evidence that women and the YA market are more likely to buy outside of the direct market, but according to ICV2, almost 60% of the book channel is still made up of men[879].

- Example: Bingo Love[880]

- **Anthology**
  - Goals: A publisher with several different shorter stories can consider an anthology as an addition to or instead of webcomics

  - Stories:
    - Anthologies lend themselves to a general theme or concept, or unrelated stories about a specific character or set of characters. Similar to a short story, the narratives don't have to be ongoing or finite. They can end abruptly or leave the door open for further exploration.
    - Anthologies can be used to test experimental stories, since there is less of a commitment on the part of the publisher and the reader to invest in a new idea.

  - Budget: $480- $20,000+. The cost is based on the amount you pay per page multiplied by the total number of pages.

  - Team Capabilities:
    - Anthologies can utilize multiple creative teams to tell each story, but there still needs to be editorial oversight for the complete publication and a business team ready to market and sell the final product.
    - Anthologies are often a showcase for new talent to prove themselves before they "graduate" to larger projects.

---

[879] Alverson, B. (2017). NYCC Insider Sessions Powered by ICv2: A Demographic Snapshot of Comics Buyers. Retrieved May 25, 2020, from https://icv2.com/articles/news/view/38709/nycc-insider-sessions-powered-icv2-a-demographic-snapshot-comics-buyers

[880] Franklin, T., St-Onge, J., San, J., & Rae, C. (2018). *Bingo love*. Portland, OR: Image Comics.

- Market Preferences: Anthologies work well for markets willing to experiment with different types of stories and new talent in the direct market, online, conventions, book channel, and libraries

- Distribution Channels: book channel, conventions, digital distribution, direct market, libraries

- Time Table: Comixology approvals, Diamond acceptance, and solicitations, book channel solicitations, printing, and shipping all need to be taken into account.

- Other Considerations:
  - If there are multiple creative teams working on a project, extra care must be taken to secure contracts with each member of each creative team to ensure there are no claims of infringement after publication.
  - If there is going to be a split of royalties based on the sales of the book, then it is important that the share for each creative team, and each member of each creative team, is clearly laid out in the contract to avoid confusion and hostility if the book makes a profit

- Example: All We Ever Wanted[881]

The comic book format you choose is not an all or nothing situation. It is often possible, if not preferable, to employ multiple formats for your book, depending on your goals and your market. As long as you own (or have the right to use) the underlying IP, you can mix and match formats at will. The next chapter will explore the sequencing of using each of the comic book formats in a way that can benefit your marketing, your distribution, and your sales.

---

[881] Miner, M., Palicki, E., & Chin-Tanner, T. (2018). *All we ever wanted: Stories of a better world.* New York: A Wave Blue World.

Releasing a single story in multiple formats can often build the momentum of your marketing, expose multiple groups of readers to your work, and increase the potential revenue of your publishing. **The industry has developed traditional and logical patterns for this sequence of releases that an independent publisher can alter and modify depending on the situation.**

Some models are challenging to alter, but nothing is prohibited. For example, it doesn't usually make sense to release a trade paperback before releasing the single issues in the same distribution channels, because the narrative suspense of the later issues is lost when the reader can just look at the last page of the trade. However, an anthology of comics can be re-released as webcomics because the accessibility, time, and price commitments are different for each format and some readers might be interested in certain stories of the overall work and not in others. It all depends on what you can produce and how your target market wants to read your story. The sequence of the formats, are like the formats themselves, they need to fit the story you are telling.

So, **the sequence I provide below can be considered as a suggestion, not a rule**. It is based on arrangements I've witnessed as both a comic reader and working in the industry. It also has similarities to the evolving release window considerations of modern film, television, and video games[882].

- <u>Preview Art</u> (Teaser): Developmental and promotional art or sample pages released on your website or social media for free can be similar to the release of teaser trailers[883] because they can arouse interest without giving away too much of the story.

- <u>Webcomic</u> (Trailer[884]): A scene, short sequence or selected segments of your story can be released on your website along with the cover art to convey the pitch, hook, and mood of the story

- <u>Digital Single Issue</u> (Episodic Release): Each issue of an ongoing or limited series can be released incrementally as a webcomic, digital single issue in the same manner as network,

---

[882] McClintock, P., & Keegan, R. (2019, August 27). Netflix Forgoes Wide Release for Martin Scorsese's 'The Irishman'. Retrieved May 25, 2020, from https://www.hollywoodreporter.com/news/netflix-forgoes-wide-release-martin-scorseses-irishman-1234382

[883] Teaser. (n.d.). Retrieved May 25, 2020, from https://www.merriam-webster.com/dictionary/teaser

[884] Trailer. (n.d.) Retrieved May 25, 2020, from https://www.merriam-webster.com/dictionary/trailer

cable, and certain streaming services[885] without absorbing the costs or dealing with the challenges of the direct market.

- Print Single Issue (Episodic Release): After the digital release has captured a certain segment of the target market and generated revenue, the digital issues can be released in print, either through the direct market or convention distribution or as part of a crowdfunding campaign.

- Digital Trade Paperback (Binge Release): At the end of the episodic release cycle, the collected story can be released in a collected digital format for those readers who prefer to read their stories all at once[886]. The digital trade can be a straight compilation of the single issues, or they could include bonus material (such as alternative cover artwork, wallpapers, or short stories) as an incentive to entice episodic readers to buy the story again in the same way DVDs used to add deleted scenes and commentary to the main film.

- Print Trade Paperback (Home Video Release): Depending on your business model, it might make sense to release your single issues in a digital format first and then print them for the first time in a collected trade, instead of fighting for space on direct market shelves with printed floppies. This will allow you to use the single issues to gain momentum without the associated print costs, but still participate in print distribution channels after you have built a following and covered a portion, if not all, of your creative costs. As we'll see in Chapter 68, the printing and shipping costs of the print trade can also be covered by crowdfunding, provided the proper marketing has been done before the book is ready to print.

- Digital graphic novel or one-shot (Theatrical Release): Because this format doesn't involve any incremental steps between the online "trailers" and the full release, it often makes sense to have multiple trailers to do the work of building momentum for the release. But remember that graphic novels often have different life cycles compared to single-issue comics. Where the continuous novelty of single issues often translates into higher initial sales, graphic novels (and trade paperbacks) often have longer ordering life because of bookstore and library orders[887].

- Print Graphic Novel (Home Video Release): Because the higher page count can raise the price of the printing of this format, and because there are no other incremental commercial releases to help offset these cost, you need to be secure in your investment before going to print with your graphic novel. Crowdfunding, Diamond orders, POD, sales funnel management (that we

[885] Rawden, J. (2019, October 23). Is Disney+ Making The Right Choice By Not Using The Binge Model? Retrieved May 25, 2020, from https://www.cinemablend.com/television/2482856/is-disney-making-the-right-choice-by-not-using-the-binge-model

[886] Hanafi, M. (2017, November 17). Binge-Watching is Killing Television. Retrieved May 25, 2020, from https://medium.com/overstimulated/binge-watching-is-killing-television-93714e8b7433

[887] Allen p. 31

will explore in Chapter 69) and other options can be used to manage this cost, but the prestige of releasing a print graphic novel needs to be balanced against the financial realities of the format.

Once you understand the formats that work best for your book and the different ways you can combine them, the next production question directly impacts the content of your story. Some comic narratives last thirty seconds, others go on for thirty years, so the duration of your story will also factor into the types of formats you can use. Of course, when your publishing program is getting off the ground, the goal is to tell one good story and release it in the best way to reach the right audience. But knowing where you want your story to go and how long the journey will take needs to be considered as your first story takes shape.

Comics have some of the shortest stories in all of narrative art. Newspaper strips like *The Far Side*[888] and modern political cartoons[889] often contained a setup and a punchline in a single panel, with characters and situations that are singular in their expression. On the other end of the spectrum, comics have some of the longest-running stories ever told. Todd McFarlane earned a Guinness World Record with his 27 year, 300 issue run of *Spawn*[890], the baseball manga *Dokaben* has 205 volumes since 1972[891] and Batman's *Detective Comics* celebrated its 80 year, 1000 issue run in 2019[892]. Your comic will probably fall somewhere between one panel and a thousand issues. Deciding on the proper length is a function of your creative vision and your production resources.

As you consider the different options, remember that the length of your story is not meant to be a burden to your creativity. **The number of issues has no bearing on the quality of the narrative**. Great stories can be long or short. Longer isn't necessarily better. And you can theoretically use any format to tell any story of any length. If you want to publish a multi-year epic in four-panel increments, no one can stop you, as long as you do it well and deliver it to the right audience. Finally, the vision for your story can change over time, along with the creative team, the owner of the IP, and the world around it. Scott Synder's Batman is a very different concept existing in a very different world from Bob Kane's original idea[893]. Your comic can and will evolve, but let's consider the four different alternatives available to the independent comic book publisher.

- A **single shot** (sometimes referred to as a gag of the day) lends itself to webcomics and social media.
  - The upside of single shots is that they are fast to create, easy to consume and they can be a good selection for current events, pop culture, and politics.

---

[888] The Far Side Comic Strip by Gary Larson - Official Website. (n.d.). Retrieved May 25, 2020, from https://www.thefarside.com/

[889] See editorial cartoons at The Week. (n.d.). Retrieved May 25, 2020, from https://theweek.com/cartoons

[890] taff. (2019). SPAWN #301 Earns Todd McFarlane a Guinness World Record. Retrieved May 25, 2020, from https://www.newsarama.com/47132-spawn-301-earns-todd-mcfarlane-a-guinness-world-record.html

[891] Dokaben (manga). Retrieved May 25, 2020, from https://www.animenewsnetwork.com/encyclopedia/manga.php?id=6852

[892] Jirak, J. (2019, April 01). Kevin Smith and Jim Lee Celebrate Batman's 1000th Issue of 'Detective Comics'. Retrieved May 25, 2020, from https://comicbook.com/dc/2019/03/31/kevin-smith-jim-lee-celebrate-batman-1000th-issue-detective-comics/

[893] Batman at 75: Highlights in the Life of the Caped Crusader. (2014, July 22). Retrieved May 25, 2020, from https://www.dccomics.com/blog/2014/07/22/batman-at-75-highlights-in-the-life-of-the-caped-crusader

- The downside is that they have a very fast shelf life and little lasting value beyond the instant of publication, but the more popular releases can evolve into memes and merchandise[894].
- Example: *The Lockhorns*[895]

- A **single-story** is a narrative with a clear beginning, middle, and end. This fundamental story structure has a home in every format of comics, but it is most common in limited series and graphic novels.
    - The upside of a single story is the balance between creative space for the narrative to develop and a definitive ending to allow closure for both the creative team and the reader.
    - The downside is a lack of long-term revenue potential outside of reprints and reorders.
    - Example: *Fun Home*[896]

- An **ongoing series**[897] (sometimes referred to as a franchise[898]) is a narrative that has no predetermined end. The ongoing series is a staple of American superhero comics and this type of narrative can be found in single issues and trade paperbacks from all the major companies. While most ongoing series do end eventually, the ending is often the result of low sales or creative fatigue[899].
    - The upside of an ongoing series is the potential for long term revenue and the mainstream appeal of the characters. Ongoing comic stories can tap into the emerging concept of the "perpetual middle" stories found in video games, social media, and legacy network television[900].
    - The downside comes in the conflict between creative closure and IP value. The value of a franchise is based on the perception that the market has to the character and their relationship to that perception. The value of many stories can be found in the change and growth the characters experience from the beginning of the story to the end. A franchise character that doesn't change can retain their market value, but can't really evolve[901].

---

[894] The best comic memes :) Memedroid. (n.d.). Retrieved May 25, 2020, from https://www.memedroid.com/memes/tag/comic

[895] The Lockhorns. (n.d.). Retrieved May 25, 2020, from https://www.comicskingdom.com/lockhorns

[896] Wilsey, S. (2006, June 18). The Things They Buried. Retrieved May 25, 2020, from https://www.nytimes.com/2006/06/18/books/review/18wilsey.html

[897] Ongoing series. (2019, October 31). Retrieved May 25, 2020, from https://en.wikipedia.org/wiki/Ongoing_series

[898] Franchise. (n.d.). Retrieved May 25, 2020, from https://www.merriam-webster.com/dictionary/franchise

[899] Wigler, J., & Goldberg, L. (2020, April 18). 'Walking Dead' Comics - Source of Multibillion-Dollar Franchise - Ends With Surprise Finale. Retrieved May 25, 2020, from https://www.hollywoodreporter.com/live-feed/walking-dead-ends-robert-kirkman-comic-book-ends-surprise-finale-1222097

[900] Bauer, J. (Writer). (2019). *Why Avengers: Endgame Did What Game of Thrones Couldn't* [Video file]. Retrieved May 25, 2020, from https://www.youtube.com/watch?v=cbUlgyHep-s&feature=youtu.be

[901] Manning, p. 21

Attempts to alter franchise characters, even on a temporary basis, can create a backlash that can damage the IP and the publisher[902].

- **Alternative narratives** attempt to bridge the gap between single stories and ongoing franchises. They might take the form of reboots[903] (The New 52[904]), linear updates (*Grendel*[905]), a reimagining of an established story (*What If?*[906]), or company crossover with a separate publisher (*Power Rangers/ Teenage Mutant Ninja Turtles*[907]), but all of them give the publisher space to move the story in a new direction without major interference with the existing IP. Independent publishers working to publish their first book aren't in a position to take advantage of alternatives, but knowledge of your options can be an asset as your publishing plans mature.

Your first comic might not last for fifty years, but that is not a bad thing. Not every book has to last forever to be successful. One of the reasons creators like Alan Moore stand out is because they are constantly telling new stories in addition to ongoing narratives[908]. Starting small and building your stories in line with the capabilities of your team makes more sense than trying to make your first publication your magnum opus. Finding the best fit between your talent and your time is more important than trying to publish a thousand issues of the same comic.

[902] Riesman, A. (2019, April 28). That Time Captain America Said 'Hail Hydra' and Geekdom Imploded. Retrieved May 25, 2020, from https://www.vulture.com/2019/04/marvel-hydra-captain-america-nick-spencer.html

[903] Reboot. (n.d.). Retrieved May 25, 2020, from https://www.merriam-webster.com/dictionary/reboot

[904] DC Comics: The New 52. (2019, January 16). Retrieved May 25, 2020, from https://www.dccomics.com/graphic-novels/dc-comics-the-new-52-2011/dc-comics-the-new-52

[905] Grendel (Character). (n.d.). Retrieved May 25, 2020, from https://comicvine.gamespot.com/grendel/4005-29748/

[906] Kistler, A. (2019, September 24). Living brains and anti-fascist odes: The greatest What If...? stories in Marvel history. Retrieved May 25, 2020, from https://www.polygon.com/2019/9/24/20880521/best-marvel-what-if-comics-spider-man-wolverine-captain-america-hulk-mcu

[907] O'Grady, C. (2019, October 02). Mighty Morphin Power Rangers/Teenage Mutant Ninja Turtles #1 First Look. Retrieved May 25, 2020, from https://www.boom-studios.com/archives/mighty-morphin-power-rangers-teenage-mutant-ninja-turtles-1-first-look/

[908] Alan Moore. (2018, October 30). Retrieved May 25, 2020, from https://www.dccomics.com/talent/alan-moore

The major task of an independent publisher is to create the best book you can make and deliver it to your market on time.

This job is manageable if you already secured your investment, gathered the right team, identified your market, determined how the book will be delivered, and decided what kind of book you're making. Pulling all those resources together into a discreet plan of action begins when you create your production schedule.

A **production schedule** is the timetable for the use of resources and processes required by a business to produce goods or provide services[909]. As an independent publisher, your production schedule needs to take into account the major business and creative milestones of comic book creation, and factor in other realities of your business. This chapter will outline each of the elements in a comic production schedule and provide two examples you can use to model your efforts.

What Are the Major Milestones in Comic Book Production?

We spent some time considering milestones when we discussed talent management, now we can use that same concept in the context of making your comics. **Whether you are publishing the book on your own or as part of a large group, every stage of comic production can be considered a distinct milestone**. The production schedule places all milestones in a defined linear order depending on its relationship to the other steps in the process. In the ICP method, there are four elements to every milestone:

1. Who is responsible for completing the milestone?
2. The date the milestone needs to be completed
3. Who is responsible for approving the milestone before it proceeds to the next step?
4. The date the milestone needs to be approved

Creative Milestones: Ten creative milestones in comic book production progressively combine several artistic disciplines to produce the final book:

1. Scriptwriting including overall plot, scene descriptions, and dialogue
2. Character designs of the major characters and any other distinct visual aspects of the story
3. Thumbnail layouts[910] of the script
4. Logo design

---

[909] What is production schedule? (n.d.). Retrieved May 25, 2020, from
http://www.businessdictionary.com/definition/production-schedule.html

[910] Thumbnails are defined as "small, rough sketches of the script to determine if the artist's interpretation of the script will work on the finished page". Love and Withers p. 62

5. Line art based on the thumbnails
6. Cover art based on the overall script
7. Flatting of the line art and cover art
8. Coloring of the line art and cover art
9. Lettering of the colored pages
10. Production design of the final pages

Business Milestones: Ten business milestones use aspects of the creative process to position the book in the market:

1. Website creation and management
2. Social media management
3. Convention management
4. Comic book press marketing
5. Printing, shipping, and storage
6. Digital solicitations
7. Direct market solicitations
8. Library solicitations
9. Advertising
10. Sales

It should be noted that **business and creative milestones are not designed to operate in isolation**. They overlap and support each other from a very early stage of production. Also, depending on the type of book you're creating and the way you plan to publish it, some steps may be eliminated. For example, if you are producing a black and white webcomic, then you don't need to add flatting, coloring, printing, direct market, or library solicitations to your production schedule.

What Are Some Examples of a Comic Production Schedule?

I've added a sample production schedule at the end of this chapter that you can modify for your book, but I also wanted to offer two examples to show a production schedule in action. In the first example, Bruce, Clark, and Diana are working on a book called *Crisis*. Bruce is the writer, Clark is the artist and Diana is the editor and publisher. Because their group is small, each one needs to juggle both the business and creative milestones. Their production schedule might look like this:

Crisis Production Schedule 1

Milestone	Role	Responsibility to Create	Creation Date	Responsibility to Approve	Approval Date
Script	Creative	Bruce		Diana	
Character Designs	Creative	Clark		Diana	

Website Management	Marketing	Diana		Bruce	
Thumbnails	Creative	Clark		Bruce	
Logo Design	Creative	Clark		Diana	
Social Media Management	Marketing	Bruce		Diana	
Line Art	Creative	Clark		Diana	
Cover Design	Creative	Clark		Diana	
Convention Management	Marketing	Bruce		Diana	
Flatting	Creative	Clark		Diana	
Coloring	Creative	Clark		Diana	
Comic Book Press	Marketing	Diana		Bruce	
Lettering	Creative	Clark		Diana	
Production Design	Creative	Clark		Diana	
Printing, Shipping, and Storage	Distribution	Diana		Bruce	
Digital Solicitations	Distribution	Bruce		Diana	
Direct Market Solicitations	Distribution	Diana		Bruce	
Bookstore Solicitations	Distribution	Diana		Bruce	
Library Solicitations	Distribution	Bruce		Diana	
Advertising	Advertising	Clark		Bruce	
Sales	Sales	Bruce		Diana	

Notice that Clark has most of the creative work and that Bruce and Diana have essentially split the business roles. They are also approving each other's work, so that everything has a second pair of eyes on it. Clark will have to do most of the heavy lifting at the beginning of the process, but he'll have more time to relax once the production design is complete.

In our second example, Charles is the writer and publisher of a book called *Hates and Fears*. He has the investment to organize a larger team comprised of Scott the artist, Jean the social media expert, Warren an editor, Hank the tech wizard, and Bobby a colorist. This group allows each team member to focus on their strengths and work less while working together. Their production schedule might look like this:

Hates and Fears Production Schedule 1

Milestone	Role	Responsibility to Create	Creation Date	Responsibility to Approve	Approval Date
Script	Creative	Charles		Warren	
Character Designs	Creative	Scott		Charles	
Website Management	Marketing	Hank		Charles	
Thumbnails	Creative	Scott		Warren	
Logo Design	Creative	Scott		Charles	
Social Media Management	Marketing	Jean		Charles	
Line Art	Creative	Scott		Warren	
Cover Design	Creative	Clark		Charles	
Convention Management	Marketing	Jean		Charles	
Flatting	Creative	Bobby		Warren	
Coloring	Creative	Bobby		Warren	
Comic Book Press	Marketing	Jean		Charles	
Lettering	Creative	Bobby		Warren	
Production Design	Creative	Scott		Warren	
Printing, Shipping, and Storage	Distribution	Hank		Charles	
Digital Solicitations	Distribution	Hank		Charles	
Direct Market Solicitations	Distribution	Jean		Charles	
Bookstore Solicitations	Distribution	Jean		Charles	
Library Solicitations	Distribution	Jean		Charles	
Advertising	Advertising	Hank		Charles	
Sales	Sales	Jean		Charles	

Things are not divided equally in this production schedule, perhaps because Charles insists on controlling most of the approvals as publisher or because Scott and Jean dominate the creative and business aspects of the production. This shouldn't be a problem if their overall compensation is more than Bobby, Hank, and Warren.

You might have noticed that in both scenarios, I didn't mention anything about the columns for creation or approval dates. That's because timing is such an important aspect of production schedules that it deserves a separate chapter that you can find after the production schedule template.

Independent Comic Book Publishing

Form 6: Production Schedule Template

Milestone	Role	Responsibility to Create	Creation Date	Responsibility to Approve	Approval Date
Script	Creative				
Character Designs	Creative				
Website Management	Marketing				
Thumbnails	Creative				
Logo Design	Creative				
Social Media Management	Marketing				
Line Art	Creative				
Cover Design	Creative				
Convention Management	Marketing				
Flatting	Creative				
Coloring	Creative				
Comic Book Press	Marketing				
Lettering	Creative				
Production Design	Creative				
Printing, Shipping, and Storage	Distribution				
Digital Solicitations	Distribution				
Direct Market Solicitations	Distribution				
Bookstore Solicitations	Distribution				
Library Solicitations	Distribution				
Advertising	Advertising				
Sales	Sales				

Comic book publishing is a time-sensitive business. Your readers expect a regular output if you want to maintain a following in webcomics or floppies. The direct market shops who take a chance on ordering your book will dump you if you burn them with late products. There is a little more flexibility with graphic novels, but since comic production is often a linear collective effort, time management is always important if you're going to deal with everyone's schedules and secret identities.

There is a natural tension between art and commerce when it comes to time. On one hand, artists struggle with creative pressures that resist the rigid confines of schedules and deadlines. But the realities of business require accepting the structure of distribution and marketing. How you decide to resolve this tension is a personal and professional choice, but it makes little sense to sabotage your idea and your investment with poor time management. You are striving to create art, but **good work on time will almost always beat great work that is late**.

There are two basic methods of time management, each with its benefits and disadvantages. This chapter will look at both options as well as the outside considerations before we revisit our previous examples.

What Are the Two Methods of Time Management?

I define the two methods of time management as open or closed.

Open Timing is a time management method that focuses on producing the book without any specific release date. The basic mantra here is "*the book will come out when it is ready to come out.*" This mentality is often used in situations where the art has just as much influence as the business side of publication. It is sometimes seen in the development stages of video game releases like *Cyberpunk 2077*, where a premature release date can ruin the quality of the final product[911].

There are three major benefits of open timing in independent comic book publishing:

1. Creative: The business and creative teams aren't rushed and have the time to create the best book possible.

2. Business: Without a hard deadline in the production process, there can't be any missed deadlines so there won't be any negative impact on distribution. With open timing, marketing

---

[911] Hood, V., Leger, H., & Boyle, E. (2020, May 07). Cyberpunk 2077 release date, price, trailers, gameplay and news. Retrieved May 25, 2020, from https://www.techradar.com/news/cyberpunk-2077-release-date-trailer-and-news

can develop normally, but you wouldn't make any solicitations to your distribution channels until the print-ready files were available[912].

3.   <u>Financial</u>: If you don't have the total investment for your book available at the start of production, open timing allows you to produce the book as the money comes in so you can avoid paying out or owing funds faster than you can cover them.

As with most aspects of independent publishing, open timing has its downsides to counterbalance the benefits, including:

1.   <u>Creative</u>: A creative team can lose momentum without a hard deadline, depending on the dispositions and schedules of everyone in the group.

2.   <u>Business</u>: There are key dates that can benefit the marketing and sales of a book, both in the general sense and based on specific elements of your story. With open timing, you might miss those dates and undercut your book in the short term. For example, if you had a horror book, the time just before Halloween could be a key marketing period that you might not be able to take advantage of with open timing. Of course, major holidays are cyclical, and you could keep the book on the shelf until next Halloween, as long as your financial commitments allow you to wait a whole year.

3.   <u>Financial</u>: If you decided to take advantage of third-party financing for your investment, then you might be responsible for paying back those funds on or before a specific date. In the alternative, your investors might not be willing to wait indefinitely for your artistic inspiration to reach its full potential. Depending on the language of your investment agreements, closed timing might be a better option for you.

Closed Timing is a time management method that focuses on producing the book on a specific release date. That date can be based on any factor relevant to your story, your market, or your distribution plans, but once you determine that date, you have to work backward to establish all the other production milestones. This back-casting method[913] is often seen in film, where the release date is announced before the movie

---

912 Manning p. 102

913 What is backcasting? (n.d.). Retrieved May 25, 2020, from
http://www.businessdictionary.com/definition/backcasting.html

even has a script[914] or annual sports video game releases that are released just before the start of the real-world seasons[915].

The three benefits of closed timing are a funhouse mirror image of the open timing benefits:

1. Creative: Deadlines can spur certain artists to focus and innovate. They can also help maintain the momentum of a project that might otherwise falter.

2. Business: Choosing the right release date can improve the marketing of your book. Whether you're launching right before a major con or taking advantage of a holiday season, your release date can have an impact on your market[916]

3. Financial: Publishing your book at the right time can also improve your overall sales. If you have books available for your cons, you have a revenue stream that you wouldn't enjoy with open timing. If you publish your book during the holiday season, your target market might take advantage of the timing to share the book with someone in the potential market, which can help your bottom line.

The three downsides of closed timing are easy to guess:

1. Creative: The stress of deadlines can hurt both the quality of the art produced and the relationships among the different team members.

2. Business: If you set a publication deadline and you miss it, the book will suffer. This is true whether you look at the early Image titles[917] or massive crossovers like Marvel's *Secret Wars 2*[918]. If late books hurt the major players, they can kill a brand-new book.

---

[914] Lambie, R., Zutter, N., Knight, R., Crow, D., Kaye, D., & Clough, R. (2013, February 13). 10 films that began filming without a finished script. Retrieved May 25, 2020, from https://www.denofgeek.com/movies/24456/10-films-that-began-filming-without-a-finished-script

[915] Kobek, P. (2019, July 28). Madden Never Changes, But I Continue To Buy It Every Year. Retrieved May 25, 2020, from https://www.thegamer.com/madden-never-changes-but-i-buy-it-every-year/

[916] Rinzler, A., (2012, November 01). Timing your book's launch date for maximum impact. Retrieved May 25, 2020, from https://alanrinzler.com/2012/11/timing-your-books-launch-date-for-maximum-impact/

[917] Reed, P. (2016, February 01). Today in Comics History: The Start Of The Image Revolution. Retrieved May 25, 2020, from https://comicsalliance.com/tribute-image-comics/

[918] McMillan, G. (2020, May 23). When Titans Miss Deadlines: What Marvel's 'Secret Wars' Schedule Slip Really Means. Retrieved May 25, 2020, from https://www.hollywoodreporter.com/heat-vision/titans-miss-deadlines-what-marvels-800490

3. <u>Financial</u>: A specific release date might force you to pay more money to meet that deadline. Whether it's more money going out to creative teams, increased shipping costs, or other expedited services, the pressure of time could translate into a monetary loss.

What Other Considerations Does the Schedule Need to Include?

Your production dates can't exist in a vacuum. As we've already seen, **resource management and secret identities will play a role in your time management**. While you won't be able to predict every bump in the road without precognition, there are at least three points to keep in mind as you develop your production schedule:

1. <u>Cash flow</u>: Look back at all your contracts in relation to your investment. If your legal obligation to pay is based on a creative or business milestone, avoid creating a schedule where you have to pay for services before you have the funds available to cover that cost.

2. <u>Secret identities</u>: Comic publishing can take a considerable amount of time to complete. During the process, you and the members of your team will have planned or surprise personal and professional obligations that can interfere with your schedule. Take a look at the plans for your secret identity and communicate with your team to try and anticipate any potential disruptions to the production process.

3. <u>Talent management</u>: If you have each team member working on multiple aspects of production, it makes more sense to spread out the work as much as possible so that one member of the team isn't responsible for the entire book for long periods of time. You can't give a job to a team member who doesn't have the disposition, skills, or time to handle a role they're not suited for, but the more balance you can build into the schedule, the more potential problems you can avoid.

How Does Time Management Factor into the Previous Examples?

Let's assume Bruce has a lot of extra time and money on his hands, so *Crisis* is going to use open timing. He doesn't know exactly when the book will come out, but bases his estimates on a production rate that is longer than the informal industry average of 22 pages in 6 weeks[919] to take the teams secret identities into account, and he staggers the other production milestones in one-month increments without bothering to ask Clark or Diana if this will work for them. While it might be a bit rude, it's not detrimental here, because open timing is designed to absorb delays. So, if the production starts on January 1st (1/1), it might look like this:

---

[919] Cooke, S. (2019, September 24). Standard Timeline Template for Artists in Comics. Retrieved May 25, 2020, from http://www.creatorresource.com/standard-timeline-template-for-artists-in-comics/

Milestone	Role	Responsibility to Create	Creation Date	Responsibility to Approve	Approval Date
Script	Creative	Bruce	1/1	Diana	2/1
Character Designs	Creative	Clark	3/1	Diana	3/15
Website Management	Marketing	Diana	3/1	Bruce	4/1
Thumbnails	Creative	Clark	4/1	Bruce	4/15
Logo Design	Creative	Clark	4/15	Diana	5/1
Social Media Management	Marketing	Bruce	4/1	Diana	5/1
Line Art	Creative	Clark	6/1	Diana	7/1
Cover Design	Creative	Clark	7/1	Diana	7/15
Convention Management	Marketing	Bruce	5/1	Diana	6/1
Flatting	Creative	Clark	8/1	Diana	8/15
Coloring	Creative	Clark	10/1	Diana	10/15
Comic Book Press	Marketing	Diana	8/1	Bruce	9/1
Lettering	Creative	Clark	11/1	Diana	12/1
Production Design	Creative	Clark	12/1	Diana	12/30
Printing, Shipping, and Storage	Distribution	Diana	7/1	Bruce	8/1
Digital Solicitations	Distribution	Bruce	7/1	Diana	8/1
Direct Market Solicitations	Distribution	Diana	9/1	Bruce	10/1
Bookstore Solicitations	Distribution	Diana	10/1	Bruce	11/1
Library Solicitations	Distribution	Bruce	10/1	Diana	12/1
Advertising	Advertising	Clark	12/15	Bruce	12/20
Sales	Sales	Bruce	12/30	Diana	12/30

On the other side, Charles doesn't have the luxury of open timing, because the themes of *Hates and Fears* coincide with a major political election and the impact of the book would be lost if it was released after Election Day on November 4th (11/4). Thankfully, Charles has a larger team, so multiple aspects of production can happen at once. He's also worked with this group before, so he knows his team as if he were a mind reader. He's confident they can stick to the following schedule to make sure the book is available by October 15th (10/15):

<u>Hates and Fears Production Schedule 2</u>

Milestone	Role	Responsibility to Create	Creation Date	Responsibility to Approve	Approval Date
Script	Creative	Charles	1/1	Warren	2/1
Character Designs	Creative	Scott	2/1	Charles	2/15
Website Management	Marketing	Hank	2/1	Charles	3/1
Thumbnails	Creative	Scott	2/15	Warren	3/1
Logo Design	Creative	Scott	3/1	Charles	3/15
Social Media Management	Marketing	Jean	2/1	Charles	3/1
Line Art	Creative	Scott	4/1	Warren	4/15
Cover Design	Creative	Scott	6/1	Charles	6/15
Convention Management	Marketing	Jean	3/1	Charles	4/1
Flatting	Creative	Bobby	5/1	Warren	5/15
Coloring	Creative	Bobby	6/1	Warren	6/15
Comic Book Press	Marketing	Jean	4/1	Charles	
Lettering	Creative	Bobby	7/1	Warren	7/15
Production Design	Creative	Scott	7/15	Warren	8/1
Printing, Shipping, and Storage	Distribution	Hank	7/1	Charles	7/15
Digital Solicitations	Distribution	Hank	9/1	Charles	9/15
Direct Market Solicitations	Distribution	Jean	8/1	Charles	8/15
Bookstore Solicitations	Distribution	Jean	9/1	Charles	9/15
Library Solicitations	Distribution	Jean	10/1	Charles	10/15
Advertising	Advertising	Hank	9/1	Charles	9/15
Sales	Sales	Jean	10/1	Charles	10/15

Open or closed time management can work for your book, depending on what you want to accomplish and who you are working with. But no matter which method you choose, coordinating the activity of a geographically scattered group of people requires effective communication. While interpersonal communication skills are beyond the scope of this book, the next chapter will look at the obstacles to staying in contact with your team and the project-based and technical tools you can use to overcome them.

One of the unique aspects of comic book publishing is the level of geographic freedom available to creators. Unlike film, theater, and other forms of **collaborative art**[920], comic book creators can live anywhere and work with anyone, as long as they have a reliable internet connection. This allows independent publishers to avoid the higher costs of living in urban centers and gives them access to a worldwide talent pool. **Virtual teams**[921] provide the flexibility to make independent comic book production more viable.

At the same time, virtual teams create a unique set of challenges for comic creators. Clear communication is a key component in collaborative art. Coordinating multiple business and creative schedules requires synchronized efforts that are difficult to achieve if the team isn't talking to each other. If an independent publisher can't compensate for the tensions of a scattered production team, then the problems can overshadow the benefits and the production of the book can suffer.

What Are the Challenges of Virtual Teams?

Dave Nevogt is the co-founder of an employee management firm called Hubstaff. According to him, there are five common issues related to managing virtual teams[922]:

1. Language and cultural barriers
2. Tracking performance
3. Lack of team cohesion
4. Conflict within the team
5. Scheduling

In addition, collaborative artists also have to handle creative criticism which can be intensified with a lack of face to face connection[923]. Each of these complications can be reduced with a combination of interpersonal techniques or digital tools that depend on the nature of the publisher and the circumstances of the team.

---

[920] What is Collaborative Art-Making. (n.d.). Retrieved May 25, 2020, from https://www.igi-global.com/dictionary/collaborative-art-and-relationships/65158

[921] Ferrazzi, K., Edmondson, A., Brett, J., Behfar, K., & Kern, M. (2015, March 10). Getting Virtual Teams Right. Retrieved May 25, 2020, from https://hbr.org/2014/12/getting-virtual-teams-right

[922] Nevogt, D. (2020, May 21). 5 Common Challenges of Virtual Teams. Retrieved May 25, 2020, from https://blog.hubstaff.com/remote-management-problems/

[923] Lepsinger, R., (n.d.). Why Your Organization Shouldn't Abandon Virtual Teams. Retrieved May 25, 2020, from https://www.business2community.com/human-resources/organization-shouldnt-abandon-virtual-teams-01938722

What Techniques Can You Use to Improve Communication?

There are several aspects of the pre-production process that can reduce the strains created by virtual teams:

- Contracts: If you are clear in your RFP and contractual terms, then you'll have a benchmark for the performance of each team member

- Compensation: If you create links between performance and payment, you'll establish ongoing incentives for team members to get their work in on time because they want to be paid.

- Small Projects: If you start the team with one or two development projects before you start working on the main book, you can get a feel for each team member's personal interaction, language styles, and work habits to build team cohesion. This could be anything from 2-5 page projects set in the world of your story, to building the ideal reader profile, to determining the form and structure of the book itself.

- Normal Meetings: If you have regularly scheduled contact with each team member individually and the team as a whole, you can monitor progress and address any potential conflicts before they hinder production. These don't have to be long soul-destroying corporate style meetings. You just need to make sure your team knows you are available.

- Special Meetings: Whenever possible, try to meet members of your team in person on a periodic basis, both individually and as a group. As we saw in the chapter on conventions, setting aside time for your team to grab coffee, dinner, or drinks is a great way to build rapport within your team. But you don't have to wait for a con or even a physical meeting. Digital tools can be used to strengthen virtual teams.

What Tools Can You Use to Improve Communication?

Virtual teams are possible because there are a variety of applications and tools you can use to stay connected to your team and share your work. Depending on your team and the nature of your book, you can mix or match the solutions that work best for your group[924]. The key here is redundancy, since any one communication tool can fail at the worst possible moment. But if you don't rely on just one platform, and you don't rely exclusively on the internet, you can avoid losing contact with your team and missing your

---

[924] CanvasFlip. (2018, February 16). Best apps and tools for managing remote teams. Retrieved May 25, 2020, from https://medium.com/@CanvasFlip/best-apps-and-tools-for-managing-remote-teams-f730dfdf3ec2

production deadlines[925]. There are dozens of choices for connection based on the nature and the method[926], and new tools are being developed all the time. Just make sure you have multiple individual and group methods to reach your team.

- <u>Individual communication methods</u>
  - Phone (audio or visual)
  - Email
  - Instant message
  - Physical mail
  - Text

- <u>Group communication methods</u>
  - Group chat
  - Group text
  - Private message boards
  - Virtual meetings

There are dozens of different decisions and discussions your comic will need before it is ready for publication. While the techniques and tools contained in this chapter can help you navigate your team management, one of the most essential elements of comic book communication is the script for the book. Because this aspect of production is so vital, it deserves its own analysis and examination.

---

[925] Manning p. 56

[926] Best Collaboration Software of 2019. (n.d.). Retrieved May 25, 2020, from https://www.getapp.com/p/sem/web-collaboration-software?t=Best+Collaboration+Software+of+2019

We've mentioned scripts several times so far, but it makes sense to take a moment to focus on the importance of creating the right script for your book.

A **script** is the underlying written text of a piece of visual narrative art, such as a stage play, screenplay, or broadcast[927]. In comics, a script is a tool used to describe the plot so the other artists can represent the images and dialogue visually[928]. The script is nothing less than the foundation and the blueprint your book will be built on.

Your script needs to convey the narrative of your story in a sequence that can be understood. It should impart the overall tone of the story, the setting in every scene, as well as the choreography, expression, and information contained in every panel[929]. It also needs to show the turning points[930], and any foreshadowing or underlying information needed for the story to make sense as a finished product. In other words, your script needs to tell the entire story of your comic to your creative team[931].

The importance of a script can't be overstated for the art you are trying to create, but there are two unfortunate ironies you need to be aware of as you write it. The first is that **while a great script can't guarantee a superior comic, it is very difficult to produce a great comic without a great script**. Poor art, lettering, or coloring can undermine an otherwise amazing script, but a poor script can ruin the whole project. The second irony is that **what defines a great script is different for every team and every book**. There is no universal formula to get it right.

What Are the Major Types of Comic Book Scripts?

While there is an unlimited number of variations to script creation, the industry has developed two major types of scripts over the years. In the **full script** (sometimes referred to as the DC method), the writer creates detailed descriptions of each panel and dialogue and then asks the artist to follow that narrative direction[932]. In the **loose script** (referred to as the Marvel Method), the writer creates a general description of the plot and direction of the story and it is up to the artist to flesh out and develop the panels and pages.

---

[927] Script. (n.d.). Retrieved May 25, 2020, from https://www.merriam-webster.com/dictionary/script

[928] McCloud, Making Comics p. 149

[929] Mooney, R. (2018, May 10). A Picture is Worth 1000 words – how to write a comic script that your artist can use Part 1. Retrieved May 25, 2020, from https://richardmooneyvi.wordpress.com/2018/05/06/a-picture-is-worth-1000-words-how-to-write-a-comic-script-that-your-artist-can-use-part-1/

[930] Schmidt, p. 12

[931] Bendis, p. 73

[932] De Pues, D. (2014, April 01). Marvel Method or Full Script? • Comic Book Daily. Retrieved May 25, 2020, from https://www.comicbookdaily.com/columns/tales-from-the-comicdenn/marvel-method-full-script/

The industry has recently been shifting more towards the Marvel Method[933], but your script, like your comic, doesn't need to follow the trends. If your writer has a better grasp of the story, or is a more experienced storyteller, then a full script might make more sense. If your writer has too many other tasks on their plate, or the artist has an inspired vision for the story, then a loose script can help shift some of the creative burden.

Full scripts and loose scripts represent the extremes, but you don't have to choose one or the other. **The best script for your comic might tap into elements from both methods**. You just have to find the right combination for your team.

What is the Best Method for Building a Script for Your Team?

Musicians, actors, and athletes practice together before their main performance. Independent publishers can steal this idea for their book. Whether you consider it a dry run, a sample, or a session in the Danger Room, **getting your team to develop art together before they start working on your book can save you a lot of aggravation and stress.**

This exercise works best if it is a smaller scale than your planned format and mimics your actual production process as closely as possible. So, if you're planning to have a 22-page full-color book, set up a project where your team does a single page from start to finish. When the process is over, the entire team, but especially the editor, can take a step back and evaluate what went right and what needs improvement with both the ways the team handled the script and the overall production process. The team can take this information, refine the process, and try again. Maybe the next exercise will be another page. Maybe you can level up to five pages. It all depends on how comfortable the team is working together.

When you are building this exercise, there are four concepts to keep in mind:

1. <u>Cost</u>: Your team should not be producing work for free. Whatever page rate or compensation they have for your book should be replicated on a **pro-rata basis**[934]. This cost might be an initial drain on your investment, but it can save you money in the long run if you find your chosen team can't work well together. Besides, you don't want to poison your relationship with your artist by asking for free work right off the bat.

2. <u>Creativity</u>: Your script is the foundation of your comic, but your artists add life and individuality to your words. The key is to strive for a balance between getting exactly the work you are

---

[933] Johnston, R. (2017, November 14). DC Comics Moves To Artist-Focused "Marvel Method" That Marvel Doesn't Use Anymore. Retrieved May 25, 2020, from https://www.bleedingcool.com/2017/11/13/dc-comics-move-artist-focused-marvel-method-that-marvel/

[934] Pro-rata. (n.d.). Retrieved May 25, 2020, from https://dictionary.law.com/Default.aspx?selected=1653

paying for and getting creative vision you could have never imagined[935]. You are working with artists, not robots, so manage their work, but give them space to provide their unique expression.

3. Flexibility: The practice is an opportunity to refine your process and your team, but nothing will change if you refuse to act on the results. If you find out after your single page run that the script doesn't work, or the final product isn't right, then you have to figure out how to solve the problem before you try again. If you find that a member of your team is a weak link, you have to be willing to address that fact or the book will suffer. Newsflash: you could be the problem with your team. While this revelation isn't easy to handle, it makes more sense to find that out when creating one page instead of spending thousands of dollars and years of your life coming to the same conclusion.

4. Utility: Your team exercises are useful for developing the right script format and refining your process, but there's no reason you can't repurpose this art in other areas of your publishing. As long as you contractually own the samples, you can use these pages as perks for your crowdfunding, marketing materials for your website and social media, or actual pages in the final book. The multiple uses for every exercise can take the sting out of paying for them, since they can have economic value beyond the production evaluation.

Where Can You Learn to Develop Comic Book Script Techniques?

Comic book scripts are unique documents in collaborative art. They are part instruction manual, part inspirational text, and incomplete by definition. **Many veterans agree that it takes time and practice to become a competent comic writer**, but there are things you can learn from both inside and outside comics to make that development easier.

Within the comic book industry, there are several veterans willing to share their work and their techniques. Some writers post samples of their scripts online[936]. Others maintain blogs about the basic process of scriptwriting[937] and working with other comic professionals[938]. There are classes available for the art of

[935] O'Keefe, M., (2020, January 10). Making Comics: The role of the letterer and responsibilities of their collaborators. Retrieved May 25, 2020, from https://www.comicsbeat.com/making-comics-letterer-role/

[936] Sample Comic Book Scripts. (n.d.). Retrieved May 25, 2020, from https://www.scriptsandscribes.com/sample-comic-scripts/

[937] Mooney, R. (2018, May 10). A Picture is Worth 1000 words – how to write a comic script that your artist can use Part 1.

[938] O'Keefe, M., O'Keefehttp, M., & Brandon Schatz & Danica LeBlanc. (2019, November 05). Making Comics: Writing scripts people actually want to read. Retrieved May 25, 2020, from https://www.comicsbeat.com/writing-comic-scripts/

comic scriptwriting[939]. There are also several books on the market about comic scriptwriting including *Writing for Comics*[940] by Alan Moore and *Words for Pictures*[941] by Brian Michael Bendis.

Techniques for comic scriptwriting can also be found in other forms of narrative art. Your script writing can gain nuance and depth by utilizing concepts from film, plays, and prose. While there is probably a limit to how much you can transfer from all these art forms, it pays to explore a few books on the subject such as:

- *Dialogue* by Robert McKee[942]
- *Elements of Fiction Writing: Conflict and Suspense* by James Scott Bell[943]
- *Making a Scene* by Jordan Rosenfeld[944]
- *On Writing* by Stephen King[945]
- *Story* by Robert McKee[946]
- *Twenty Master Plots and How to Build Them* by Ronald Tobais[947]
- *World-Building* by Stephen Gillett and Ben Bova[948]
- *Writing for Emotional Impact* by Karl Ignlesias[949]
- *Writing Subtext: What Lies Beneath* by Linda Seger[950]

Your script is a valuable component of your comic, but the other output your team creates is also valuable to your publishing business. You need to access the character designs, thumbnails, final pages, and other assets of your book and share it with your team and your distribution partners. If those assets are lost or difficult to find, you could lose substantial amounts of your investment and your time. The next chapter will introduce ways you can manage the assets of your publishing and complete the production process.

---

[939] Comics Expereince Writing & Lettering Courses. (n.d.). Retrieved May 25, 2020, from https://www.comicsexperience.com/courses/writing-lettering/

[940] Moore, A., & Burrows, J. (2010). *Alan Moore's writing for comics*. Rantoul, IL: Avatar Press.

[941] Bendis, B. M. (2014). *Words for pictures: The art and business of writing comics and graphic novels*. Berkeley, CA: Watson-Guptill.

[942] McKee, R. (2016). *Dialogue: The art of verbal action for the page, stage, and screen*. New York: Twelve

[943] Bell, J. S. (2012). *Elements of Fiction Writing - Conflict and Suspense*. F & W Media, Incorporated.

[944] Rosenfeld, J. E. (2008). *Make a scene: Crafting a powerful story one scene at a time*. Cincinnati, OH: Writer's Digest Books.

[945] King, S. (2010). *On writing: A memoir of the craft*. New York: Scribner.

[946] MacKee, R. (2010). *Story: Substance, structure, style, and the principles of screenwriting*. New York, NY: ItBooks

[947] Tobias, R. B. (2003). *20 Master plots (and how to build them)*. Cincinnati, OH: Writer's Digest Books

[948] Gillett, S. L., & Bova, B. (1996). *World-building*. Cincinnati, OH: Writer's Digest Books.

[949] Iglesias, K. (2010). *Writing for emotional impact advanced dramatic techniques to attract, engage, and fascinate the reader from beginning to end*. Livermore, CA: WingSpan Press.

[950] Seger, L. (2017). *Writing subtext: What lies beneath*. Studio City, CA: Michael Wiese Productions

Modern comic book publishing relies on digital files. It doesn't matter how your book is created, who is in your market, or how you plan to distribute. You need reliable digital assets. Whether you're uploading PDFs to your website or Comixology, sending files to your printer, or artwork to an influencer, you need to be able to send information about your book anywhere at any time. If your team doesn't have the right files when they need them, your vision, your investment, and your effort can be lost. As an independent publisher, you need to control the final digital version of your book.

Digital assets are computer files like documents, photos, and other media[951]. For independent publishers, your digital assets will include the final artwork after the editor has approved the contributions of the entire creative team. It will also include documents and spreadsheets related to your corporate formation, IP and talent management, marketing, advertising, sales, and revenue.

Digital asset management (DAM) is a computer application or system that stores, shares and organizes digital assets in a central location[952]. Independent publishers don't need expensive or elaborate DAM systems for their publishing, but they do need to develop an organization system for their assets and select a storage solution that best serves the needs of the company.

How Should Digital Assets Be Organized?

Scripts, panels, and pages evolve during the production process. There will probably be dozens of drafts and versions of your comic as it moves from the artist to the letterer to the colorist and each team member might make several alterations to the same image. But what happens if everyone is working on a different version of the page, or if an earlier version full of errors and unfinished art is sent to the printer while the latest and greatest version is still with the editor? It's unmitigated chaos. One of the benefits of DAM is organizing files in ways that bring order to your work in several different ways[953]:

- Streamlining of file creation and editing
- Creating a more efficient workflow
- Ensuring product consistency
- Reducing file search times

---

[951] What Is Digital Asset Management (DAM)? (2020, May 12). Retrieved May 25, 2020, from https://www.canto.com/digital-asset-management/

[952] Id

[953] Digital Asset Management Essentials. (n.d.). Retrieved May 25, 2020, from https://www.smartsheet.com/essential-guide-digital-asset-management

The basis of DAM organization is creating naming conventions for your files and folders that are consistent and descriptive[954]. They should include any information that will help a member of the team quickly find and understand what the file contains. Folders are grouped in a similar fashion to organize information in a coherent and informative manner.

For example, when I'm sharing files with my clients, I always follow the same naming convention: the initials of the client, the title that the document is about, the type of contract contained in the document, the current version, the date the document is being sent, and then the three-letter extension for application-specific files. So if I'm working on a work for hire agreement for Bram Stoker's Dracula today, then the file would be named "BS.Dracula.WFH.v1.12.29.19.doc".

A similar structure can be adopted for independent publishing files. For example, if Bruce is working on a script update for *Crisis* then the convention could be the initials of the person working on the file, the title of the book, the name of the artwork, the current version, the date the document is being sent, and then the three-letter extension for application-specific files. So, the third version of the script will be "BW.Crisis.Script.v3.12.29.19.doc"

You can develop any system you want as long as it makes your files easier to find and update. Just make sure that once you decide on a system, everyone on the team understands and uses the same format. **A naming convention system is useless if each team member is saving files in a different way**.

What Storage Solutions Are Available?

The three options for storing your independent publishing files and folders include cloud, remote and hybrid solutions[955].

- Cloud systems collect all your digital assets in remote internet servers. They tend to be cost-effective and simple to use[956]. Some cloud-based DAM also includes a component to allow team members to communicate as well as share files. Examples of Cloud-based systems include Dropbox[957], Evernote[958], Google Docs[959], and Slack[960].

---

[954] Best practices for file naming. (n.d.). Retrieved May 25, 2020, from https://library.stanford.edu/research/data-management-services/data-best-practices/best-practices-file-naming

[955] Digital Asset Management Essentials.

[956] Digital Asset Management Essentials.

[957] DropBox. (n.d.). Retrieved May 25, 2020, from https://www.dropbox.com/install?trigger=_footer

[958] Best Note Taking App - Organize Your Notes with Evernote. (n.d.). Retrieved May 25, 2020, from https://evernote.com/

[959] Google Docs. (n.d.). Retrieved May 25, 2020, from https://docs.google.com/

[960] Slack. (n.d.). Slack: Where work happens. Retrieved May 25, 2020, from https://slack.com/

- <u>Remote systems</u> collect your digital assets on a single hard drive that you own and control. This could be the editor's or the publisher's computer or a hard drive not connected to the internet. The benefit of this method is that the files are still available even if an app isn't available[961]. The downside is that if that particular computer crashes, or if the owner of the computer isn't available, or if they are not consistently collecting files from the entire team, the system is compromised.

- <u>Hybrid systems</u> collect your digital assets both in a cloud-based system and back them up on a remote system. This gives you the flexibility of a cloud system and the independence of a remote system. The main consideration here is making sure all the files are up to date in both systems to maximize the value of the redundancy.

What Security Measures Should You Include in Your DAM?

Whichever system you decide to use, security measures and periodic backups of all your publishing files are useful techniques to protect your digital assets. This means:

- Limiting access to all files to only members of your team
- Only allowing access of specific files to the team members that need them
- Promptly removing access to any team member who leaves the team
- Copying all files to a separate hard drive on a weekly, monthly or bi-monthly basis

It is highly unlikely that hackers, spies, ninja, or your competitors are roaming the internet looking to steal your digital assets. But your final pages are the culmination of your vision, your investment, and the time and effort of your team. It deserves protection before you release it to your readers.

---

[961] Manning p. 151

STAGE 3: POST-PRODUCTION

PART 9: ADVERTISING

Or How Will You Inform Your Target Market About Your Comic?

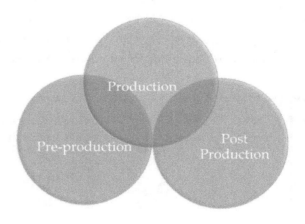

Completing the production of your comic is a major milestone in your publishing business. Taking a step back to review your progress can provide some perspective on the process and show you how far you've come as an independent publisher.

At this point, you have:

- Decided why you wanted to make comics
- Cultivated an idea you love
- Figured out how to pay for everything
- Created legal and financial protection for your book
- Assembled the best team possible
- Connected with your target market
- Decided how to get your book into their hands
- Created the best comic for your story

You deserve to be proud when your comic is ready to go out into the real world. This is the kind of event your target market wants to know about. Your excitement and their interest create the perfect environment for advertising your book.

What Is Independent Comics Advertising?

The formal definition of **advertising** is the action of calling public attention to one's product or service[962]. Advertising in the traditional sense involves messages delivered through print, mass media, or out of home methods like billboards[963]. Modern advertising also includes things like display ads, social media, and email[964].

As an independent publisher, your advertising is less about harassing the general public about your book in a scattershot fashion and more about **continuing the conversation you started with your niche marketing**. In many ways, informing your target market about your book is just as important as finding your target market in the first place. If a tree falls in the forest, does it make a sound? If you make a comic and never tell the right people, did you even make a comic?

---

[962] Advertising. (n.d.). Retrieved May 25, 2020, from https://www.dictionary.com/browse/advertising

[963] LaMarco, N. (2019, February 11). 10 Kinds of Advertising. Retrieved May 25, 2020, from https://bizfluent.com/info-7736409-10-kinds-advertising.html

[964] Id

Yes you did, but if you want anyone to read your comic, it makes sense to advertise it.

Why Does Your Comic Need Advertising?

The right advertising message can overcome modern challenges for reaching your core market. At the same time, it can create opportunities to expand the reach of your message to your potential market.

Attention has been a business commodity for at least 180 years[965]. The evolution of available content, the expansion of wireless technology, and the proliferation of information devices has intensified this situation over the past thirty years, to the point where some people don't even know where to start in consuming the content they are interested in, much less screen out everything they don't want[966]. As we saw in Chapter 31, your target market can consume their preferred type of stories from several different media, so the potential for **information overload**[967] makes it difficult to maintain **top of mind status**[968] long enough for them to buy your comic. But the right advertising message at the right time can cut through the noise and connect your reader to your book.

Using advertising to inform your target market about your book is also one of the best ways to build excitement and a sense of connection among your ideal readers. Film critic, editor, and producer John Campea believes "…one of the main goals of advertising is to raise the emotional excitement for a story to a higher level than what the viewer felt before they encountered the advertising."[969]

Evidence of this dynamic can be seen in 2018-2019 with the advertising campaign of *Avengers: Endgame*. In spite of the fact that the movie was the sequel to one of the highest-grossing movies ever[970], and the culmination of a decade of the most popular and successful series of movies in history[971], Disney still

---

[965] Barrett, N. (2017). Has our attention been commodified? Retrieved May 25, 2020, from https://medium.economist.com/has-our-attention-been-commodified-abc178e34826

[966] Wallenstein, A. (2017, November 06). Too Many Shows? Peak TV Overwhelms Viewers, Survey Finds. Retrieved May 25, 2020, from https://variety.com/2017/digital/news/too-many-shows-peak-tv-overwhelms-viewers-survey-finds-1202606620/

[967] Information overload. (n.d.). Retrieved May 25, 2020, from https://www.dictionary.com/browse/information-overload

[968] Top-of-mind. (n.d.). Retrieved May 25, 2020, from https://www.yourdictionary.com/top-of-mind

[969] Campea, J. (Producer). (2019). *Black Widow Trailer Review* [Video file]. Retrieved May 25, 2020, from https://www.youtube.com/watch?v=4_Whw22bURo

[970] Avengers: Infinity War (2018) - Financial Information. (2018, April 25). Retrieved May 25, 2020, from https://www.the-numbers.com/movie/Avengers-Infinity-War

[971] How the Marvel Cinematic Universe shaped pop culture. (2019, January 24). Retrieved May 25, 2020, from https://little.agency/2019/01/24/how-the-marvel-cinematic-universe-shaped-pop-culture/

released six trailers in the US for the film[972], escalating collective anticipation with each new release. *Endgame* advertising helped establish it as the highest-grossing movie in the history of film[973].

Advertising doesn't need to be aggressive or intrusive to be effective. If you approach it as part of your ongoing dialogue with the target market, it can generate the same mood as the invitation to a party. In the same way your friends want you to tell them about your parties, your market wants to know about your comic.

How Can You Advertise Your Comic?

Independent publishers have several advertising methods open to them, each with their own positive and negative traits. The approaches I'm going to cover in the following chapters include:

- Online ads
- Endorsements and reviews
- Sponsorships
- SWAG[974]
- Comic book press
- Print advertising

This isn't an exhaustive list by any means, and some of the ideas I'm going to suggest haven't been proven successfully in the comic book industry as of the writing of this book. Because comic book advertising has room to grow, I would suggest **considering any advertising idea that informs the right people about your book**. You can use competitive intelligence to see what works and doesn't work for your competitors. You would also be well served to look outside the comic book industry to explore ideas that make sense for your target market[975]. Of course, you don't have to use all the advertising types discussed here. Only focus on what fits your book, your budget, and your market.

Whatever you do, don't rely on advertising to replace the time and effort required to find and build a target market. **Comic book advertising is an extension of marketing, not a replacement for it.**

---

[972] Marvel Studios (Producer). (2019). *Avengers: Endgame (All Trailers)* [Video file]. Retrieved May 25, 2020, from https://www.youtube.com/watch?v=mx9TjGVW59Q

[973] Avengers: Endgame (2019) - Financial Information. (2019, April 23). Retrieved May 25, 2020, from https://www.the-numbers.com/movie/Avengers-Endgame-(2019)

[974] SWAG is an acronym for Stuff We All Get. In comics, it often includes promotional items like stickers, artwork or mini comics What does SWAG mean in General Business? (n.d.). Retrieved May 25, 2020, from https://www.abbreviations.com/term/95393

[975] Nastos p. 101

Before we unpack each advertising technique, let's establish the essentials you'll need no matter what type of advertising you decide to use.

The two major goals of advertising are getting the *attention* of your target market and prompting *action* in the future[976]. As an independent publisher, you also need to create an effective *hook* to connect your story and the potential reader's interests. **Every element you choose to place in your ads should facilitate attention, connection, or action.**

What are the Attention Elements of Your Ad?

Human beings tend to have stronger and more visceral responses to images than text[977]. Because comics are primarily a visual medium, this tendency is even more pronounced. If you want your reader to notice your book amid the clutter of their existence, the visual aspects of your story can be your strongest tool.

The cover of a comic is usually the primary visual used to promote the book. It can, through a single image, let the reader know why they would enjoy reading your story[978]. Comic book covers are an art form in their own right, and the most iconic covers have the power to define the character, the story, and the evolution of the entire industry[979]. This is one of the main reasons comic book covers are often paid at a higher rate than other pages in the book. Sample pages, character designs, and other art can also be used in advertising, but cover design is an important aspect.

When you create your cover, imagine it as the first, last, and most important image for your story. Imagine yourself as a member of the target market and what appeals to them. Consider the major themes, tone, climax, or turning point of your story. Use the most powerful art for your cover, just don't give away the ending or use images in the cover that can't be displayed in public.

From a practical standpoint, make sure your cover is visible and understandable in a thumbnail format. If your cover is going to appear on someone's phone or tablet screen, you want them to be able to understand what's going on in your story.

[976] Suttle, R. (2019, January 31). Goals & Objectives in Advertising. Retrieved May 25, 2020, from https://smallbusiness.chron.com/goals-objectives-advertising-25273.html

[977] Alexis, C. (2018, November 12). Email is the Greatest - a Real Conversation is Even Better! Retrieved May 25, 2020, from https://movableink.com/blog/29-incredible-stats-that-prove-the-power-of-visual-marketing/

[978] Mansfield, A. (2019, August 23). What Makes A Good Comic Book Cover? Retrieved May 25, 2020, from https://bookriot.com/2019/08/22/what-makes-a-good-comic-book-cover/

[979] Schedeen, J. (2018, May 01). The 25 Most Iconic Comic Book Covers of All Time. Retrieved May 25, 2020, from http://www.ign.com/articles/2018/05/01/the-25-most-iconic-comic-book-covers-of-all-time

What are the Connection Elements of Your Ad?

Your readers often know what they like. **If what they like appears in your ad, you have a better chance of increasing their interest** in your story. There are several different ways to connect your ad to your reader, but some of the more common tactics in modern entertainment include:

- Your title
- Your pitch
- Your tagline
- Members of the <u>creative team</u> who are well regarded by the target market. For example, if you have a horror book and your artist has done a lot of horror titles in the past, a line like "from the artist who brought you…" can lure in more readers.
- Your <u>competition</u>, especially when they are well established. For example, a new zombie story could try to position themselves as the next *Walking Dead*.

What are the Action Elements of Your Ad?

If your ad gets your reader's attention and connects with them on an intellectual or emotional level, then you can **convert that interest into action if you provide the right information**. For comics, this means letting your reader know:

- When the book will be available for sale,
- Where they can buy it and
- How much it costs.

Depending on the ad format and available space, you can refer to specific bookstores, comic shops, and online stores that carry your book, but at the very least your website should appear somewhere in the ad.

Different advertising formats allow for different types of information. You'll have to tailor your ads to fit each platform you choose, but this list of core elements can be manipulated to capture attention, create connection and inspire action whether your ad is online or in the real world.

If attention, connection, and action are the goals of advertising, then engaging the target market online is essential to your efforts. In the 21st century, the average American spends almost 15% of their week, or 24 hours a week, devoted to online activity, whether it involves email, internet searches, online shopping, or social media[980]. Almost 80% of Americans connect with each other on social media[981]. Finally, buyers around the world take economic action online. The projection for global e-commerce spending in 2021 is projected to be around 4.8 billion dollars[982]. If you avoid **online advertising**[983], you give up a major opportunity to reach your target market.

But online advertising can be confusing, costly, and counter-productive if it isn't managed in a way that makes sense for your business. Leveraging your existing marketing network and your knowledge of the target market can reduce some of the risks and get your message in front of the right people.

How Do You Leverage Your Marketing Network?

If you are continuously connecting with your ideal readers as a part of your marketing efforts, then adding advertising to the overall message can be painless and effective. Adding a special ad page to your website, periodically reposting your ad in your social media feed, and sending an ad announcement to your mailing list are natural extensions of your ongoing conversation.

This kind of advertising can help because it reaches the specific audience that wants to hear your message with very little cost, or no cost at all. Just be sure not to abruptly change tone when you shift from marketing to advertising in your online posts. If you go from posting reviews, commentaries, and chats to an endless barrage of "BUY MY BOOK!!!" you can wind up sabotaging the community you built up over those long weeks, months, or years.

How Do You Leverage Your Target Market Knowledge?

When you defined your ideal reader, you selected the demographics, psychographics, genre, and generation of the person most likely to read your story. You determined which keywords would be most

---

[980] Condliffe, J. (2020, April 02). The average American spends 24 hours a week online. Retrieved May 25, 2020, from https://www.technologyreview.com/f/610045/the-average-american-spends-24-hours-a-week-online/

[981] Clement, J. (2020, May 19). U.S. population with a social media profile 2019. Retrieved May 25, 2020, from https://www.statista.com/statistics/273476/percentage-of-us-population-with-a-social-network-profile/

[982] Duncan, E. (2019). Topic: E-commerce worldwide. Retrieved May 25, 2020, from https://www.statista.com/topics/871/online-shopping/

[983] What is Online Advertising? (n.d.). Retrieved May 25, 2020, from https://www.techopedia.com/definition/26362/online-advertising

effective in finding them online and you determined the specific comics and other media that form the competition for your book. This information builds the foundation of your online advertising arsenal.

Online ad platforms[984] utilize keywords to create specific audiences for every product or service. For example:

- **Amazon** allows advertisers to target custom audiences in the form of sponsored products that appear while people are searching the Amazon store[985].

- **Facebook**[986] and its subsidiary **Instagram**[987] create custom audiences based on demographics, psychographics, and location.

- Mobile advertising platforms like **AdColony**[988] can place your ad within mobile apps and games that cater to your target market.

- **YouTube**[989] takes advantage of Google ad technology to create custom audiences based on the videos people watch.

If you elect to advertise online, **direct your attention to your ideal reader, and don't worry about reaching anyone else**. If you want your message to appear in the right place at the right time, use your genres to pop up when your readers are looking for something new. While it is often a violation of both terms of service and trademark law to use a competitor's trademark as a keyword in your ad[990], you can focus on the unique elements of your book to offer readers what your competitors don't.

[984] Yaioa. (2020, February 10). 10 Best Online Advertising Platforms To Advertise and Grow Your Business (Updated 2020). Retrieved May 25, 2020, from https://www.yaioa.com/blog/best-online-advertising-platforms/

[985] Wright, J. Amazon Advertising. Retrieved May 25, 2020, from https://services.amazon.com/advertising/faq.html

[986] Facebook Advertising Targeting Options. (n.d.). Retrieved May 25, 2020, from https://www.facebook.com/business/ads/ad-targeting

[987] Advertising on Instagram: Instagram Business. (n.d.). Retrieved May 25, 2020, from https://business.instagram.com/advertising/

[988] AdColony for Advertisers. (2020, January 07). Retrieved May 25, 2020, from https://www.adcolony.com/advertisers/

[989] Google Find My Audience. (n.d.). Retrieved May 25, 2020, from https://www.thinkwithgoogle.com/feature/findmyaudience/

[990] Smith, B. (2018, May 12). AdWords Competitor Targeting: Everything You Need To Know To Do It Right. Retrieved May 25, 2020, from https://adespresso.com/blog/adwords-competitor-targeting/

How Do You Select the Right Online Advertising Mix?

Some types of advertising might make more sense for your book than others. Your **advertising mix**[991], or the combination of ad methods you will use for your book, will be dependent on several factors. Before we develop tactics to navigate this industry, it will help to understand a few basic definitions in addition to the concept of keywords:

- **Conversion rate** (CVR): is the percentage of visitors to your website that complete a desired goal (a **conversion**) out of the total number of visitors[992]. For example, if your desired action was pre-ordering your book online, your CVR would be the percentage of visitors to your website who completed the pre-order. The average CVR in Google Ads in 2019 was about 3%[993].

- **Cost per click** (CPC): a method that websites use to bill based on the number of times a visitor clicks on an advertisement[994]. Going back to our *Crisis* example, if Bruce buys a CPC ad that 1,000 people see, but only 10 people click on the link in the ad, then Bruce only pays for the clicks, not for the number of people who saw the ad.

- **Cost per thousand** (CPM): is the number of impressions, or viewers, in thousands, regardless of whether each viewer clicks on the advertisement or not[995]. So, if Charles buys a CPM ad that 1,000 people see and no one clicks on, he still has to pay for the number of people who saw the ad.

- **Real-time bidding** (RTB): refers to the buying and selling of online ad impressions through real-time auctions for keywords that occur in the time it takes a webpage to load[996]. So, if Bruce and Charles bid on the same keywords, whoever made the higher bid (in addition to other elements of their ad) would get the ad placement.

---

[991] Advertising Mix. (n.d.). Retrieved May 25, 2020, from https://dictionary.cambridge.org/us/dictionary/english/advertising-mix

[992] What Is a Conversion Rate? (n.d.). Retrieved May 25, 2020, from https://www.wordstream.com/conversion-rate

[993] Id.

[994] Frankenfield, J. (2020, January 29). Cost Per Click (CPC). Retrieved May 25, 2020, from https://www.investopedia.com/terms/c/cpc.asp

[995] Id.

[996] What is Real-Time Bidding, or RTB? (2018, November 29). Retrieved May 25, 2020, from https://digiday.com/media/what-is-real-time-bidding/

- **Return on investment** (ROI) is a performance measure used to evaluate the efficiency of an investment or compare the efficiency of several different investments[997]. In this case, it is the difference between the value of a conversion and the cost of the conversion. So, if Charles spent more on advertising for one book than the money he made from that book, he would have a negative ROI.

So how does all this tech jargon help you decide what ad platform to use?

- First, you need to decide what to consider as your conversion. If you want your target market to see your ad and be aware that your book exists, then bidding based on CPM might make more sense. If you want them to pick up a copy when they see the ad, then a CPC bid could be a better option.[998]

- Next, based on your marketing research, determine if your target market spends time in one online forum more than others. It makes sense to advertise where the market will see it, but keep in mind that some ad networks only have one bidding option, so you might not get to decide between CPC and CPM.

- Determine how much you are willing to bid per keyword for the duration of your advertising campaign. This will help you control costs and avoid overspending. For example, let's say Bruce wants to spend $100 per month on his ads. That breaks down to about $3 per day. If he bids $.50 per click, then the highest number of ad generated traffic he can expect is about five or six clicks per day.

- Start small and track the progress of your ad campaign so you can make adjustments to protect your investment. Most aspects of your ads can be changed in real-time, so you don't need to throw money away on a strategy that isn't working. You should give your keywords, ad copy, and audience choices a chance to succeed or fail before you pull the plug, but when you decide something isn't working, feel free to change it or stop the campaign completely.

- Make sure your sales can justify your ads based on a simple ROI. Remember, not every click you pay for guarantees a sale. If your conversion rate is 5% (higher than average), that means 95% of the ad traffic to your website will not result in a sale. So, if you pay a $.50 CPC and you need 20 clicks to make 1 conversion, then the profit from the book needs to be more than $10

---

[997] Chen, J. (2020, April 27). Return on Investment (ROI). Retrieved May 25, 2020, from https://www.investopedia.com/terms/r/returnoninvestment.asp

[998] CPC Bidding vs. CPM Bidding: What's The Difference? (2020, April 06). Retrieved May 25, 2020, from https://www.honchosearch.com/blog/paid-media/cpm-cpc-bidding/

to avoid a negative ROI. The CPC bid might be fine to sell a $25 OGN, but it won't make any sense for a $4 single issue.

- Remember to track all of your advertising costs for your taxes and possible deductions.

The ROI for using your marketing network for ads will almost always make sense, but other ad platforms and paid options require more thought and analysis depending on the book. Paid advertising can't solve all of your challenges. No matter how much you spend, **"ad blindness"**[999] (or the subconscious disregard for online advertising) can undermine all your efforts. As we noted earlier, people are more likely to pay attention to and take action based upon personal referrals over ads, so it makes sense to consider reviews and endorsements as part of your online advertising mix.

---

[999] Ryan, T. (2017, November 21). Examples of Advertising Blindness. Retrieved May 25, 2020, from https://smallbusiness.chron.com/examples-advertising-blindness-35729.html

Imagine for a moment that former president Barack Obama posted a positive tweet about your historical comic to his 111 million followers[1000].

What if the cast of *Game of Thrones* got on stage during the 2018 SAG awards and thanked you for your great fantasy OGN?

How many copies of your book would you sell if the winning quarterback of the Super Bowl mentioned your sports comic as one of the inspirations that helped him win the biggest game in America?

I think if any of these scenarios happened, and only one percent of those audiences responded to these messages, you would have one of the biggest selling comics of the year, if not the decade.

Unfortunately, you probably don't have the clout to DM a former president or send preview copies of your book to NFL locker rooms. But you can increase the attention, connection, and action associated with your book on a smaller, more realistic scale through the use of endorsements.

An **endorsement** is a public statement in support of something or someone[1001]. In the past, endorsement deals were exclusively for the famous and influential. Corporations routinely pay millions of dollars per year for a positive connection with an actor or athlete[1002]. But the internet age has given everyone a platform for their opinions. Now, anyone can endorse almost any product or service through their reviews. Part of the goal of **online reputation management** (ORM) is using reviews to grow your business[1003]. Sites like

---

[1000] Pope, L. (2019). The 10 Most Followed Twitter Accounts in 2020. Retrieved May 25, 2020, from https://learn.g2.com/most-followed-twitter-accounts

[1001] Endorsement. (n.d.). Retrieved May 25, 2020, from https://dictionary.cambridge.org/us/dictionary/english/endorsement

[1002] Lisa, A. (2020, April 27). Celebrity Endorsement Deals With Insane Payouts. Retrieved May 25, 2020, from https://finance.yahoo.com/news/celebrity-endorsement-deals-insane-payouts-090030383.html

[1003] Bowman, M. (2019, January 16). Council Post: Online Reviews And Their Impact On The Bottom Line. Retrieved May 26, 2020, from https://www.forbes.com/sites/forbesagencycouncil/2019/01/15/online-reviews-and-their-impact-on-the-bottom-line/

Yelp[1004] and Trip Advisor[1005] are built on public reviews, and most comic book distribution platforms like Amazon[1006] and Webtoons[1007] include a rating system for readers to endorse a book.

Online reviews are more than the expression of a random personal opinion. According to various research, 70% of global consumers trust online reviews to make their purchases[1008], 84% of people trust online reviews as much as a personal recommendation from a friend[1009], and 91% of them are more likely to buy from a business with positive reviews[1010]. Positive reviews and endorsements can mean the difference between a best seller and just another comic.

Who Can Provide a Useful Review for Your Book?

The best reviews for your book will probably come from your ideal readers. They are interested in both your medium and your message. They might be the group most enthusiastic about your story. If you have created and maintained a dialogue with your community through your marketing efforts, they will probably be the easiest reviewers to find, as well. These reviews won't always be positive and they usually won't be professional[1011], but their passion can often make up for their prose.

There is a good chance you can also find professional and semi-professional bloggers, vloggers, and reviewers for the medium of comics and the specific genres of your story. These reviews can have a greater impact on your advertising than any individual review, because while an ideal reader might post a review and forget about it, this group is actively blasting their message online to get more clicks on their site. Again, if you spend time during the marketing phase finding the discussions and personalities relevant to your ideal reader, then you probably know where to find these people. Once you know who they are, the goal is to make a review request as part of your ongoing conversation.

[1004] Yelp Investor Relations. (n.d.). Retrieved May 26, 2020, from https://www.yelp-ir.com/

[1005] Trip Advisor Inc. 10K Report. (2018). Retrieved May 26, 2020, from https://www.sec.gov/Archives/edgar/data/1526520/000156459019003889/trip-10k_20181231.htm

[1006] Amazon Customer Reviews FAQ. (2011). Retrieved May 26, 2020, from https://www.amazon.com/gp/help/customer/display.html?nodeId=G3UA5WC5S5UUKB5G

[1007] Webtoons Popular Titles. (n.d.). Retrieved May 26, 2020, from https://www.webtoons.com/en/top

[1008] Lagarde, J. (2015, December 29). 6 Reasons Why Amazon Product Reviews Matter to Merchants. Retrieved May 26, 2020, from https://www.entrepreneur.com/article/253361

[1009] Bloem, C. (2017, July 31). 84 Percent of People Trust Online Reviews As Much As Friends. Here's How to Manage What They See. Retrieved May 26, 2020, from https://www.inc.com/craig-bloem/84-percent-of-people-trust-online-reviews-as-much-.html

[1010] Clement, J. (2020, January 09). Effect of online reviews on local business customer opinion 2019. Retrieved May 26, 2020, from https://www.statista.com/statistics/315751/online-review-customer-opinion/

[1011] Marz, R. (2015, September 11). Review 101: Tools for Reviewing Comics. Retrieved May 26, 2020, from https://www.cbr.com/review-101-tools-for-reviewing-comics/

How Do You Get Reviewers to Focus on Your Book?

If you continue to work under the marketing theory that people do things for the indirect feeling they get from the action and not the direct action itself, then you can use the concept to motivate potential reviewers. While there are two general motivators you can focus on, there is one you should avoid in the context of reviews.

- Use increased status: people are constantly attempting to increase their standing within their tribe or sub-culture[1012]. This is no different in comic book fandom. Reviewers who get the chance to see the book before anyone else might be encouraged enough to give you a review[1013]. This might also work for reviewers who feel they will have more influence within your genre by offering their opinion, or who simply want to get access to something for free.

- Use increased attention: this is related to the issue of status, but it deserves a separate mention. Because attention is a commodity in the internet age[1014], many reviewers are looking for those books that will attract more eyeballs. If you offer a book appealing to their peer group or you already have a community that would go to their site, then you increase the chances they'll review your book.

- Avoid offering cash: Businesses that rely on reviews often prohibit publishers paying for reviews[1015]. While some people might use their reviews to indirectly make money (through online advertising or affiliate marketing) you can't pay someone to give you a good review, or prevent them from giving you a bad review.

When you are ready to reach out to potential reviewers, there are a variety of methods you can use to find them individually or collectively[1016]. Modify your query letter to take their motivations into account, give them the time, information, and sample copies they need to function, then sit back and see if your book gets a good review or a bad review.

[1012] Greene 48 Laws of Power

[1013] Winkie, L. (2019, June 07). Who are these people who write thousands of Amazon product reviews? Retrieved May 26, 2020, from https://www.vox.com/the-highlight/2019/6/7/18645784/amazon-product-reviews-reviewers-vine

[1014] Barrett, N. (2017). Has our attention been commodified? Retrieved May 25, 2020, from https://medium.economist.com/has-our-attention-been-commodified-abc178e34826

[1015] Amazon Customer Reviews FAQ. (2011).

[1016] Penn, J. (2018, August 29). Book Marketing: 10 Ways To Get Reviews For Your Book. Retrieved May 26, 2020, from https://www.thecreativepenn.com/2018/08/29/book-marketing-10-ways-to-get-reviews-for-your-book/

How Do You Deal with Negative Reviews?

Even if you create the best book possible, focus only on your target market, and carefully select ideal readers as your reviewers, **all of your reviews may not be positive**. *Hamlet*, one of the most influential stories in Western literature, currently has more than 110 one-star reviews on Amazon[1017]. While the emotional effect of bad reviews can be stressful for the artists involved[1018], as an independent publisher, it helps to understand the potential positive impact of any review, good or bad.

According to the *Harvard Business Review*, bad book reviews can increase sales of an unknown author by up to 45%[1019]. The possible reason for this surge is awareness. Any review has the potential to inform people about a book that they otherwise would not know about. And although positive reviews make people more confident about buying a product, negative reviews do not have the same ability to discourage purchases[1020]. You only have to look at the 100 million copies *Fifty Shades of Gray* sold [1021] to see how well a book can do despite bad reviews[1022]. Negative reviews aren't fun, but bad press is often better than no press at all.

How Can You Secure Larger Endorsements for Your Book?

If you are looking beyond the consumer or blogger review, you are entering the modern world of endorsements. The influencers we discussed in the marketing chapter might not be actors or athletes, but they can drive sales in your target market[1023].

If you already have influencers in your marketing program, shifting to advertising can be a straightforward process that is seamless to their audience. If this is your first attempt at using an influencer, you'll have to

[1017] Hamlet Amazon Page. Retrieved May 26, 2020, from https://www.amazon.com/Hamlet-Folger-Library-Shakespeare-William/dp/074347712X/ref=sr_1_3?keywords=hamlet

[1018] Alvear, M. (2017, February 03). Real Writers Get Bad Book Reviews. Here's Why That's OK. Retrieved May 26, 2020, from https://thewritelife.com/real-writers-get-bad-book-reviews/

[1019] Berger, J. (2014, August 01). Bad Reviews Can Boost Sales. Here's Why. Retrieved May 26, 2020, from https://hbr.org/2012/03/bad-reviews-can-boost-sales-heres-why

[1020] Clement, J. (2020, January 09). Effect of online reviews on local business customer opinion 2019. Retrieved May 26, 2020, from https://www.statista.com/statistics/315751/online-review-customer-opinion/

[1021] Statista Research Department. (2014, February 27). Fifty Shades of Grey - number of copies sold worldwide 2014. Retrieved May 26, 2020, from https://www.statista.com/statistics/299137/fifty-shades-of-grey-number-of-copies-sold/

[1022] Odell, A. (2017, October 09). The 11 Meanest Things Critics Said About the New "Fifty Shades of Grey" Book. Retrieved May 26, 2020, from https://www.cosmopolitan.com/entertainment/news/a42274/meanest-reviews-of-grey/

[1023] Wiley, D. (2018, May 29). Council Post: More Than Awareness: Influencer Marketing's Role In The Sales Funnel. Retrieved May 26, 2020, from https://www.forbes.com/sites/forbesagencycouncil/2018/05/29/more-than-awareness-influencer-marketings-role-in-the-sales-funnel/

find and build a relationship with the right people before you can expect them to share your story with their followers[1024].

- Find one who fits your potential reader and follow them to see if their message matches the feeling you intend to generate for your reader.

- When you find a potential fit, only then should you reach out and work out a deal for both compensation and creative control of the ad campaign. As always, get a signed contract to cover any work associated with your comic.

- Decide on the best time to launch your ad campaign, based on the release schedule of your book.

- Finally, because this activity is governed by the Federal Trade Commission, be sure to conform to all the relevant rules about social media influence[1025] and consult with your attorney if you have questions.

Reviews from library level services can also act as a form of endorsement advertising when you're focusing on the bookstore and library markets[1026]. We covered those companies in chapter 46, so refer back to them to determine which ones fit your overall advertising program.

Creating a buzz for your book with reviews is standard operating procedure in the Amazon world of publishing, but strong associations with the brands, events, and locations your target market enjoys can separate you from your competition. That kind of association often comes from sponsorships, so we'll look at that method of advertising in the next chapter.

[1024] Newberry, C. (2020, March 05). Influencer Marketing in 2019: How to Work With Social Media Influencers. Retrieved May 26, 2020, from https://blog.hootsuite.com/influencer-marketing/

[1025] The FTC's Endorsement Guides: What People Are Asking. (2019, May 15). Retrieved May 26, 2020, from https://www.ftc.gov/tips-advice/business-center/guidance/ftcs-endorsement-guides-what-people-are-asking

[1026] Thorn, P. (n.d.). How to Get Book Reviews to Market Your Self-Published Book. Retrieved May 26, 2020, from https://www.ingramspark.com/blog/book-review-checklist-what-to-do-before-submitting-for-review

A **sponsorship** is a form of marketing in which a payment is made by a company for the right to be associated with a project or program[1027]. It is a common feature in the sports industry, where players, games, stadiums, and entire leagues generate billions of dollars by selling corporate sponsorships[1028].

The psychology of sponsorships is based on ideas we covered in the marketing chapter. Because people spend money with companies they like and identify with, associating a car, a beer or an insurance company with a prominent franchise or a local stadium can create a **halo effect** in the mind of a sports fan[1029]. Independent comic book publishers can create a similar effect on a smaller scale, creating positive connections with the target market by becoming a corporate sponsor.

What are the Benefits of Sponsorship?

Finding the right sponsorship for your book or your publishing company as a whole can help **achieve the advertising goals of garnering attention, creating connection and prompting action** in a variety of ways all at once including:

- Enhancing your image and visibility
- Differentiating you from competitors
- Developing closer relationships with ideal readers
- Providing a positive showcase for your books
- Allow you to compete more effectively against established companies[1030]

What are the Downsides of Sponsorship?

Associating your book with **the wrong sponsorship deal can undermine both your project and your company**. Potential problems include:

[1027] Kenton, W. (2020, March 23). Corporate Sponsorship. Retrieved May 26, 2020, from
https://www.investopedia.com/terms/c/corporate-sponsorship.asp

[1028] Fuller, S. (n.d.). Topic: Sports Sponsorship. Retrieved May 26, 2020, from
https://www.statista.com/topics/1382/sports-sponsorship/

[1029] Kenton, W. (2020, March 23). Corporate Sponsorship.

[1030] Corporate Sponsorship. Retrieved May 26, 2020, from https://www.inc.com/encyclopedia/corporate-sponsorship.html

- Poor representation of your book, either because your sponsorship is not prominent or the event or organization you decide to partner with generates negative publicity[1031].

- Wasting advertising efforts by targeting the false market or the non-market.

- Diluting the sponsorship message because your book or logo is buried among too many disparate companies. The common analogy of this is the race car driver who has so many sponsors on her uniform that they all just blend into a logo tapestry.

- Loss of control over how the sponsorship investment is spent.

- The cost of sponsorship outweighing the potential benefits to the book[1032].

What Criteria are Important for Comic Sponsorship?

When deciding on a potential sponsorship opportunity, the key is to **increase the potential benefits and minimize the potential risks**. The editors of Inc. Magazine suggest a four-part test for any potential sponsorship deal[1033]:

- Relevance: Does the sponsorship mean anything to the ideal reader?

- Branding Fit: Does the sponsorship fit with the overall concept of the book or the company?

- Mission Alignment: Does the sponsorship align with your goals?

- Business Result: Do you think the sponsorship can achieve some measurable business results (website visits, mailing list signups, purchases, etc.)?

How Can You Create Sponsorship Opportunities?

Because sponsorships are a form of marketing, it makes sense to **revisit some of the ideas in the marketing chapters and convert them into opportunities for branding**. Since your goal is to connect only with your target market, you're probably not trying to sponsor an NBA team or a NASCAR race. You can stay small, focusing on the apps, events, and media your target market cares about. By retaining a tight

---

[1031] Wilson, B. (2015, May 28). Fifa scandal 'a disaster' for sponsors. Retrieved May 26, 2020, from https://www.bbc.com/news/business-32912445

[1032] McQuerrey, L. (2019, February 11). The Disadvantages of Sponsorship. Retrieved May 26, 2020, from https://bizfluent.com/info-8335114-disadvantages-sponsorship.html

[1033] Corporate Sponsorship. Retrieved May 26, 2020

focus, you can try to control costs by using free giveaways, barter agreements, and the management of events in place of investment dollars.

Sponsorships, like marketing, can occur online or in the real world. You can explore different virtual events and act as their official sponsor. Different online platforms are always looking for sponsors to help defer costs and generate traffic[1034], just make sure to conduct your due diligence on the potential partner's online traffic, followers and unique visits before you make a deal. Online sponsorships are only limited by your imagination and the interests of your target market, but some ideas include:

- Blog or YouTube sponsorships
- Book giveaways or discount codes for purchases
- Genre related reviews
- Genre related art contests
- Genre chats/hangouts
- Interviews

Remember to post all your online sponsorship activity to your social media to increase exposure and maintain momentum.

Real-world sponsorships can occur at comic shops, libraries, bookstores, or any other venue relevant to your target market. The types of events are also numerous, including:

- Comic book reading club
- Cosplay contests
- Educational classes
- Game nights
- Family nights
- Local panel discussions
- Local conventions
- Trivia contests

[1034] Gumpel, E. (2010, February 24). How to Attract Corporate Sponsors. Retrieved May 26, 2020, from https://www.entrepreneur.com/article/217913

What Are the Costs of Sponsorship?

Unlike other types of marketing, sponsorship falls under the concept of advertising because there are usually some investment costs involved with being a sponsor. But **there is huge variation in those costs based on what you're trying to do and who you're trying to reach**. As the editors of Inc. pointed out "*…the fees involved in event marketing can range from a few hundred dollars to hundreds of thousands of dollars, depending on the scale of the event and the level of the sponsor's involvement. In addition to the cost of staging the event itself, there are also associated advertising, publicity, and administrative costs to consider.*[1035]"

As an independent publisher, it makes more sense to **keep the scale small, both to control costs and to focus your efforts solely on the target market**. In addition, you might want to consider co-sponsoring an existing event[1036]. This will allow you to take advantage of the experience of other sponsors, in addition to keeping costs down, as long as your message isn't lost in the crowd.

What Are the Contractual Requirements of Sponsorship?

Because sponsorship involves both your intellectual property and your investment, **you need a sponsorship agreement spelling out the terms and conditions of the business relationship**. What you want to ask for in every deal will be unique[1037], but there are business and foundation terms[1038] you and your attorney can ask for in the written deal including:

- Full or partial ads in a relevant publication or app
- Blog posts featuring your book
- A booth, tent or table at the event
- The event named for you or your book
- A guest post on an organization blog
- Inclusion in any press release
- Links in their email newsletter
- Links on their website
- Your logo on event t-shirt or other swag
- Your logo on event signage
- Your logo or name on their website

[1035] Corporate Sponsorship. Retrieved May 26, 2020

[1036] Id.

[1037] Cruz, C. (2018, April 03). The Guide to Local Sponsorship Marketing. Retrieved May 26, 2020, from https://moz.com/blog/guide-to-local-sponsorship-marketing

[1038] Kenton, W. (2020, March 23). Corporate Sponsorship.

- Video spots featuring your book
- Mention of your book in publicity materials, such as programs and other printed materials
- Social media mentions
- Speaking opportunities at an event
- Tickets to the event
- Verbal recognition during the event

Sponsorship is an advanced and more involved form of advertising that can gain prominence for an otherwise overlooked property. The use of sponsorships can also generate the kind of publicity that the comic book press will take notice of and cover. Contacting and working with the comic book press can be another useful component of your advertising efforts, so we'll focus on them in the next chapter.

Although the internet gives everyone a platform for expression and opinion, more established and organized forms of news media can have a major influence on the attention, connection, and action of ideal readers in relation to independent comics.

The news media, more commonly referred to as the **press**, delivers various types of information to large audiences[1039], to help them make the best decisions on a variety of subjects[1040]. In the past, the press was dominated by newspapers, radio, and television[1041]. Today, online journalism has become an important addition to the flow of information[1042], offering narrow and specific **filter bubbles** of curated reality[1043]. While these self-selected silos of information might not be beneficial to the public discourse in terms of politics or government, it can help your potential readers make decisions about how they want to spend their entertainment time and money.

Who Makes Up the Comic Book Press?

In my experience, the majority of the journalists who cover the comic book industry are currently online. There are bloggers[1044], podcasters, and vloggers who work both independently[1045] and as part of larger organizations. While there is some debate on the professional experience and training of these writers[1046], they do contribute to the ongoing coverage of comics. Specific comic book press sites currently include:

- Ain't It Cool News[1047]

[1039] News media. (2020, May 14). Retrieved May 26, 2020, from https://en.wikipedia.org/wiki/News_media

[1040] What is the purpose of journalism? (2017, July 18). Retrieved May 26, 2020, from https://www.americanpressinstitute.org/journalism-essentials/what-is-journalism/purpose-journalism/

[1041] Lawlor, J. (2018). 5 major differences between traditional media and social media. Retrieved May 26, 2020, from https://muckrack.com/blog/2018/08/01/differences-between-traditional-media-and-social-media

[1042] News media. (2020, May 14).

[1043] Leetaru, K. (2017, December 18). Why 2017 Was The Year Of The Filter Bubble? Retrieved May 26, 2020, from https://www.forbes.com/sites/kalevleetaru/2017/12/18/why-was-2017-the-year-of-the-filter-bubble/

[1044] Top 100 Comics Blogs & Websites For Comic Fans: Comic Websites. (2020, May 25). Retrieved May 26, 2020, from https://blog.feedspot.com/comics_blogs/

[1045] Google Search: Indie Comic Reviews. (n.d.). Retrieved May 26, 2020, from https://www.google.com/search?rlz=1C1GCEA_enUS885

[1046] "Perch" (Producer). (2019). *A look at the curious "state" of Comics "Journalism".* [Video file]. Retrieved May 26, 2020, from https://www.youtube.com/watch?v=txYiT4Uy6Yc

[1047] Ain't It Cool News: The best in comic book news. (n.d.). Retrieved May 27, 2020, from https://www.aintitcool.com/section/comics/

- Bleeding Cool[1048]
- Book Riot[1049]
- Comics Beat[1050]
- Comic Book Resources[1051]
- Deadline[1052]
- ICV2[1053]
- IGN[1054]
- IO9[1055]
- Hollywood Reporter[1056]
- Newsarama[1057]
- Newsweek[1058]
- The New York Times[1059]
- Publishers Weekly[1060]
- Wired[1061]

In addition to these general comic news sites, it makes sense for every independent publisher to seek out niche news and reviews sites that cater to their specific genre and ideal reader, even if they don't normally

---

[1048] Bleeding Cool. (n.d.). Retrieved May 27, 2020, from https://www.bleedingcool.com/

[1049] Book Riot Comic Books. (n.d.). Retrieved May 27, 2020, from https://bookriot.com/tag/comic-books/

[1050] Leblanc, P., Leblanchttps, P., Leblanc, & Kaplan, A. (2020, February 04). Small Press & Indie Comics News – A Fresh Start. Retrieved May 27, 2020, from https://www.comicsbeat.com/small-press-indie-comics-news-a-fresh-start/

[1051] CBR - The World's Top Destination For Comic news. (n.d.). Retrieved May 27, 2020, from https://www.cbr.com/

[1052] Deadline: Comics. Retrieved May 27, 2020, from https://deadline.com/results/

[1053] The Business of Geek Culture: Comics. (n.d.). Retrieved May 27, 2020, from https://icv2.com/articles/comics

[1054] IGN Comics Reviews, News, Heroes, Villains, Superheroes & Toys. (n.d.). Retrieved May 27, 2020, from https://www.ign.com/comics

[1055] Gizmodo Comics - Tech and Science Tips, Reviews, News (n.d.). Retrieved May 27, 2020, from https://gizmodo.com/c/comics

[1056] Hollywood Reporter Comic Book & Sci-Fi Movie News - Heat Vision. (n.d.). Retrieved May 27, 2020, from https://www.hollywoodreporter.com/blogs/heat-vision

[1057] Newsarama Comic Book News, TV, Movies. Retrieved May 27, 2020, from https://www.newsarama.com/

[1058] Newsweek Comic Books. (n.d.). Retrieved May 27, 2020, from https://www.newsweek.com/topic/comic-books

[1059] NYT: Comic Books (n.d.). Retrieved May 27, 2020, from https://www.nytimes.com/topic/subject/comic-books-and-strips

[1060] Comics and Graphic Novel News: Publishers Weekly. (n.d.). Retrieved May 27, 2020, from https://www.publishersweekly.com/pw/by-topic/industry-news/comics/index.html

[1061] Comic Books | Latest News, Photos & Videos. (n.d.). Retrieved May 27, 2020, from https://www.wired.com/tag/comic-books/

cover comics. This can provide more access to the potential market that might not be aware of what's happening in the comic book press.

What Are the Benefits of Using the Comic Book Press for Your Advertising?

As an advertising vehicle, press coverage can satisfy the three goals of attention, connection, and action by:

- Attention: Generating buzz that can excite readers, comic shop owners, and librarians.

- Connection: Reaching the target market with a level of social proof based on the perceived legitimacy of the site.

- Action: Driving significant traffic to your distribution channels when your book is ready for sale.

- Cost: Reducing the cost of advertising because press coverage is often free. Because the sites ostensibly generate revenue based on traffic and their advertising efforts, there is no cost to the independent publisher for submitting a story.

What Are the Downsides of Using the Comic Book Press for Your Advertising?

The benefits of press coverage are, like most other things in comics, counterbalanced by the detrimental elements:

- Control: Because you are not paying for the site to pick up your story, and because there is significant weekly competition for press coverage, **there is no guarantee that any site will run a story on your book**. If they do post a story, it might not come out in a time and in a manner that is beneficial or flattering to your book.

- Coverage: Because the comic book press is motivated to generate as much traffic as possible, I sense a natural hierarchy in terms of which stories they cover that looks something like this:
  - Coverage of movie, television, or video game-related comics news
  - Coverage of the Big Two
  - Coverage of major comic-related events like conventions
  - Coverage of major independent creator-owned books
  - Coverage of established independent publishers
  - Coverage of established talent
  - Coverage of independent publishers

This doesn't mean that the comic book press will never write about your book. It does mean that you can't expect or rely on press coverage to be your only advertising strategy, even if you hire a publicist to help you[1062].

- Diluted Audience: Depending on the news outlets you contact you might be reaching fans of comics in general and not your type of story specifically. This potential overemphasis on the false market reduces the value of press coverage for niche stories.

How Do You Contact the Comic Book Press?

There are three general ways to contact comic book journalists; formal, informal, and hybrid.

The formal method involves sending a press release to the proper organizations. A **press release** is a public relations announcement issued to the news media to announce specific events[1063]. The standard format of a press release includes a headline, an opening sentence, the body of the press release (what is the story about and the hook for why it matters to the target market), and contact information for the organization issuing the press release[1064]. Whenever possible, your press release should also include your key artwork. You can have your press release issued through an established service[1065], but in my experience, these services skew heavily toward the non-market. It makes more sense to send the release directly to either the comic book news sites or the individual writers yourself or through your publicist.

Contacting journalists directly is easier if you have a connection to them before you need a story. If you develop an informal relationship with comic book writers as part of your marketing in the same manner as other types of influencers, then reaching out to them to offer them the scoop on your story can be a natural by-product of your communication.

Since you probably can't have pre-existing connections to every comic book journalist who might cover your book, a hybrid approach is often the best bet. Writing a strong press release, sending it directly to your press contacts, and then more generally to the overall comic book press can yield better results than either method individually.

[1062] Talley, J. (2018, October 29). What Does a Publicist Do? Retrieved May 30, 2020, from https://www.mediabistro.com/be-inspired/advice-from-the-pros/what-does-a-publicist-do/

[1063] Sorensen, M., Rose, J., & Marks, G. (n.d.). Press Release Definition - Entrepreneur Small Business Encyclopedia. Retrieved May 30, 2020, from https://www.entrepreneur.com/encyclopedia/press-release

[1064] Wynne, R. (2016, June 14). How To Write A Press Release. Retrieved May 30, 2020, from https://www.forbes.com/sites/robertwynne/2016/06/13/how-to-write-a-press-release/

[1065] Rudder, A. (2020, May 19). 6 Best Press Release Distribution Services 2020. Retrieved May 30, 2020, from https://fitsmallbusiness.com/best-press-release-service/

When Should You Contact the Comic Book Press?

The timing for reaching out to the comic book press depends on three factors:

- The developments of your book
- The schedule of the particular site
- The needs of the target market

There is no reason to contact the press unless there is something newsworthy going on with your book[1066]. Depending on the site, this could be anything from the release of the book, to the announcement of the crowdfunding campaign, to the signing of well-known talent, to your sponsorships. Every post that you make on social media won't warrant a press release. Save them for the major events.

When considering timing from the press perspective, try getting on their radar as soon as possible, especially if you are going to use the press release as a tie-in to the publication date or crowdfunding. Keep in mind that there are internal as well as external time factors for every site, including convention season, holidays, major media events, and publishing deadlines -so don't reach out to a reporter at the last minute and expect them to drop everything for you[1067].

Finally, think about the potential reader of the article and the action you want them to take. If you're targeting comic shops or librarians who need several months of advanced lead time so they can order your book before the street date, your press contact needs to happen a lot earlier than the article designed to get an ideal reader to click a link and buy the book immediately[1068].

How Do You Measure the Results of Press Advertising?

One of the benefits of online advertising is the ability to see how different tactics impact your goals. Your use of the comic book press can produce the same results if you keep track of the data over time.

On the first level, you can see which sites ran your story and which ones didn't. Depending on your website or your use of URL analytics[1069], you can determine which press sites generated the most traffic. When you compare the traffic from each site with your existing conversion goals, it can start to paint a picture of which press sites give you the biggest return on investment for your efforts.

[1066] Wynne, R. (2016, June 14). How To Write A Press Release.

[1067] Derek Becker, Comic Pros and Cons Interview [Telephone interview]. (2017, December 21).

[1068] Allen p. 149

[1069] Kranz, J. (2020, April 22). What Is a UTM Code? The Complete Guide Everyone Can Love. Retrieved May 30, 2020, from https://buffer.com/library/utm-guide/

An advertising vehicle that doesn't offer the same type of analytics is print advertising. But this traditional form of getting the word out still has a place in an industry where 80% of the revenue comes from physical products. The next chapter will take a quick look at how print ads can fit into your advertising mix without spending too much of your investment.

Print advertising includes advertising messages placed in print media like newspapers or magazines[1070]. For our purposes, I'm also going to include **outdoor advertising** in this broader concept because most public real-world advertising messages also have to be printed so people can see them[1071]. Examples of print advertising include ads in magazines. Examples of outdoor ads include billboards or ads on taxis.

Are Print Ads Relevant to Independent Comics?

There is a strong argument against spending time and money on print advertising in the 21st century. Traditional print publications like magazines have been losing readers and revenue at an accelerated pace for the past two decades[1072]. Newspapers, like the newsstands that supported them, are close to extinct thanks to online news sources[1073]. Even if the mainstream print publications were healthy, their usefulness to comics in general and independent comics in particular would be questionable for at least three reasons. First, it is too difficult to generate attention, connection, or action with print ads[1074]. Second, print publications target too much of the false market or non-market to justify the cost. Finally, it is difficult to track the results of a print campaign, even if URL analytics are used to guide traffic online[1075].

Despite all this negative evidence, there are still print advertising considerations an independent publisher needs to factor into their advertising mix. While it may not be an effective advertising method on its own, print ads can be a useful supplement to your other offline marketing efforts.

How Can Print Ads Be a Useful Investment?

There are several instances where some form of print advertising can bolster the awareness of your book:

- Diamond Previews: Taking out an ad in your local newspaper might not make sense for your independent comic, but ads in more targeted publications can be a good investment. For

---

[1070] Print Advertising. (n.d.). Retrieved May 30, 2020, from https://dictionary.cambridge.org/us/dictionary/english/print-advertising

[1071] Sorensen, M., Rose, J., & Marks, G. (n.d.). Outdoor Advertising Definition - Entrepreneur Small Business Encyclopedia. Retrieved May 30, 2020, from https://www.entrepreneur.com/encyclopedia/outdoor-advertising

[1072] Silber, T. (2018, May 29). Big Ideas For A Magazine Newsstand Industry In Distress. Retrieved May 30, 2020, from https://www.forbes.com/sites/tonysilber/2018/05/29/big-ideas-for-a-magazine-newsstand-industry-in-distress/

[1073] Douglas McLennan, J. (2018, March 21). Opinion | A once unimaginable scenario: No more newspapers. Retrieved May 30, 2020, from https://www.washingtonpost.com/news/theworldpost/wp/2018/03/21/newspapers/

[1074] Editors (2010, July 01). Print Advertising Pros and Cons. Retrieved May 30, 2020, from https://www.allbusiness.com/print-advertising-pros-and-cons-2590-1.html

[1075] Knapp, S. (2018). 6 Ways to Measure the Success of Your Print Campaigns. Retrieved May 30, 2020, from https://marketing.sfgate.com/blog/6-ways-to-measure-the-success-of-your-print-campaigns

example, if you decide to work with Diamond to reach the direct market, they will list your book in their print catalog Diamond Previews[1076]. This is essential if you want LCS to order your book, but if your independent titles are listed with thousands of other products, one small ad might not be enough to capture attention. Diamond offers several other advertising options to help publishers stand out, including catalog pack inserts, additional ads, and Previews Adult for an additional charge[1077]. This can potentially raise the profile of your book, as long as you can conform to their advertising requirements[1078].

- <u>Convention Programs</u>: Many conventions have printed programs and many of those programs include advertising for the books and publishers associated with the event. Downloading available media kits from the shows you are attending will give you an idea of the options and requirements for each show[1079].

- <u>Signage</u>: **Signage** includes any public visual images that advertise a product[1080]. Examples of signage include banners, flyers, and posters. If you are going to run events at libraries, it helps to have some element of signage up during the event. If you are going to be tabling at a convention, you'll need signage to attract people to your booth. If your book is going to be on sale at a comic shop, signage might be a welcome bonus for the store.

What Are Your Options for Print Advertising?

While your print ads and outdoor advertising needs to be printed, the considerations are different than deciding on the various printing options for your actual book.

When thinking about print ads for Diamond or convention programs, there are three major considerations:

1. <u>Cost</u>: Get the largest ad for the lowest price you can absorb.

2. <u>Conformity</u>: Adhere to the guidelines and deadlines for each publication to reduce stress during the process.

3. <u>Impact</u>: Make sure your ad has all the elements necessary to attract attention, create connections, and inspire action.

[1076] Diamond Distribution Marketing and Promotional Services. (n.d.). Retrieved May 30, 2020, from https://vendor.diamondcomics.com/public/default.asp?t=1

[1077] Id

[1078] Id

[1079] New York Comic Con Media Kit. (2017, July 12). Retrieved May 30, 2020, from https://www.newyorkcomiccon.com/Media-Kit/Main/

[1080] Signage. (n.d.). Retrieved May 30, 2020, from https://dictionary.cambridge.org/us/dictionary/english/signage

Your outdoor advertising has several additional requirements you need to balance before moving forward:

4. Acceptability: If your book is risqué, special attention must be paid to any print ad that will be available for public consumption. If the cover art for your book is controversial from a political, sexual, or violence perspective, you have to confirm that the printer is willing to print it and the convention or comic shop is willing to display it. You don't want to spend money on ads that you can't use.

5. Printing specs and timing: Whether you use online or local printers, you need to manage the look and feel of the final product as well as the timing of delivery. You don't want your ideal reader's first experience with your book to be a substandard image and you don't want to order a run of flyers only to get them after the event is over.

6. Expendability: Some physical advertising has a short life span. Convention banners and signage should be reusable, but print ads like flyers and postcards are often thrown away, lost, or destroyed once you give them out. Promotional posters are eventually torn down and replaced with new images. Keep this in mind when considering the size, paper stock, and weight of your printed material. You want a print ad you can be proud to associate with your book, but you don't want to break the bank on something that will eventually wind up in the trash.

Print ads still have a place in independent publishing, but their utility has to be balanced in terms of cost versus their ability to generate attention, connection, and action. The other major factor for print ads or any other element of your advertising mix is timing. Because different types of ads require different levels of planning, set-up, and scheduling, we'll close out the advertising portion of ICP focusing on that aspect of the process.

One of the major mantras in advertising is *"get the right message in front of the right people at the right time.*[1081]*"* We've spent several chapters focusing on both the message in terms of your content and the people in terms of your target market. It makes sense to close the loop with a short discussion about internal and external timing.

What Internal Factors Go into Independent Comic Book Advertising Timing?

Your ads are going to be part of the communication between your team and your target market. **Before you can determine when to deliver your ads, you have to manage all the steps needed to prepare for the ad campaign,** including:

- <u>Planning</u> the advertising mix based on your goals and the options available.

- <u>Developing</u> the ad materials and securing any investment required.

- <u>Gathering</u> the proper information on the right people to contact and the requirements for advertising in each of the channels you're planning to work in.

- <u>Placing</u> the ads at the right time based on the action sought. If the action you want involves a distributor ordering your book for their store or library, you'll need to start advertising much earlier than the ads designed to get ideal readers to instantly order the book. You don't want to advertise so far in advance of the desired action that the audience forgets you, but you also don't want to advertise after the window for action has passed. The following is a general rule of thumb, but you should check the cut-off dates and other requirements of each distribution channel:

  - *Book market*: eight months prior to your book's release date
  - *Library market*: eight months prior to your book's release date
  - *Direct market*: four months prior to the release date
  - *Consumer Pre-Orders*: two months prior to the release date
  - *Sponsorships*: One month prior to the release date
  - *Press release*: Two weeks prior to the release date
  - *Endorsements*: Two weeks prior to the release date

[1081] Lacoste, J. (2016, March 22). Micro-Moments: The New Right Moment, Right Message, and Right Time. Retrieved May 30, 2020, from https://www.inc.com/jonathan-lacoste/micro-moments-the-new-right-moment-right-message-and-right-time.html

- *Social Media*: One week prior to the release date
- *Blog Posts*: One week prior to the release date

All this activity needs to be coordinated with the other elements in your production schedule, in addition to the external factors that can impact your advertising.

What External Factors Go into Independent Comic Book Advertising Timing?

The events of the real world will always have an impact on the advertising for your book. We've already mentioned the challenges created by secret identities and unforeseen events. There are also annual occurrences that may compel you to alter your advertising schedule to capitalize on favorable conditions or avoid negative ones. Think about how the following could enhance or detract from the effect of your ads:

- Convention season
- The launch of a competitive comic, TV show, movie or game
- Events specifically related to the target market (like a major sports event for a sports comic or a political event for a political comic)
- The work, school or holiday schedule of your target market
- The holiday season observed by your target market

Without pre-existing data and the analytics to take advantage of that data, it is difficult to pinpoint which ad is shown to which ideal reader at what time is going to trigger a click or a purchase. That's why advertising - like marketing- is an ongoing interaction between your book and your target market. Once you do get the word out and your ideal reader is willing to exchange their time and money for your book, you're ready for the next major milestone…making money from your comic.

STAGE 3: POST-PRODUCTION

PART 10: SALES

Or How Can You Make Money from Your Comic?

It takes a lot of work to bring a comic to market. Under the ICP method, all these steps put you in position to sell your comic to your target market:

- You chose a goal for your publishing
- You found a story to publish
- You collected investment dollars to get the idea off the ground
- You created a structure to protect your idea and your investment
- You assembled a team to create your comic
- You found readers for your book
- You decided how to get your book to your readers
- You created the best comic you could
- You informed your readers that your comic is ready to read

Now that you're at the stage where you start to collect money for your efforts, it helps to understand the financial condition of your book before and after it goes on sale. The three basic economic questions you need to answer for each of your comics are:

1. How many copies do you need to sell to recover your investment?
2. How do you know if your comic is profitable?
3. How can you keep track of your comic's financial performance?

Answering each of these questions involves understanding a few basic definitions and formulas that can be explained using the examples and scenarios we introduced in prior chapters.

How Many Copies Do You Need to Sell to Recover Your Investment?

To understand how much you need to sell to **recoup**[1082] your investment, you need to understand the break-even number. We'll walk through the necessary definitions and provide examples of the concept.

- Fixed Costs
  - Definition: A **fixed cost** is a cost that does not change with an increase or decrease in the amount of goods or services produced or sold[1083].

[1082] Recoupment. (n.d.). Retrieved May 30, 2020, from https://www.dictionary.com/browse/recoupment

[1083] Kenton, W. (2020, May 29). Fixed Cost. Retrieved May 30, 2020, from https://www.investopedia.com/terms/f/fixedcost.asp

- Translation: For independent publishers, fixed costs include overhead like legal fees, loan repayments, marketing, and advertising, IP registration fees, staff member salaries, and freelance creative costs

- Example: If Bruce spends $5,000 to set up his company, get contracts drafted, set up his website, and attend conventions and another $5000 to pay Clark and Diana, then his fixed costs are $10,000

- Variable Costs

  - Definition: A **variable cost** is an expense that changes in proportion to production output[1084].

  - Translation: For independent publishers, variable costs include printing costs and distribution costs.

  - Example: Bruce pays $2,000 for printing 2,000 copies of *Crisis*. The variable costs in this case is $1 per copy ($2,000/2000).

- Break-even Number

  - Definition: **Break-even analysis** tells you what level an investment must reach to recover your initial investment[1085].

  - Explanation: The break-even point is calculated by dividing the total fixed costs of production by the price of a product per individual unit less the variable costs of production.

  - Formula: *(Breakeven = Fixed Costs/ Price per book - Variable cost per book)*

  - Example: In Bruce's case, the breakeven number for his $10 comic is 1,111 copies ($10,000/9 ($10-1))

    - Note that if the comic was $5, he would have to sell 2,500 copies to break-even ($10,000/4 ($5-1), which is more than his initial print run for the book.

[1084] Kenton, W. (2020, January 29). Understanding Variable Cost. Retrieved May 30, 2020, from https://www.investopedia.com/terms/v/variablecost.asp

[1085] Hayes, A. (2020, January 29). Break-Even Analysis. Retrieved May 30, 2020, from https://www.investopedia.com/terms/b/breakevenanalysis.asp

- At the current comic book revenue level for a direct market on a $4 comic ($1.60) the breakeven point is 16,666 units (10,000/ 1.60-$1), which is far more than Bruce printed. This indicates that Bruce couldn't break-even just from his initial print run of direct market comics.
- He might need multiple revenue streams to break even.

- Multiple Revenue Break-even: Because independent publishers can release their book across multiple distribution channels, the break-even formula can be more complex to take into account multiple revenue streams[1086].

  - Formula: *Multiple Break-even = (Fixed cost / Average price - Average cost)*

  - Example:
    - Bruce's Fixed Costs are still $10,000
    - Bruce decides to sell *Crisis* as a print graphic novel for $10 at comic shops, $8 at conventions, and $5 as a digital comic. This makes the average price per book $7.70 ($23/3)
    - The average cost per book is now $.66 ($1 +$1 + $0 for the digital issue)
    - This means the multiple break-even number is 1,420 (10,000/ $7.04 ($7.70-$.66)
      - Every unit sold after the breakeven amount contributes to profit.

How Do You Know If Your Comic Is Profitable?

- Profits

  - Definition: **Profit** describes the financial benefit when the revenue generated from a business activity exceeds the expenses, costs, and taxes involved in sustaining the business[1087].

  - Translation: Independent comics see a profit when the total revenue generated from the book is greater than the total expenses to publish and distribute the book

  - Formula: *Profit = Revenue - Costs*

  - Example:

[1086] Mushi, E., (2019, December 21). Break-even analysis with multiple products. Retrieved May 30, 2020, from https://www.accountingformanagement.org/break-even-analysis-with-multiple-products/

[1087] Kenton, W. (2020, January 29). Understanding Profit. Retrieved May 30, 2020, from https://www.investopedia.com/terms/p/profit.asp

- If Bruce paid fixed costs of $10,000 for *Crisis*, and had printing costs of $2000, then his total costs are $12,000.
- If he then sold all 2,000 copies of his $10 book, his total revenue would be $20,000.
- The profit on Crisis in this example would be $8,000 ($20,000 - $12,000)
- If Bruce changes the price to $5, then selling out the initial print run would create a **net loss**, where expenses are greater than income[1088].

How Can You Keep Track of Your Comic's Financial Performance?

You can keep track of income and expenses by using a Profit and Loss statement

- <u>Definition</u>: The **Profit and Loss (P&L)** statement is a financial statement that summarizes the revenues, costs, and expenses incurred during a specified period, usually a fiscal quarter or year[1089].

- <u>Sample:</u> Below is a sample P&L that covers all the income and expense concepts covered in ICP on an annual basis. If you decide to recreate this, keep in mind that it will work better in a spreadsheet program like Excel or Google Sheets than as a text document.

[1088] Smart Business Owners Need to Understand About Net Loss. Retrieved May 30, 2020, from https://www.investopedia.com/terms/n/netloss.asp

[1089] Reiff, N. (2020, April 28). Profit and Loss Statement (P&L) Definition. Retrieved May 30, 2020, from https://www.investopedia.com/terms/p/plstatement.asp

Sample P&L Form

Title			
Cover Price			
	Year 1	Year 2	Year 3
INCOME			
Digital Income			
Webcomics			
Digital Single Issue			
Digital Trade Paperback			
Digital Graphic Novel			
Advertising Revenue			
Crowdfunding			
Sponsorships			
Patreon			
Affiliate Marketing			
Digital Subtotal: (Add all Digital Income)			
Print Income			
Direct Market Single Issue			
Direct Market Trade Paperback			
Direct Market Graphic Novel			
Book Store/ Library Trade Paperback			
Book Store/ Library Graphic Novel			
Convention Single Issue			
Convention Trade Paperback			
Convention Graphic Novel			
Merchandise			
Other			
Print Subtotal (Add all Print Income)			
Total Income (Add Digital and Print Subtotals)			
EXPENSES			
Labor Costs			
Editing			
Cover Art			
Line Art			
Flatting			

Coloring			
Lettering			
Production Design			
Legal			
Accounting			
Marketing			
Distribution			
Printing			
Advertising			
Sales			
Labor Subtotal			
Marketing Costs			
Competition Research			
Website Costs			
Social Media Costs			
Email List Costs			
Comic Shop Event Costs			
Book Store Event Costs			
Library Event Costs			
Convention Costs			
Target Market Events Costs			
Influencer Costs			
Marketing Subtotal			
Distribution Costs			
Single Issue Print Costs			
Trade Paperback Print Costs			
Graphic Novel Print Costs			
Single Issue Shipping Costs			
Trade Paperback Shipping Costs			
Graphic Novel Shipping Costs			
Crowdfunding Costs			
Sales Costs			
Storage Costs			
Distribution Subtotal			
Advertising Costs			
Review Copies Costs			

Advertising Creative Costs			
Digital Advertising Costs			
Sponsorship Costs			
Print Advertising Costs			
Advertising Subtotal			
Total Expenses (Add Labor, Marketing, Distribution, Advertising, and Sales Subtotals)			
Profit/Loss (Total Income - Total Expenses)			

When developing a P&L for your publishing, there are several things to keep in mind:

- Not every source of income or every expense applies to every comic. Relevance is dependent upon your goals, your market, your team capability, and your investment level.
- Not all expenses occur at once. Pre-production expenses can be stretched out over time and the investment to pay for them can be collected over time.
- Not all income comes in at once, Sales can continue over time after the initial costs are absorbed.
- Keep costs down to raise the profit potential.
- Work with your accountant to deduct expenses from taxes and reduce the initial financial impact.
- Remember most comics and most businesses run at a loss, especially at the beginning[1090].

If you want to take a much deeper dive into the dynamics of an independent publishing P&L, The University of South Florida published a paper entitled *The Financial Aspects of Comic Book Self-Publishing*[1091], but I'm going to provide a simpler example using Bruce and his *Crisis* comic.

In this example, any cell with an "X" is either not being used to collect revenue in this example (like webcomics), or not being spent as an expense (like influencer costs}. Any cell with a $0 means Bruce is handling that work himself so there is no cost.

[1090] McIntyre, G. (n.d.). What Percentage of Small Businesses Fail? Retrieved May 30, 2020, from https://www.fundera.com/blog/what-percentage-of-small-businesses-fail

[1091] Harden, C. (2005). *The Financial Aspects of Comic Book Self-Publishing* [PDF].

Title	Crisis			
Cover Price	$10			
	Year 1	Year 2	Year 3	Total
INCOME				
Digital Income				
Webcomics	X	x	x	
Digital Single Issue	X	x	x	
Digital Trade Paperback	X	x	x	
Digital Graphic Novel	$2,000	$1,500	$500	
Advertising Revenue	X	x	x	
Crowdfunding	X	x	x	
Sponsorships	X	x	x	
Patreon	X	x	x	
Affiliate Marketing	X	x	x	
Digital Subtotal	$2,000	$1,500	$500	$4,000
Print Income				
Direct Market Single Issue	X	x	x	
Direct Market Trade Paperback	X	x	x	
Direct Market Graphic Novel	$5,000	$2,500	$1,500	
Book Store/ Library Trade Paperback	X	x	x	
Book Store/ Library Graphic Novel	$5,000	$2,500	$1,500	
Convention Single Issue	X	x	x	
Convention Trade Paperback	X	X	x	
Convention Graphic Novel	$1,000	$750	$250	
Merchandise	X	X	x	
Other	X	X	x	
Print Subtotal	$11,000	$5,750	$3,250	$20,000

	$13,000	$7,250	$3,750	$24,000
Total Income				
EXPENSES				
Labor Costs				
Editing	$500	X	x	
Cover Art	$500	X	x	
Line Art	$3,000	X	x	
Flatting	$500	X	x	
Coloring	$500	X	x	
Lettering	$500	X	x	
Production Design	$500	X	x	
Legal	$1,500	X	x	
Accounting	$1,500	$500	$500	
Marketing	$0	$0	$0	
Distribution	$0	$0	$0	
Printing	$0	$0	$0	
Advertising	$1,000	$500	$250	
Sales	$0	$0	$0	
Labor Subtotal	**$10,000**	**$1000**	**$750**	**$11,750**
Marketing Costs				
Competition Research	$100	X	x	
Website Costs	$200	$100	$100	
Social Media Costs	x	X	x	
Email List Costs	$100	X	x	
Comic Shop Event Costs	$200	X	x	
Book Store Event Costs	$200	X	x	
Library Event Costs	x	X	x	
Convention Costs	$700	$700	$700	
Target Market Events Costs	x	X	x	
Influencer Costs	x	X	x	
Marketing Subtotal	**$1,500**	**$800**	**$800**	**$3,100**
Distribution Costs				

Single Issue Print Costs	X	X	x	
Trade Paperback Print Costs	X	X	x	
Graphic Novel Print Costs	$1,300	X	x	
Single Issue Shipping Costs	X	X	x	
Trade Paperback Shipping Costs	X	X	x	
Graphic Novel Shipping Costs	$500	X	x	
Crowdfunding Costs	X	X	x	
Storage Costs	$200	$200	$200	
Distribution Subtotal	**$2,000**	**$200**	**$200**	**$2,400**
Advertising Costs				
Review Copies Costs	$300	X	x	
Advertising Creative Costs	$100	X	x	
Digital Advertising Costs	$100	$50	$50	
Sponsorship Costs	$200	X	x	
Print Advertising Costs	$300	X	x	
Advertising Subtotal	**$1,000**	**$50**	**$50**	**$1,100**
Total Expenses (Add Labor, Marketing, Distribution, Advertising and Sales Subtotals)	**$14,500**	**$2,050**	**$1,800**	**$18,350**
Profit/Loss (Total Income - Total Expenses)	**-$1,500**	**$5,200**	**$1,950**	**$5,650**

In this example, notice that *Crisis* runs at a loss during the first year even though that year has the highest sales. This is because all the revenue is being absorbed by upfront costs. Profit comes in at Year 2, when all the upfront costs are covered after the breakeven point.

We've already looked at the various expenses covered in the pre-production and production process. It's time to review different income sources and how they can be applied to your comic.

It might seem counterintuitive to try making money from your comic by giving it away. You've spent a lot of time and investment dollars to bring your book to market. Why would you offer it to your target market for free? The answer is **monetization**, or turning a non-revenue generating asset into cash[1092].

Traditional broadcast television[1093] in America makes money from selling the eyeballs of their viewers to advertisers[1094]. People don't have to pay money to watch NBC, but they do have to deal with commercials, one way or another. One of YouTube's business models is similar, where short ads are placed in front of or inside videos to generate revenue[1095]. Many mobile apps use the same monetization methods to generate money from the attention of their users[1096]. **As an independent publisher, you have the opportunity to capture the attention of your target market and turn that interest into revenue[1097].**

This method of making money goes beyond giving your comic away for free. By leveraging the traffic on your website, you may find that your artwork, your marketing content, and your perspective on topics of interest to your target market all become monetization content. Depending on which method you use, you can begin to make money from your comic before it is made, but if and only if you develop a relationship with your target market. Without an audience, you have nothing to monetize.

The three major methods of monetization are website advertising, affiliate marketing, and sponsorships.

[1092] Ganti, A. (2020, January 29). Monetize Definition. Retrieved May 30, 2020, from https://www.investopedia.com/terms/m/monetize.asp

[1093] Sheffer, R. (2015, March 10). How do media networks make money? Retrieved May 30, 2020, from https://finance.yahoo.com/news/media-networks-money-180605757.html

[1094] Pearson, P. (2015, May 31). Eyeballs vs Engagement. Retrieved May 30, 2020, from https://medium.com/@philgpearson/eyeballs-vs-engagement-the-struggle-of-digital-advertising-301ffd61c773

[1095] Edinger, E. (2017, December 18). The five ways YouTubers make money. Retrieved May 30, 2020, from http://www.bbc.co.uk/newsbeat/article/42395224/evan-edinger-the-five-ways-youtubers-make-money

[1096] Varshneya, R. (2019, May 17). How to Make Money from Your Free App. Retrieved May 30, 2020, from https://www.business.com/articles/why-free-apps/

[1097] Pahwa, A., Aashish, & Pahwa, A. (2018, December 12). The Attention Monetization. Retrieved May 30, 2020, from https://www.feedough.com/the-attention-monetization/

How Can Website Advertising Generate Revenue?

Banner advertising[1098] refers to the use of unused space on a website or online media property to display advertising. There are various types, sizes, and aspect ratios depending on the nature of your website[1099], and different sizes can generate different levels of income.

What Are the Benefits of Banner Advertising?

1. Revenue can be generated before production of the book is complete[1100].
2. Ads often come from third-party networks, so you don't have to spend extra time and effort finding ad partners[1101].
3. You make money without asking for your ideal reader to spend any of their money.

What Are the Downsides of Banners?

1. Ads can detract from the visual and narrative appeal of your website[1102].
2. Ads can slow down the performance of your website, leading to lost traffic and lost readers[1103].
3. Ads can often drive traffic away from your site, unless you have the option to open the ad link in a new window.

How Do You Make Money with Banners?

As we saw in the chapter on buying advertising, revenue is calculated on a cost per thousand (CPM) or cost per click (CPC) basis[1104]. Rates can vary from as little as $0.15 to $2.75 depending on the ad network you are using and the target market you are bringing in[1105]. Keep in mind that ad networks retain 40%-50% of

---

[1098] Hayes, A. (2020, February 05). The Ins and Outs of Banner Advertising. Retrieved May 30, 2020, from https://www.investopedia.com/terms/b/banneradvertising.asp

[1099] *IAB New Standard Unit Portfolio* [PDF]. (2017). IAB Technology Library.

[1100] Paulson, M. (2016, November 02). How to Make Money by Running Display Ads on Your Website. Retrieved May 30, 2020, from https://medium.com/@matt_25083/how-to-make-money-by-running-display-ads-on-your-website-6f570ed6bda6

[1101] Google AdSense - Earn Money From Website Monetization. (n.d.). Retrieved May 30, 2020, from https://www.google.com/adsense/start/

[1102] Oricchio, R. (2007, November 01). What's the Harm? Allowing Ads on Your Website. Retrieved May 30, 2020, from https://www.inc.com/internet/articles/200711/webads.html

[1103] Jacobsen, T. (2020, January 02). Should You Put Ads On Your Website? Retrieved May 30, 2020, from https://marketingartfully.com/put-ads-on-website/

[1104] See Chapter 60

[1105] Allen p. 87

the money made from the ads[1106], and some networks require a minimum amount of traffic before they allow you to place ads[1107].

Where Can You Find Advertisers for Your Website?

Ad networks change or rebrand frequently, so this is only a sample to start your due diligence. Keep in mind that it may be possible to use more than one network to maximize your potential revenue and add it to your website[1108].

- Exponential[1109]
- Google Ads[1110]
- Open X Exchange[1111]
- Rubicon[1112]

When considering which network to use for your monetization, give some consideration to the content of your book and your overall marketing message. Some advertisers and networks are sensitive to sexual depictions, violence, or other adult themes. It doesn't make sense to try and run ads for PG products if your site is NSFW.

How Can Affiliate Marketing Generate Revenue?

Affiliate marketing[1113] is an advertising model in which a company compensates third-party publishers to generate traffic or leads to the company's products and services. As a third-party publisher, you are the affiliate, and the commission fee incentivizes you to find ways to promote the company. It is your job to post ads on your site that will appeal to your target market. When an ideal reader clicks on the ad and buys something, you get a portion of that sale as a commission.

[1106] Paulson, M. (2016, November 02). How to Make Money by Running Display Ads on Your Website.

[1107] Jacobsen, T. (2020, January 02). Should You Put Ads On Your Website?

[1108] Lofgren, L. (2019). Create a Website. Retrieved May 30, 2020, from https://www.quicksprout.com/how-to-add-adsense-to-your-website/

[1109] Exponential Home. (2019, July 31). Retrieved May 30, 2020, from http://exponential.com/

[1110] Grow your business with Google Ads. (n.d.). Retrieved May 30, 2020, from https://ads.google.com/

[1111] OpenX Ad Exchange for Demand Partners. (n.d.). Retrieved May 30, 2020, from https://www.openx.com/demand-partners/adexchange/

[1112] Rubicon Project Programmatic Advertising Exchange. (2020, March 25). Retrieved May 30, 2020, from https://rubiconproject.com/

[1113] Frankenfield, J. (2020, January 29). How Affiliate Marketing Works. Retrieved May 30, 2020, from https://www.investopedia.com/terms/a/affiliate-marketing.asp

For example, Amazon has an extensive affiliate marketing program[1114] and a large selection of vampire cosplay products[1115]. If the publisher of *Blood Bond* sets up an affiliate marketing program with Amazon, they could potentially make money from all their readers who might also be into cosplay as part of their fandom[1116].

What Are the Benefits of Affiliate Marketing[1117]?

1. There is a low cost of entry to get started.
2. You don't have to buy, store or ship the products being sold[1118].
3. You can start generating revenue before your comic is finished.
4. Your revenue is based on the relationship between your target market and the goods and services they are interested in, not just your book.

What Are the Downsides to Affiliate Marketing[1119]?

1. Affiliate marketing doesn't lend itself to every type of comic.
2. You have very little control over the quality of the product or the customer service of your marketing partner[1120].
3. There is very little control over the commission amounts.
4. Some marketing partners resist or avoid paying commissions.
5. There is often little support from the marketing partners.
6. There is often a high degree of competition in the market.
7. Affiliate marketing can be a long-term revenue stream, but it is not a short-term income solution.

[1114] Earn up to 10% advertising fees with Amazon, a trusted e-commerce leader. (n.d.). Retrieved May 30, 2020, from https://affiliate-program.amazon.com/

[1115] Hennessy, G. (n.d.). Amazon Search: Vampire Cosplay. Retrieved May 30, 2020, from https://www.amazon.com/s?k=vampire+cosplay&ref=nb_sb_noss_1

[1116] Interest in vampires boosts the fang trade. (2019). Retrieved May 30, 2020, from https://www.economist.com/united-states/2019/10/30/interest-in-vampires-boosts-the-fang-trade

[1117] Ocasio, K., Kevin, & Fernando, J. (2018, January 05). 7 Benefits of Affiliate Marketing as a Source of Income. Retrieved May 30, 2020, from https://thimpress.com/7-benefits-affiliate-marketing-source-income/

[1118] Duermyer, R. (2020, January 17). Is Affiliate Marketing Really Profitable? Retrieved May 30, 2020, from https://www.thebalancesmb.com/can-you-really-make-money-with-affiliate-marketing-1794168

[1119] Disadvantages Of Affiliate Marketing - Know The Good & The Bad. (2018, March 06). Retrieved May 30, 2020, from https://www.affiliatemarketertraining.com/disadvantages-of-affiliate-marketing%E2%80%A8/

[1120] Duermyer, R. (2020, January 17). Is Affiliate Marketing Really Profitable?

How Do You Make Money with Affiliate Marketing?

Commissions vary by partner and product. For example, Amazon offers 10% commissions for their program[1121], but you can make anywhere between 5-20% per item purchased[1122], depending on your marketing partner.

How Do You Get Started with an Affiliate Marketing Program?

There are dozens of affiliate marketing programs available in 2020[1123]. Running an affiliate marketing program on your website involves four basic (but potentially time-consuming) steps:

1. Maintain your relationship with your target market so you have an audience to provide to your marketing partner.
2. Perform your due diligence so you understand who your partners are in terms of their performance, payments, and products.
3. Understand the business and legal requirements of your affiliate marketing relationship.
4. Track your traffic and your earnings to ensure that you are getting paid properly for your efforts.

How Can Sponsorships Generate Revenue?

When we looked at sponsorships in Chapter 62, your book acted as the sponsor for some group or event. **Sponsorships in this context involve someone acting as your sponsor and providing funds in exchange for a halo effect with your readers**. There are two types of sponsors your comic can employ, single sponsors (often corporate sponsors) and public sponsorship (or crowdfunding).

What Are the Benefits of Corporate Sponsorship[1124]?

1. Revenue for your comic is not tied to reader spending.
2. Social proof to your target market.
3. Special deals or discounts for your target market.

[1121] Earn up to 10% advertising fees with Amazon, a trusted e-commerce leader.

[1122] Lake, R. (2020, January 29). Make Money With Affiliate Marketing. Retrieved May 30, 2020, from https://www.investopedia.com/personal-finance/affiliate-marketing-can-you-really-make-money/

[1123] Saint-Juste, D. (n.d.). 43 of the Best Affiliate Programs That Pay the Highest Commission. Retrieved May 30, 2020, from https://blog.hubspot.com/marketing/best-affiliate-programs

[1124] Staff (2020, April 23). How to Get Sponsors for Your Blog (at Any Level). Retrieved May 30, 2020, from https://doyouevenblog.com/rachel/

What Are the Downsides of Corporate Sponsorship[1125]?

1.   Sponsorship dollars are extremely competitive[1126].
2.   The sponsor could dictate the marketing or even the content of your comic.
3.   The deal could be exclusive and limit your other sources of revenue.
4.   Disclosure is legally required for all sponsors[1127].

How Do You Make Money with Corporate Sponsorship?

The amount you can make from a sponsorship is based on your website and social media traffic, what the sponsor wants, and how much work you are willing to do for that sponsor[1128]. For example, you might charge $30 for a social media blast, $50 for a mention on your latest post, or $1,000 for a banner ad on your website. The only limits of what you can do are what you can produce and what your sponsor is willing to pay. Just make sure the rights and responsibilities on both sides are included in the sponsorship agreement.

How Do You Find a Corporate Sponsor?

There are several discreet steps in securing sponsorship dollars[1129]:

1.   Build a media kit for your book. This is a variation on your sell sheet[1130] that is clear about who your ideal reader and target market are, and what your book offers them in relation to the sponsor.

2.   Create a sponsorship "hit" list. Consider the brands and organizations that you support and would like to sponsor your comic. This could be anything from the comic shops and conventions you work with, to a product or organization related to your story, or any other criteria that makes sense for you. Just don't pick potential sponsors that aren't relevant to your target market.

[1125] Bair, A., (n.d.). How to Find Sponsorships for Your Blog. Retrieved May 30, 2020, from https://www.dummies.com/social-media/blogging/how-to-find-sponsorships-for-your-blog/

[1126] Campea, J. (Director). (2020). *Can Big Multi Staffed Channels Survive on Youtube Ads?* [Video file]. Retrieved May 30, 2020, from https://www.youtube.com/watch?v=Ajq7oaBdJoc

[1127] Truex, L. (2019, March 02). How to Make Money With a Blog Sponsored Post. Retrieved May 30, 2020, from https://www.thebalancesmb.com/how-to-make-money-with-a-blog-sponsored-post-4177880

[1128] Id.

[1129] Staff (2020, April 23). How to Get Sponsors for Your Blog (at Any Level)

[1130] See Chapter 44

3. Find potential sponsors based on existing sponsor networks or your professional network[1131].

4. Pitch your sponsorship proposal to them using your media kit.

5. Negotiate and sign a sponsorship agreement with the help of your attorney.

What Are the Benefits of Public Sponsorship?

Public sponsorship programs like **Patreon** enable fans (or patrons) to pay and support artists for their work[1132]. There are several benefits for independent publishers who want to monetize their target market with Patreon or similar systems[1133]:

1. It works well for niche creators with passionate fans.
2. It allows you to set up flexible funding goals.
3. It provides an interface to track and interact with your ideal readers and might be the closest approximation of your true fans.

What Are the Downsides of Public Sponsorship?

1. The majority of creators only generate between $1 and $100 per month[1134].
2. The sites charge a fee which further reduces your revenue[1135].
3. Some creators are banned based on their content[1136].

[1131] Truex, L. (2019, March 02). How to Make Money With a Blog Sponsored Post.

[1132] Sraders, A. (2019, February 21). What Is Patreon? History, Controversies and How It Works. Retrieved May 30, 2020, from https://www.thestreet.com/lifestyle/what-is-patreon-14865916

[1133] McGee, L. (2019). 6 Patreon Alternatives for Your Startup in 2019. Retrieved May 30, 2020, from https://sumup.com/blog/6-patreon-alternatives-for-your-business/

[1134] Sanchez, D. (2018, January 03). Less Than 2% of Content Creators on Patreon Earn Monthly Minimum Wage. Retrieved May 30, 2020, from https://www.digitalmusicnews.com/2018/01/02/patreon-content-creators-monthly-minimum-wage/

[1135] Pricing: Patreon: Build Your Own Membership Business. (n.d.). Retrieved May 30, 2020, from https://www.patreon.com/product/pricing

[1136] Curtis, C. (2019, June 28). Patreon continues to crack down on NSFW content creators. Retrieved May 30, 2020, from https://thenextweb.com/tech/2019/06/27/patreon-continues-to-crack-down-on-nsfw-content-creators/

How Do You Make Money with Public Sponsorship?

The average amount donated by a patron is $12[1137] on a one time or monthly basis[1138]. So, if Charles brainwashed 1,000 true fans to donate $12 per month, his comic would generate $12,000 per year or $144,000 per year as long as the patrons continued to support *Hates and Fears*.

Just remember that **true fans don't magically appear all at once** unless you have some sort of mind control. They will appear over time based on your marketing message and your call to action.

What Are the Alternatives to Patreon?

Patreon is one of the larger crowdfunding platforms, with approximately three million current users[1139]. Independent publishers looking for alternatives can consider these public sponsorship methods[1140]:

- BMC[1141]
- Liberapay[1142]
- Memberful[1143]
- Podia[1144]

What is the Best Monetization Method for Your Comic?

Monetization isn't normally an instant success or failure. It is often not based on a single solution. Many independent publishers test different monetization mixtures to find the right combination for their market and their website[1145]. Comparing the CPM revenue to the commission from merchandise might be a process you explore throughout the marketing cycle. You might not be able to land a significant sponsor until after your book is ready for release. It might take time to find the right formula.

[1137] Sraders, A. (2019, February 21). What Is Patreon?

[1138] How to Make a One-Time Donation. (2017). Retrieved May 30, 2020, from https://www.patreon.com/posts/how-to-make-one-15076061

[1139] Patreon. (2020, May 26). Retrieved May 30, 2020, from https://en.wikipedia.org/wiki/Patreon

[1140] McGee, L. (2019). 6 Patreon Alternatives for Your Startup in 2019.

[1141] Buy Me A Coffee: Where creators make money doing what they love. (n.d.). Retrieved May 30, 2020, from https://www.buymeacoffee.com/

[1142] Liberapay. (n.d.). Retrieved May 30, 2020, from https://en.liberapay.com/

[1143] Sell memberships to your audience. (n.d.). Retrieved May 30, 2020, from https://memberful.com/

[1144] Sell Online Courses, Memberships, and Downloads. (n.d.). Retrieved May 30, 2020, from https://www.podia.com/

[1145] Allen p. 93

Monetization isn't for every publisher. Some independent publishers might decide to avoid generating money using these methods to avoid alienating fans or diluting the message of their story, but artistic integrity needs to be balanced against profit and loss. If you're only using online distribution like webcomics and you need a way to get a return on your investment, monetization could be a viable option.

This chapter started the discussion of crowdfunding, but this topic deserves in-depth attention. While ongoing patronage works for some comic creators, others have found success with a more project-based crowdfunding method. This is currently the largest source of growth in independent comic book publishing, so we're going to take a look at what platforms like Kickstarter can offer. We will also walk through the steps to conduct a successful crowdfunding campaign.

What is Project-Based Crowdfunding?

Crowdfunding is the process of raising money from a large group of people online[1146]. The secret to using crowdfunding as an independent comic book publisher is hidden in the name. **If you do not have a crowd, it is very difficult to secure funding.** One of the reasons I waited until this stage of the process to discuss this specific source of revenue is because independent publishers should avoid launching crowdfunding campaigns until they are consistently engaged with their target market[1147].

The good news is that if you've been building a relationship with your marketing and advertising, you've put your book in a better position to succeed. The bad news is that you have to drive traffic for your crowdfunding to have a chance[1148]. You can't rely on the random browsing of potential backers or even discoverability because most of those people will probably be in your non-market or the far edge of your false market.

What is the Current State of Crowdfunding for Comics?

Crowdfunding has become a beneficial alternative for independent publishing in general and comic book publishers in particular over the past ten years[1149]. In 2018, it is estimated that a single platform, generated up to sixteen million dollars for all the successful comic book projects combined[1150]. Camilla Zhang, the former Comics Outreach Lead at Kickstarter offered these data points to paint a picture of the state of affairs in 2019[1151]:

- The average comics campaign pulls in $3,900.
- A 30-day campaign for $10,000 has a 35% chance to succeed.
- Campaigns with videos make 115% more than ones without video.
- Campaigns with multiple images (3-6) succeed more than ones with only one image.
- Campaigns that get 30% of their goal in the first week are more likely to succeed.

[1146] Hyatt, A. (2016). *Crowd start: The ultimate guide to a powerful & profitable crowdfunding campaign.* New York: Hunter Cat Press. line 234

[1147] Hyatt, lines 68 and 353

[1148] *New Publishing Frontier Panel.* (2018). Lecture presented at New York Comic Con, New York.

[1149] Rowe, A. (2019, June 11). How Kickstarter Is Reshaping The Publishing Industry. Retrieved May 30, 2020, from https://www.forbes.com/sites/adamrowe1/2019/06/11/how-kickstarter-is-reshaping-the-publishing-industry/

[1150] Arrant, C. (2019). Kickstarter Boasts $16m Comics Funding in 2018, Wants More Marginalized Creators. Retrieved May 30, 2020, from https://www.newsarama.com/43590-kickstarter-boasts-16m-in-comics-funding-in-2018.html

[1151] Zhang, C. (2019, June 12). *Introduction to Kickstarter.* Lecture presented at Comic Arts Workshop, New York.

- The most popular pledge amount is $25. The average pledge amount is $70.
- For every order of magnitude of your target market (10, 100, 1000, etc.), the probability of success increases dramatically (10%, 20%, 40% respectively).
- Consistent engagement produces more successful campaigns.
- March and October are big months, especially if you want to count the funds in the same tax year.

What Are the Advantages of Crowdfunding?

The main advantages of crowdfunding are marketing and revenue generation[1152].

- Marketing: The independent publisher who can complete a successful campaign offers the target market an opportunity to interact and impact content they enjoy. The campaign becomes an event they can be involved in, transforming them from passive consumers to active participants and creating the positive emotional connection that is essential for marketing. It also provides concrete proof that your book has a market of ideal readers and true fans willing to invest time and money into your book.

- Revenue Generation: Crowdfunding circumvents the traditional distribution channels of comics and allows independent publishers the chance to get books to their ideal readers without the gate-keepers of Diamond or Comixology and without the time commitment and expense of conventions.

What Are the Disadvantages of Crowdfunding?

The downsides of crowdfunding are competition, labor, and the impact of disappointment:

- Competition: At any given time, there can be between 50 and 200 other comic book campaigns running on any given platform[1153]. This level of competition reinforces the necessity of bringing your own crowd to the campaign and not relying on being discovered among all the other books.

- Labor: The amount of planning, management, and fulfillment of a crowdfunding campaign is significant (as we shall see) and can strain the resources of a small independent publishing team.

[1152] Hyatt, 245

[1153] Fowler, B. (2020). Is 2020 the Year Crowdfunding Comics on Kickstarter Stops Working? Retrieved May 30, 2020, from http://www.comixlaunch.com/session234/

- Disappointment Impact: Estimates suggest that more than 60% of all crowdfunding campaigns fail[1154]. The sense of rejection, combined with the lost time and apparently wasted efforts associated with the campaign, can cause publishers to doubt their book, their market (or both), and derail an otherwise confident publishing team.

What Crowdfunding Platforms Are Available?

There are three major crowdfunding platforms in the United States at the time of this writing[1155]. Each one has distinct pros, cons, and fee structures you need to consider when choosing one for your book.

- **Kickstarter**[1156]
  - Fees:
    - 8% of the funds raised from a successful campaign,
    - $.20 per pledge for payment processing

  - Pros: With over 9 million users, Kickstarter is the largest and most well-known crowdfunding platform. This isn't a guarantee of success, since you need to drive your traffic to the campaign, but enough people have heard of and used Kickstarter to make it a trusted platform for your crowdfunding.

  - Cons: Kickstarter is an all-or-nothing program, meaning if the money your crowd promises to provide is less than your funding goal, you don't get any money.

- **Indegogo**[1157]
  - Fees:
    - 4% of funds raised for a successful campaign
    - 8% of funds raised for an unsuccessful campaign
    - Credit card processing fees of up to 5% of each donation

  - Pros: You can collect funds even if you miss your funding goal

  - Cons: High fees reduce your overall funding compared to other platforms

---

[1154] Zhang, C. (2019, June 12). *Introduction to Kickstarter*

[1155] Hyatt, line 4060

[1156] Comics & Illustration on Kickstarter. (n.d.). Retrieved May 30, 2020, from https://www.kickstarter.com/comics-illustration?ref=section-homepage-nav-click-comics-illustration

[1157] Comics at Indiegogo. (n.d.). Retrieved May 30, 2020, from https://www.indiegogo.com/explore/comics?project_type=campaign

- **GoFundMe**[1158]
  - Fees
    - 8% of total funding
    - $.30 per pledge for payment processing

  - Pros: No restrictions on when or if publishers can have access to the funds

  - Cons: No fixed campaign duration, making it closer to a public sponsorship program.

What Are the Elements of a Successful Crowdfunding Campaign?

No matter which crowdfunding platform you choose, there are common components you'll need to pull from your pre-production development to build your campaign[1159]:

- The story in your book[1160]: You need to be able to **concisely explain how your comic will benefit your crowd**. Go back to your pitch, synopsis, and hook to create compelling connections.

- The story of your team: The story of how your book came about is an important element of inspiring crowdfunding donations[1161]. Successful campaigns share the personal side of their creative teams. This can occur in an organic fashion as part of your marketing efforts, and you should consider building this momentum over a period of up to eighteen months before your campaign launches[1162].

- The perks: Perks are incentives offered to backers in exchange for their support[1163]. Independent comic book publishers can offer seven to nine perks of various types[1164], including:

[1158] Browse fundraisers on Go Fund Me. (n.d.). Retrieved May 30, 2020, from https://www.gofundme.com/discover/creative-fundraiser

[1159] Quora. (2017, November 02). How Do You Run A Successful Crowdfunding Campaign? Retrieved May 30, 2020, from https://www.forbes.com/sites/quora/2017/10/30/how-do-you-run-a-successful-crowdfunding-campaign/

[1160] Telling your story. (n.d.). Retrieved May 30, 2020, from https://www.kickstarter.com/help/handbook/your_story?ref=handbook_started

[1161] Hyatt, line 2098

[1162] Hyatt, line 519

[1163] Perks: How to Use Perks to Raise Funds. (n.d.). Retrieved May 30, 2020, from https://support.indiegogo.com/hc/en-us/articles/205157097-Perks-How-to-Use-Perks-to-Raise-Funds

[1164] Hyatt, line 2268

- Digital rewards (digital copies of the book, art, etc.)
- Physical rewards (physical copies of the book, bookmarks, posters)
- Insider rewards (early access to the book, behind the scenes material)
- Experiential rewards (backers name or image in the book, etc.)

- The crowd: The people that will provide your funding consists of your core market along with members of your potential market and even your false market, because this is the one instance where your network of personal and secret identity connections might support you, even if they don't like comics or your particular story.

- The timing of the campaign: The scheduling for your campaign needs to align with the other aspects of your publishing schedule. If you don't have the time or the resources to run a campaign because of what is going on with the book or with the secret identities of you and your team, or if it's going to cause conflicts with outside events like conventions or holidays, then it makes more sense to reschedule the campaign for a more opportune moment.

How Do You Determine Your Crowdfunding Goal?

The amount you attempt to raise in a crowdfunding campaign will be a function of two distinct factors[1165]:

- The *overall expenses* (or whatever portion of your expenses) in your P&L that you are trying to generate from the campaign.

- The *fees* associated with running the campaign, including:
    - Credit card processing fees (estimated to be 2-4% of the total goal)
    - The fees charged by whatever platform you decide to use
    - Any taxes associated with the campaign
    - Shipping supplies for any physical campaign perks
    - Shipping expenses for any campaign perks

It makes sense to set a funding goal high enough to cover both these factors, plus a cushion to cover unforeseen expenses. You don't want to run a successful crowdfunding campaign that loses money for you overall because you didn't consider all the relevant costs.

[1165] Building rewards. (n.d.). Retrieved May 30, 2020, from
https://www.kickstarter.com/help/handbook/rewards?ref=handbook_story

Who Makes Up Your Crowdfunding Team?

Crowdfunding, like comic book publishing in general, is often easier when the tasks are divided between different individuals. If you plan to run a crowdfunding campaign for your book, it makes sense to modify the production schedule to leverage your available talent.

For example, the publisher can oversee the crowdfunding campaign. The writer can create the copy for the crowdfunding page and the social media posts. The artist can create perks in the form of special artwork or the design of swag. The marketing manager can oversee the changes to the website and respond to social media inquiries. Finally, everyone on the team can repost messages from the crowdfunding campaign on their personal and professional social media pages. Just **make sure that additional work on the crowdfunding campaign is compensated accordingly and spelled out in the contract.**

At the same time, your target market can also help make the campaign a success. Asking your most enthusiastic fans, influencers, media contacts, and even comic shop partners to spread the word can help you reach more people likely to make your campaign a success.

How Do You Prepare Before Launch?

Think of your crowdfunding campaign as a miniature version of your overall publishing cycle. **The successful campaign will have pre-campaign, campaign, and post-campaign elements.** Each element builds on the prior one to help you reach your funding goals[1166].

- Talent Management: Determine who from your creative and business teams will be able to assist in the campaign. Figure out what their schedule is going to be during the time you plan to crowdfund, and how you are going to compensate them for their work.

- Timing: Building a schedule for the campaign that takes the following dynamics into account[1167]:
    - The launch date of the campaign
    - The length of the campaign
    - The end date
    - The date before the campaign when press releases go out
    - The dates during the campaign when social media and email posts go out
    - The outside obligations of you and your team
    - Any holidays or seasonal events that might impact your target market

---

[1166] Hyatt, line 2291

[1167] Kickstarter Creator Handbook: Promotion. (n.d.). Retrieved May 30, 2020, from https://www.kickstarter.com/help/handbook/promotion?ref=handbook_funding

- Marketing: Your crowdfunding campaign is another aspect of the ongoing communication between you and your target market. All the tools you have developed in this aspect of your publishing can be modified to assist the campaign:

  - *Your website*: can be updated to focus on the campaign. Your home page should feature your campaign front and center. Links to your crowdfunding page need to be easy to find and all the links need to work. Experts also suggest creating 2-4 blog posts before the campaign that can be posted at key intervals such as the launch of the campaign, funding milestones, or focus pieces on your perks[1168].

  - *Your social media*: can be used as a platform to disseminate art and copy promoting the campaign. Again, 5-10 posts created beforehand can be used strategically at major points of the campaign to keep the momentum strong, and a link directly to the crowdfunding page is essential.

  - *Your email list*: can be used to reach your true fans and encourage them to recruit others. As with the other marketing tools, writing 5-10 emails to support the campaign before it launches can drive traffic to your crowdfunding page.

  - *Your campaign video:* is a unique component to your marketing if you weren't using YouTube on a day-to-day basis. The crowdfunding video is normally 90 seconds to 3 minutes and uses a combination of members of the team in front of the camera, art from the comic, or a combination of the two[1169]. You can say and do whatever you want in the video to get your target market excited, but the video needs to address the following questions somehow:

    - Who are you?
    - What is the book about?
    - Why should your target market pay attention (What's in it for them)?
    - What will you do with the money?
    - What are the best rewards?
    - How can they back your campaign?

[1168] Hyatt

[1169] *Webinar: Running a Comics project on Kickstarter* [Video file]. (2018). Retrieved May 30, 2020, from https://kck.st/ComicsWebinar

It's a good idea to pre-screen your video to a select group before it goes out into the world and put your best face forward in the video copy and production[1170]. Videos play a large role in campaign success, so you want to produce the best clip you can.

- <u>Distribution</u>: Kickstarter and other crowdfunding platforms require submission of your page for review and approval before the campaign goes live. If you want a professional review of your page by a crowdfunding expert, you need to submit your page up to one month before the campaign launch date. If you just want your page approved, then the submission time is about a week for sites like Kickstarter[1171].

- <u>Advertising</u>: Modifying your existing ad campaign to temporarily focus on your crowdfunding can help drive your target market to your campaign site. Your pre-existing contacts in the comic book press might also be willing to post something about your campaign on their social media. Whichever ad mix you decide to use, modify your press kit for the campaign by including things like:

  - Your crowdfunding press release
  - Bios for you and your team
  - Key artwork for the campaign
  - Links to your video and the crowdfunding site

How Do You Manage the Crowdfunding Campaign?

Running your crowdfunding campaign is the production aspect of the process. **Your goal is to combine your talent with your marketing and advertising to inspire your target market to support your campaign before the end date[1172].**

Just before the campaign begins and on the launch date, try to draw as much attention to the campaign as possible. Treat this like an event, similar to a movie premiere or a gallery opening for your target market[1173]. Remember, campaigns that get 30% of their goal in the first week are more likely to succeed, so you want to launch with a splash.

[1170] Id

[1171] Zhang Lecture

[1172] Communicating with backers. (n.d.). Retrieved May 30, 2020, from
https://www.kickstarter.com/help/handbook/updates?ref=handbook_promotion

[1173] Fowlkes, M., (2019, February 11). The Ultimate Guide On How To Launch An Epic Crowdfunding Campaign. Retrieved May 30, 2020, from https://foundr.com/crowdfunding-launch-plan

In the days and weeks following the launch, you're going to have to set aside time each day to market your campaign, answer any questions, and generally oversee your progress. You can use either your weekly milestones or your percentage milestones to celebrate your gains, highlight your perks, or ask your community for support[1174]. Combine both your pre-planned marketing messages with some real-time reactions from you and your team to adapt to changing conditions as the campaign progresses. Remember to get your team, your core market, and even members of your false market to spread the word until the campaign ends.

What Do You Do After the Campaign Ends?

When the campaign is over, your post-production phase begins. If you reached your goal, you have a reason to celebrate. If you missed your goal, you have a chance to learn from your mistakes. In either case, there are several things you need to deal with:

- Communicate the results of your campaign to your target market and thank everyone who supported you.

- Set up a method to collect funds after the campaign is over in case some supporters missed the deadline.

- Maintain communication with your target market as part of your ongoing conversation with them.

- Analyze the results of the campaign to determine what went right, what went wrong, and what factors were out of your control.

If you reached your funding goal, there are two additional steps you need to complete before your campaign is finished. You need to utilize the backer reports and surveys to collect all the relevant information you need to deliver your perks. And you need to deliver your perks on time or early, either on your own or through a fulfillment service[1175]. In the same way a customer wants what they paid for in a normal sale, your supporters will turn on you if they give you money for a book and you never deliver.

[1174] Entrepreneur Media, Inc. (2017, March 08). 9 Steps to Launching a Successful Crowdfunding Campaign. Retrieved May 30, 2020, from https://www.entrepreneur.com/article/288277

[1175] Rheude, J. (2019, December 06). Best Crowdfunding Fulfillment Companies of 2019. Retrieved May 30, 2020, from https://redstagfulfillment.com/best-crowdfunding-fulfillment-companies/

In most cases, selling your comic to your target market will generate more revenue than monetization or crowdfunding. As we saw in the distribution chapters, the bulk of the industry's revenue comes from the various types of digital and print sales channels. The good news is that if you've been developing your book through the pre-production, production, and post-production phases, then you are well-positioned to sell your comic in a classic process known as the **sales funnel**[1176].

What is a Sales Funnel?

A **sales funnel** is a theoretical, multi-step process that transforms prospective browsers into long-term buyers[1177]. As an independent publisher, **your sales funnel can transform ideal readers into true fans**. While a sales funnel is not the only approach to selling[1178], the idea does have long term benefits the other methods lack.

Why is a Sales Funnel Necessary?

Because of the medium you've chosen to tell your story, the competition for your book, and the price point you selected, you can't rely on **impulse buying** to sell comics, like a kid picking up a book from the spinner rack in the 1970s[1179]. Independent comic book sales require a certain amount of persuasion to overcome the barriers we discussed in the marketing chapters[1180]. Once those obstacles are overcome, the impact on your publishing can be intense. In entertainment, the obsessive **fandom** of anything[1181] is the result of a well-developed sales funnel. It can transform a piece of intellectual property into a core aspect of a true fan's life[1182] by:

- Harnessing the power of your marketing and advertising

[1176] McGinnis, D. (2019). What Is a Sales Funnel? Retrieved May 30, 2020, from https://www.salesforce.com/blog/2019/04/what-is-a-sales-funnel.html

[1177] Adams, R. (2017, July 28). What Is a Sales Funnel? The Guide to Building an Automated Selling Machine. Retrieved May 30, 2020, from https://www.entrepreneur.com/article/296526

[1178] Shaw, J. (2017, November 21). Different Sales Approaches. Retrieved May 30, 2020, from https://smallbusiness.chron.com/different-sales-approaches-41299.html

[1179] Impulse buying is defined as a spur of the moment unplanned decision to buy that is made just before the act of buying. What is impulse buying? (n.d.). Retrieved May 30, 2020, from http://www.businessdictionary.com/definition/impulse-buying.html

[1180] Greene, Art of Seduction

[1181] Fandom. (n.d.). Retrieved May 30, 2020, from https://dictionary.cambridge.org/us/dictionary/english/fandom

[1182] Kresnicka, S. (2016, April 02). Why Understanding Fans is the New Superpower (Guest Column). Retrieved May 30, 2020, from https://variety.com/2016/tv/columns/understanding-fans-superpower-troika-1201743513/

- Allowing you to form a lasting connection with your target market

- Helping you build trust with ideal readers and nurture them towards purchasing multiple books, merchandise and other swag related to your IP[1183]

- Increasing the lifetime value of customers, allowing you to sell again and again to the same core group.

What is the Sales Funnel Process?

I've added the diagram below to help you visualize the sales funnel as it relates to the five-step process of selling your comics.

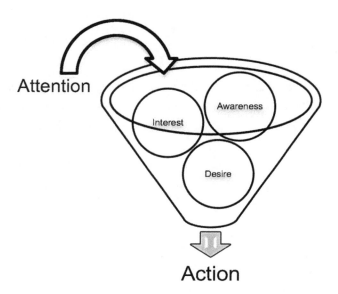

1. **Getting the attention of your ideal reader**: This is one of the main goals of your marketing efforts. You're not trying to sell anything to them at this stage. You're attempting to establish a connection that will inspire them to start the sales process. Whether you are using social media, in-store events, or sponsorships, you are simply trying to distinguish yourself from the other marketing messages your ideal reader is receiving.

2. **Making your ideal reader aware of your comic**: This is one of the main goals of your advertising, where you put the comic on the radar of your ideal reader in a positive fashion.

[1183] Adams, R. (2017, July 28). What Is a Sales Funnel?

Just as movie trailers and celebrity interviews increase the profile of a film, your digital and print ads let your ideal reader know that your book exists.

3. **Increase the ideal reader interest in your comic**: This is the main purpose of your hook. Once the ideal reader knows your book is out there, they need to know how your book relates to what they like and the feelings they want to experience. You can use your key artwork, your pitch, and other promotional material to create connection and curiosity.

4. **Create a subconscious desire for your book**: Members of your target market can be influenced on an emotional level based on one or more conditions you create[1184]:

   a. *Reciprocity*: Your ideal reader is willing to give you what you want (i.e. money) in exchange for what they want (the feeling your book can provide).

   b. *Liking*: If people like you because of the feeling you help them experience, there is a good chance they will buy comics from you.

   c. *Commitment*: If you continue to show up over time to provide the feeling that people want to experience through your social media presence, your mailing list, and your offline marketing, people might be willing to pay to keep you around.

   d. *Authority*: If you can show, through your marketing, that you are in command of your story and the wider genre your story fits in, people who enjoy that kind of story are more likely to buy yours.

   e. *Social Proof*: Humans are social creatures who often imitate one another[1185], so once members of your target market accept you, especially online, other ideal readers will follow them to become true fans.

5. **Ideal readers take the action to buy your comic**: This is the main goal of your distribution. You want to make your comic available in all the channels where your ideal reader can acquire it with as little **sales friction**[1186] as possible.

[1184] Id.

[1185] Greene, Art of Seduction

[1186] Friction here is defined as anything that impedes the sales process
Wingo, S. (2018, July 19). How a Zero-Friction Approach Can Make You Money. Retrieved May 30, 2020, from https://www.business.com/articles/zero-friction-approach/

The sales funnel I described above works for a single comic or graphic novel. The number of steps in your sales funnel will depend on how many levels of action you want your ideal reader to take. If you have multiple comics, or a combination of comics, merchandise, and other media, then you'll need to repeat the procedure multiple times. In this case, there is often an indirect relationship between the price of each item and the number of actions taken[1187]. A certain number of people might buy your $4 comic, but fewer people will buy your $40 custom t-shirt and fewer still will pay for your $400 Kotobukiya statue.

We can use one of our previous examples to illustrate the multiple action idea. When Charles markets his book *Hates and Fears*, he uses social media to brainwash 100,000 people to visit his website in a year. Once they visit his website, 10,000 people join his mailing list and download his free content. When the $4 comics are released, he might sell 1,000 copies of each one. When the $25 trade comes out, sales might drop to 100. When the $100 hardcover prestige edition drops, he might only sell 10.

What is the Timeframe for a Sales Funnel?

A sales funnel is not a magical formula for making money.

It is not a singular sudden event for your entire target market at once, because it might take weeks or months for your ideal reader to make it through your sales funnel to buy your comic.

The sales funnel isn't a smooth linear process either[1188]. Ideal readers need to be guided through the process. You have to earn each true fan with attention and effort. While there might be a tipping point created by a viral event or an influential fan, the majority of your sales will be the result of your ongoing marketing, advertising and sales efforts both online and in the real world. The amount of money you make will depend in large part on how well you connect with your target market, the quality of your comic, and the price you ask people to pay for it.

[1187] Platt, S., Truant, J. B., & Wright, D. (2013). *Write. Publish. Repeat.: The no-luck-required guide to self-publishing success.* United States: Realm & Sands.

[1188] McGinnis, D. (2019). What Is a Sales Funnel?

When your ideal reader decides to buy your comic, one of their first logical questions will be "how much does this cost?" Your answer to that question involves a delicate balance of conditions that is more art than science. While you could sell your comic for any price you want, some prices may prove more beneficial than others.

How Are Prices Determined?

Price theory[1189] is an economic concept that states the optimal market price, or *equilibrium*, is the point at which the total number of products available for sale can be reasonably consumed by potential customers. As an independent comic book publisher, your equilibrium price is the highest amount you can charge your target market to buy all the available copies of your comic. The price of your book should be high enough to make it financially worthwhile to publish comics, but not so high that it creates friction for your ideal reader.

The equilibrium price is determined by the perceived value of your book to the target market. Joe Field, owner of Flying Colors Comic shop stated it this way in 2018: "*A $3.99 comic book by an unknown talent on an unknown property with little to no promotion is too expensive. A $3.99 title by popular creators on well-known properties is a good deal. So when it comes to my preference on price, it's always about whether the comic sells or not.*"[1190]

What Are the Current Prices for Comics?

Each of the various formats of comics has its price conventions that fluctuate slightly from year to year:

- Single issues: According to Comichron, the average price of the top 300 single issues sold by Diamond in February of 2020 was $4.16[1191], with the majority of titles priced at $3.99.

- Trade paperbacks and graphic novels: Because there is a large amount of variety in page counts, paper stock, and other considerations, there is a significant range in the price of trades and OGN. According to *Publisher's Weekly*, graphic novels aimed at younger markets tend to be priced in the $10 to $15 range, while superhero and literary graphic novels can range from

---

[1189] Banton, C. (2020, February 19). Theory of Price Definition. Retrieved May 30, 2020, from
https://www.investopedia.com/terms/t/theory-of-price.asp

[1190] Rogers, V. (2017). What Price Is Too High? Comics Retailers Talk Pricing. Retrieved May 30, 2020, from
https://www.newsarama.com/32826-what-price-is-too-high-retailers-talk-pricing-2017-state-of-the-business.html

[1191] Monthly Comic Book Cover Prices. (n.d.). Retrieved May 30, 2020, from
https://www.comichron.com/vitalstatistics/monthlycoverprices.html

$15 to $30 or more[1192]. Without doing a statistical analysis the way Comichron did with single issues, we're going to say the average GN price is around $20.

- Webcomics have the highest amount of variance because as we have seen in earlier chapters, the revenue from webcomics is often indirectly tied to microtransactions, monetization, sponsorship, or related merchandise sales.

What Are the Pricing Options for Comics?

Once you understand the current prices for comics, the next step as an independent publisher is choosing a price option based on the format you plan to distribute. In general, there are three options: discount, competitive, and premium pricing.

- **Discount pricing** (sometimes referred to as loss leader pricing) means selling your comic for a price that is not profitable and often less than the competition[1193]. For example, this could mean selling a single issue of your comic for $1.99 instead of the standard $3.99.

  - *Advantages*
    - Lower prices (or no price at all) can stimulate more traffic to your site for digital comics, increasing your monetization opportunities.
    - Lower prices of single issues can provide advertising and anticipation for the trade.
    - Lower prices can increase market share by drawing readers away from higher-priced competition.

  - *Disadvantages*
    - Lower prices require you to sell significantly more copies to break-even or make a profit compared to other pricing.
    - Lower digital prices can alienate the direct market and book channel[1194].
    - Lower prices can be detrimental to the perception of your book, since some readers use price as a determination of quality[1195]

[1192] Middaugh, D. (2019). What We Know About 2018 Graphic Novel Sales. Retrieved May 30, 2020, from https://www.publishersweekly.com/pw/by-topic/industry-news/comics/article/79818-what-we-know-about-2018-graphic-novel-sales.html

[1193] Banton, C. (2020, February 05). How Loss Leader Strategies Work. Retrieved May 30, 2020, from https://www.investopedia.com/terms/l/lossleader.asp

[1194] Johnston, R. (2019, January 11). Comic Store in Your Future: Cheaper Comics Would Mean No Comic Shops. Retrieved May 30, 2020, from https://www.bleedingcool.com/2019/01/10/comic-store-in-your-future-cheaper-comics-would-mean-no-comic-shops/

[1195] Dholakia, U. (2018, February 05). When High Prices Attract Consumers and Low Prices Repel Them. Retrieved May 30, 2020, from https://www.psychologytoday.com/us/blog/the-science-behind-behavior/201802/when-high-prices-attract-consumers-and-low-prices-repel-them

- **Competitive pricing** (sometimes referred to as the standard price) means selling your comic for the same price that your competition sells their comics[1196], so if the common price of a single issue is $3.99, then your comic sells for the same price.

  - *Advantages*[1197]
    - A standard price requires fewer copies to break-even compared to discount pricing.
    - Standard pricing suggests parity in quality with the competition and reduces sales friction.

  - *Disadvantages*
    - Standard pricing provides no differentiation between your book and the competition.
    - Standard comic book pricing offers comparatively lower entertainment value than other media and may not be sustainable in the long term[1198].

- **Premium pricing** means selling your comic at a higher price than your competition[1199]. This practice is not uncommon among established publishers, who use crossovers, "major events", and relaunches to charge between $4.99 and $7.99 for a single-issue comic[1200].

  - *Advantages*[1201]:
    - Premium pricing reduces your breakeven number and increases the potential profit per issue sold.
    - Premium pricing increases the perceived value of the book for some readers.

  - *Disadvantages*:
    - Premium pricing can discourage web traffic and reduce monetization opportunities.
    - Premium pricing can discourage price-conscious readers who can't afford to spend higher prices on discretionary entertainment.

[1196] Chappelow, J. (2020, January 29). Competitive Pricing Definition. Retrieved May 30, 2020, from https://www.investopedia.com/terms/c/competitive-pricing.asp

[1197] Prisync. (2018, April 10). The Advantages and Disadvantages of Competitive Pricing Strategy. Retrieved May 30, 2020, from https://medium.com/@PrisyncCom/the-advantages-and-disadvantages-of-competitive-pricing-strategy-9466a117ac92

[1198] Griepp, M. (2019). ICv2 Interview: Image's Eric Stephenson. Retrieved May 30, 2020, from https://icv2.com/articles/news/view/43847/icv2-interview-images-eric-stephenson

[1199] Woodruff, J. (2019, February 06). What is Premium Pricing Strategy? Retrieved May 30, 2020, from https://smallbusiness.chron.com/premium-pricing-strategy-1107.html

[1200] Johnston, R. (2018, August 30). Comic Book Prices, Inflation Over The Decades and Why Spawn Bucks the Trend. Retrieved May 30, 2020, from https://www.bleedingcool.com/2018/08/27/comic-book-prices-inflation-spawn-batman/

[1201] Parikh, V. (2018, January 03). Advantages and Disadvantages of Premium Pricing. Retrieved May 30, 2020, from https://www.letslearnfinance.com/advantages-disadvantages-premium-pricing.html

- Premium pricing can push ideal readers to select a competitor's book or another form of media entirely if they feel the perceived value doesn't match the price.

Does the Digital Price Need to Match the Print Price?

No matter which pricing option you choose, there is one other decision you have to make if you plan to publish both digital and print versions of your comic. As we have seen, digital comics have no print cost, lower distribution costs, and more attractive revenue splits than print. Despite that, the cost of digital comics and print comics are often the same for many publishers[1202]. The reasons for this range from covering the cost of digital staff, to avoiding conflict with comic book shops, to a desire to increase profits for digital comics[1203].

But **just because other publishers decide to price match doesn't mean you have to make the same decision**.

- Consider the financial realities of your book in terms of staff, market, distribution, and costs[1204].

- Test different scenarios for digital and print pricing to see where your risk tolerance and your sales funnel can benefit from charging different prices for digital and print comics.

- Estimate how much more of the market you can capture at a lower price, either as direct competition or as promotion for the print trade.

- Find out which digital platforms allow you to set your own price.

- Figure out if you're going to be able to get into comic book shops in the first place.

After this analysis, you might conclude that price matching makes sense for your comics. There is nothing wrong with that conclusion, as long as it comes from a firm understanding of your different sources of revenue.

[1202] Wilson, J. (2019, September 30). Everything You Need to Know About Digital Comics. Retrieved May 30, 2020, from https://www.pcmag.com/news/everything-you-need-to-know-about-digital-comics

[1203] Ibid

[1204] Kandell, Z. (2017, May 08). Why I Switched to Digital Comics. Retrieved May 30, 2020, from http://www.indiecomicnews.com/home/2017/4/25/why-i-switched-to-digital-comics

STAGE 3: POST-PRODUCTION

PART 11: REVENUE

Or How Do You Manage the Money from Your Comic?

From a technical standpoint, you are now an independent publisher. You have completed your pre-production, production, and post-production by achieving several milestones:

- You selected a goal for your publishing
- You chose a story to publish
- You found investment money
- You protected your idea and your investment
- You built a publishing team
- You found a market for your book
- You developed a distribution system
- You produced your comic
- You advertised your comic to your target market
- You generated sales for your comic

From a practical standpoint, there is still work to do to complete the post-production process. Depending on your distribution channels and your sales model, **selling a comic and receiving the money from that sale are two different things**. If you find yourself in a situation where your readers have your comic but you didn't get paid for that transaction, it's difficult to consider your book a financial success.

How Do You Collect the Revenue from Your Sales?

Accounts receivable (A/R) are sales made but not paid for by the customers until after the products are delivered[1205]. They are different from **direct sales**[1206], which is the simultaneous exchange of money and products. The distinction between accounts receivable and direct sales is found in the **payment terms**, which are the conditions under which a sale is made[1207].

For an independent comic book publisher, direct sales occur at convention tables and on your website, where the payment terms are immediate **cash on delivery**[1208]. Accounts receivable make up the bulk of

---

[1205] Accounts receivable (A/R). (n.d.). Retrieved May 31, 2020, from
http://www.businessdictionary.com/definition/accounts-receivable-A-R.html

[1206] What is direct selling? (n.d.). Retrieved May 31, 2020, from http://www.businessdictionary.com/definition/direct-selling.html

[1207] Payment terms. (n.d.). Retrieved May 31, 2020, from http://www.businessdictionary.com/definition/payment-terms.html

[1208] What is cash on delivery (COD)? (n.d.). Retrieved May 31, 2020, from
http://www.businessdictionary.com/definition/cash-on-delivery-COD.html

your sales in the direct market, book channel, and on digital sales platforms like Comixology, where payment is **deferred** to you until a later date[1209].

Keep in mind that multiple payment terms can exist in the same distribution channel. For instance, when you sell your comics to a comic shop through Diamond (or another distributor), the payment terms are deferred. When a comic shop sells that same book to a customer in their store, the payment terms in that transaction are cash on delivery.

The comic book industry has different payment terms depending on the distribution channel. These are some of the common conditions, but you should always confirm the payment terms of your specific deal and consult your attorney and your accountant if you are unsure about anything.

- Bookstore sales: are part of your accounts receivable sales and the payment terms are dependent on the distributor that you use. For example, Ingram Spark currently pays 90 days from the end of the month in which sales are reported[1210].

- Convention sales: are direct. Your reader gets the book and you get the money.

- Comixology payments: are A/R sales. They are made 45 days after the end of each quarter[1211].

- Diamond payments: are A/R sales. They are made weekly and within 30 days after your release date[1212].

You need to understand the different criteria of the distribution methods you select. Some accounts receivable sales are dependent on a date threshold or schedule. Others require you to accrue a certain threshold of sales, like $50 or $100. Some distribution channels are based on a sales threshold and a schedule[1213]. Some payment methods are automatic. Others require you to send an invoice before you can be paid.

[1209] Deferred payment. (n.d.). Retrieved May 31, 2020, from http://www.businessdictionary.com/definition/deferred-payment.html

[1210] Reports, Distribution Sales Payments, Payment Schedule, Invoices and Returns. (n.d.). Retrieved May 31, 2020, from https://help.ingramspark.com/hc/en-us/articles/210654983-Reports-Distribution-Sales-Payments-Payment-Schedule-Invoices-and-Returns

[1211] How will I get paid and how often? (n.d.). Retrieved May 31, 2020, from https://support.comixology.com/hc/en-us/articles/360042721674-How-will-I-get-paid-and-how-often-

[1212] The Diamond Comics Distribution Agreement as of June, 6, 2019

[1213] Amazon. (n.d.). Getting Paid with KDP. Retrieved May 31, 2020, from https://kdp.amazon.com/en_US/help/topic/G200641050

What Is an Invoice?

An **invoice** is a written account of the details of a sale[1214]. It is an important document in the accounts receivable process for both the independent publisher and the comic shop or bookstore because it helps both sides keep track of transactions that occurred in the past where money is still owed. Many accounts will not pay for books without a proper invoice, so you need to be able to generate them in a consistent and professional manner to avoid any friction in getting paid[1215].

The person on your team generating the invoices needs to coordinate with the people on your team making the sales through each channel and the person in charge of making sure the product is shipped. This will ensure the right books and the right number of books get to the right location at the right time before you attempt to collect money.

There is no one correct way to design an invoice. Whatever program you use to create documents probably has several templates to use. But while the style of your invoice can reflect the image of your publishing company, **there are several components[1216] you need to include** to avoid complications or payment delays.

- Header: A clear indication that this document is an invoice, and not a sell sheet or some other kind of business document.

- Your Company Information: including your business name, physical address, email, phone number, and website need to be easy to find in case the store or client has to contact you.

- Company Information of the Recipient of the invoice to ensure you are asking for payment from the right store or distributor.

- Dates: both the date that the invoice was sent and the date that payment is due

- Invoice Number: Because you might send multiple invoices to any one store over time and both sides might need to go back and review past invoices, it is important to create some kind

---

[1214] What is invoice? Black's Law Dictionary. (2011, November 04). Retrieved May 31, 2020, from https://thelawdictionary.org/invoice/

[1215] Sullivan, M. (2015, February 18). How to Make an Invoice: 8 Essential Elements. Retrieved May 31, 2020, from https://quickbooks.intuit.com/r/bookkeeping/invoices-everything-you-need-to-know-2/

[1216] Totka, M. (2019, September 29). How to Write an Invoice. Retrieved May 31, 2020, from https://www.business.com/articles/how-to-write-an-invoice/

of sequence or designation for each invoice. Many businesses just list invoices in chronological order by account to make them simple to find later[1217].

- Itemized list of products: The details of what the store received, which should match exactly what the store ordered. The details should include:

  - The name of the book(s)
  - The date the books were sent
  - The number of books ordered
  - The cost of each book
  - The total amount due for the entire order

- Itemized fees that are not included in the cost of the book. This could include shipping fees, taxes, or any other money the store needs to pay.

- Payment instructions: This gives the store the ability to pay you. This information includes:

  - When payment is due (for example, an invoice can be payable upon receipt, or within a certain timeframe like 30 or 60 days)
  - How payment can be made (whether it's PayPal, credit card or some other method)
  - Penalties for late payment (whether you charge late fees, refuse to ship additional product or referral to a collection agency[1218])

The following page contains a sample invoice for *Hates and Fears* issue #1 and a set of posters. Please feel free to modify it for your purposes.

[1217] Id.

[1218] Kagan, J. (2020, May 18). Collection Agency. Retrieved May 31, 2020, from https://www.investopedia.com/terms/c/collectionagency.asp

Invoice

**Independent
Publishing
Group**

321 Freedom Street
New York, NY 11111
(phone number)
(email)
(website)

To   Big Two Comics

100 Convention Street
New York NY
(phone number)
(email)
(website)
Customer ID: BTC

Ship Date	Number Copies	Description	Unit Cost	Line Total
1/3	200	Hates and Fears Issue #1	$2.00	$400.00
1/3	25	Hates and Fears Premium Poster	$10.00	$200.00
Total			**Total**	$600.00

__Independent and Proud!__

How Do You Keep Track of All the Different Revenue Streams?

Because different distribution channels have different time frames and different thresholds for payment, and because sales of your book may occur over time, **it will be difficult to keep track of what you are owed if you don't keep some kind of record**. Depending on your publishing program, it might make sense to use both a spreadsheet and a calendar to coordinate payments.

The spreadsheet can keep track of:

- Each distribution channel you use
- Each distributor, platform, store, or website in that channel
- When each entity makes payments
- How much you sold to each entity
- How much you are owed from that entity
- The date you should be paid from that entity
- The date the store paid
- The amount the store paid
- The total amount you made

The calendar can help you keep track of the dates you should be paid. Most entities pay their bills on time, but you might have to remind others more than once to ensure payment[1219]. The calendar can also remind you when to follow up with delinquent accounts.

Where Should the Money Go?

The business account that you created to hold your investment should be the same account you use to receive the revenue from your publishing. This will make it easier to reconcile your profits and your losses and keep track of your accounts payable without interfering with the money from your secret identity.

[1219] Caramela, S. (2018, March 16). How to Prevent and Handle Non-Paying Customers. Retrieved May 31, 2020, from https://www.business.com/articles/overdue-and-over-you-what-actions-can-you-take-when-a-client-hasnt-paid/

Keeping track of the money owed by your publishing company is just as important as overseeing the revenue coming in from the sales of your comic. As an independent publisher, **the five main types of payments include accounts payable, loan repayments, incentive or royalty payments, recoupment, and taxes**. Any funds left over after these payments are made constitute your profit.

What Are Accounts Payable?

Accounts payable (sometimes referred to as AP) are amounts due for goods or services[1220]. Independent publishers may or may not have extensive AP accounts in their business because of the three economic realities of comic book publishing. Vendors and service providers are often reluctant to offer credit to a new business attempting to establish itself in a competitive market[1221]. In cases where you do have AP there are four general concepts to follow:

1. Work with your accountant to ensure all AP payments conform to the accounting principles your business uses and any relevant tax laws.

2. Confirm that only valid and accurate demands for payment are honored. Some accountants use a process called **three-way matching**[1222] which reconciles:

   a. Your purchase orders (or contracts),
   b. The goods or services you received
   c. The invoice from the vendor or supplier

3. Follow the payment terms contained in the contracts between you and your vendors.

4. Consider paying all outstanding bills as close to their due dates as possible if that will improve your **cash flow**[1223].

[1220] Tuovila, A. (2020, May 26). Accounts Payable (AP). Retrieved May 31, 2020, from https://www.investopedia.com/terms/a/accountspayable.asp

[1221] Caramela, S. (2018, March 16). How to Prevent and Handle Non-Paying Customers

[1222] Accounts Payable Process: AccountingCoach. (n.d.). Retrieved May 31, 2020, from https://www.accountingcoach.com/accounts-payable/explanation/2

[1223] Tuovila, A. (2020, March 05). Cash Flow. Retrieved May 31, 2020, from https://www.investopedia.com/terms/c/cashflow.asp

What Are Loan Repayments?

Loan repayment is paying back the money previously borrowed from a lender[1224]. Depending on your sources of investment, this could be the repayment of a personal loan, credit cards, or other types of debt. Your repayment terms will be defined in your loan agreement and may include periodic payments of both the **principal** (the amount you borrowed)[1225] and the **interest** (the amount the lender charges you for using the principal)[1226]. Failure to pay back a loan is referred to as a **default** and can result in lawsuits against you or your company, possession of your collateral, harassment by credit agencies, or a reduction in your credit score[1227].

What Are Incentive Payments?

Depending on how you structured your talent management contracts, there may be royalty payments owed for creative work or incentive payments tied to business milestones. You can use the terms of your contract to determine how often you need to pay royalties, what (if anything) needs to be included in the **royalty report**, and what sources of revenue are being measured.

If your royalties are based on net revenue, you can pay any outstanding royalties after your AP, loans, and taxes are paid. If your royalties are based on gross revenue, you may have to pay them before any other outstanding liabilities are paid. The definition of royalties based on gross amounts can limit your available cash flow and increase the risk of default, which is another reason to define all royalty payments based on net revenue.

What Are Recoupment Payments?

Recoupable expenses (recovering amounts paid upfront in a business venture) are another amount which may be deducted from the gross revenue, depending on how your company is set up and how your contracts have been drafted. The major difference between recoupable expenses and other kinds of outstanding costs is the recipient. Where incentive payments and loans need to be disbursed outside the company, recoupable expenses are repaid to individuals in the company to give them back the money they provided to get the business off the ground.

[1224] Twin, A. (2020, March 31). Repayment Is Paying Back Money Borrowed from a Lender. Retrieved May 31, 2020, from https://www.investopedia.com/terms/r/repayment.asp

[1225] Chen, J. (2020, February 13). Principal. Retrieved May 31, 2020, from https://www.investopedia.com/terms/p/principal.asp

[1226] Banton, C. (2020, May 17). Interest Rate: What the Lender Gets Paid for the Use of Assets. Retrieved May 31, 2020, from https://www.investopedia.com/terms/i/interestrate.asp

[1227] What Happens if You Default on a Loan? (n.d.). Retrieved May 31, 2020, from https://loans.usnews.com/what-happens-if-you-default-on-a-loan

What Taxes Do You Need to Pay?

The type and amount of tax you will need to pay as an independent publisher will be specific to you and best determined by your accountant. They will consider all of your valid deductible expenses, the type of company you chose to set up, and the relevant local, state, and federal tax code to determine what (if anything) you will need to pay in taxes and when those taxes need to be paid. If you kept accurate records of the business transactions of your company, this can be a straightforward task. If there are any discrepancies or irregularities, there is a chance you and your publishing company could be subjected to an audit.

What Is an Audit?

An **audit** is an examination of the financial statements of an organization to determine if they accurately represent the business of that company[1228]. While tax audits from the IRS can be the most intimidating type of business examination, your creditors, investors, and even your freelance contractors might have the ability to audit the records of your business depending on the language in the housekeeping terms of each contract. Even if they aren't a signal of wrongdoing[1229], audits can disrupt a business and take an emotional toll on the independent publisher if it is not handled in a professional manner.

Of course, the best way to deal with an audit is to avoid business practices that raise red flags[1230], but even the most scrupulous record-keeping can't completely prevent this from happening. If your business is subjected to an audit, there are four major steps you can make to handle the situation[1231].

1. Keep your accountant and (if necessary) your attorney involved in the process.
2. Review the audit demand to determine exactly what information is being requested.
3. Organize your records for the relevant period of the audit.
4. Answer all questions from the auditor, but do not offer any additional information or explanations.

There are three possible outcomes of an audit[1232]. If your financial records are found to be accurate, then there is no further action that needs to happen. If your records are found to be inaccurate and you accept the inaccuracy, then you may have to pay the additional taxes or royalties that weren't paid. If your records

---

[1228] Tuovila, A. (2020, February 05). What is an Audit? Retrieved May 31, 2020, from https://www.investopedia.com/terms/a/audit.asp

[1229] Ibid

[1230] Taylor, J. (2020, March 13). 20 IRS Audit Red Flags. Retrieved May 31, 2020, from https://www.kiplinger.com/slideshow/taxes/T056-S001-20-irs-tax-audit-red-flags/index.html

[1231] Hedreen, S. (2020, January 16). How to Handle a Business Audit. Retrieved May 31, 2020, from https://www.businessnewsdaily.com/8993-handle-tax-audit.html

[1232] Tuovila, A. (2020, February 05). What is an Audit?

are found to be inaccurate and you disagree with the findings, then the result could include appeals, mediations, or lawsuits.

What Do You Do with Your Profits?

After you have collected all the money from your distribution, after you have paid your loans and your taxes and your royalty payments, you might be surprised to find there is money left over from your publishing efforts. This is not common, because as we said in the beginning **the majority of small businesses both in comics and in the wider world do not generate profits in the short term**. But if you do generate profits from your business, you need to decide what to do with them.

First, any contractual obligations you have to pay investors or the other people who might own a piece of your IP or your publishing company need to be satisfied. Then all of you have a choice. You can walk away with your profits and enjoy the fruits of your labor, or you can reinvest those profits back into your publishing company, turning the profits from the first comic into the investment that will fund any future business. This decision can bring your independent publishing full circle, where the post-production process leads back to the pre-production process.

But before you decide where to put your possible profits, you need to decide what you want to do in the future in terms of your career in comics.

STAGE 3: POST-PRODUCTION

PART 12: GROWTH

Or What Happens After You Publish Your Comic?

When the dust settles and the smoke clears…when your books are in your reader's hands and their money is in your business account, you deserve to celebrate. Take yourself out for a nice meal, a good drink, or even a mini-vacation. You have accomplished something that many people only talk about.

But during the celebration of your achievement, ask yourself this question: "Can you achieve your goals with only one comic?"

If you had a story to tell, or if you wanted to see your book on the shelf next to your favorite titles, then one book might be all you need. But **if you plan to have a career in comics, one book is just the beginning**. In the same way, it's difficult for an athlete or musician to reach the Hall of Fame with one good game or one good song. You can't define a career with a single book. Consider these examples from the recent history of the industry[1233]:

- Jim Lee could have just drawn best-selling versions of *Punisher* and *X-Men*, but he went out on his own and built Image into one of the largest independent comics companies, before going to DC and taking a major leadership role there[1234].

- Frank Miller could have been happy to redefine characters like *Batman* and *Daredevil*, but he kept pushing, creating independent properties like *Sin City* and *300* that made it to the big screen.[1235]

- Joe Quesada could have been content to draw *Batman* and create characters like Azrael and Ninjak, but he went further, first with Marvel Knights, then becoming Editor-in-Chief at Marvel and helping move the company into the golden age of comic book media.[1236]

The book you published can be a major element of social proof in the industry. Travis McIntire, president of Source Point Press, sees independent comics as the launchpad for other work. "*Doors open when you*

[1233] Hennessy, G. (2014, August 15). How to Break into (and Stay In) Comics. Retrieved May 31, 2020, from https://www.creativecontractconsulting.com/c3blog/2014/8/14/mp4gfnq28r2zauvx4fs3z6g3oyoll6

[1234] Jim Lee. (2020, May 05). Retrieved May 31, 2020, from https://en.wikipedia.org/wiki/Jim_Lee

[1235] Frank Miller (comics). (2020, May 31). Retrieved May 31, 2020, from https://en.wikipedia.org/wiki/Frank_Miller_(comics)

[1236] Joe Quesada. (2020, May 05). Retrieved May 31, 2020, from https://en.wikipedia.org/wiki/Joe_Quesada

create a comic, just from a proof of survival factor. People in the industry recognize the effort that goes into publishing."[1237]

Mark Richardson, the publisher of Dark Horse Comics, cautions against ending your publishing efforts prematurely. According to him, "if you're going to put money into something and commit to something, you have to do it and not just go halfway."[1238] So if you already spent the time creating a company, building a market, constructing a distribution system, and organizing a unique business model, does it really make sense to abandon it all after your first book?

Your first experience of independent publishing is an educational process as much as it is a business endeavor. Like any artistic creation, it probably wasn't perfect and it isn't supposed to be. You had to make multiple decisions for each step of your comic's development. Each one impacted the final result. But luck and other external forces also shaped the outcome of your book in ways that you can't control or understand[1239]. If you continue to publish comics over time, your experience with real-world decisions can make you a better publisher and generate more successful comics. But **your publishing can only improve if you continue your career in comics**.

Independent publishing isn't the only career path in this industry. Your comic can be the springboard to other opportunities, depending on your goals and what type of work fits your personality.

[1237] Becker, D. (2017). Listen to the Comic Pros & Cons Episode - Episode 085: Travis McIntire on iHeartRadio. Retrieved May 31, 2020, from https://www.iheart.com/podcast/256-comic-pros-cons-30981514/episode/episode-085-travis-mcintire-37202328/

[1238] McLauchlin, J. (2017). Business 3x3: Mike Richardson at Dark Horse Comics. Retrieved May 31, 2020, from https://icv2.com/articles/news/view/37287/business-3x3-mike-richardson-dark-horse-comics

[1239] Duke, A. (2018) Thinking in Bets. Portfolio

Your published comic is a key to opening doors in the comic book industry, but which door you decide to open depends on your goals, your personality, and your experience with independent publishing. In general, there are five paths you can pursue in comics:

- Independent publishing
- Freelance comic creation
- Creator-driven comic creation
- Multimedia content creation
- Diversified comic creation

Why Pursue More Independent Publishing?

If you find yourself working on the sequel to your book before the first one has gone on sale, then being an independent comic book publisher is probably in your DNA.

The benefit of choosing this path comes from your ability to streamline the initial process you just completed. It won't be the same, of course. The pre-production, production, and post-production process for each book might vary with each new book if the goals, target market, format, distribution channels, or sales environment are different. Some steps, like forming a company, can be skipped. Other steps, like negotiating contracts or analyzing competition, can go faster because it's not your first rodeo. **The method you developed for your first book offers a guide to future books, even if it's not an exact formula.**

The path of the independent comic book publisher requires you to take the model for your single book and expand it into the development of your publishing catalog. This decision requires creative choices on the macro level. Are you going to build a connected narrative universe like DC, Marvel, Valiant, and AWA, or are you going to publish diverse unconnected stories like AfterShock, A Wave Blue World, Dark Horse, and Image? Whichever model you chose to follow, the business of publishing the comics remains the same:

- Secure the rights for the IP you want to use, either by getting a license or owning it outright.
- Stick to a budget for each book. You can use the funds from a profitable book to finance the less successful ones, as long as you don't overextend yourself.
- Build the best team you can with collaboration or work for hire agreements.
- Connect with the target market for each book.
- Distribute your books where your target market consumes content.
- Produce your book on time with a realistic and manageable schedule for each element of each book.

- Inform the market about your books and consider cross-promoting books in the catalog (if it makes sense for the market).
- Sell your comics in ways that leverage the new books to help older books sell.
- Collect the revenue for all your sales.
- Distribute funds to everyone you are obligated to pay.
- Repeat.

A variation on building a catalog from your publishing efforts is to form a broader publishing company with other independent publishers. This would be similar to what Rob Liefeld, Marc Silvestri, Todd McFarlane, and other creators did in forming Image Comics[1240]. If you built a business model that works, you can use your team and your process to bring in new partners, expand your market reach, and ultimately increase your revenue.

If you read this book in a linear fashion, you can probably guess that there are benefits and liabilities that come with building a company alongside other publishers.

Potential benefits include:

- **Economies of scale**, or the cost advantages that come from increased production[1241].
- Diversified catalogs that can attract different target markets.
- Increased reputation in the comic book industry.
- Increased inspiration is generated when different creators and publishers share ideas.
- Coordination in everything from marketing, distribution, and advertising, or crossover events and storylines.

Potential pitfalls include:

- Incompatible business practices or personalities.
- Incompatible visions and goals for the company.
- Increased complication and complexity in legal issues, management, or production.

In the same way you managed your potential team members in your talent management, you need to conduct the same due diligence, negotiation, and administration of any coordinated publishing effort. Make sure your accountant, attorney, and editors are involved and don't do anything without the proper contracts in place.

[1240] Reed, P. (2016, February 01). Today in Comics History: The Start of The Image Revolution. Retrieved May 31, 2020, from https://comicsalliance.com/tribute-image-comics/

[1241] Kenton, W. (2020, January 29). What You Need to Know About Economies of Scale. Retrieved May 31, 2020, from https://www.investopedia.com/terms/e/economiesofscale.asp

Why Pursue Freelance Comic Creation?

If you enjoyed the creative experience of publishing your comic, but you're not in love with the responsibility of pre- or post-production, you should consider becoming a freelance comic creator. This allows you to use your independent comic as proof of your creative talents and professional skills. CB Cebulski, Editor in Chief at Marvel, has said on several occasions that editors in the Big Two use original material from potential creators as one method for evaluating talent[1242].

As we've discussed earlier, **the freelance creator trades independence for control**. A freelance artist gets paid for their contribution to the book whether it is financially successful or not, but they probably don't share in the financial success of the book if it becomes a best-seller or spawns movies and video games for generations to come. A freelance artist contributes their artistic sensibilities to the story, but they normally don't have final authority in terms of what the story will be about, what happens in the story, or even what stories they work on. Being a freelance creator requires a certain amount of professional detachment that isn't suited to every independent comic book publisher.

Your experience in independent publishing can increase your value as a freelance creator if you decide on this path. In addition to your creative skills, you may have contacts, experience, and business skills that can help in a variety of ways:

- Talent management: If your publisher is looking for other members of their team, you can tap into the pool of people who you worked with or considered working with for your book.

- Marketing: You can help define the target market for any project you work on because you understand the fundamentals of marketing. Depending on the books you work on, you can bring some of your press contacts and the target market from your book to your new projects to increase market share.

- Distribution: Your existing relationships with bookstores, comic shops, and libraries can help get new books into the market.

- Production: Your research and relationships with printers can assist in navigating the wide world of printing.

Freelance comic creators who can provide business support in addition to their creative talent, professional demeanor, industry reputation, and time deserve to be compensated for everything they bring to a project.

[1242] Chronicles of the Nerds (Producer). (2011). *How to become a Marvel Comic Writer/Artist (with C.B. Cebulski)* [Video file]. Retrieved May 31, 2020, from https://www.youtube.com/watch?v=mNWj61J_gZs

Remember to work with your accountant and attorney to negotiate compensation for the work you do and **avoid doing any work for free no matter what publisher you work for**[1243].

Why Pursue Creator-Driven Comic Creation?

If you enjoy the pre-production and production aspects of comics, but you don't want to worry about the distribution or post-production responsibilities, you can consider a career in creator-driven comics[1244]. The combination of creator-driven publishing companies[1245] and the rise of graphic novel imprints in traditional publishing houses[1246] provide a variety of opportunities for an independent publisher to deliver stories to their readers without managing the distribution, sales, and revenue functions of publishing.

In theory, the ownership and rights to a creator-driven comic remain with the creative team and not the publisher. This means that you can control the IP and focus more of your time on the artistic aspects of the book by licensing various publishing rights to your publisher. In reality, this means that when you develop creator-driven comics, you still have to manage the entire pre-production process, especially the marketing. It also means navigating around the various gatekeepers of publishing, which may require an agent or long periods of query letters, pitch meetings, or dilution of your original idea[1247]. **In the worst-case scenarios, publishers try to use creator-driven deals to gain complete control over your IP, leaving you with no money and limited legal recourse**[1248]. When faced with this type of abusive agreement, your BATNA could be going back to the independent publishing path.

There are other ways that your experiences as an independent publisher can help you navigate and thrive in creator-driven publishing:

- Foundation: When you understand why you're making your comic, you'll understand which deals make sense and which ones to walk away from.

[1243] "Perch" (Director). (2020). *Never ever, ever, ever work for free in comics* [Video file]. Retrieved May 31, 2020, from https://www.youtube.com/watch?v=vy67EsSXfsk&list=WL&index=8&t=0s

[1244] Crowell, T. A. (2015). *The pocket lawyer for comic books: A legal toolkit for indie comic book artists and writers.* Burlington, MA: Focal Press. P. 224

[1245] Verrillo, E. (2018, May 01). 7 Graphic Novel Publishers Accepting Manuscripts Directly From Writers. Retrieved May 31, 2020, from https://medium.com/@ericaverr/7-graphic-novel-publishers-accepting-manuscripts-directly-from-writers-1366132b04d2

[1246] Cronin, B. (2020, January 22). Random House Children's Books Launches Imprint to Promote Graphic Novels. Retrieved May 31, 2020, from https://www.cbr.com/random-house-graphic-novels-launch-line-books/

[1247] Vicente, M. (2019, February 19). A Literary Agent's Guide to Querying Your Graphic Novel. Retrieved May 31, 2020, from http://www.mariavicente.com/blog/query-graphic-novels

[1248] Hennessy, G. (2013, July 10). Deal with the Devil (How Comic Creators Get Their Rights Stolen). Retrieved May 31, 2020, from https://www.creativecontractconsulting.com/c3blog/2013/07/deal-with-devil-how-comic-creators-get.html

- IP Management: Once you publish your independent comic, you'll be able to explain your new comic ideas with confidence.

- Talent Management: You can tap into your pool of proven professionals and approach publishers with a fully vetted creative team.

- Marketing: You'll understand who is in your target market and how to deliver them to the publisher.

- Advertising: You can use your existing press contacts and marketing relationships to help the publisher inform the market.

When considering the creator-driven path or analyzing any contract with another publisher, it is important to evaluate three aspects of the agreement:

- Compare what you are getting from the publisher in relation to what you are giving away to understand if the deal makes legal sense[1249].

- Understand where the money is or isn't coming from to understand if the deal makes financial sense[1250].

- Perform your due diligence to determine how much creative control you can expect to have over the art and story in the comic.

It's not an accident that these considerations match the expertise of your accountant, attorney, and editor. You should get input from each of these professionals, in addition to your agent, when evaluating any creator-driven deal.

Why Pursue Multimedia Content Creation?

It's one thing to love comic book publishing before you've gone through the process. It's another situation entirely after you've negotiated contracts, spent weekends on your feet at cons, fought for endorsements, and chased bookstores for money. To paraphrase Anthony Bourdain, it pays to look at your experience as

---

[1249] Hennessy, G. (2016, August 31). Get What You Give (Rights and Revenue in Comics). Retrieved May 31, 2020, from https://www.creativecontractconsulting.com/c3blog/2016/8/31/get-what-you-give-rights-and-revenue-in-comics

[1250] Hennessy, G. (2015, August 01). How a Lawyer Beat Darth Vader. Retrieved May 31, 2020, from https://www.creativecontractconsulting.com/c3blog/2015/8/1/how-a-lawyer-beat-darth-vader

an independent publisher as an experiment to determine if you want a career in comics or if you'd rather be a "normal person"[1251].

I started this book with the premise that you should only make comics if you love the medium of comics. But at the end of your independent publishing experience, you might decide that while you love your story and your characters, you might not be in love with the business and process of publishing comics. You might decide that your story needs to be told in other media, whether that is film, novels, television, or video games. Your independent publishing could lead you on a path out of comics and into other media.

This isn't a unique proposition. Companies from Aspen[1252], AWA[1253], Millar World[1254], and Valiant[1255] all have multimedia distribution as a significant aspect of their business model. Ticket sales for each film in the MCU have generated close to what the entire comic book industry generates in a year[1256], not counting merchandise and marketing tie-ins. Some commentators see comic book publishing as little more than idea farms for more lucrative media properties[1257]. **For some publishers, the ideas in the comics are more important than the media itself.**

So, the upside of multimedia productions is clear. Because of the limitations on comic growth we discussed in Chapter 31, there is currently more potential for exposure to larger audiences outside of comics. This means there are bigger budgets and more potential revenue in other media. But the downsides of multimedia are significant.

From the beginning of the medium, comic creators have not usually enjoyed the success of their work outside of comics[1258]. It is not uncommon for comic creators to have little or no ownership or control over

---

[1251] Spirit and Place (Producer). (2011). *Chefs Anthony Bourdain & Eric Ripert discuss the value of cooking school* [Video file]. Retrieved May 31, 2020, from https://www.youtube.com/watch?v=14eFoQYXe0I

[1252] Montgomery, S. (2018, June 01). Scooter Braun Wants His New Film Studio to Be the Next Marvel. Retrieved May 31, 2020, from https://www.complex.com/pop-culture/2018/03/scooter-braun-starts-film-company-to-make-comic-book-movies-with-former-marvel-chairman

[1253] Reid, C. (2019). Bill Jemas Returns with a New Comics Venture. Retrieved May 31, 2020, from https://www.publishersweekly.com/pw/by-topic/industry-news/comics/article/80472-bill-jemas-returns-with-a-new-comics-venture.html

[1254] Netflix Acquires Millarworld. (2017). Retrieved May 31, 2020, from https://media.netflix.com/en/press-releases/netflix-acquires-millarworld-1

[1255] Outlaw, K. (2018, January 29). Here's How Valiant Will Be Affected by the DMG Entertainment Deal. Retrieved May 31, 2020, from https://comicbook.com/movies/2018/01/29/valiant-dmg-entertainment-deal-details-terms-changes/

[1256] Hennessy, G. (2019, November 7). *Comic Book Law: An Introduction*. Lecture presented at Comic Book Law: An Introduction in New York Law School, New York.

[1257] Elbein, A. (2017, May 25). The Real Reasons for Marvel Comics' Woes. Retrieved May 31, 2020, from https://www.theatlantic.com/entertainment/archive/2017/05/the-real-reasons-for-marvel-comics-woes/527127/

[1258] Lopes, P. D. (2009). *Demanding Respect*. Temple University Press.

their multimedia properties[1259]. Hollywood accounting is also an ever-present concern, especially when a comic creator, who may or may not understand the financial realities of publishing, is thrust into the more complex economics of film and television. Finally, the competition for multimedia opportunities remains ferocious, even in the golden age of comic book media we live in.

Consider this: if a hundred comic book properties are transitioning to various media every year, it is still a small fraction of the total number of comics being published. If there are close to five thousand comics and graphic novels released per year, a hundred comic film and television shows would only account for two percent of the total available comics. And that ratio only considers current comics. Most comic related films and television being released today are based on properties that began twenty to forty years ago. This means that if you're trying to get your independent comic optioned for multimedia, you not only have to compete with all the current comics from established publishers. You have to consider the entire history of comic IP that might be available, in addition to all the other screenwriters and other narrative artists trying to secure a limited amount of funding and distribution.

This is not to say that your independent comic can't become a multimedia property. One of my former clients got his crowdfunded comic optioned for a film before the book was even published[1260]. But that is the exception and not the rule. My original premise still stands. **If you are going to publish independent comics, your business model needs to utilize your comic for something more than a farm system for narrative ideas[1261].** If and when you own characters and stories that build a strong following for ten or twenty years, then the transition to multimedia can evolve as a natural extension of your comic's concomitant popularity[1262].

Why Pursue Diversified Comic Creation?

One of the unique aspects of a career in comics is the ability of the creator to flow between the different types of comic book publishing. Once you understand the process of independent comic book publishing, **nothing is stopping you from creating different kinds of business relationships and different publishing models for each new project.** You could, in theory, work in creator-driven, freelance, independent, and multimedia publishing all at the same time, depending on the stories you want to tell and the deals you can create. As long as you remember the fundamental business concepts and work with your

---

[1259] Elbein, A. (2016, September 06). How Marvel Mistreated One of Its Biggest Stars. Retrieved May 31, 2020, from https://www.theatlantic.com/entertainment/archive/2016/09/marvel-jack-kirby-and-the-plight-of-the-comic-book-artist/498299/

[1260] McMillan, G. (2020, May 30). 'Black' Comic Book Movie Coming From Studio 8 and Black Mask. Retrieved May 31, 2020, from https://www.hollywoodreporter.com/heat-vision/studio-8-black-mask-studios-team-black-movie-1105037

[1261] Francisco, E. (2020, July 06). Netflix 'The Old Guard' writer: Comic books aren't just movie fodder. Retrieved July 07, 2020, from https://www.inverse.com/entertainment/old-guard-netflix-comic-book-writer-interview

[1262] Jenkins, H. (2015, June 14). Comic Books and Convergence Synopsis. Retrieved May 31, 2020, from https://wolfhumanities.upenn.edu/comic-books-and-convergence-synopsis

accountants, agents, attorneys, and editors, you can pursue all your comic book goals in an ever-evolving industry.

The United States Marine Corps has a motto that is as relevant to small business as it is to warfighting:

Adapt. Improvise. Overcome[1263].

When I originally planned this chapter, I envisioned a theoretical discussion of managing your long-term comic book goals amid inevitable changing circumstances[1264]. But as I write this sheltered in my apartment for eight weeks straight, the reality of the novel coronavirus (also known as Covid-19), is forcing everyone in the comic book industry to make dramatic adjustments during an unprecedented health and economic crisis[1265]. Creators, publishers, distributors, and retailers are trying to apply the Marines' motto to their business. I'm going to try and apply it to the redesign of this chapter.

Comic book publishing exists in a multi-level ecosystem. **Throughout your comic book career, there will be change on various levels that will impact your business**. Positive and negative events will occur in the secret identities of you and your team. Competition in your genre will rise and fall. Changes large and small will emerge in the industry as a whole. Larger economic trends will alter the wider world of publishing and recreational entertainment. Social and political changes in the country and the world can also trickle down and affect your business. Unique events, like Covid-19, can occur overnight and impact every level at once[1266]. While you can't anticipate every storm or go back in time to prevent every extinction-level event with a snap of your fingers, you can prepare for changes in the publishing landscape before they happen and follow the Marine example.

How Do You Prepare for Industry Changes Before They Happen?

Our old friend Heraclitus spent a lot of his life contemplating the nature of change. He is one of the philosophers credited with the idea that change is the only constant aspect of life[1267]. As an independent comic book publisher, your experience of publishing your first book provides a personal perspective and understanding of your industry. But **the business, economic, legal, and social realities that were true for your first book are not constants**. When you start to think about publishing comics for the next few

---

[1263] Mission of the Marine Corps. (n.d.). Retrieved May 31, 2020, from https://www.marines.com/who-we-are/our-purpose.html

[1264] Greene, Laws of Human Nature

[1265] Itzkoff, D. (2020, April 10). Can Comic Books Survive the Coronavirus Era? Retrieved May 31, 2020, from https://www.nytimes.com/2020/04/10/arts/comic-books-coronavirus.html

[1266] Griepp, M. (2020). World According to Griepp: Geek Winter Is Coming. Retrieved May 31, 2020, from https://icv2.com/articles/columns/view/45635/world-according-griepp-geek-winter-is-coming

[1267] Beris, A.N. and A.J. Giacomin, "Everything Flows", Cover Article, Applied Rheology, 24(5), 52918 (2014), pp. 1–13; .

decades, it becomes clear that the comic book industry of 2060 might be very different than the one you see today.

Adjusting to changing circumstances depends on the decisions you make in relation to new situations. Those choices are influenced by your goals, your resources, and your personality. They are also shaped by the time you have to decide. Shorter timeframes for mental activity increase stress, which can reduce the quality of any given decision[1268]. You have an opportunity to increase the time you have to choose if you consider your potential options before the critical moment arrives. This is referred to as pre-situational decision making, or a **pre-decision**[1269].

Pre-decisions for independent comic book publishing involve taking time to think about how you would respond to sweeping changes to the business of comics. When we discussed your goals, I suggested taking yourself out for a contemplative cocktail to think about what you wanted to achieve. Now that you are an independent publisher, this thought experiment involves asking yourself what you would do with your comics and your company in various potential scenarios. The number of potential events is infinite, but I'll offer a few ideas to spur your imagination.

For example, write down what you would do as an independent comic book publisher, if;

- The Big Two suddenly stopped publishing new comics for some reason.[1270]
- An emerging new comic book format became the new standard across the industry[1271].
- New distribution players suddenly entered the market[1272].
- The multimedia popularity of comic book related content came to an end[1273].

[1268] McLeod, L. (2016, July 13). Pre-Decision Making: How to Make Better Decisions Under Stress. Retrieved May 31, 2020, from https://www.huffpost.com/entry/predecision-making-how-to_b_7788014

[1269] Ibid.

[1270] Hennessy, G. (2019, March 05). Are Independent Comics Worth Making If Marvel Stops Publishing? Retrieved May 31, 2020, from https://www.creativecontractconsulting.com/c3blog/2019/3/4/are-independent-comics-worth-making-if-marvel-stops-publishing

[1271] GlobalComix. (2020). GlobalComix Launches Pro-Comics Publishing Services for Digital Comic Sales, Angel Funding. Retrieved May 31, 2020, from https://www.prlog.org/12809432-globalcomix-launches-pro-comics-publishing-services-for-digital-comic-sales-angel-funding.html

[1272] MacDonald, H., (2020, April 17). DC announces return to shipping comics for 4/27 with alternative distributors. Retrieved May 31, 2020, from https://www.comicsbeat.com/shocker-dc-announces-return-to-shipping-comics-for-4-27-with-alternative-distributors/

[1273] Rose, S. (2019, April 15). A pocketful of kryptonite: Are superheroes dying out? Retrieved May 31, 2020, from https://www.theguardian.com/film/2019/apr/15/a-pocketful-of-kryptonite-are-superheroes-dying-out

- A new generation of film, television, and video game makers began looking for independent comic book content in the same way many current film directors grew up on the Big Two now look to those stories for inspiration[1274].

You may find some of these potential changes (and the ones you come up with on your own) don't change anything about your publishing plans or your career in comics. Others might force a radical re-evaluation of your goals and plans. Either way, **if you come to grips with inevitable change and uncertainty before it happens, you can be in a better position to adapt, improvise, and overcome new conditions.**

How Do You Adapt to Industry Changes When They Happen?

Evolving business and social conditions require both decisions and actions from independent comic book publishers. But before you make your choices and navigate your enterprise to boldly go where no publisher has gone before, it makes sense to look at both the context and the consequences of your decisions.

First and foremost, **you need to protect the secret identities of yourself and your publishing team.** If you can't afford to eat or pay your rent, publishing comics becomes a trivial concern. If a hurricane destroys your city or a pandemic washes over the world, you might need to evacuate or horde toilet paper before you can worry about meeting your production schedule.

If and when you can turn your attention to comics, it helps to take a breath and **consider how the current situation alters your business reality.** For example, Covid-19 disrupted offline marketing when most conventions were canceled[1275]. It crippled print distribution when comic shops were forced to close with other non-essential businesses and Diamond shut down its distribution centers to help flatten the curve[1276]. The domino effect of all these events led to a severe reduction in direct market revenue collection from comic shops and Diamond[1277].

Once you understand how an event alters the publishing environment, you can **consider all your options for responding to the situation.** During the pandemic, independent publishers could try to shift their

---

[1274] Evry, M. (2018, June 15). 11 Movie Directors Who Are Hardcore Comic Book Fans. Retrieved May 31, 2020, from https://www.comingsoon.net/movies/features/953047-11-movie-directors-who-are-hardcore-comic-book-fans

[1275] Booker, B. (2020, April 17). Coronavirus Forces Organizers To Cancel San Diego Comic-Con. Retrieved May 31, 2020, from https://www.npr.org/sections/coronavirus-live-updates/2020/04/17/837354657/coronavirus-forces-organizers-to-cancel-san-diego-comic-con

[1276] Salkowitz, R. (2020, March 24). Final Crisis? Diamond Comic Distributors Halts Shipments Of New Comics In Response To COVID-19 Shutdowns. Retrieved May 31, 2020, from https://www.forbes.com/sites/robsalkowitz/2020/03/24/final-crisis-diamond-comic-distributors-halts-shipments-of-new-comics-in-response-to-covid-19-shutdowns/

[1277] Griepp, M. (2020). World According to Griepp: Distributor Cash Flow 101. Retrieved May 31, 2020, from https://icv2.com/articles/columns/view/45542/world-according-griepp-distributor-cash-flow-101?

marketing efforts online[1278], suspend their production and distribution completely[1279], explore alternative distribution and sales methods[1280], or alter payment terms to reflect the new reality[1281]. Whatever set of options are available, it pays to consider the potential reactions from various interested parties for each decision. A decision that benefits you and your team might be seen as negative by your market, your distributors, your printers, or anyone else with an emotional or financial stake in your comics[1282]. You have to be able to look beyond the current situation and maintain the long-term public image and relationships that are best for your publishing program.

It also helps to **remain cognizant of all those aspects of independent publishing that are not affected** by whatever situation you find yourself in. Once your basic needs of safety and health are met, there will almost always be things that you can continue to do for your comic regardless of the situation. Covid-19 didn't prohibit most elements of pre-production or production, so independent publishers sheltering at home could continue to develop their books and continue to produce new content[1283].

Above all, independent publishers can take advantage of their relatively smaller size and fewer decision-makers to remain flexible and nimble in the face of changing circumstances. When your goals are clear and your resources are protected, you can put yourself in a position to adapt, improvise, and overcome changes in the industry, and thrive no matter what the comic book industry evolves into[1284].

Of course, there is one inescapable change that is less about the comic book industry or world events and more about you and your finite reality. Not every comic book creator survives major shifts in the environment. We lost comics luminaries to Covid-19[1285]. There is a cliché that nothing is certain except death and taxes. Since we already discussed taxes in earlier chapters, we need to move onto the other certainty...

[1278] Marston, G. (2020). Mainframe Comic Con Brings Con Season Online. Retrieved May 31, 2020, from https://www.newsarama.com/49753-mainframe-comic-con-brings-con-season-online.html

[1279] Hennessy, G. (2012, November 01). Catastrophe and Contracts (Understanding the "Act of God" Clause). Retrieved May 31, 2020, from https://www.creativecontractconsulting.com/c3blog/2012/11/catastrophe-and-contracts-understanding.html

[1280] MacDonald, (2020, April 17). DC announces return to shipping comics for 4/27 with alternative distributors

[1281] Levitz, P. (2020). Suggestions for Comic Publishers and Retailers on the Coronavirus Pandemic. Retrieved May 31, 2020, from https://icv2.com/articles/columns/view/45420/suggestions-comic-publishers-retailers-coronavirus-pandemic

[1282] MacDonald, H., (2020, April 21). Retailers have poor reaction to DC's new distribution plan – extremely bad, like I mean it is BAD. Retrieved May 31, 2020, from https://www.comicsbeat.com/retailers-react-to-dcs-new-distribution-plan/

[1283] Quaintance, Z., (2020, April 16). 'Business as Usual,' AfterShock Comics assures market. Retrieved May 31, 2020, from https://www.comicsbeat.com/business-as-usual-aftershock-comics-assurances-market/

[1284] Sardo, M., (2020, March 27). What Will A Post-Crisis Comic Book Industry Look Like? Retrieved May 31, 2020, from https://monkeysfightingrobots.co/what-will-a-post-crisis-comic-book-industry-look-like/

[1285] MacDonald, H., (2020, April 03). RIP: Metabarons artist Juan Gimenez passes away from COVID-19. Retrieved May 31, 2020, from https://www.comicsbeat.com/rip-metabarons-artist-juan-gimenez-passes-away-from-covid-19/

Intellectual property rights can last up to seventy years after the death of the creator[1286].

Companies are theoretically perpetual[1287].

You are not.

Eventually, you will die, but your comic and the company you built can live on. **What happens to the work you've done and the revenue it creates depends in part on how you plan for a future without you.**

This chapter obviously isn't an in-depth analysis of the complexities of estate planning. It is meant to provide an introduction to estates as it relates to your independent publishing.

What Is an Estate?

An **estate** is the economic valuation of all the investments, assets, and interests of an individual. This includes a person's belongings, physical and intangible assets, land and real estate, investments, and collectibles[1288]. As an independent publisher, your assets could include the following:

- Ownership (percentage of total) of IP related to the comics
- Control of your publishing company
- Ongoing revenue streams from your comics
- Other personal assets not connected to comics
- Your personal debt or any taxes you are liable for

Estate planning is the preparation of tasks that serve to manage an individual's asset base in the event of their incapacitation or death[1289]. Estate planning often uses the legal mechanisms of wills and trusts to manage estate assets.

[1286] United States Copyright Office. (2011). *Duration of Copyright* [PDF].

[1287] Kenton, W. (2020, February 21). Articles of Incorporation. Retrieved May 31, 2020, from https://www.investopedia.com/terms/a/articlesofincorporation.asp

[1288] Kagan, J. (2020, March 06). Estate. Retrieved May 31, 2020, from https://www.investopedia.com/terms/e/estate.asp

[1289] Kagan, J. (2020, January 29). Estate Planning. Retrieved May 31, 2020, from https://www.investopedia.com/terms/e/estateplanning.asp

What Is a Will?

A will[1290] is a legal document that spells out your wishes regarding the distribution of your assets to your heirs[1291] after your death:

Why Should an Independent Publisher Have a Will?

When you make a will, you have to consider the end of your life. While it is hard for many people in modern society to think about their death[1292], there are several benefits for those independent publishers who are interested in what happens to their creations in the future. When you have a will[1293]:

- You can be clear about who receives your assets after you die. You can decide who gets what and how much.
- You can keep your assets out of the hands of people you don't want to have them (like an estranged relative).
- Your heirs will have a faster and easier time getting access to your assets.
- You can plan to save your estate money on taxes. You can also give gifts and charitable donations, which can help offset the estate tax.

What Happens If You Don't Have a Will?

A person who dies without a will is referred to as **intestate**[1294]. If you die intestate, a **probate court**[1295] will have to determine what happens to your remaining assets and liabilities. The most common division of assets involves a distribution among surviving spouses, children, and family members, but every case in every state is different, so you can't rely on this outcome.

[1290] Smith, L. (2020, April 21). What Is a Will and Why Do I Need One Now? Retrieved May 31, 2020, from https://www.investopedia.com/articles/pf/08/what-is-a-will.asp

[1291] Kagan, J. (2020, January 29). Heir. Retrieved May 31, 2020, from https://www.investopedia.com/terms/h/heir.asp

[1292] Lewis, R. (2018, November 22). Facts to Calm Your Fear of Death and Dying. Retrieved May 31, 2020, from https://www.psychologytoday.com/us/blog/finding-purpose/201811/facts-calm-your-fear-death-and-dying

[1293] Smith, L. (2020, April 21). What Is a Will and Why Do I Need One Now?

[1294] Kagan, J. (2020, May 12). Intestate Definition. Retrieved May 31, 2020, from https://www.investopedia.com/terms/i/intestate.asp

[1295] Kagan, J. (2020, January 29). What is Probate Court? Retrieved May 31, 2020, from https://www.investopedia.com/terms/p/probate-court.asp

According to recent studies, more than fifty percent of Americans don't have a will, and many famous people with sizable assets died intestate, including Bob Marley, Tupac Shakur, and Prince[1296]. While it might be aspirational and inspirational to emulate these artists from a creative standpoint, it doesn't make sense to use them as role models of estate planning if you want the fruits of your independent publishing to benefit someone specific when you die.

What is a Trust?

A **trust** is a business relationship in which one party, known as a **trustor**, gives another party, the **trustee**, the right to hold title to property or assets for the benefit of a third party, the **beneficiary**[1297]. As an independent publisher, you act as the trustor. You can place your assets in a trust for the benefit of your beneficiaries to protect them from taxes and creditors when you die or even when you are still alive.

Can Wills and Trusts Always Be Used to Protect Your Estate?

In many cases, the assets that can be protected by a will can also be protected by a trust, and it is not uncommon to use both legal vehicles together where the assets from a will are automatically added to a pre-existing trust in what is known as a **pour-over will**[1298].

But wills, trusts, and the other mechanisms of estate planning are not foolproof. **People can contest these legal structures and depending on who is involved and what is at stake, court cases might be inevitable**[1299]. The estate of Stan Lee, for example, has been the subject of several court cases since his death[1300].

How Do You Manage Your Estate Planning?

Estate planning is similar to other financial and legal aspects of your independent publishing. **You don't want to sign anything or commit your assets to any course of action without consulting your accountant and your attorney.** Don't be surprised if the professionals you used to build your publishing empire don't specialize in estate planning, but they should be your first points of contact to find referrals.

[1296] Erb, K. (2016, April 28). 17 Famous People Who Died Without A Will. Retrieved May 31, 2020, from https://www.forbes.com/sites/kellyphillipserb/2016/04/27/17-famous-people-who-died-without-a-will/

[1297] Kagan, J. (2020, April 05). Trust Definition. Retrieved May 31, 2020, from https://www.investopedia.com/terms/t/trust.asp

[1298] Kagan, J. (2020, January 29). Pour-Over Will. Retrieved May 31, 2020, from https://www.investopedia.com/terms/p/pour-overwill.asp

[1299] Beattie, A. (2020, April 07). What to Do When You're Left Out of a Will. Retrieved May 31, 2020, from https://www.investopedia.com/articles/pf/12/left-out-of-the-will.asp

[1300] Gardner, E. (2020, April 18). Stan Lee's Daughter Sues to Reclaim His Intellectual Property. Retrieved May 31, 2020, from https://www.hollywoodreporter.com/thr-esq/stan-lees-daughter-sues-reclaim-his-intellectual-property-1243840

They should also remain in the loop to the extent that they can help you understand the fees involved and the process of setting up your estate planning.

Once you find the right people to establish your will and /or trust, consider informing all the interested parties about what you are doing and how it affects them. The transition for them can be easier if the grief from losing you isn't compounded with the uncertainty about the future of your comics and your company.

What Happens to Your Company After You're Gone?

The future of the company you created can be more complex than your estate planning based on your long-term plans and the other parties that might be involved long after you are gone. We'll look at three common options, dissolution, succession, and various corporate exit strategies.

What Is Dissolution?

If formation is the birth of your company, **dissolution** is the death of a business. The purpose of dissolution is to sell off assets, pay any remaining debts, and distribute whatever is left over to interested parties[1301]. The terms of dissolution are often built into the housekeeping terms of operating agreements. Requirements often include the triggers for dissolution, the documents required to be filed with the appropriate state agencies, and general instructions for the disposal of assets and the payment of creditors. If the goal of your independent publishing company was simply to provide a legal entity for your comic career while you are alive, then it might make sense for your company to end when you do.

What Is Succession?

Succession planning is a strategy for passing on leadership roles or the ownership of a company to another person[1302]. If you want your independent publishing company to live on after you die, then pre-decisions will have to be made. Without a succession plan firmly in place, your business partners can lose confidence in the company when you die and refuse to continue the relationship, effectively killing the company or forcing your eventual successor to rebuild everything from the ground up[1303].

As an independent publisher, you might decide that your collaboration partner is a natural successor and build that into the collaboration agreements. If you don't have a collaboration partner, your succession plans

---

[1301] Kenton, W. (2020, February 05). What Does Winding up a Business Mean? Retrieved May 31, 2020, from https://www.investopedia.com/terms/w/windingup.asp

[1302] Kenton, W. (2020, February 05). Understanding Succession Planning. Retrieved May 31, 2020, from https://www.investopedia.com/terms/s/succession-planning.asp

[1303] Rosenberg, J. (2019, June 23). Uncertainty can follow grief when small business owner dies. Retrieved May 31, 2020, from https://www.telegraphherald.com/news/business/article_79f7f9d1-20a6-5439-af46-2f57eb136272.htm

could be included as part of your estate planning, so your company is left to an heir or trust beneficiary[1304]. Alternatively, you might have a specific exit strategy as an independent publisher for when you're ready to cash out and retire from comics.

What Is an Exit Strategy?

An **exit strategy** is a conscious plan to dispose of an investment in a business venture or a financial asset[1305]. **Exit strategies are complex legal transactions and require the expertise of accountants and attorneys who specialize in those kinds of deals**. Don't attempt any exit strategy without getting referrals from professionals and performing due diligence on the people who might be working on the most important deal of your comic book career.

What Are the Different Types of Exit Strategies?

There are three general types of exits: sales, mergers, and initial public offerings.

- A sale of a company occurs when an outsider purchases complete or partial ownership of the corporate entity[1306]. Depending on the status of the company and the structure of the deal, a sale can be for the assets of the company (including tangible assets like inventory and equipment and intangible assets like IP, revenue streams, AR and goodwill), or the shares of the companies. For example, Valiant was purchased by the entertainment company DMG in 2018 to control the IP library for multimedia content[1307].

- In an **acquisition,** one company takes over another company, establishes itself as the new owner, and the target company ceases to exist. In a **merger**, two companies join forces to move forward as a single new company[1308]. An acquisition example from the world of comics

[1304] Fershteyn, I. (2019, November 11). Succession and Estate Planning for Businesses. Retrieved May 31, 2020, from https://brooklyntrustandwill.com/succession-estate-planning-businesses/

[1305] Hayes, A. (2020, March 26). What is an Exit Strategy? Retrieved May 31, 2020, from https://www.investopedia.com/terms/e/exitstrategy.asp

[1306] Sorensen, M., Rose, J., & Marks, G. (n.d.). Selling Your Business Definition - Entrepreneur Small Business Encyclopedia. Retrieved May 31, 2020, from https://www.entrepreneur.com/encyclopedia/selling-your-business

[1307] Kit, B. (2020, April 19). Comic Book Shake-Up: DMG Entertainment Acquires Valiant (Exclusive). Retrieved May 31, 2020, from https://www.hollywoodreporter.com/heat-vision/valiant-acquired-by-dmg-entertainment-comic-book-shake-up-1078980

[1308] Hayes, A. (2020, February 05). How Mergers and Acquisitions – M&A Work. Retrieved May 31, 2020, from https://www.investopedia.com/terms/m/mergersandacquisitions.asp

can be seen when Disney acquired Marvel in 2009[1309]. On the other side, Oni Press merged with Lion Forge in 2019[1310].

- An **Initial Public Offering** (IPO) refers to the process of offering shares of a private corporation to the public[1311]. As an independent publisher, your initial company, whatever the type, will start as a private entity. "Taking the company public" will place shares of ownership on one of the various stock exchanges (Dow, Nasdaq, S&P 500). Companies must meet financial and legal requirements by whatever exchanges you decide to join and the Securities and Exchange Commission (SEC) before you can hold an initial public offering. These requirements make going public a complex, time consuming, and expensive process involving underwriters[1312], specialized accountants, attorneys, and investment experts. The cost and complexity of IPOs, when coupled with the three economic realities of comics, has historically limited comic IPOs to major publishers, including DC, IDW, and Marvel[1313].

Any individual company might go through multiple transactions in the history of its existence. The exit strategy for one publisher might be the initial investment of the next one, if the underlying IP is valuable enough. For example, Marvel was sold to Perfect Film and Television Corporation in 1969[1314], went public in 1989, and was then acquired by Toy Biz[1315] before the entire entity was purchased by Disney for four billion dollars[1316].

[1309] Goldman, D. (2009, August 31). Disney to buy Marvel for $4 billion. Retrieved May 31, 2020, from https://money.cnn.com/2009/08/31/news/companies/disney_marvel

[1310] Rowe, A. (2019, May 09). What The Oni Press-Lion Forge Merger Says About The Shifting Comic Book Industry. Retrieved May 31, 2020, from https://www.forbes.com/sites/adamrowe1/2019/05/09/what-the-oni-presslion-forge-merger-says-about-the-shifting-comic-book-industry/

[1311] Hayes, A. (2020, April 28). Learn About Initial Public Offerings (IPOs). Retrieved May 31, 2020, from https://www.investopedia.com/terms/i/ipo.asp

[1312] Banton, C. (2020, February 05). How Underwriters Assess the Risk of Insurers. Retrieved May 31, 2020, from https://www.investopedia.com/terms/u/underwriting.asp

[1313] Gerber, G. (2018). Investing in the Future of Comics: Entertainment Industry and Market Demand. Retrieved May 31, 2020, from https://icv2.com/articles/news/view/41815/investing-future-comics-entertainment-industry-market-demand

[1314] Daniels, Les (September 1991). Marvel: Five Fabulous Decades of the World's Greatest Comics, Harry N Abrams. p. 139

[1315] Reuters. (1997). Marvel Reaches Agreement to Emerge from Bankruptcy. Retrieved May 31, 2020, from https://www.nytimes.com/1997/07/11/business/marvel-reaches-agreement-to-emerge-from-bankruptcy.html

[1316] Wilkerson, D. (2009, August 31). Disney to acquire Marvel Entertainment for $4B. Retrieved May 31, 2020, from https://www.marketwatch.com/story/disney-to-acquire-marvel-entertainment-for-4b-2009-08-31

Is Doing Nothing an Option?

Most independent publishing companies are not ultimately absorbed into one of the largest conglomerates in the history of business. As we have seen, most independent publishers fail financially. The ones that don't often do not outlive their publishers.

Many publishers have no estate planning, no succession plans, and no exit strategy. Depending on your goals, you might decide you don't care what happens to your comic or your company when you die. You might decide you want the IP to go into the public domain and the crumbs of your empire should be fought over by your heirs in a *Mortal Kombat* style tournament. You might think that your comics and your company will never be worth anything anyway. But if you thought that, you probably wouldn't have made comics in the first place and you certainly wouldn't have finished reading this book. So, plan ahead. You never know if your books will be the next big thing.

Chapter 77: What Did You Learn in this Book?

When you started reading ICP, I said that this book could help you get the following things:

- Intellectual property that you own
- A business plan for publishing comics
- Experience in the comics publishing industry
- Contacts within the industry
- A market for your ideas
- A process you can replicate with other books
- A finished product
- Maybe a little cash left over

If you've followed the process in this book and turned your decisions into real-world actions for your comic, then you now have the skills and, more importantly, the options of an independent comic book publisher.

What Skills Have You Learned?

Reading this book doesn't make you an expert in any particular aspect of comic book publishing. You don't understand all the intricacies of contract negotiation, web design, affiliate marketing, or estate planning. But you do know enough to get started.

- You learned what steps and decisions go into publishing a comic.
- You learned about the history and realities of the industry you're trying to break into.
- You learned to ask the right questions at each stage of the process
- You learned what your options can be and how to choose what's best for your circumstances, goals, and story.

What Options Have You Gained?

Understanding the business associated with your art gives you a level of true creative freedom. While you still might be limited by political censorship based on the country you live in, you are now free from what Prince referred to as economic censorship[1317] imposed either by the comic book establishment or the wider entertainment industry.

When you understand the business of independent comic book publishing, you're not at the mercy of gatekeepers or established publishers. You don't have to wait months or years for approval from an agent or an editor. You don't have to put up with sexual abuse[1318], racial harassment[1319], or political blacklisting. You don't have to limit or repress any controversial aspect of your story that you feel is important. You can tell whatever story you want to anyone who wants to read it. You can publish the comic you want to make, not the comic that someone else lets you make.

Knowing the business of comics means you don't have to accept the comics you see on the shelf of the comic shop as the only comics people can read. You're not limited to the characters, narratives, or voices embraced by the mainstream. To paraphrase award-winning author Chinua Achebe, *"If you don't like someone else's comic, you can publish your own.*[1320]*"*

What you don't have is a perfect formula for creative and financial success. The comic book industry isn't like chess where there are clear (but complex) finite steps to victory. Publishing comics has more in common with poker, where many of the variables for success are based on a combination of luck, skill, and timing. Comics, narrative art, and life, in general, are more like poker than chess[1321]. Even the best script using the most popular characters and produced by the best creative team doesn't guarantee a successful book, movie, or video game. All those elements simply improve the odds.

Because there is no perfect formula and the results of your publishing are based on the options you choose, you also have the option to ignore everything in this book. Thousands of publishers released independent comics long before this book was written. Many of the lessons they learned the hard way have been included here so you can avoid the pitfalls they faced. But you have the right to publish your comics your way. Nothing in this book can change that.

[1317] Piepenbring, D. & Prince (2019) *The Beautiful Ones*. One World

[1318] Elbein. A. (2020, July 12). Retrieved July 14, 2020, from Inside the Comic Book Industry's Sexual Misconduct Crisis- and the Ugly, Exploitative History That Got It Here. https://www.thedailybeast.com/warren-ellis-cameron-stewart-and-the-storm-of-sexual-misconduct-allegations-roiling-the-comic-book-industry

[1319] Lopes, P. D. (2009). Chapter Six. In *Demanding respect: The evolution of the American comic book.*

[1320] Chinua Achebe At 88: Ten Inspiring Quotes. (2018, November 16). Retrieved May 31, 2020, from https://guardian.ng/life/chinua-achebe-at-88-ten-inspiring-quotes/

[1321] Duke, A. (2018) *Thinking in Bets*. Portfolio

Whatever aspects of this book you decide to use, you now have the option to publish your comics armed with both the creative inspiration of the story you love and the business concepts to support it.

So, go have some fun and publish your comics.

I referred to a wide range of articles, books, and interviews to write this book, but if you decide you'd like to explore a particular aspect of business or comics in-depth, please consider this list for more information.

Book	Author
Book Yourself Solid	Port
Comic Book Marketing 101	Nastos
Comic Book Start-Up 101	Vanover
Comic-Con and the Business of Pop Culture	Salkowitz
Comic Shop	Gearino
Crowd Start	Hyatt
Demanding Respect	Lopes
Do the Work	Pressfield
Economics of Digital Publishing	Allen
From Panel to Publisher: Transactional Law for Comics	Crowell
Getting Past No	Ury
Getting to Yes	Ury
How to Self-Publish Comics	Blaylock
How to Self-Publish Your Own Comic	Caputo
Insider's Guide to Creating Comics	Schmidt
Is $.99 the New Free?	Scott
Laws of Human Nature	Greene
Making Comics	McCloud
Pros and Comic Cons	Nicholson
Story	McKee
The Art of Seduction	Greene

The Complete Guide to Self-Publishing Comics	Love
The 48 Laws of Power	Greene
The Law for Comic Book Creators	Sergi
The Long Tail	Anderson
The Pocket Guide for Comics Creators	Crowell
This is Marketing	Godin
Understanding Comics	McCloud
Unnatural Talent	Brubaker
Words for Pictures	Bendis
Write or Wrong	Manning
Write, Publish, Repeat	Truant
The Perfect Pitch	Rotcop
Selling Your Comic Book Concept	Wampler
Your First 1,000 Copies	Grahl

Acknowledgments

To the family, friends, and colleagues who have supported my life and my work over the years, I appreciate the impact you've had on my career and the development of this book.

Paul Azaceta

Nicola Black

Russ Brown

Chris Carter

C.B. Cebulski

Thomas Crowell

Sara Erickson

David Gallaher

Ramon Gil

David Hyde

Joseph Illidge

Bill Jemas

Michael Lent

Mike Marts

John O'Donnell

Stephen Pakula

Nelson Pinero

Peter Robbins

Wilson Ramos

Andy Schmidt

Joe Sergi

Tim Smith

Eric Tapper

Dirk Vanover

Eugene Wainwright

Tim Werenko

Camilla Zhang

Dorothy Hennessy

Michael Hennessy

Michael Benjamin Hennessy

Rebecca Hennessy

Vincent Hennessy

Yussef Hennessy

Dwaine Wintz

Romayne Wintz-Banberger

Sean Wintz

Trish Budhu

Brittany Caruso

Lauren Caruso

Gina Gonzalez

Staisha Hamilton

Alysse Jordan

Celesta Sligar

Colleen Edwards

Shonali Bhowmik

Shana Pederson

Mee-Lise Robinson

Michael Palin

Elece Green

Matt Blank

Dwight Coye

James Hollowman

Burt Hubbard

William Lindsay

Damon Samuel

Roberto Stewart

Robert Taylor

$400.00

Printed in the USA
CPSIA information can be obtained
at www.ICGtesting.com
LVHW012324121023
760666LV00013B/370

9 780578 72